THE
MAFIA, CIA &
GEORGE BUSH

BY
PETE BREWTON

S.P.i.
BOOKS

A division of Shapolsky Publishers, Inc.

The Mafia, CIA & George Bush

S.P.I. BOOKS

A division of Shapolsky Publishers, Inc.

For any additional information, contact:

S.P.I. BOOKS/Shapolsky Publishers, Inc.
136 West 22nd Street
New York, NY 10011
(212) 633-2022
FAX (212) 633-2123

ISBN: 1-56171-203-5

10 9 8 7 6 5 4 3 2 1

Printed and bound in the United States of America

*To my mother, and in memory of my
father, Fred O. Brewton, Jr.,
who loved a good story.*

TABLE OF CONTENTS

INTRODUCTION

Something very significant happened during our country's savings-and-loan crisis, the greatest financial disaster since the Great Depression. It happened quietly, secretly, without any fanfare and attention. It happened before our very eyes, yet we knew it not.

What we all missed was the massive transfer of wealth from the American taxpayers to a select group of extremely rich, powerful people. What these people had in common—unknown to the American public—were their symbiotic relationships to the Mafia and the CIA, and to the two most prominent, powerful politicians from Texas, President George Bush and Senator Lloyd Bentsen.

This small cabal of businessmen realized that the S&Ls were going the way of the dinosaurs. They recognized that S&Ls couldn't survive under rapid inflation and high interest rates. So they decided to exploit the situation for their own purposes, with help from, and rewards for, the Mafia, the CIA and their favorite politicians. They probably figured that the insulation and protection these powerful institutions and individuals conferred upon them, in addition to all the endemic protections within the financial, judicial, political and journalistic systems, made them invulnerable. They were probably right.

For unlike Watergate and Iran-Contra, this was a bipartisan scandal. There was no opposition party to push for an independent investigation. In fact, the same group of wealthy, powerful businessmen, centered in Houston, that encircle Republicans like George Bush and James A. Baker III, also encircle Democrats like Jim Wright and Lloyd Bentsen.

This information enables one to view the 1988 elections, in which not one cross word was ever spoken about the savings-and-loan debacle, in a whole new perspective. It was not merely a fortuitous coincidence that both Bush, the Republican nominee for President, and Bentsen, the Democratic nominee for Vice President, were part of, and beholden to, the same group of Houston businessmen. Even if the Democrats lost that presidential election, as they did, Bentsen could still win re-election to his Senate seat under the so-called "LBJ rule." The Houston boys, as usual, had their bets covered.

(If the Democrats had won in 1988, this book would be entitled "The Mafia, the CIA and Lloyd Bentsen," for Bentsen and Bush are two interchangeable peas in a pod. They have many friends, business associates and campaign donors in common. The story of the most important one they share begins this book.)

But Bush won in 1988, and one of the reasons he did was his ability to keep the S&L scandal out of the political debate. He was assisted in this by none other than Bentsen, as we shall see. They both had much to hide, Bush in particular. Not only were many of the President-to-be's friends involved—along with two of his sons—but Bush himself, as Vice President, had personally intervened in the federal regulation of a dirty Florida savings and loan that was being looted by people with connections to the Mafia and the CIA. This S&L ultimately failed, costing taxpayers nearly $700 million.

The S&L scandal is the vehicle for telling the story about these leading American politicians and businessmen. But the relationships between these individuals and how they control and manipulate public and private institutions is the bigger story. Unless we know who these people are and understand how they operate, we can all look forward to more S&L-type debacles to come.

The S&L scandal was almost the perfect crime. The layers of protection and insulation between what the public discovered was going on at the savings and loans and what actually happened with the money were so many and so thick that the crimes and theft would never be completely figured out. And even if the truth were ultimately unearthed, there were additional layers between that revelation and the bringing of those responsible to the bar of justice and recovering the money.

The first and foremost layer of protection is the difficulty in tracking the money from the savings and loans to its ultimate destination. That is why almost no FBI agent, federal prosecutor, S&L regulator, congressional committee or journalist has been able to track the money. Yet where the money went is really the only thing that matters. The rest of the "facts" that, typically, got investigated, prosecuted and written about were mostly smoke and mirrors, set up to shield who really got the hundreds of billions of dollars that taxpayers must pay back and to hide what the money was used for.[1]

The five years that went into this book represent my efforts to peel back all the layers of insulation and protection to get to the real culprits. I have organized this book with that process in mind, to help the reader understand a complicated and confusing subject.

In general, the bulk of the money lost in the S&L crisis that American citizens must now pay for went to the owners of the property and assets that the more notorious borrowers purchased with money from S&Ls run by equally infamous owners. This seems to be obvious, yet it somehow got lost in all the hype and hysteria. While Congress, the Justice Department and the press concentrated on the flamboyant borrowers and managers of the S&Ls, the big recipients of the money—the wealthy, powerful landowners and property owners—crept off quietly with their profits.

In the second half of this book, a number of examples will be detailed to show how this happened, and who got the money. For example, one later chapter deals with a $200 million, 21,000-acre land transaction in Florida in which much of the borrowed S&L money went to a paper company owned by the Du Pont empire, one of the oldest, richest, most powerful bastions of wealth in this country.

We know this because many of the lending documents were pursued by a lone, shrewd, tenacious federal regulator named Kenneth Cureton. However, the unraveling of this transaction was a rare and exceptional event. But even it could not be called a complete victory. The Department of Justice's International Division, the government body through which subpoenas to offshore banks must pass, inexplicably became a brick wall for Cureton's efforts to obtain records on the Isle of Jersey in the English Channel, where a big chunk of the money went—possibly to buy weapons for Iraq.

---

[1] A notable exception is the book *Inside Job,* by Stephen Pizzo, Mary Fricker and Paul Muolo, which nailed down the fact that the savings-and-loan debacle was caused primarily by fraud.

Since so many of the crucial documents in this scandal are not available, we are left with the second-best avenue of investigation: finding out who the original property owners were and everything we can about them, and then doing the same thing for the S&L proprietors and borrowers. The bulk of this book consists of that enterprise.

The evidence uncovered is clear, convincing and compelling: Members and associates of the Mafia and the United States Central Intelligence Agency were key participants in our nation's savings-and-loan debacle, and some of the richest, most powerful people in the country did business with these participants and profited from the S&L crisis.

That members of the Mafia and the CIA, two organizations that operate in secrecy and whose members take sacred oaths—one supposedly dedicated to the national security, the other simply to their organizations' security—may have been working together is not unprecedented in this country. But that fact doesn't make their cooperation any less outrageous.

It is well known that members of the Mafia and the CIA conspired to try to assassinate Fidel Castro. There are other, less substantiated, although credible, allegations regarding the two groups' involvement together in drug smuggling and money laundering in Southeast Asia, Australia and the Caribbean.[2] There are also some curious, ominous connections between members of these groups and JFK-assassination figures Lee Harvey Oswald and Jack Ruby.

Drawing a straight, direct line from the CIA operatives discussed in this book to the top officials of the CIA and on to the President is extremely difficult because of the way the CIA works. Most of the characters in this book are not the card-carrying bureaucrats and bean counters at CIA headquarters in Langley, Virginia. They are what are called CIA "assets," who can be someone who turns over an occasional piece of information to the CIA, without even knowing it is for the CIA, all the way up to someone who is continually working for the CIA in covert operations.

A similar and, likewise, important cog in CIA operations is what is known as a cutout. A cutout is a front man or middle man set up to protect the identities of the primary participants. Like an asset, a cutout

---

[2] *The Politics of Heroin in Southeast Asia,* by Alfred W. McCoy (New York: Harper and Row, 1972); *The Crimes of Patriots,* by Jonathan Kwitny (New York: Norton, 1987); and *In Banks We Trust,* by Penny Lernoux (Penguin Books, 1986).

may or may not know for whom he is working and the actual purpose of his work. (The Mafia also makes use of such cutouts, except they call them "mustaches" or "beards.")

The CIA uses assets and cutouts to maintain one of its prime directives: plausible deniability, or, in other words, "Don't get caught embarrassing the President." (The CIA is the intelligence-gathering and covert-action arm of the President. Perhaps that is the definition journalists should always refer to, rather than just throwing the general term "CIA" around as if it were some sort of independently run mythical loose cannon.) So . . . if an asset or cutout is caught breaking the law, the CIA can deny that its operative was working for it at that particular time.

This leads to one difference between the Mafia and the CIA, particularly in this story. Once it is established that members and associates of the Mafia are involved in a failed savings and loan, that is usually enough to establish, prima facie, the involvement of the Mafia. Members and associates of the Mafia don't do such things without the knowledge, permission and the sharing of the spoils, with their superiors.

The destruction of the savings and loan industry in Texas, and in some other parts of the country, worked basically like an organized-crime bustout or burnout. This is a mob scam in which a failing company is taken over, built up on credit, then drained of all its assets and purposely put into bankruptcy, leaving the creditors holding the bag.

In the case of savings and loans, the credit was federally insured deposits injected by money brokers, like mob associate Mario Renda, and the creditors are the taxpayers. The front men, the cutouts and the "mustaches," like Don Dixon, Tyrell Barker, Ed McBirney, Jarrett Woods, Roy Dailey, Mike Adkinson and Robert Corson, are left to take the blame. But don't feel sorry for them, for they have usually skimmed enough off to offshore bank accounts to make it well worth a couple of years in jail, keeping their mouths shut.

However, because of the CIA's doctrine of plausible deniability, the involvement of a CIA asset in a failed savings and loan does not make a prima facie case for the involvement of the CIA. In fact, I know of no independent test a journalist can conduct to determine whether the involvement of a CIA asset means the CIA has sanctioned it or whether the asset is just freelancing for his own gain. Both possibilities would look the same to an outside observer.

The only way to tell would be if the CIA admitted its involvement or if there were unassailable, documented evidence showing S&L money going from an asset to a CIA operation. This is attainable only by subpoena, if at all. Even in such a case the CIA might deny that it knew the asset was pumping money into the operation or that it knew the money came from an S&L. But if the CIA admitted that, it would be admitting that it is both incompetent and stupid.

In the case of the failed S&Ls, the CIA has categorically denied its involvement. The CIA did admit to a congressional committee that it had a relationship to five individuals connected to failed savings and loans, and that it had also done business with four savings and loans that later failed. But the spy agency claimed that its business with these S&Ls was legitimate. However, there are several cases in which there are clear indications that S&L money went directly to operations that the CIA took part in, even if it didn't overtly control them—for example, the cases of Iran-Contra and of weapons shipments to the Middle East.

But one thing we can say, categorically: The CIA either knew or didn't know what its operatives were doing at S&Ls. If it knew, why didn't it stop them or alert the proper authorities? If it didn't know, how effective an intelligence agency could it really be?

Finally, a word about the circumstantial evidence in this book. Circumstantial evidence must necessarily be used because of the secretive nature of the CIA and the unavailability of S&L documents. The evidence appears many times in *this* way: A failed S&L was owned and controlled by people who have done business with Mafia associates and CIA operatives; many of the borrowers were Mafia and CIA associates; many of the original property owners have done business with Mafia and CIA operatives and some of the money disappears in foreign accounts controlled by Mafia and CIA associates.

What does such evidence prove? Based on my research and knowledge of the CIA, I believe it makes it more likely than not that someone in the CIA hierarchy knew about and approved, if not instigated, the S&L actions of its operatives. In any event, journalists are not in the proof business, we are in the information business. Proof is for mathematicians and courts of law, and even in those arenas, there are great disputes about what constitutes proof. The readers of this book, and the American public, can evaluate the evidence and information in this book for themselves and decide whether it should be acted upon or ignored.

Introduction

There is nothing intrinsically wrong with circumstantial evidence. In our country's courts of law, fortunes and lives can be won or lost, fairly and squarely, on the basis of circumstantial evidence. Juries, as well as readers of this book, may infer facts and conclusions from circumstantial evidence. I have attempted to set out all the facts and circumstantial evidence that I know. In some cases the meanings are clear and conclusions can be drawn. In other places the going gets a little tough, because there is not enough data and evidence to draw meanings and reach conclusions. For this I apologize; I wish I had found more information.

In all, I have tried to follow the injunction of our forefathers, who in proclaiming their thesis in the Declaration of Independence, stated: ". . . let facts be submitted to a candid world."

Admittedly, it is easy to be cynical and discouraged about the situation presented in the following chapters. One question I am constantly asked is: "What can we, the American people, do about this?" There are no quick-and-easy solutions or panaceas. However, like our founding fathers, we should have faith in the liberating power of knowledge and information. If we know how and why something happened, and who benefitted by it, then we will know the right thing to do.

PROLOGUE

The roar of gunfire reverberated through the saloon. As the smoke cleared, a young deputy sheriff lay dead on the floor, shot down in the prime of life by a fellow lawman. It was 1934 in Gillett, Karnes County, Texas, some 40 miles southeast of San Antonio—a rough, dirt-poor country, whose monotony was relieved only by live oak, prickly pear, bony cattle, Germans and Poles.

No one knows for sure what caused the gunfight between Walter C. Mischer, the thirty-three-year-old Deputy Sheriff, and Walter Patton, the sixty-three-year-old Justice of the Peace. Some of the old-timers said a poker game led to the fatal fight. Others whispered it was the whiskey that was flowing that Saturday night at the dance. A few said the fight was over control of bootleg hooch. The Mischers claimed the tragedy was caused by the J.P., who thought the deputy was interfering in his family disputes.

The facts are these:

There had been some earlier bad blood between the two lawmen. In a previous fight, Mischer had allegedly hit Patton over the head with a bottle. But there was testimony that several days before the shootout Mischer ran his car off the road into a ditch and hurt himself. It was Patton who came to his aid.

Anyway, it was Saturday night and a dance was being held at Nick Richter's place. Patton was upstairs watching the dance, while Mischer was downstairs drinking and carousing. A beer bottle dropped to the floor and Mischer kicked it up against the bar.

Someone went upstairs to get Patton, claiming that Mischer was causing a disturbance. Patton, who had been hired to help keep the peace that night, came down and began having words with Mischer, who hauled off and slugged Patton in the face, knocking his hat and glasses off. The J.P. pulled his revolver and pistol-whipped the deputy. Blood began flowing profusely from the blows inflicted on Mischer's head.

A friend assisted Mischer to the door of the saloon to take him to a doctor to get his wounds tended. All the while, Patton kept his revolver trained on the deputy, taunting him to go for his gun. Just as Mischer got to the doorway, he drew his gun, whirled, crouched down and fired. The bullet hit the judge just inches below his heart and went right through him. He then calmly fired two bullets into Mischer.

Whether it was poker or whiskey or women or family affairs, or all of those things and more, the deputy sheriff was dead, leaving behind a wife, an eleven-year-old son and two younger daughters. The old judge, whose own wife had died at an early age, leaving him to raise their six children, survived his bullet wound and was indicted for murder.

The justice system served up another bitter pill for the Mischers to swallow. The widow had to dig into her own pocket to hire a special prosecutor to handle the case. And even though a jury convicted Patton of murdering Mischer, it only sentenced him to two years in the penitentiary, at a time and in a place where the usual punishment for murder was at the end of a rope. Perhaps the jury looked with leniency on the judge's claim of self-defense, a plausible assertion, but a claim that usually won't work as a defense when the altercation is provoked by the defendant.

Patton appealed his conviction to the Texas Court of Criminal Appeals, which reversed the verdict and remanded it back for a new trial—on the grounds that the trial judge failed to instruct the jury that Patton was entitled to carry a pistol that night because he was a duly-constituted peace officer. A year later there was another trial, and the verdict was the same: guilty, two years in jail with a recommendation by the jury that the sentence be served and not suspended. But the trial judge disregarded the jury's recommendation and suspended the sentence.

Old Judge Patton never spent a day in jail, died with his boots on at the age of seventy-seven and was buried under the cedar and live oaks in the tiny Gillett cemetery not 100 yards from the man he killed.[1]

The deputy's eleven-year-old boy, Walter Max Mischer, had a tough go of it. The shooting turned him from a child into the man of the house; his mother had to return to teaching to support him and his sisters. Creditors then carved their 13,000-acre cattle ranch down to 400,[2] hardly enough land to support a milk goat.

The boy was bitter, and sometimes depressed, about his father's death and the killer's escape from the hangman's noose. Many times during his junior high and senior high school days he had to be restrained by his friends and teachers from his threats to take revenge: get a gun and kill the judge.

And if that were not enough, when he was two years old he had been kicked in the head by a horse, leaving him with a vulnerable soft spot, where curious schoolboys could upon close inspection see his pulse. His injury prevented him from participating in two of the most important rites of passage for Texas teen-age boys at that time: football and World War II. He was the lowly waterboy for the football team, and, rejected by the Navy, he joined a private firm and helped build naval bases in the Caribbean. But decades later, after Walter Mischer became one of the most powerful men in this country, the joke was that everybody in Karnes County was trying to find that horse so they could get kicked too.

However, his early exposure to violence and injustice taught him well: No parent or law or badge or court could protect him against the luck of the draw. And it left him vulnerable to the siren songs of two organizations in which this country's laws need not necessarily be obeyed, where no badge is required and where justice can be bought with blackmail, bribes or bullets—the Mafia and the Central Intelligence Agency.

---

[1] Based on interviews with Walter M. Mischer, Sr., his childhood friend Steve Crews, his teacher Viola Johnson, a profile on Mischer in the *Houston Post*, November 22, 1987, and criminal case in Karnes County, State of Texas vs. Walter Patton, 1934.

[2] *Texas Big Rich*, by Sandy Sheehy (New York: Morrow, 1990).

CAST OF PRINCIPAL CHARACTERS
(IN ALPHABETICAL ORDER)

WILLIAM MICHAEL "MIKE" ADKINSON, con man and good old boy from the Florida panhandle; built houses in Houston and sold arms with some Kuwaitis to Iraq; borrowed close to $200 million from a half-dozen dirty S&Ls; convicted for fraud in a $200 million S&L land deal in Florida and sentenced to 11 years in prison; associate of Robert Corson.

ROBERT O. ANDERSON, former chairman of Atlantic Richfield; land-owner with Walter Mischer; borrowed from Hill Financial Savings with Richard Rossmiller.

GEORGE AUBIN, Kappa Sigma frat rat who named most of his companies after his fraternity; took E. F. Hutton for $48 million and several Texas S&Ls for more; always just hanging around Louisiana mobster Herman K. Beebe; one place he never hung around was the inside of a jail, despite vow by several FBI agents to put him there.

FARHAD AZIMA, Iranian native close to Pahlavi family; Kansas City airline owner; board member and stockholder of Kansas City bank controlled by the mob; CIA asset protected by CIA from criminal prosecution.

JAMES A. BAKER III, White House Chief of Staff, former Secretary of the Treasury and Secretary of State; former partner at Andrews & Kurth, which investigated Raymond Hill and Mainland Savings and then did nothing; longtime good friend of Raymond Hill.

JOHN BALLIS, Beaumont dentist who moved to Houston and married a rich man's daughter; developer; associate of John Riddle; pleaded guilty to savings-and-loan fraud and turned state's evidence against Roy Dailey.

BEN BARNES, former Texas lieutenant governor; business associate of Herman K. Beebe, Walter Mischer and John Connally.

JIM BATH, Houston airplane company owner; CIA asset; front man for rich Saudis; associated with Reza Pahlavi, the Shah's son, and business partner with Lan Bentsen, the senator's son, and George W. Bush, the President's son; borrowed from Lamar Savings and Mainland Savings.

CHARLES BAZARIAN, Oklahoma con man, convicted felon and associate of numerous S&L crooks and mobsters, including Morris Shenker, Mario Renda and Don Dixon.

HERMAN K. BEEBE, SR., Louisiana financier, convicted felon and Mafia associate; many connections to the intelligence community; godfather of the dirty Texas S&Ls; did nine months in Club Fed.

JAKE BELIN, former head of the largest private landowner in Florida, St. Joe Paper Co., which is owned by the A. I. DuPont Trust; protegé of Ed Ball, right-wing fanatic and most powerful man Florida has ever known; Belin liked doing business with fellow Florida redneck Mike Adkinson; he also liked the $80 million St. Joe got from Hill Financial Savings.

LLOYD BENTSEN, senior Democratic senator from Texas; an owner of three Texas S&Ls that later ended up in the hands of CIA or Mafia associates; close to Walter Mischer.

FERNANDO BIRBRAGHER, convicted drug-money launderer at Marvin Warner's Great American Bank; got probation amid rumors of connections to a higher authority (CIA); helped Jack DeVoe launder his drug money; now building hush kits for DC-8s; bought Farhad Azima's interest in two DC-8s in Spain; business partner with Miguel Acosta, a former associate of Ron Martin.

WILLIAM BLAKEMORE, Midland oilman and fierce Contra supporter; head of Gulf & Caribbean Foundation, set up to lobby Congress for aid to Contras; good friend of George Bush; his Iron Mountain ranch the site of paramilitary training and alleged transshipment of weapons.

ROBERT BOBB and DOUGLAS CROCKER, Chicago businessmen who worked for Gouletas family; bought Bellamah Associates from Gouletases; had business dealings with Robert Corson, Larry Mizel's MDC Corp., Silverado Savings and Key Savings.

RICHARD BRENNEKE, renegade intelligence operative and gun dealer; told press about Iran-Contra deals and S&L deals; worked for CIA,

Israeli intelligence, Customs and others; acquitted of perjury charges for claiming to work for the CIA; laundered Mafia and CIA money with Robert Corson.

NORMAN BROWNSTEIN, Denver attorney; "Mr. Fix-it"; worked with Kenneth Good, Bill Walters, Larry Mizel, Marvin Davis, Michael Milken, Burton Kanter, Neil Bush and the Gouletas family; good friend of Senator Ted Kennedy, who called him this country's one hundred and first senator.

GEORGE BUSH, President of the United States.

JOHN ELLIS "JEB" BUSH, the President's son; Contra supporter; business associate of Camilo Padreda, who escaped S&L conviction (with Guillermo Hernandez-Cartaya) with possible help from the CIA.

NEIL BUSH, the President's son; director of Silverado Savings; partner with Bill Walters and Ken Good; friend of Walt Mischer, Jr.

LEONARD CAPALDI, reputed Detroit Mafia associate; borrower at Mainland Savings and Hill Financial Savings.

EULALIO FRANCISCO "FRANK" CASTRO, Cuban exile and Bay of Pigs veteran; CIA operative who helped train and supply Contras; part of drug-smuggling ring that bought Sunshine State Bank.

JACK CHAPMAN, Omaha lawyer and former CIA operative; represented Mario Renda; took half a million in cash from CIA-connected Haitian, Clemard Joseph Charles, for Renda to bribe union officials.

CLEMARD JOSEPH CHARLES, Haitian exile who laundered money for Mario Renda to bribe union officials; CIA asset; mob money launderer; associate of Miami lawyer who represented Lawrence Freeman.

ROBERT CLARKE, former U.S. Comptroller of the Currency; lawyer with Houston firm Bracewell and Patterson; involved with Walter Mischer and Mischer's Allied Bank; associated with Louisiana bank connected to Herman K. Beebe; helped charter West Belt National Bank, where Mike Adkinson and E. Trine Starnes, Jr., were stockholders.

JOHN CONNALLY, former Texas governor; Charles Keating worked on his 1980 Republican presidential race; he and his partner, Ben Barnes, borrowed tens of millions of dollars from dirty S&Ls.

RAY CORONA, former head of "Mafia" bank—Sunshine State Bank in Miami, which he fronted for drug smugglers; convicted felon; borrower from Peoples Savings in Llano, Texas; associate of mobsters and CIA operatives, including Leonard Pelullo, Frank Castro, Guillermo Hernandez-Cartaya and Steve Samos.

ROBERT L. CORSON, Houston good old boy and developer who

owned Vision Banc Savings in Kingsville; Walter Mischer's former son-in-law; CIA mule; indicted along with Mike Adkinson for $200 million S&L land deal in Florida.

ROY DAILEY, Robert Corson's first cousin; former business associate of Walter Mischer; convicted for fraud at First Savings of East Texas, which he owned with money borrowed from Herman K. Beebe.

MARVIN DAVIS, Denver and Beverly Hills oil billionaire; neighbor of Norman Brownstein; did business with John Dick; his daughter was in the cookie business with Neil Bush's wife, Sharon.

JACK DEVOE, convicted cocaine trafficker and CIA-connected arms smuggler; used Lawrence Freeman to launder money, which went to same trust in Isle of Jersey that was used by Robert Corson and Mike Adkinson; involved in drug-smuggling and money-laundering operation that included Fernando Birbragher and Marvin Warner's Great American Bank.

JOHN DICK, who lives on a manor on the Isle of Jersey; Denver attorney by way of Russia and Canada; business partner with Silverado borrower Bill Walters; associate of Marvin Davis and Robert O. Anderson; borrowed from Hill Financial Savings; involved in Isle of Jersey trust company that was laundering drug money for Jack DeVoe and Lawrence Freeman and S&L money for Robert Corson and Mike Adkinson; sells wheat to the Russians; uses Youth for Christ as cover.

DON DIXON, former head of Vernon Savings, which he bought with a little help from his friend Herman K. Beebe; associate of John Riddle.

LAWRENCE FREEMAN, disbarred Miami attorney and convicted money launderer for cocaine smuggler Jack DeVoe; set up $200 million S&L land deal for Jake Belin and Mike Adkinson; former law partner of CIA super-operative Paul Helliwell and alleged money launderer for Mafia boss Santo Trafficante.

BILLIE JEAN GARMAN, Robert Corson's mother and business partner; indicted along with her son in $200 million S&L land deal in Florida; first person publicly banned by feds from S&Ls.

THOMAS GAUBERT, big Democratic fundraiser from Dallas; former head of Independent American Savings; owned a piece of Sandia Federal Savings in Albuquerque; head of Telecom.

KENNETH GOOD, developer in Texas, Colorado and Florida; borrower at Silverado Savings and Jarrett Wood's Western Savings; helped set up Neil Bush in business.

GOULETAS FAMILY—NICHOLAS, EVANGELINE GOULETAS-CAREY and

VICTOR GOULET—condo developers from Chicago; have alleged organized crime ties; owned Imperial Savings in San Diego; sold Bellamah Associates to Robert Bobb and Douglas Crocker.

JOSEPH GROSZ, Chicago mob associate; worked for Gouletas family; ran Southmark's San Jacinto Savings; director of Thomas Gaubert's Telecom.

MARVIN HAASS, San Antonio contractor; co-owner of Peoples Savings in Llano, Texas; associate of Morris Jaffe.

JAMES HAGUE, former owner of Liberty Federal Savings, Leesville, Louisiana, which lent to Morris Shenker; associate of George Aubin and John Riddle.

STEFAN HALPER, co-founder with fellow George Bush supporter Harvey McLean of Palmer National Bank, which was financed by Herman K. Beebe and funneled private donations to the Contras; former son-in-law of past CIA deputy director Ray Cline; helped set up legal defense fund for Oliver North.

J. B. HARALSON, former head of Mercury Savings and Ben Milan Savings, where he was fronting for his close associate George Aubin; old Surety Savings hand and managing officer of two other Texas S&Ls that later failed.

RAYMOND SIDNEY RICHARD HARVEY, Isle of Jersey money manager; handled drug money for Jack DeVoe and Lawrence Freeman and S&L money for Mike Adkinson and Robert Corson; associate of John Dick.

GUILLERMO HERNANDEZ-CARTAYA[1], Cuban exile and Bay of Pigs veteran; convicted of fraud at Texas S&L he bought from Lloyd Bentsen's father; CIA and Mafia money launderer; protected by CIA from certain criminal charges.

RAYMOND HILL, Houston attorney and scion of old, rich Houston family; owner of Mainland Savings, which lent money to Mafia associates and CIA operatives; did business with Walter Mischer, "his mentor"; close friend of James A. Baker III.

JERRY HOLLEY, Waco contractor; co-owner with Marvin Haass of Peoples Savings; convicted for perjury involving his S&L.

K. C. HOOD, Western Savings officer; convicted felon; associate of

[1] Many hispanics are characters in this book. For those who are citizens of Spanish-speaking nations, the editors have maintained the Spanish accent marks in their names. For names of American hispanics, the accents have not been retained since for American usage they are customarily omitted.

Herman K. Beebe; House Speaker Jim Wright rode in his plane.

MONZER HOURANI, Lebanese native and Houston businessman; close friend of U.S. Senator Orrin Hatch (Republican-Utah); did business with Robert Corson; borrowed from Lamar Savings and Mainland Savings.

MORRIS and DOUG JAFFE, father-and-son businessmen from San Antonio, Morris is an associate of Marvin Haass and Carlos Marcello, the New Orleans Mafia boss. Doug borrowed from Ed McBirney's Sunbelt Savings and provided jet airplane noise-limitation equipment for Farhad Azima and others.

BURTON KANTER, Chicago tax attorney and reputed organized crime associate; founded Castle Bank & Trust with CIA mastermind Paul Helliwell; close associate of Lawrence Freeman; his law firm set up trusts for Larry Mizel.

CHARLES KEATING, S&L looter; spawned by Carl Lindner; worked on John Connally's 1980 presidential campaign; controlled Lincoln Savings (the first big deal Lincoln Savings did was with John Connally); Lincoln involved in daisy chain with Larry Mizel's M.D.C. Holdings, Silverado Savings and San Jacinto Savings (Joseph Grosz); lent more than $30 million to Father Ritter's Covenant House; his chief pilot in 1979 was CIA operative Ken Qualls.

CARROLL KELLY, who epitomized his Kappa Sigma fraternity; owner of Continental Savings and associate of Herman K. Beebe ("I'm Beebe's man in Texas," he bragged to S&L regulators).

ADNAN KHASHOGGI, Saudi Arabian arms dealer, Iran-Contra middleman and borrower at Raymond Hill's Mainland Savings and Lamar Savings.

ART LEISER, chief examiner for Texas S&L Department; discovered S&L daisy chains with Herman K. Beebe at center in 1983; challenged Guillermo Hernandez-Cartaya to a tennis match to try to get him out of Texas S&Ls.

CARL LINDNER, Cincinnati conglomerateer; gave Charles Keating his start; associate of Michael Milken and Marvin Warner; business ties to Walter Mischer; owns Ocean Reef club on Key Largo where Jack DeVoe would bring in his cocaine from Colombia; Florida police report said Lindner would not be happy with DeVoe's income tax problems.

JON LINDSAY, county judge of Harris County; top Republican figure in Houston; close friend of George Bush; helped Robert Corson get his savings and loan and got $10,000 campaign contribution from Corson.

Cast of Principal Characters

DONALD LUNA, convicted S&L looter and union pension fund scam artist; caught at Flushing Federal S&L with mobsters; worked loan brokerage deal with Herman K. Beebe, Ben Barnes and Richard Rossmiller.

CARLOS MARCELLO, New Orleans Mafia boss, who also ruled over the Texas underworld; recently returned from a seven-year vacation at Club Fed; close associate of Santo Trafficante.

RONALD J. MARTIN, Miami gun dealer who provided arms to the Contras for the CIA; alleged business partner with Robert Corson in a casino in Grand Canary Island.

ED MCBIRNEY, "Fast Eddie" from Dallas; former head of Sunbelt Savings; associate of Jarrett Woods and George Aubin.

JOE MCDERMOTT, Houston developer; protege' of Walter Mischer; business partner of John Connally; borrower at Robert Corson's Vision Banc Savings.

HARVEY MCLEAN, Shreveport, Louisiana, businessman and close associate of Herman K. Beebe; owned Paris (Texas) Savings and Loan; founded Palmer National Bank with Stefan Halper and Beebe's money.

JOHN MECOM, SR. and JR., Houston oilmen; Sr. organized a charitable foundation that laundered money for the CIA; Jr. allegedly associated with New Orleans mobsters.

WALT MISCHER, JR., the son, tapped to take over his father's empire; friend of Neil Bush; Kappa Sigma president.

WALTER M. MISCHER, SR., Houston developer, banker, power broker, who headed Allied Bank; Corson's former father-in-law; did business with the Mafia and the CIA; fourth largest landowner in Texas; owns 12 percent of Caribbean nation of Belize with partners; friend and fundraiser for LBJ, Lloyd Bentsen, Ronald Reagan and George Bush, among many others.

LARRY MIZEL, Republican fundraiser and head of M.D.C. Holdings, a Denver homebuilder, which did more than $300 million of business with Silverado Savings and owned stock in the Gouletas family's Imperial Savings; used Burton Kanter's law firm for family trusts.

JACK MODESETT, Houston real estate investor; headed company that did business with Howard Pulver and owned land in far west Texas by a guns-for-drugs landing strip (close to Walter Mischer's land).

LLOYD MONROE, former Kansas City organized-crime strike force prosecutor; told to back off Farhad Azima because he had CIA-issued get-out-of-jail-free card.

MURCHISON, CLINT, SR. and JR., Dallas oilmen and wheeler-dealers; Clint Sr. was involved in business in Haiti with a CIA operative; Clint Jr. purchased Mischer's interest in sawmills in Honduras; Jr. was involved with a CIA operative in Libya and did business with Herman K. Beebe and Adnan Khashoggi.

MARVIN NATHAN, Houston attorney who served on Carroll Kelly's Continental Savings' board; related by marriage to Robert Strauss; his law firm represented Robert Corson and Mike Adkinson; bought Texas ranch from the family of late Nicaraguan dictator Anastasio Somoza, which in turn had purchased it from one of George Bush's best friends.

WILL NORTHROP, Israeli army officer and military intelligence operative; worked in Central America with CIA; associate of Richard Brenneke; indicted with Adnan Khashoggi's attorney in scheme to sell arms to Iran; said Robert Corson "rode the CIA mule in with the Republican party."

LEONARD PELULLO, Philadelphia Mafia associate; borrower at Ray Corona's Sunshine State Bank; indicted in Ohio S&L scam with a member of the Herman K. Beebe circle; tried to buy an Atlantic City casino from another S&L looter; charged with fraud at American Savings in California.

ALBERT PREVOT, Houston and Louisiana businessman; associate of Herman K. Beebe and borrower at Mainland Savings and Continental Savings.

HOWARD PULVER, Long Island apartment syndicator who got money from Mainland Savings and Sandia Federal Savings; did business with mob associate Seymour Lazar; neighbor of Martin Schwimmer.

WAYNE REEDER, California developer; associate of Herman K. Beebe; borrower at Silverado Savings; his CIA-connected associate tried to make guns for the Contras on an Indian reservation.

MARIO RENDA, Long Island money broker with Martin Schwimmer, convicted felon and Mafia associate with a number of CIA buddies.

JOHN C. RIDDLE, a University of Texas Kappa Sigma who tried to emulate his fraternity brother George Aubin; Houston lawyer, developer, banker and title-company owner; close associate of Robert Corson; borrowed several hundred million dollars from Texas S&Ls that later failed.

JOHN B. ROBERTS, San Antonio developer who owned Summit Savings in Dallas and Commerce Savings in San Antonio; associate of George Aubin, Jarrett Woods and Adnan Khashoggi; convicted felon.

Cast of Principal Characters

VICTOR J. ROGERS II, scion of Beaumont's Rogers family, which owned Texas State Optical; former law partner of John Riddle; former co-owner of an Austin savings and loan; former officer of Caesar's Palace casino in Las Vegas; his uncles were the third largest stockholders of Caesar's Palace; two uncles served as directors of a Beaumont S&L that lent money to Harvey McLean on his Palmer National Bank stock.

RICHARD ROSSMILLER, Denver developer, Herman K. Beebe associate and borrower at Hill Financial Savings; alleged to be the largest debtor to the Federal Deposit Insurance Corp. in the country; John Dick's neighbor.

HEINRICH RUPP, Denver gold dealer and CIA operative; convicted of bank fraud with mobsters; associate of Richard Brenneke.

JOE RUSSO, noted Houston developer; good friend of George Bush and Lloyd Bentsen; owned Ameriway Savings; big borrower at five failed S&Ls; minority owner of United Press International; Kappa Sigma.

STEVE SAMOS, convicted drug trafficker; helped Ray Corona set up Sunshine State Bank for drug smugglers; helped set up companies that funneled money and weapons to the Contras.

KENNETH SCHNITZER, noted Houston developer; business associate of Walter Mischer; owned BancPlus Savings; allegedly associated with mobsters.

MARTIN SCHWIMMER, convicted Long Island money broker with Mario Renda; Ph.D. and author; Mafia money launderer; neighbor of Howard Pulver.

BARRY SEAL, murdered drug smuggler, gun runner, DEA informant and CIA asset; used by CIA on drug sting of Sandinistas; had owned C-123K used to resupply the Contras; caught in 1972 guns-for-drugs operation with Cuban exiles in Mexico that included a Texas rancher, a Gambino family associate and Herman K. Beebe.

MORRIS SHENKER, deceased mob lawyer and casino owner; several of his properties ended up in the hands of Southmark, a Dallas real estate firm that was a mob dumping ground and owner of San Jacinto Savings.

REBECCA SIMS, former accountant for Robert Corson turned freelance investigator and journalist.

ELLISON TRINE STARNES, JR., Houston con man and son of famous evangelist; borrower at Mischer's Allied Bank; second largest borrower at Silverado Savings ($77 million); associate of John Riddle; borrowed more than $27 million from Carroll Kelly's Continental Savings; one of the biggest private donors to the Contras.

ROBERT STRAUSS, Dallas attorney; U.S. Ambassador to Moscow and former chairman of Democratic National Committee; friend of George Bush and former business partner with James A. Baker III; he and his son, Richard, were involved in a number of failed Texas S&Ls, including Lamar and Gibraltar.

SANTO TRAFFICANTE, the late Tampa Mafia boss; worked with CIA to try to assassinate Fidel Castro; involved in narcotics trafficking in Southeast Asia with CIA operatives; close to Carlos Marcello; one of his money launderers was Lawrence Freeman.

JACK TROTTER, Houston investor and close associate of Walter Mischer; headed Lloyd Bentsen's trust; business partner of Jim Bath.

BILL WALTERS, Denver developer; borrower at Silverado Savings; helped set up Neil Bush in business; associate of Richard Rossmiller and John Dick.

MARVIN WARNER, native Alabaman who was involved in a number of failed S&Ls in Ohio and Florida; former U.S. ambassador to Switzerland; former chairman of Great American Bank and American Savings of Florida; convicted of S&L fraud in Ohio; had business ties to Robert Corson.

STEPHEN CASS WEILAND, Robert Corson's attorney; former chief counsel to Senate Permanent Subcommittee on Investigations; expert on narcotics trafficking, money laundering and offshore banks; makes cameo appearance in Oliver North's notebooks regarding a White House project in Belize.

JARRETT WOODS, former head of Western Savings; childhood buddy and close associate of George Aubin; sentenced to 25 years in jail for S&L fraud.

1

GOOD OLD WALTER MISCHER

On February 28, 1992, George and Barbara Bush strolled out of their home-away-from-home at the Houstonian Hotel on the west side of Houston. Surrounded by their Secret Service entourage, they passed through a small gate into a new residential development called Stablewood. It was a quiet, private walk, unnoticed by the press.[1] Ostensibly, the Bushes were looking at new houses, perhaps with a purchase in mind.

The First Couple headed straight for the spec house of Dempsey and Paula Watson, where they arrived at the back entrance, spent some 30 minutes inside, and then returned to the Houstonian. The visit was no random occurrence of a president and his wife dropping in unexpectedly on Joe Citizen. Nor was it a coincidence that the Watsons had their home in the new development. For Paula Mischer Corson Cook Watson is the only daughter of Walter Mischer, Sr., the Houston millionaire banker-developer and political power broker. And Stablewood is Mischer's new project, a residential development he began after he sold his Allied Bank to First Interstate.

Several months later, when Mischer was questioned about this visit, he denied any advanced knowledge of it. "I didn't have anything to do with it. He [Bush] stays over there in the Houstonian, and that deal [Stablewood] wraps around the Houstonian and he very often come

---

[1] Except that it was mentioned by gossip columnist Betsy Parish several days later in the *Houston Post*.

[sic] over there and walked. I'd like to sell him a lot or two over there."

If so, it would not be the first time Mischer and Bush sat down together. But their relationship is not well known, nor is it one they publicize. Mischer has always liked to stay in the shadows, pulling strings and manipulating, away from the light of public view. Bush, for his part, would not be anxious to have his relationship to Mischer exposed, for Mischer leads to the Mafia, the CIA, the savings-and-loan scandal, and also to the Democratic party. At Mischer's level all of these entities meld together into one prodigious pursuit of public power and private profit.

Walter Mischer is a small, quiet, self-effacing man who talks in a low, slow mumble as if he has a mouthful of grits and gravy. He tends to speak in rural cliche's and ungrammatical good-old-boy homilies, giving the overall impression that he's really not too bright. His non-threatening shtick of the country bumpkin who came to the big city and outwitted the city slickers by being naive and pure endears him to many Texans. But they know it is just a put-on. As one of his friends, Jerry J. Moore, the strip shopping center king and reputedly the richest man in Houston, told *Forbes* magazine, "He's the only guy I've ever met who has a better dumb act than me."[2]

But Mischer's behavior belies his power. In terms of his influence and presence in business, financial, criminal, intelligence, international and political circles he is without peer in Texas and perhaps in the entire country.

Little known outside Texas, Mischer regularly places on *Texas Monthly* magazine's list of the most powerful Texans. In fact, he is one of only two people who made the magazine's list of most powerful Texans in 1976 and in 1987. (The other one was Dallas oilman Ray Hunt, son of H. L. Hunt and half-brother of Nelson Bunker Hunt.)

Mischer is first and foremost a master buyer and manipulator of political influence for private gain. Known as a pragmatist, he has neither ideology nor party loyalty. He usually supports incumbents, but will work both sides of the fence to cover his bets—if he publicly supports one candidate, some of his employees or close associates support the opposing one. And he is noted for inventing a famous expression in the Texas political lexicon: "There's always time to buy a ticket

---

[2] *Forbes*, "2% and friends," by Robert H. Bork, Jr., April 9, 1984.

on the late train." This means that if he has supported one candidate over another and his candidate loses, he can always make a campaign contribution to the winner after the election.

Among the politicians who have benefitted from Mischer's largess are Lyndon B. Johnson, Ronald Reagan, Democrat-turned-Republican John Connally and almost every Texas governor since Connally, including Democrats Preston Smith and Mark White and Republican Bill Clements. The current governor, Ann Richards, is the only exception.

Every Texas governor since Connally (except Richards) has appointed Mischer to some board or commission. In 1966, Connally appointed Mischer to the board of the Texas Department of Corrections, which oversees the state prison system. He was reappointed to that board by Preston Smith in 1971. Governor Dolph Briscoe appointed Mischer to the Texas Deepwater Port Authority in 1978, and Bill Clements in 1981 appointed him to the Governor's Task Force on Water Resource Use and Conservation.

Mischer flip-flopped in his support of Democrat Mark White and Republican Bill Clements in their bitter races for governor, depending on which one was the incumbent. And in 1978 he was a member of the steering committee of Democrats for Tower, supporting incumbent Republican U.S. Senator John Tower in his race against Democrat Bob Krueger.

"Walter is a pragmatic Texan who basically supports the incumbent," Governor Clements has said. "He doesn't let ideology get in his way."[3] Governor Connally claimed that Mischer was involved in politics for partially unselfish reasons. "He's not devoid of self-interest, but he's in it for the state too."[4]

Mischer has had just about every Houston mayor in the last 30 years in his hip pocket, except for Kathy Whitmire. He and his developer friends also control the Harris County Commissioners Court, which determines flood-control policy and projects in the greater Houston area and road projects in unincorporated areas outside Houston.

Of all his political alliances, Mischer is closest to U.S. Senator Lloyd Bentsen. "Lloyd Bentsen is a very good friend of Mischer," said someone who should know—Ben Barnes, the former Texas politician, Mischer minion and big savings and loan borrower. Mischer has served

---

[3] *Houston Post*, November 22, 1987.
[4] Ibid.

in various official capacities on Bentsen's campaigns through the years: in 1976 as treasurer of Bentsen's senatorial re-election committee[5] and in 1981 as co-chairman of a benefit dinner for Bentsen that raised $750,000.[6]

And, in 1988, when Bentsen was running as the Democratic candidate for Vice President and also running to retain his Senate seat in case the Dukakis/Bentsen team lost, Bentsen's senatorial campaign headquarters were in the Mischer Corporation headquarters building. Although Mischer has denied ever doing any straight business with Bentsen, on November 11, 1979, the Mischer Corp. and two partners purchased an apartment building in a Houston suburb from Bentsen for an undisclosed sum of cash and a $243,000 promissory note due on January 2, 1980.[7]

There are other indirect business connections between Senator Bentsen and Mischer. John Tillman "Jack" Trotter, Mischer's close business associate and former chairman of Mischer's flagship Allied Bank of Houston, was an administrator of one of Bentsen's blind investment trusts. One of Bentsen's investments was in the J. T. Trotter No. 2 Limited Partnership, which controlled 2,167 acres southwest of Houston.[8]

What's more, Mischer's company ended up owning a Houston savings and loan that had belonged to Bentsen's company. Benjamin Franklin Savings was owned by Bentsen's holding company, Lincoln Consolidated, an insurance company. In 1971, after Bentsen took office as a senator, Lincoln sold the S&L to IC Industries of Chicago. In 1978, the Mischer Corp. bought Benjamin Franklin Savings from IC Industries.[9] (Mischer presciently sold this S&L in 1981 before the bottom dropped out of the industry.)

In his remarkable new book, *Who Will Tell the People*, author William Greider reports that when Democratic presidential candidate Michael Dukakis tried to bring up the savings-and-loan crisis as a campaign issue against the Republicans in 1988, Bentsen "communicated to campaign headquarters that this was not going to be a winning issue for their ticket."

---

[5] *Houston Post*, October 5, 1975.
[6] *Houston Post*, April 23, 1981.
[7] Deed records of Harris County, film code 144-81-1387.
[8] Senator Bentsen's financial disclosure statements.
[9] *Houston Post*, September 22, 1978.

As we shall see, Bentsen's connections to the S&L industry and to those who caused taxpayers to lose hundreds of millions of dollars extend far and wide.

The exact relationship between Mischer and President Bush is something of a mystery. Mischer acknowledges having known Bush for a long time, but says he has never been particularly close to him. There are no public records showing the two ever did business together.

Several people who are familiar with the CIA believe that Mischer engineered the involvement of his former son-in-law, Robert Corson, with the CIA around the time Bush was CIA director. A Washington lawyer familiar with the CIA told me that Corson's work for the CIA began in 1976, when Mischer's friend Bush was director of the CIA. In addition, a former federal law enforcement official familiar with Corson's money-laundering activities believes that Corson's participation began around the time Jimmy Carter won the 1976 presidential election.

This official stated that after Carter's victory, Bush begged Carter to keep him on as CIA director. When Carter refused, Bush returned to Texas, met with Mischer and they decided, among other things regarding their private activities, to use Corson as their cutout, or front man. (This story may be apocryphal. A noted Washington journalist who publishes a newsletter printed an almost identical story some two years after I was told the story, except in place of Mischer she named Midland oilman William Blakemore, a good friend of Bush and Mischer.)

When the story of his alleged meeting with Bush was related to Mischer for comment, he denied it, focusing on the first part: "I can testify that Bush wouldn't go to Carter and ask him to stay on."

If Mischer so testified under oath, then he could be prosecuted for perjury, for that's exactly what happened, although I didn't know it when I was interviewing Mischer. Several months later, I found an article in the *Washington Post*, dated August 10, 1988, stating that after Carter defeated Gerald Ford: "Bush wanted to stay on at the agency—'desperately'—according to one of his closest former associates. On November 19, Bush visited Carter in Plains, Georgia.

"Knoche, Bush's CIA deputy," the article continued, "who accompanied him to Plains, recalled that 'Bush offered to stay on a short-time, transitional period. He was a little shocked that there was no interest in that' on Carter's part.

"Robert Mosbacher, a longtime Bush friend from Texas and the current finance chairman of the Bush presidential campaign, said in an interview that Bush went further and told Carter, 'If I stay on, I won't run in 1980' for president. But Carter wasn't interested."

The *Washington Post* also reported that Bush maintained his CIA contacts during the Carter Administration, stating there were "several occasions in 1978-79 when Bush was living in Houston and traveling the country in his first run for the Presidency that he set aside periods of up to 24 hours and told aides he had to fly to Washington for a secret meeting of former CIA directors."

The day after the First Couple's February 1992 visit to Paula Mischer Watson's (Walter Mischer's daughter's) house, an event occurred in Mexico that revealed another side to the Walter Mischer-George Bush relationship and exposed the close ties between Mischer and some of the stalwarts of the Republican party in Houston (those who started and nurtured Bush's political career). The event was the death of Albert Bel Fay, who passed away in Cuernavaca while on vacation.

Bush described the late Houston businessman Bel Fay, former U.S. ambassador to Trinidad and Tobago and former Republican candidate for Texas governor, as his "political mentor."[10] Bush said Fay was his "close, personal friend, and a leader in building the Republican party in Houston."

Mischer has also acknowledged that Fay was a good friend of his. Fay served on the board of directors of Westside National Bank in Houston, a bank partly controlled by Robert Corson.[11] Paula, Mischer's daughter, was married to Corson (whom Mischer allegedly introduced to the CIA). Fay also did business and owned property in Belize, the small Central American country where Mischer is very active.

Mischer's circles of business associates and friends continue to intersect in a number of other places with those of President Bush. For example, one of Bush's oldest and closest friends is the previously mentioned Midland, Texas, oilman William Blakemore II.

Blakemore, a fierce supporter of Nicaraguan Contras, was president of the Gulf and Caribbean Foundation, which raised private money to lobby for congressional aid to the Contras. A paper found in Oliver North's White House safe diagramming the private aid network to the

---

[10] Fay's obituary in the *Houston Chronicle*, March 3, 1992.
[11] Texas Banking Red Book, 1987-88; *Houston Post*, February 27, 1985.

Contras shows that the Gulf and Caribbean Foundation was one of the key organizations. North's diaries also list several meetings with Blakemore and Gulf and Caribbean's front man, Dan Kuykendall, a Texas native, Washington lobbyist and former Tennessee congressman. The Gulf and Caribbean Foundation hired Michael Ledeen to write a booklet on the situation in Latin America, particularly in Nicaragua. Ledeen, a part-time adviser to Reagan's National Security Council, was one of the leading instigators of the Iranian arms-for-hostages deals. And one of Blakemore's Houston attorneys is a lawyer who represents the Houston interests of the family of the late Nicaraguan dictator, Anastasio Somoza Debayle, the ousted predecessor to the Contras. (We will see a number of people in this book who also aided the Contras.)

Blakemore married a daughter of eccentric Houston oilman Jim "Silver Dollar" West, noted for carrying around huge quantities of silver dollars and pressing them upon startled Houstonians. The other West daughter and her husband were a major financial force behind Tracor, the Austin-based electronics firm and defense contractor. Their partner, a large stockholder and board member at Tracor, was Jack Trotter, Mischer's associate and Bentsen's trustee. In 1969, Trotter, along with the Blakemore-Somoza attorney, was named one of the three trustees of most of the West family's trusts.

Blakemore has said he knows Mischer "reasonably well. I gave a little money to his foundation"—one supporting a desert museum at Lajitas in far west Texas. But Mischer, when asked if he knows Blakemore, said, "Yeah. I just know who he is. He's got a ranch by Alpine."

Mischer's response is laughable, and obviously intended to convey the impression he knows nothing about Blakemore or his Iron Mountain ranch, which allegedly was used for CIA training of Latin American assets and transshipment of weapons to Latin America. Blakemore's ranch is actually outside Marathon, 30 miles east of Alpine. Mischer, a man who has owned hundreds of thousands of acres in that area and probably knows the ownership of every square inch of land there, could not have made such a mistake of geography.

Another strong Contra supporter and Houston Republican who has also supported Bush from his earliest political races is Jimmy Lyon. Lyon, a banker, is mentioned at least four times in Oliver North's White House diaries in connection with fundraising for the Contras. Lyon and Mischer are also longtime good friends. Lyon said they have done business together for many years.

Robert Mosbacher, Bush's close friend, former Secretary of Commerce and Bush-Quayle campaign chairman, is no stranger to Mischer either. In 1984, Mischer began one of his most grandiose developments west of Houston by buying Cinco Ranch, a 5,416-acre development, from Mosbacher and several other wealthy Houstonians.

And, in 1980, Walter Mischer was the biggest fundraiser in the country for Ronald Reagan and George Bush, collecting more than $3 million for their campaign,[12] including $2.8 million in one fund-raising dinner in Houston, which Mischer headed. The *Houston Chronicle* also reported in March 1992 that Mischer donated $1,000 to Bush's campaign, making him one of the President's "major Harris County contributors."

A longtime Houstonian who has followed Mischer's career over the years said Mischer was introduced to the circle of Brahmin Houston Republicans like Bush, James A. Baker III and Mosbacher by Lyon and Tommy Robinson. Robinson, a banker and contractor who owned First Mortgage, and Lyon controlled a right-wing newspaper in the city called the *Houston Tribune*.

The money for Mischer's first construction jobs came from Tommy Robinson, said the longtime Houstonian, who stated that Robinson, Mischer, Bush and Baker all relaxed together at the Houston Country Club. It is well known that Bush and Baker first became good friends on the tennis courts of the club.

In addition, two sons of Bush and Mischer, Neil Bush and Walt Mischer, Jr., are friends—"asshole buddies," according to one Houston businessman who has known Mischer since the 1950s. On several occasions, the Houston newspaper gossip columns have confirmed this by noting that Neil and Walt Jr. have had lunch or dinner together in Houston.

Two sons of Neil and Walt Jr. also attend the first grade together at Kinkaid School, a ritzy private school in Houston. Neil also attended Kinkaid, along with the children of Baker and Mosbacher, before his family moved to Washington. And Mischer Sr. has served on Kinkaid's investment foundation.

However, for some reason, Walt Mischer, Jr., denies being close to Neil. "I have met him one time in my life," he said of Neil. When told about being named together in gossip columns, the younger Mischer said, "I've never had lunch with Neil Bush in my life."

---

[12] Sandy Sheehy, op. cit.

When Neil Bush was charged by the Office of Thrift Supervision (OTS) with conflicts of interest in his actions as a director of Silverado Banking, Savings and Loan Association in Denver, Charles M. Pickett appeared as one of the two expert witnesses on his behalf. Pickett was the former general counsel to Mischer's Allied Bancshares. Even though the OTS knew this and knew of Neil's relationship to Walt Jr., and their fathers' friendship, the OTS attorneys incredibly did not question either Neil or Pickett about it.[13]

Before joining Allied Bancshares, Pickett was the regional counsel for the Dallas region of the Federal Deposit Insurance Corp., and on at least one occasion oversaw the selling of a defunct bank to none other than Mischer and his partners.[14]

Walt Mischer, Jr., said he knows who Pickett is, but that he didn't have anything to do with arranging Pickett's testimony for Neil. Mischer Sr. initially denied knowing who Pickett was. Later he said he remembered him, but he didn't think his first name was Charles. Mischer then denied having anything to do with Pickett's testimony.

Walter M. Mischer, Sr., was born in Gillett, Texas, on the Fourth of July, 1922. His family was doing quite well before that fatal day of January 20, 1934, when his father, Walter C. Mischer, was killed in a shooting incident. Mischer's father was not only the deputy sheriff but also a big cattle rancher and owner of a car repair shop.

The killing of his father must have taken a terrible toll on Mischer and his family. One of his teachers, Viola Johnson, said many times through high school Mischer would complain about being poor, even though "he actually wasn't that poor—but he didn't like not to have money. He hated being a poor boy." His buddy Steve Crews said Mischer's primary interest was in getting out of school and starting his own construction company. "He was always making signs that said 'Mischer Construction Company,' " Crews said.

After Mischer graduated from high school, he attended Texas A&I, a small Texas college in the small south Texas town of Kingsville. He supported himself by doing surveying work and building fences on the

---

[13] United States of America before the Office of Thrift Supervision, in the matter of Neil Bush, a former director of Silverado Banking, Savings and Loan Association, Denver, Colorado; hearing in Denver before Administrative Law Judge Daniel J. Davidson, September 1990.

[14] *Houston Post*, October 23, 1975.

mammoth King ranch. When Japan bombed Pearl Harbor he tried to sign up with the Navy, but was rejected because of his earlier head injury. So he joined the construction firm of Stone & Webster and helped build small naval installations in the Caribbean.[15]

After the war was over, he went back to his hometown of Gillett, surveyed the situation and thought to himself, "Even if I had it all here, I wouldn't have much. I'm going to Houston." He landed a job there working for Foster Wheeler, on the construction of refineries along the Houston Ship Channel. It was there he met his first partner, Pat Harris, a construction superintendent. They formed the Mischer-Harris Co. and tried their hand at building homes. But Mischer soon decided that home building was not for him, and turned to the construction of utilities for new houses, primarily sewers.[16] Since then, when the Walter Mischer success story is recounted in Houston, it usually begins, "He started out down in the sewers. . . ."

When Jim McConn, a former Houston mayor whom Mischer supported, asked Mischer, "Walter how did you get so much goddamn money," Mischer reportedly replied, "Digging ditches. I dug them deeper and cheaper." (This is the same Jim McConn who got in over his head running up gambling debts in Las Vegas and called the Houston city purchasing agent Jack Key, saying he needed $6,000 immediately. Key promptly extorted the $6,000 from a city contractor. Key went to jail and Kathy Whitmire defeated McConn, reportedly prompting Mischer to say of McConn, "I like my mayors dumb, but not that dumb.")

Although Mischer preaches the virtues of the free market and the unfettered entrepreneur, he has sucked a lot of juice from the government teat. He made his first big money in real estate development by taking advantage of quasi-governmental entities called municipal utility districts, which were established by the Texas legislature and allowed a private developer to issue tax-exempt bonds to put in the utility systems for new developments.

In some cases, Mischer would have the bonds issued, buy them himself to take advantage of the tax-free interest and then use the proceeds to pay his company to install the utilities. After the homes were built, the city of Houston would annex the area, assume the bonded indebtedness and pay it off with its tax collections. A pretty good deal,

---

[15] *Houston Post*, November 22, 1987.
[16] Ibid.

if you could get it. The trick was to have the political connections in the Texas Legislature and the Houston City Council to get the utility district established and then annexed.[17]

Mischer also made a bundle in the city's cable television scandal. In the late 1970s the Houston City Council awarded the city's cable TV franchises to select privileged groups of local investors. Mischer was a prominent member of one of these groups, which had to put up very little front money. As soon as they received their franchises, these groups sold them for millions of dollars to national cable TV outfits.[18]

Mischer also turned up as one of the investors in a company that owned part of the local Yellow Cab company, which had a virtual monopoly on the city's taxi-cab business, courtesy of the City Council.[19] And he owned a good-sized stake in a local municipal bond underwriting company that was getting city and county contracts to underwrite their tax-exempt bonds.

As local activist, watchdog and gadfly Virgil Knox told the *Houston Press* in 1990, "I don't think there are many things that go on in the city of Houston that Walter Mischer doesn't notice. Everyone is afraid of Walter Mischer. Politicians, developers, engineers. No one wants to stand up to him. If there's a toll road, a Grand Parkway, whatever it is, if it doesn't benefit Walter Mischer in some way, it probably won't get built."

County election records show that Mischer has rarely voted in local, state or national elections. When asked about this by *Houston Post* reporters, Mischer first replied, "I vote most every time." But when told that county records show that he has not voted regularly since 1980, Mischer said he sometimes votes absentee, and "a lot of times I don't vote, particularly when it is not close." The county election records show that Mischer has not voted absentee since 1980.

"Why vote when all you have to do is pick up the phone and get what you want," one county politician said, when told of Mischer's voting record.[20]

Mischer got his start in real estate development and still owns his own company, the Mischer Corporation, which buys raw land and prepares it for the construction of homes and commercial buildings by

---

[17] *Shadow on the Alamo,* by Harvey Katz (New York: Doubleday, 1972).
[18] *Houston Post,* April 5, 1980; December 7, 1980.
[19] *Houston Post* February 1, 1990.
[20] *Houston Post,* November 22, 1987.

putting in the streets and utilities. His company owns thousands of acres of prime development land in the Houston area, while affiliate companies do street paving and sell air-conditioning units to home builders.

Although the Mischer Corp. is a medium-sized company of less than $100 million in assets, Mischer has run with some of the biggest businessmen in the country. At one time in the early 1980s he served on the board of Braniff Airlines, and he and his close, longtime partner, Howard L. Terry, were large stockholders in Marathon Manufacturing Corp., which was purchased by Cincinnati billionaire Carl Lindner's Penn Central. Mischer and Terry's stock in Marathon was swapped for Penn Central stock, and Terry was named to the Penn Central board of directors. In 1986, Mischer and Terry sold their Penn Central stock for $106 million.[21]

At one time, Mischer was the fourth largest private landowner in Texas.[22] He may have lost that position in 1988 when he sold more than 200,000 acres in far west Texas near Big Bend National Park to the state of Texas to be used as a park. His partner, and co-owner of the land, was oilman Robert O. Anderson, the former chairman of Atlantic Richfield.

What's more, when novelist James Michener came to Texas to research his novel on the Lone Star State, Mischer squired him around. "I found Mischer a delightful friend and I'm indebted to him," Michener told the Houston Chronicle.

Other than real estate development, Mischer's primary business interests lie in another field that has extensive government protection and intrusion: banking. Mischer has been a big collector of banks since the late 1950s. In the mid-1970s, he consolidated them into Allied Bank of Texas, which was the fourth largest bank in Houston with assets approaching $10 billion and more than 40 subsidiaries across the state. He was the largest stockholder of the bank with 5 percent of the common shares and was chairman of the holding company, Allied Bancshares, when he sold out in 1988 to First Interstate Bank of California.[23]

Mischer is known for hiring former federal examiners to run his banks and has had longtime connections to the top echelons of the federal banking regulatory system. His son, Walt Jr., has been a director

---

[21] Forbes, December 1, 1986.
[22] Sandy Sheehy, op. cit.
[23] Houston Post, January 30, 1988; November 22, 1987; April 12, 1987.

of the Houston branch of the Dallas Federal Reserve bank. Further, the former U.S. Comptroller of the Currency, Robert Clarke, who was not reconfirmed by the Senate in 1991, but stayed on into 1992 because Bush had not named a replacement, is a friend of Mischer's. Clarke was an investor, borrower and director of Allied Bank.

In 1974, Clarke, then an attorney in Houston, and his brother-in-law, D. Kent Anderson, a top executive at Allied Bank, invested together in a bank that was later sold to Allied.[24] Before he was named Comptroller in late 1985, by Treasury Secretary James A. Baker III, Clarke was a lawyer with Bracewell and Patterson, a Houston law firm that has done legal work for Mischer and his companies.

At one time, Clark was buying and selling stock in First Continental Real Estate Investment Trust, a mortgage financing firm where Mischer Jr. was a director. Clarke also had dozens of outstanding loans at Allied after he became Comptroller. Although Clarke's Office does not oversee state-chartered banks like Allied, he did sit on the board of the Federal Deposit Insurance Corporation, which is responsible for all banks with deposit insurance.

Clarke also had an investment in a Louisiana bank with his brother-in-law and Gerald Smith, Mischer's right-hand man at Allied Bank. Another investor in this bank was Louisiana Mafia associate Herman K. Beebe, Sr. (More on these connections later.)

One last regulatory connection worth noting: in the 1970s Mischer had some questionable loans with Houston First Savings, an S&L that was owned by his friend, sometime partner and Allied Bank board member, Eddie Dyche. The Texas Savings and Loan Department criticized the loans as being imprudent and forced the S&L to move them out. The woman who ran that S&L for Dyche, Mary Grigsby, was later appointed by President Jimmy Carter to a place on the Federal Home Loan Bank Board, which oversees savings and loans.[25]

After deregulation, Grigsby served on the FHLBB with Ed Gray, who was the chairman. It was Grigsby who told Gray in November 1985 that Charles Keating of Lincoln Savings wanted to hire him. This was a time when the S&L industry in general was criticizing Gray for taking a hard line on some of their questionable practices, and also when

---

[24] *Houston Post*, December 18, 1987.
[25] Interview with Art Leiser, former chief examiner of Texas Savings and Loan Department.

federal regulators were examining Lincoln Savings. Gray found out later that Keating wanted him out of the way.[26] And it was Grigsby who had been selected to deliver the message.

Mischer has also been involved in some not-so-legitimate enterprises. He was on the fringes of two of the biggest scandals in Texas and Houston history: the Sharpstown scandal of the early 1970s that toppled several of his favorite politicians and the Hermann Hospital Estate scandal of the mid-1980s that came close to engulfing his son and namesake who had taken his place on the estate board.

The Sharpstown scandal was about two things near and dear to Mischer: banking and politics. Houston banker Frank Sharp had been running his bank fast and loose and wanted to get out from under the oversight of the federal deposit insurance system. Sharp made some sweetheart loans and stock deals to favored Texas politicians to get a law passed by the Texas Legislature. Sharp got caught and pleaded guilty and took a bunch of Texas politicians down with him.[27]

One of those politicians was the speaker of the Texas House of Representatives, Gus Mutscher, who was convicted of taking a bribe. In 1970, a year before the scandal broke, Mutscher appointed Mischer to his committee of 100 to study the duties, responsibilities, ethics and compensation of state legislators.[28] Years later, after Mutscher got himself rehabilitated and elected county judge of Washington County, he was borrowing money for questionable land deals from Mischer's Allied Bank.[29]

The politician closest to Mischer who got swept away by the reaction to Sharpstown was the boy wonder of Texas politics, Ben Barnes. The golden-haired boy from Brownwood had risen faster than all the other greats of Texas politics before him. At the age of 26, he became the youngest Speaker of the House and was Texas lieutenant governor and bucking for governor when the Sharpstown scandal hit. Although he wasn't directly implicated, he was tarred as part of the network of good-old-boy politics and was defeated in the 1972 Democratic primary for governor.

---

[26] *Inside Job,* by Steve Pizzo, Mary Fricker and Paul Muolo (New York: McGraw-Hill, 1989).
[27] Harvey Katz, op. cit.
[28] *Houston Post,* October 24, 1970.
[29] Washington County deed records.

Barnes was Mischer's boy. Not only did Mischer support him politically, he loaned him money for business ventures, including a sweetheart loan for an interest in a radio station.[30] Years later, Barnes would reminisce wistfully about how Mischer advised him not to run for governor in 1970 but wait until 1972, which turned out to be a fatal mistake because he lost the election.

Many of the details of the Sharpstown story can be found in the 1972 book *Shadow on the Alamo*, by Washington investigative reporter Harvey Katz, who picked up on the significance of Mischer faster than most of his Texas counterparts. Katz missed something very important about Mischer, though: his reputed relationship to one of the most powerful Mafia families in the country, the Marcello family in New Orleans.

I was first told about Mischer's connections to the New Orleans Mafia family by a former deputy sheriff who had worked for a Harris County commissioner in Mischer's hip pocket. He, in turn, referred me to a number of retired Houston police officers who had worked in the old Criminal Intelligence Division. This division followed Carlos Marcello, the New Orleans Mafia don, and his relatives, when they came to Houston to look after their numerous business interests.

The retired CID officers confirmed that Mischer and the Marcellos knew each other, met together and had mutual business interests. They also said that the Marcellos had contact with other powerful Houstonians, including noted developer Kenneth Schnitzer and prominent oil man John Mecom, Jr.[31]

When Marcello and family came to Houston they would sometimes stay at the Stouffer Hotel in the Greenway Plaza, which had been developed by Schnitzer. Schnitzer, who had a number of business connections with Mischer, bought a savings and loan in a suburb of Houston that had been controlled by Tommy Adkins, who was a partner with Mischer in the purchase of the apartment complex from U.S. Senator Lloyd Bentsen.

"Walter Mischer and I have been close friends for many years," Schnitzer said in a letter to me. "I think the only business transaction we did together was the development of the office/merchandise mart which is known as Innova," Schnitzer stated. "I have never done any other

---

[30] Katz, op. cit.
[31] Mecom is named in congressional organized crime hearings because of his attendance and gambling at a mobbed-up restaurant in New Orleans.

business with Walter Mischer or his son." However, Schnizter's development company built the 71-story Allied Bank building, where Mischer's bank holding company was headquartered. (And where the notorious, scandal-plagued Bank of Credit and Commerce International (BCCI) had its Houston branch.) Also, in 1990 Schnitzer was a partner with Walt Mischer, Jr., in a group of Houston investors vying for the $1 billion-plus rail transit contract.

Schnitzer also said he has "never associated with the Marcellos." And, he said, "If the Marcellos were ever comped into the Greenway Stouffer, I did not arrange any such comping or have connection with it or know about it."

One former Houston police officer with the Criminal Intelligence Division stated unequivocally to me that Schnitzer had contact with and associated with Joseph Marcello, Carlos Marcello's son. He said the Marcellos would register into the Greenway Stouffer and then go and party with Schnitzer in Schnitzer's penthouse.

"I do not have and never had a penthouse at the Greenway Stouffer, and the Marcellos never attended any party in any such non-existent penthouse or any other living quarters I have occupied," Schnitzer also stated in his letter.

The former police officer said the penthouse was either in the Stouffer or in one of the high-rise office buildings in Greenway Plaza.

When Mary Flood and I interviewed Mischer in 1987 for an article in the *Houston Post*'s Sunday magazine, I asked him about his relationship to Carlos Marcello, which a number of people had told us about. Surprisingly, he admitted he met Marcello when a Houston real estate man—he couldn't remember who—brought the Mafia don to his office.

Mischer said Marcello, whom he described as a "short, squatty Italian" (Marcello's nickname is "The Little Man"), wanted to buy two Houston hotels from him. Mischer and his partner, Howard Terry, owned the Coronado Hotel and the Carrousel Hotel. The Coronado was located in a older neighborhood west of downtown and was noted for its poker games, gambling and prostitution, according to undercover Houston police officers. It later burned down.

The Carrousel opened in 1960 to great fanfare. The hotel was located between downtown Houston and Hobby Airport. It was supposed to be a hip, swinging place, but instead evolved into a gaudy and semi-sleazy motel. It had its share of prostitution too. NASA would hide the Mercury astronauts from the press at the Carrousel, where some of them allegedly engaged in certain extracurricular activities.

The Carrousel Hotel is well known to many first-year law students across the country. A court case involving the Carrousel is used in torts classes to illustrate an unusual type of battery. Back in the early 1960s, a black man who worked for NASA was going through the buffet line at the Brass Ring Club in the Carrousel. The manager of the club jerked the plate out of his hand and said that "Negroes" couldn't be served in the club. The Texas Supreme Court ruled in favor of the black man, deciding that jerking a plate from a person's hand was harmful or offensive bodily contact, and therefore a battery.

Later, the new Houston Intercontinental Airport opened north of the city and Hobby Airport closed for a time. The Carrousel died on the vine and was shuttered in 1975. That's when Marcello came around. But Mischer said he didn't sell to Marcello, because "I didn't want to get run out of town."

However, it appears that Mischer sold the hotel to Marcello indirectly. In our interview, Mischer said he couldn't remember who bought the hotel. It turned out to be John Kenneth Coil, a disbarred attorney and convicted pornographer who began offering X-rated movies in the rooms. A sergeant in the vice division of the Houston Police Department said Coil was an associate of the New Orleans Mafia family. In fact, Coil had a similar X-rated hotel, the San Antonio Inn, on the Airline Highway in Metarie, Louisiana, just a few miles down the road from the Town & Country Motel, Marcello's infamous headquarters.[32]

The transaction between Coil, Mischer and Terry over the Carrousel was a strange one. Mischer said they sold the hotel on a contract for deed. This basically means that the title to the property in the form of a deed is not transferred to the buyer until the property is completely paid for. In a normal transaction the buyer gets title to the property by deed and, if the buyer owes the seller or a bank money, then the seller, or the bank, retains a lien on the property.

In the case of the Carrousel, Mischer and Terry retained title to the hotel and continued to pay the taxes while Marcello's man showed porno flicks and ran whores. Mischer said they took the hotel back around 1986 and bulldozed it down.

---

[32] Deed records and lawsuits in New Orleans and Jefferson Parish.

An independent confirmation that Marcello controlled the Carrousel Motel is contained in an upcoming book, *The Man on the Grassy Knoll*, by two Houston investigators, John R. Craig and Philip A. Rogers. The book, to be published by Avon, identifies one of the three so-called tramps who were taken into custody in Dallas after JFK was assassinated. The authors show that this man was a CIA agent. One of the other "tramps" they identify as convicted hitman Charles Harrelson.

Craig and Rogers state in their book that after the assassination the CIA agent had called Harrelson, "who was staying at another Carlos Marcello-owned rest stop, the Carrousel Motel at 3330 Reveille, across the street from the Gulfgate Mall. The Carrousel was a well-known hideout and watering hole for bandidos of all persuasions."

After the 1987 interview with Mischer, I talked to two other people in a position to know, who further confirmed Mischer's relationship to the Marcello family. One, a former Mischer employee and close personal friend, said Mischer not only dealt with the Marcellos but also with mob associates from New York and Chicago. This person said he once saw Mischer together with some of the Marcello brothers at the Hofbrau steak house in Houston. The Hofbrau is owned by a man named Browne Rice, who was a partner in the Victoria House Hotel in Belize with Albert Bel Fay, George Bush's political "mentor."

And yet another individual who confirmed Mischer's relationship to Carlos Marcello was a private investigator in Houston who has a great deal of contact with the FBI. This person said he knew of Mischer's relationship to Marcello primarily through Herman K. Beebe, Louisiana mob associate and the so-called godfather of the crooked Texas S&Ls.

Although Beebe deserves an entire book, the next chapter will suffice for our purposes. Then in Chapter 3 we will get back to the relationship between Mischer and Beebe and how their paths became intertwined in dirty savings and loans.

2

THANKS, BEEBE

S cott Susala tooled his silver BMW up Sorrento Valley Road north of
San Diego. His house is on a bluff overlooking the road, which he
and his friends jokingly refer to as "Surrender Hill," in honor of one of
the biggest drug busts in Southern California history.

In March 1985, Susala and about 100 others were charged in what
federal authorities said was a massive cocaine-smuggling ring. FBI
agents said then the group was responsible for bringing in 20 to 25
percent of the cocaine being smuggled from Peru. The two Peruvian
ringleaders were in the "highest echelon of the cocaine market in South
American and Peru."[1]

While many of his co-conspirators were getting long jail sentences,
Susala pleaded guilty to possession of cocaine, a misdemeanor, and
received a one-year probated sentence. The more serious felony charges
of conspiracy to possess cocaine with intent to distribute and the unlaw-
ful use of a communication facility were dismissed upon his plea bargain. All of the records in this case, except the docket sheet, are sealed
in the San Diego federal courthouse.[2] This was Susala's only official
brush with the law, but federal law enforcement officials knew very well
who he was because of his father and his financial mentor.

His father, Edward D. "Fast Eddie" Susala, was a manager and
general partner of La Costa Spa and Hotel, the luxury resort north of

---

[1] Associated Press, March 19, 1985.
[2] United States of American vs. Sullivan, et al., CR 85-0000252.

San Diego that was controlled by the mob and built with Teamsters Union pension funds. "Fast Eddie" was brought in as a general partner in the early 1980s by three of the four original partners, Allard Roen, Irving Molasky and Merv Adelson.[3] The fourth founding partner, Morris "Moe" Dalitz, had "retired" from La Costa in 1981.[4] Dalitz, one of the most notorious mobsters in this country's history, had risen from the old Cleveland Mayfield mob to running Las Vegas casinos for the syndicate.

An early Dalitz partner was Morris Kleinman, who was later involved with Castle Bank & Trust, the Nassau, Bahamas, money-washing, tax-avoidance bank used by the mob and the CIA.[5] And, a registered agent for La Costa Land Company, which participated in the development of the resort, was Chicago attorney Burton Kanter, one of the principals behind Castle Bank & Trust.[6] (Kanter has connections to several important people in this book, which will be discussed in later chapters.)

In 1975, *Penthouse* magazine published an exposé on La Costa saying it was established and frequented by mobsters. That article spawned a huge libel action in which a jury in 1982 cleared *Penthouse*; but a judge, who turned out to have connections to some of the witnesses, overturned the jury verdict with respect to Molasky and Adelson. The parties eventually settled out of court; *Penthouse* didn't pay a penny but gave a letter to Molasky and Adelson saying it didn't mean to imply that the two were members of organized crime. The letter said nothing about Dalitz and Roen, the latter a longtime Dalitz associate who in 1962 pleaded guilty to stock fraud.[7]

(At La Costa, Canadian money replaced the Teamsters financing in 1984, and in 1988 a Japanese company purchased the resort.)

In the early 1980s, Scott Susala was a playboy, scratch amateur golfer, tennis player and college dropout with a small bank account. He was not, by any stretch of the imagination, a businessman. But a very successful businessman picked him off the La Costa playgrounds, dusted him off and brought him into the world of big real estate deals and fast,

---

[3] San Diego County deed records.
[4] *Wall Street Journal*, September 15, 1986.
[5] *Wall Street Journal*, April 18, 1980.
[6] *Masters of Paradise*, by Alan A. Block (Transaction Publishers, 1991).
[7] *Wall Street Journal*, September 15, 1986.

easy money. The identity of that businessman could be read from the license plate on Susala's BMW: "Thnx BB."

BB was Herman K. Beebe, Sr., from Shreveport, Louisiana, and Susala was thanking him for all the money Susala had made in their real estate firm and other Beebe-connected businesses. Beebe may have picked up Susala off the Southern California grass because he liked him, or he may have helped "Fast Eddie's" son as a favor to the mob. Whatever, the two priapics became master and pupil, spending most of their time together getting drunk and chasing women.

A 1985 report on Beebe's banking activities by the Comptroller of the Currency noted, "Because Beebe owns two residences in Southern California and spends the majority of his time there, speculation abounds that he is involved with financial institutions on the West Coast. To date, none of his California operatives or operations have been identified." Despite this red flag, no other reporter that I am aware of, including some who scoff, mistakenly, at the claim presented in this book that Beebe is connected to the Mafia, has traveled to Southern California and investigated Beebe's activities there.

Susala stated on his resumé that he "formed a powerful alliance with financier H. K. Beebe to handle the bulk of TLC's real estate investments." Their company, TLC Investments, stood for Texas, Louisiana and California, the three states where they were doing real estate deals. In San Diego, Susala was also a general partner with Beebe's son, H. K. "Ken" Beebe, Jr., in a limited partnership called Branch Office Ltd. Ken Beebe listed Susala's home on Sorrento Valley Road as his California address in the partnership documents, demonstrating that they used each other's home addresses for business purposes. In addition, Beebe got Susala together with Vernon Savings & Loan owner Don Dixon, with whom he developed condominiums along the championship golf course at La Costa.

Beebe and the Susalas also got caught up in a lawsuit involving a bank loan to a La Costa travel agency. Beebe, Scott and "Fast Eddie" had guaranteed a $75,000 loan from San Dieguito National Bank to the Tour Company, headed by Steven J. Leo, who, like Ken Beebe, also listed his address on the legal documents as Scott Susala's.[8]

Also hanging out at La Costa with Beebe and the Susalas were: the

---

[8] San Dieguito National Bank vs. The Tour Company, et al., San Diego Superior Court, 31647.

former All American wide receiver from Arkansas and then star with the San Diego Chargers, Lance "Bambi" Alworth; former Texas State Senator Peyton McKnight from Tyler, who later broke with the group because of the $1 million or so he lost on a loan to Alworth; and occasionally, noted Houston developer Kenneth Schnitzer, the close Mischer business associate found by Houston police associating with the Marcello Mafia family. As stated earlier, Schnitzer has denied any such association.

In a letter to me, Schnitzer stated, "I do not know Herman Beebe. I have never done business with him. I have never socialized with him. I would not know him if he walked into this room. I do know Eddie Susala. I have known him for many years. I have socialized with him at La Costa Country Club."

In further researching Beebe's business dealing, I was told by California journalist Mary Fricker that sometime during the late 1970s or early 1980s, Beebe was negotiating with some San Diego people to buy a gambling casino in Nevada. His prospective partners were known to the San Diego Police Department as having organized-crime connections, so the San Diego police contacted the New Orleans Metropolitan Crime Commission about Beebe. The casino deal fell through and the San Diego cops apparently lost interest in Beebe.

Meanwhile, the FBI had discovered in the late 1970s that Beebe's friend and partner, Lance Alworth, had done business with Allen Glick,[9] the Chicago mob's front man in several Las Vegas casinos. Also around this time, Glick's company was the beneficiary of a fraudulent deal at a Beebe-connected Houston bank. (More on this later.)

Beebe had been coming to play at La Costa, his home away from his Shreveport home, for some time. The public record first showing Beebe's presence in La Costa was a financial statement he submitted to the Texas Insurance Department in applying for permission to start an insurance company. This statement said he owned 50 percent of a house in La Costa in 1972. San Diego deed records show that his wife, Mary, deeded him her interest in the house in 1973. The next year, a fellow Louisiana businessman, one of Beebe's early backers and mentors, deeded him and his wife a one-half interest in a lot in La Costa.[10] The older man was Charles M. Waters, an insurance man who was caught

---

[9] *The Bluegrass Conspiracy*, by Sally Denton (New York: Doubleday, 1990).
[10] San Diego County deed records, Vol. 5059, p. 200.

in 1965 by the Securities and Exchange Commission in a stock scam along with Beebe.

The two were ordered not to mislead or withhold information from investors in their company, American Motel Industries. The next year, perhaps emboldened by a mere slap on the wrist for his first known walk on the wild side or perhaps as a reward from the mob, Beebe got a piece of his first bank, Bossier Bank & Trust (across the Red River from Shreveport), with financial help from Waters.

Beebe then proceeded to build a small empire of banks, hotels, nursing homes and insurance companies. By 1985, a study by the Comptroller of the Currency found his footprints at more than 110 banks and savings and loans in eight states. He ended up doing ten months in jail for bank fraud in 1989 and became known as the godfather of the dirty Texas savings and loans.

There is little in Beebe's background to predict that he would become such a notorious financial criminal. He was born in 1927 into a family that wasn't rich, but wasn't poverty-stricken either. His father had a sawmill in Lena in central Louisiana. In 1943 Beebe went to Northwestern State University in Natchitoches, where he worked as a janitor for his room and board. His college roommate, Raymond Reed, said he remembers that Beebe was "aggressive and didn't have much respect for women."

Beebe dropped out of Northwestern to serve in the Navy at the end of World War II and then enrolled in Louisiana State University in Baton Rouge, where he finished his bachelor's degree in agriculture in 1949. His first job was assistant county agent in Winn Parish, just north of his hometown, where he tried to help farmers deal with the vicissitudes of weather and the government. The Korean War intervened, he re-enlisted in the Navy, and when he got out he no longer had any desire to help farmers. He wanted to make money, so he started selling insurance. He moved to Alexandria, Louisiana, and by 1958 was a vice president of Savings Life Insurance Co. Three years later, he formed his own company, American Motel Industries, that eventually evolved into his umbrella company, AMI.

In the late 1960s, after he had his run-in with the SEC and had bought a few banks, but before he moved to Shreveport and set up his empire there, Beebe came to the attention of the Louisiana State Police and the New Orleans Metropolitan Crime Commission.

During this time, the Louisiana State Police conducted extensive surveillance on New Orleans Mafia boss Carlos Marcello and some of his closest associates, including his personal attorney and gofer, Phillip E. Smith. On the inside of the door leading out of Marcello's office at the Town & Country Motel was a sign that read: "Three can keep a secret if two are dead."[11] Smith's office was next to this sign and down the hall from Marcello's office. Attorney Aaron Kohn, a former FBI agent and the leading expert on the New Orleans Mafia, called Smith the "messenger boy" lawyer for Marcello.

One day the Louisiana State Police tracked Smith to a meeting with a hotel and insurance man from Alexandria, Herman K. Beebe. Kohn, who was privy to the occurences of the meetings, said the contact between Beebe and Marcello's people was prolonged and significant and probably dealt with the interests each had in Holiday Inns and nursing homes. Kohn, a shrewd and courageous man, died in 1990 shortly after being diagnosed with cancer; he had survived 30 years in the heart of Marcello territory as director of the New Orleans Metropolitan Crime Commission, a respected organization founded by New Orleans businessmen who were unhappy with the lack of effective law enforcement against organized crime in the region.

Marcello controlled at least five Holiday Inns in Louisiana through his fronts and close associates, the Occhipinti brothers. And Beebe owned at least six Holiday Inns in Texas and Louisiana, including one in the mob-infested New Orleans suburb of Gretna, which he later put up as collateral for a loan guarantee for his close associate Don Dixon to buy the infamous Vernon Savings and Loan.

Another Holiday Inn Beebe owned was in the small northern Texas town of Denton, according to AMI's 1976 annual report. In a 1975 book, *Brothers in Blood*, Marcello expert David Chandler states that in the late 1960s "the wealthy Louisiana Mafiosi, hounded in their home city, spread over Texas . . . They bought controlling shares in at least three banks, and their investments reached into towns as small as Denton." Also, according to Chandler, "One of Houston's largest builders began a series of real estate negotiations with Marcello."

Although Chandler didn't name Beebe in his 1975 book, the next year the *Dallas Morning News* did. In a ground-breaking series of articles on a circle of Texas banks being looted (the so-called Texas

---

[11] *Mafia Kingfish*, by John H. Davis (New York: New American Library, 1991).

rent-a-bank scandal), reporters Earl Golz and Dave McNeely made the allegations that Beebe had associations with mobsters, including one of Marcello's personal attorneys. (It was Smith, but they didn't name him.)

In addition, the *Dallas Morning News* stated, "Usually reliable federal sources report that Bossier Bank & Trust is suspected of being a conduit for funds skimmed by organized crime from Las Vegas gambling receipts and placed in foreign bank numbered accounts."

Beebe's business partner, former Texas politician Ben Barnes, was also named in the *Morning News* stories. Barnes promptly sued the Dallas paper for libel to the tune of $20 million. Beebe then had Bossier Bank & Trust sue the newspaper in federal court for $12 million.

Both lawsuits were later dropped, and although the *Morning News* didn't run any retractions or pay any damages, it agreed to Barnes and Beebe's request to keep all the records of the case sealed in the federal court. These records allegedly contained additional information tying Beebe to organized crime, including a secret report by the organized crime division of the Texas Attorney General's Office.

In December 1988, more than 12 years after its first story on Beebe came out, the *Dallas Morning News* published a story on Beebe's interesting banking and savings and loan network, which showed connections between him and Marcello. The paper's reporters, including Allen Pusey and Bill Lodge, found that Mob boss Carlos Marcello, his son Joseph and some of their companies were regularly doing business with Beebe's Pontchartrain State Bank in Metarie. According to a deposition by Pontchartrain president James McKigney, Marcello's Pelican Tomato Company had loans from, and deposits with, Pontchartrain, as did his son Joseph.

(McKigney was a close associate of Beebe and would later become chairman of the board and chief executive officer of Beebe's flagship bank, Bossier Bank & Trust.)

The *Morning News* also discovered that a Marcello business associate, John Drew Langford, tried to purchase Beebe's Colonial Bank in New Orleans. Langford was offered the bank with the condition that he put up additional collateral for a $1 million loan at Pontchartrain State Bank. Langford put up 1,700 acres that were owned by Marcello's Marsh Investment Corp. Marcello testified that Langford was a business partner and Marcello wanted to help him with his Pontchartrain loan.

The *Morning News* also discovered another link between Beebe and Marcello through one of Marcello's attorneys, Anthony J. Graffagnino, who was a director of Sunbelt Life Insurance Co., headquartered in Beebe's Shreveport offices.

Another Beebe business deal that went bad involved one of his close associates, Richard O'dom, who in the early 1980s was chief executive officer of Beebe's umbrella company, AMI. The victim of this deal, a well-respected Mississippi businessman, received a phone call out of the blue from none other than Mafia boss Carlos Marcello, making an unsolicited, incredible offer to help settle his problem with Beebe.

The details of the case are as follows: O'dom bought First United Bank in Meridian, Mississippi, then transferred more than $13 million in loans from Bossier Bank & Trust to First United. When Bossier failed in the summer of 1986, it took down First United with it. This failure led to a lawsuit between First United's receiver, the Federal Deposit Insurance Corp., and Paul Broadhead, a noted business leader from Meridian, Mississippi, and co-owner of the Cinemark Theater chain. Broadhead, who said he once was O'dom's best friend, was brought into the suit because he had guaranteed O'dom's loan from MBank Dallas to buy First United.

Broadhead told me that during the Beebe-instigated lawsuit against him, he received a phone call from the Texarkana federal prison. It was Carlos Marcello, serving time for bribery. The Mafia don made the astounding offer to help Broadhead with his banking problems and also with a problem he had with the U.S. Customs Service in New Orleans, which had confiscated a sword owned by Broadhead.

Also, during his struggle against Beebe and First United in his effort to escape liability for First United's failure, Broadhead located a Dallas pawn shop owner named Raymond Rose, who had served time in the federal prison with Marcello. Rose informed Broadhead that Marcello told him he was involved with Beebe.

Another connecting link between Beebe and Marcello was the mob-dominated Teamsters Union. "We own the Teamsters," Marcello bragged to two undercover FBI agents in 1979. Marcello was referring to himself and his close associates in the Chicago, Detroit, Kansas City and Florida Mafia families. And the President's Commission on Organized Crime confirmed in 1986 that the Teamsters had been "firmly under the influence of organized crime since the 1950s."

Beebe's longtime presence at La Costa underscores his likely connection to the Teamsters, which financed the construction of the resort. Joe Cage, the United States Attorney for the Western District of Louisiana, and Beebe's chief nemesis, is convinced of that connection. In fact, Cage, who won two fraud convictions against Beebe, believes that "the Beeb," as he calls him, got a great deal of his power and authority from the Teamsters.

To illustrate his point, Cage told me the stories of Terry Wilkerson and William Wortley. He explained how Wilkerson is a "Beebe man from Oklahoma City" who owned a nightclub there. Wilkerson hung out at the mobbed-up Jockey Club in Miami and would stay with Beebe when he went to La Costa, according to Cage. One day, Albert Prevot, a Houston businessman who turned state's evidence against Beebe, told Cage that in 1983 Wilkerson told him that he had lost a good friend, Allen Dorfman.

Dorfman, a notorious and powerful mob associate from Chicago, helped the mob control the Teamsters Central States Pension Fund, which was used to build La Costa and many Las Vegas casinos. Dorfman was convicted of racketeering and shortly thereafter gunned down in a Chicago parking lot.

(Dorfman's longtime attorney was Chicago lawyer Harvey Silets.[12] Silets also represented Chicago mob lawyer Sidney Korshak,[13] and Chicago attorney Burton Kanter, who has represented mob associates and was involved in La Costa. Silets also represented drug smuggler Jack DeVoe and Florida money launderer Lawrence Freeman,[14] who will be discussed later regarding his involvement with the Mafia, the CIA and the previously mentioned $200 million Florida land deal.)

Cage said that another Beebe associate, William Wortley, is a "Chicago thug and a Teamsters enforcer who is now in federal prison in Kentucky on a weapons charge." Wortley and Beebe owned a barge company together, said Cage.

Art Leiser, the former chief examiner for the Texas Savings and Loan Department, who knows more about Texas savings and loans than anyone except perhaps Beebe, believes there is something to Cage's theory about the Teamsters' backing Beebe. As soon as Beebe got involved with Surety Savings in Houston in the mid-1970s, Teamsters Union pension funds started pouring in as deposits, Leiser explained.

Another connecting link between Beebe, the Teamsters and the mob

---

[12] *Mobbed Up*, by James Neff (New York: Atlantic Monthly Press, 1989).
[13] *Dark Victory*, by Dan E. Moldea (New York: Viking Penguin, 1986).
[14] Florida Department of Law Enforcement reports on Lawrence Freeman.

lies in the business dealings of the late Morris Shenker, the St. Louis attorney who owned Las Vegas casinos, represented Teamsters head Jimmy Hoffa and was associated with Mafia families in Chicago, St. Louis and Kansas City. Both Shenker and Beebe were bailed out of problem investments by Southmark, the now-dismantled Dallas real estate development company and dumping ground for bad mob investments.

Shenker was also a borrower at Liberty Federal Savings in Leesville, Louisiana, which was controlled by San Antonio businessman James Hague. Hague was a cog in a circle of Texas wheeler-dealers and savings-and-loan looters, including Houstonians John Riddle and George Aubin, who borrowed hundreds of millions of dollars from Beebe-controlled S&Ls and then defaulted on the loans, leaving taxpayers to pick up the pieces.

Well, is Beebe a mobster or mob associate? Was he fronting for the mob in his dealings with and control of dozens of savings and loans? He and his attorney, James Adams, have vociferously denied this. Unfortunately, there are not the law enforcement mob experts in Texas and Louisiana that exist in, say, New York City. The few that there have been, such as Aaron Kohn and, for a brief period in the 1970s, the organized crime strike force at the Texas Attorney General's office, have all, however, convincingly connected Beebe with Carlos Marcello.

Interestingly, the man who prosecuted Beebe for bank fraud, Louisiana U.S. Attorney Joe Cage, has testified under oath that he "never had any suspicion that Mr. Beebe was tied into the Mafia," and has no evidence of that in his files. However, Cage made these statements in July 1987 under questioning by Beebe's attorney, Gerry Spence, the cowboy lawyer from Wyoming, who was trying to show the U.S. Attorney's prejudice in an attempt to disqualify Cage from prosecuting Beebe.

But, when I asked Cage in 1989 if he had come across any evidence linking Beebe or his associates to Marcello, he noted some interesting connections. First, he said that Shreveport businessman Harry Hart had received loans from the Beebe-bankrolled State Savings and Loan in Lubbock, Texas. Hart's attorney is Mike Maroun, who is also Marcello's Shreveport attorney, Cage said. It was Maroun who traveled to Guatemala in 1961 to be with Marcello after Attorney General Robert Kennedy had the Mafia boss abruptly deported.[15]

---

[15] John H. Davis, op. cit.

In addition, when Marcello came to Shreveport he usually hung out at Ernie's Supper Club, the same place Beebe frequented, Cage revealed.

Furthermore, Cage's assertion that Beebe is an instrument of the Teamsters is tantamount to saying he is also an instrument of organized crime. And, in an affidavit by Cage in response to Beebe's attempt to disqualify him, Cage explained the connections of Edmund Reggie, a Louisiana attorney, judge, power broker and close business associate of Beebe's, with "organized crime, Mafia or La Cosa Nostra figures."

Cage further stated in his affidavit that Beebe had close connections to former and current Louisiana governor Edwin Edwards. "Beginning in 1980, shortly after Edwin Edwards left the Governor's Office, AMI, Inc. (a company in which Herman K. Beebe, Sr., was the majority stockholder), and other Beebe-owned or -controlled companies began paying Edwin Edwards $100,000 per year for some unknown reason. This $100,000 per-year payment continued through 1982."

Edwards was also close to Marcello. During a 1979 investigation of Marcello, undercover FBI agents tape-recorded Marcello talking about Edwards. ". . . Edmund [meaning Edwin Edwards] and me all right, but I can't seen him every day. He's the strongest son of a bitching governor we ever had. He fuck with women and he plays dice games, but he won't drink. How you like that?"[16]

I found additional evidence linking Beebe to the Mafia in the form of a statement by a Houston dentist filed in state court in Houston. Dr. James F. Fairleigh first discusses how he was brought into Brazosport Savings near Houston in the mid-1970s by its owner, W. Carroll Kelly, and forced to buy stock in the S&L in order to avoid the S&L's foreclosure on his real estate loan.

(Kelly had consolidated his ownership of Brazosport S&L, which later became Continental Savings and Loan, through loans at Mischer's Allied Bank that were guaranteed by Beebe. Kelly and his fellow investors purchased Brazosport from Senator Lloyd Bentsen. Kelly told Texas S&L regulators that he was Beebe's representative in Texas, and took Beebe to meet with them when Beebe was getting back into Texas S&Ls in the early 1980s.)

Dr. Fairleigh further revealed that Kelly's ex-partner, Darrell Tomblin, had done him a favor and furnished him with an affidavit linking Kelly to Mafia boss Marcello. Fairleigh used this damaging affidavit to

---

[16] Reported by John H. Davis in *Mafia Kingfish: Carlos Marcello and the Assassination of JFK* (New York: New American Library, 1991).

sever his ties with Kelly. He further tied Kelly to Marcello when he stated: "Later, a black man, Wilbert Bourdeaux, whom I first met as a construction superintendent for Tomblin and later worked for me, confirmed Tomblin's statements about Kelly and Marcello since he had gone to New Orleans to do remodeling for Kelly and Tomblin in Marcello's kitchen. These were favors to 'the Don' from Kelly and Tomblin."

Fairleigh goes on to link Beebe with Marcello by stating that "Herman Beebe was a player in the relationship between Kelly and Marcello. Also the Bossier Bank in Louisiana had a part in their financing. I met Beebe at the White Hall Hotel with Kelly. We had brunch and Kelly was like a lap dog with this man. Tomblin said later that Marcello controlled Continental through stock owned by Beebe—another 'mustache' deal."

When I reached Tomblin at a Sarasota, Florida, restaurant in 1988, he said he couldn't remember what Fairleigh was talking about. He said he only met Marcello "once."

A few months later, Tomblin was indicted by a federal grand jury in San Antonio, along with an aide to former Nevada senator Chic Hecht, on charges of conspiring to pressure federal regulators to help them buy failed S&Ls at bargain prices and on charges of conspiring to use S&L loans to corner the spice market in Grenada. (As *Miami Herald* humorist Dave Barry would say, I am not making this up.)

Even if Beebe doesn't admit to being a mobster, he certainly enjoyed acting like one and leaving the impression that he was one. Art Leiser, the former Texas S&L chief examiner, related to me that when Kelly brought Beebe in to meet him, "Beebe looked at me and said there had been some bad things said about him. And he told me, 'You let me know if someone says something bad about me. I'll squash them like a cockroach.'"

It's doubtful that Beebe ever talked to Walter Mischer that way, but their relationship, which we will now take up in the next chapter, was not something either man, or their associates, liked to discuss.

3

MISCHER, BEEBE AND SAVINGS AND LOANS

B en Barnes is smooth as glass, oozing charm and overpowering personality like a good-looking Lyndon Johnson, never at a loss for words, never flustered. Never, that is, except when the former boy wonder of Texas politics is asked about the relationship between two of his closest associates, Herman K. Beebe and Walter Mischer: "No . . . Mischer . . . I didn't have any . . . Mischer and H. K. Beebe didn't have any friendship. I don't even know that they knew one another. I don't even know that they knew one another."

They do know each other, although Mischer wasn't too sure about it in an interview in November 1989. "I don't know. I don't think I ever met Beebe," he said. Asked whether Beebe had done any business with Allied Bank, he replied, "I don't know whether he did or didn't."

But in June of the next year, Mischer called to complain about a *Houston Post* story that mentioned him and Beebe. "I haven't seen Beebe in 15 or 18 years. At one time the bank had a loan with him 15 or 18 years ago."

Then the next month, in an interview in his office at the Mischer Corp., Mischer said, "I met him [Beebe] when we were still in the old Continental Bank building, before we moved. He had an insurance company. I just spoke to him. That was the only time I met him."

(Beebe must hold the world's record for meeting people only once. Ask almost any person in the banking and savings and loan businesses if he or she has ever met Beebe, and you get the invariable response, "Yes, but I only met him once.")

One person who was at Beebe's side for ten years, Dale Anderson, said Beebe established his ties to Mischer and Allied before he began working with Beebe in 1975. Anderson said he never met with Mischer, but that "Herman met with Walter a few times." Beebe used Mischer's Allied Bank for a number of deals, Anderson revealed. "We borrowed money from Allied pretty often—$500,000 here and a million there," he said. These loans were for working capital for their companies, under the AMI umbrella, and were all paid back before AMI folded after Beebe got into legal trouble.

The only Allied loan to Beebe that Mischer mentioned was for $800,000 and was made in connection with the Allied loan on Carroll Kelly's Continental Savings stock, which Beebe's company guaranteed.

In addition to the loans, Anderson said, Allied gave Beebe's company a big hunk of the credit life insurance for car loans made by Allied. "They had two clusters of banks and they gave us one cluster," he said. About this time, Allied had some 40 member banks across Texas.

(Anytime Beebe got control of a financial institution, he would require borrowers of that institution to purchase credit life insurance from his insurance company. Such insurance pays off the loan in the event of the death of the borrower. It was very lucrative business for Beebe, and if a potential borrower declined it he was usually told that perhaps he should go somewhere else to get a loan.)

AMI also had money on deposit at Allied. "We'd buy CDs there from time to time," Anderson said. A 1976 House finance subcommittee report on the Texas rent-a-bank scandal showed that Beebe's Louisiana insurance company, Savings Life, had large certificates of deposit at Allied in the early and mid-1970s.

In addition, the 1985 Comptroller of the Currency report on Beebe lists Allied Lakewood Bank, an Allied member bank in Dallas, as being "controlled by Beebe and his associates or which conduct(s) significant correspondent banking with banks controlled by Beebe and his associates."

Beebe's primary contact at Allied was Gerald Smith, the chief executive officer, Anderson said. Smith is listed in the 1985 Comptroller's report on Beebe as part-owner of the First National Bank of Jefferson Parish in Gretna, Louisiana, where Beebe, Anderson and others owned $1.6 million in debentures in the bank's parent corporation and held warrants to buy about 14 percent of the stock.

As previously noted, Robert Clarke, the former Comptroller of the

Currency, was also involved in the bank with his brother-in-law, Kent Anderson, an Allied Bank officer, and Smith. Clarke was a shareholder in the bank, with stock holdings of between $50,000 and $100,000. He also received at least $5,000 in legal fees for work for the bank. And, as of late 1985, Clarke had an outstanding promissory note of $250,000 at the bank.[1]

Gerald Smith and Mischer go back to the early 1960s, when Mischer bought Continental Bank, where Smith was working. Smith, a former banking examiner, became Mischer's right-hand man at Allied. "If Mischer wanted something done [at Allied], he called Gerald Smith and it got done," said one Houston executive with extensive banking connections. One banking expert and Mischer-watcher for years described Smith as Mischer's "gofer."

Although Mischer denies ever owning a bank in Louisiana, a former Texas bank examiner and a veteran Houston business reporter confirm that he had extensive bank holdings in Cajun country. The bank examiner said that one time in the late 1970s he was playing poker with Mischer and some of his associates in a small town in Louisiana where Mischer owned a bank. Mischer leaned over to him and asked him if he knew the man sitting next to him. The examiner said no, and Mischer grinned and replied, "That's Edwin Edwards, the Governor of Louisiana."

This is the same Edwin Edwards who was on Beebe's payroll as a $100,000-a-year consultant and who was good friends with mob boss Carlos Marcello.

When it became obvious to insiders in the early 1980s that the savings and loan industry in Texas was in for some rough times, Mischer ordered all S&L stock loans at Allied moved out of the bank. He believed, or perhaps even knew, that the S&L industry was going to go down the tube. One of the S&L stock loans at Allied Bank was to Carroll Kelly on Continental Savings stock, with a guarantee from Beebe. Nearby San Jacinto Savings, a Houston-based subsidiary of Southmark Corp., gladly accepted the loan from Allied, even without the guarantee from Beebe.

The titular head of San Jacinto was another person with business relationships to both Mischer and Beebe. Gene E. Phillips rose from the

---

[1] *National Mortgage News*, May 1991.

ashes of the biggest personal bankruptcy in South Carolina history, took a busted-out real estate investment trust in Atlanta called Southmark and transformed it into a $9 billion company in Dallas. Helping him along the way was $1.2 billion in financing arranged by his friend Michael Milken, the junk bond king.

In the summer of 1984, when it was clear that U.S. Attorney Joe Cage in Shreveport was going to nail Beebe's hide to the wall, who should come to Beebe's financial rescue but Gene Phillips and Southmark. They agreed to buy Beebe's nursing homes for the incredible sum of $50 million, and consummated the deal after Beebe was indicted and convicted of defrauding the Small Business Administration. Then Phillips and his partner William Friedman, who was vice chairman of Southmark, bought Beebe's failing Bossier Bank and Trust for the unbelievable sum of $8 million. The bank was already on the skids when they acquired it, and failed shortly thereafter, wiping out the Southmark executives' investment.

Now nobody like Phillips throws away millions of dollars to a known mobster like Beebe unless he's been instructed to do so by the mob. There is certainly evidence that that is the case here. In 1983, Southmark bought San Jacinto Savings in Houston, and while the nominal heads of the S&L remained in place, a mob associate from Chicago, Joseph Grosz, came in to make all the big loan decisions.[2]

Anderson, Beebe's partner, said they dealt primarily with Grosz in their transactions with Southmark.

While Southmark was generously bailing Beebe out and assuming Beebe's guaranteed loan from Allied Bank, Walter Mischer and Gene Phillips were investors together in the 1984 Oak Cliff Stallion Development Program Syndicate. There were ten partners in this syndicate, each with one-twentieth interest in 13 thoroughbred colts, including some with big name sires like Ack, Alydar and Secretariat.

With the exception of Phillips, most of the partners were from Houston. The financing bank, according to statements on file at the Dade County Clerk's Office in Miami, was Allied Bank.

Continental Savings wasn't the only savings and loan whose stock was financed at Allied Bank. Raymond Hill, a Houston attorney and owner of Mainland Savings, also had his Mainland stock financed at

---

[2] Report of Examination of San Jacinto Savings, Federal Home Loan Bank Board, 1986.

Allied. And he, too, had to find alternative financing.

First, Hill went for help to Continental Savings' Carroll Kelly, who sent him to Herman K. Beebe, according to Beebe's partner, Dale Anderson. One day Beebe called Anderson and told him they were going to Houston to talk to Raymond Hill. "We stopped at New Orleans first and got us some girls," Anderson related.

"Hill was scared—a weakling. You could smell it. He was afraid to deal with us," Anderson said. "We said we could get him a million dollars tomorrow, but we wanted a piece of the action. He didn't want to do it."

Although that particular deal didn't go through, there were other connections between Beebe and Mainland. The 1985 U.S. Comptroller of the Currency report on Beebe named Mainland as one of the many savings and loans "controlled by Beebe and his associates."

Raymond Hill appeared to be a strange bedfellow for Mischer and Beebe. An arrogant, pious, cock-of-the-walk and a scion of Houston wealth and society, Hill is a fifth-generation Texan, born into a prominent, wealthy, well-respected family. His mother was a Vanden Burge from Victoria, Texas, and his father was an attorney and chief executive officer of Houston Oil Company. His brother, George Jr., was also a well-known attorney. Hill's father and brother, both deceased, are regularly called "two of the finest people you would ever want to meet." Once, when Hill was grilled about Mainland Savings' failure on a public television show in Houston, in a pathetic attempt to defend himself he invoked the memories of his father and brother and pointed to their pictures on his wall.

Hill, who was born in 1925, attended Hotchkiss prep school and then served briefly in World War II before returning to Houston, where he graduated from the University of Houston and then from the university's law school. The story is told of how Hill's mother called up a senior partner of Vinson & Elkins to ask if he would give "little Raymond" a job. He told her to send Raymond downtown for an interview.

When Hill walked into the attorney's office at Vinson & Elkins, the senior partner opened with, "So, you'd like to come to work for us, Raymond?" To which Hill was said to have replied, "Well, of course, only if I can be in charge." Needless to say, Hill was not put in charge of Vinson & Elkins. Instead, he went off and started a law firm of his own, eventually developing a reputation as an expert in real estate and corporate law.

Although generally considered to be a good attorney from a good family, there is something about Raymond Hill that attracts him to, or makes him attractive to, people of questionable background and character. Perhaps it can be explained by the schoolyard analogy of the poor little rich kid who sucks up to the bullies and thugs—either because he thinks they are cool or because he is afraid of them.

Hill got into the savings and loan business in the early 1960s, when he was riding in an airplane with a good friend of his, William Donald Shepherd, who told him that the two of them should buy an S&L. So Hill and Shepherd purchased tiny ($2 million in deposits) Mainland Savings in Texas City, a small blue-collar town southeast of Houston.

Hill's friend and partner, Shepherd, is a major character in Jonathan Kwitny's ground-breaking book on white-collar crime in America, *The Fountain Pen Conspiracy* (1973). In 1969 and 1970, Shepherd took some $1.3 million from several financial institutions in exchange for worthless checks drawn on the Bank of Sark, a shell bank set up on the British island of Sark in the Channel Islands between England and France, not far from the Isle of Jersey (which will play an important part in this book). In 1973, Shepherd was convicted for this scam and sentenced to 15 years in jail. His name also surfaced in the Sharpstown scandal of the early 1970s, as part of the SEC stock fraud investigation. It happened that Shepherd was giving rides in his Lear jet to politicians, including Mischer's buddy, then-Governor Preston Smith.

In 1975, Hill decided to move his little S&L up to the big time in Houston. He bought a pretty Spanish Mediterranean-style building with a clock tower on Allen Parkway alongside Buffalo Bayou. The property was purchased from Walter Mischer.

It is not known when, or under what circumstances, Hill and Mischer met each other. "Hill thought Walter was his mentor," said former Mainland chief executive officer Ron Bearden, who first worked as Hill's personal accountant.

Hill and Mischer have both separately attempted to downplay their relationship. "I didn't know him well, but I knew him around town," Mischer said of Hill. "I think he was a lawyer." According to Mischer, Hill is "kind of a mild-mannered little guy, kind of a meek sort of little guy." (It is not known whether Mischer was being facetious, or if that is just the way Hill acts around him.)

Hill did not return my phone calls about his relationship to Mischer. But a woman who answered the phone in his law office, identifying herself as Ms. Macy, called back saying that "Mr. Mischer is considerably older than Mr. Hill. We're certain that Mr. Hill has had no business dealings with Mr. Mischer, at least for the last 20 years."

Ms. Macy was wrong on both counts. First, Mischer is only three years older than Hill. Second, the purchase of the Allen Parkway building was in 1975, some 15 years before the date of the phone conversation. Assuming Hill told Ms. Macy what to say, it is obvious he, like Mischer, is trying to hide behind Allied Bank's corporate veil, for the fact is, Hill and Mainland had considerable dealings with Allied Bank, well into the 1980s.

First of all, Hill's Mainland stock was financed at Allied. This was confirmed by Ron Bearden, by Art Leiser, the former chief examiner at the Texas Savings and Loan Department, and by Mischer himself, who said, "I think that is correct"—which for Mischer is a resounding confirmation.

Leiser said Hill had an interesting way of dealing with Mainland's stock dividends. Hill would not pay out all the dividends in cash, but would instead reinvest them in additional stock, and then brag about how he was building up Mainland's capital that way. What Leiser found out later was that Hill would take his additional stock and use it as collateral for more loans at Allied Bank. (It is not known if Mainland's other stockholders did the same, or even knew what Hill was doing.)

After Hill moved his stock loan out of Allied, he financed it at several different Houston banks, according to former Mainland CEO, Ron Bearden. These included Suburban Bank, South Main Bank, North-Shore Bank and River Oaks Bank & Trust, the latter of which was controlled by President Bush's and Mischer's friend, Contra supporter and right-wing Republican Jimmy Lyon.

In June 1984, Mainland paid $19.2 million to Allied in a deal that showed Hill's fealty to Mischer but caused the S&L, and ultimately the taxpayers, to lose at least $14 million. It happened this way:

In 1982, Allied lent $27 million to Penaco, a Corpus Christi oil and gas company controlled by Al Pena, secured by 30 oil and gas leases in 18 South Texas counties. The following year Penaco filed for bankruptcy and by 1984 was in default on its Allied loans, still owing some $21 million.

Allied had already posted the security property for foreclosure, when Mainland stepped in and bought the loans for $19.2 million. Pena testified in a bankruptcy hearing that no other lender could be found to take over the Allied loans, and that the transaction with Mainland was a "last resort type of thing."

It was almost unheard of for a medium-sized savings and loan like

Mainland to buy a big oil and gas loan by itself, much less buy one—for 90 cents on the dollar—that was in bankruptcy and foreclosure. Also at that time, oil drilling was in the doldrums and prices were way down. Mainland basically just gave the money to Allied. A study by an outside law firm estimated that Mainland lost at least $14 million on the deal. It didn't make any sense, unless seen in the light of the relationship between Hill and Mischer.

But there was more to Mainland Savings than its relationships to Mischer and Beebe. Mainland was the first failed thrift that the *Houston Post* investigated.

In the spring of 1987, two *Houston Post* reporters (Gregory Seay and myself) were interviewing Raymond Hill. Mainland Savings, which, when it bit the dust in April 1986, was the biggest S&L failure in the country, with approximately $1 billion of illusory assets. No one paid much attention to Mainland's failure at the time. And why should they? Talk of a possible taxpayers' bailout of the industry was more than two years away, while the press release from the federal agency explaining its takeover of Mainland was soporific and mind-glazing:

"Mainland's insolvency resulted from rapid growth in its asset base from approximately $308 million to over $1 billion between October 31, 1983, and the end of 1985. The increase reflected the association's aggressive program of high-risk poorly underwritten land and construction lending funded through brokered deposits and in-house sales of high-cost jumbo certificates of deposit."

Although this explanation was like saying someone died of malnutrition by overeating, it seemed to satisfy most reporters, who never got around to asking: What loans? What deposits?

By the beginning of 1987, it was becoming apparent that something bigger than simply the failure of a few isolated S&Ls was occurring. Other forces were at work, and Seay, a business writer for the *Houston Post*, wrote a story about a fraud-riddled "daisy chain" of Texas savings and loans that were swapping bad loans among themselves and selling each other loan participations. Seay quoted the U.S. Attorney in Houston, who named Mainland Savings as one of the participants.

The story prompted an anonymous phone call to Seay, urging him to investigate the transactions between Mainland Savings and a man named Howard Pulver. That call sent Seay and myself on a two-year journey into a labyrinth of real estate transactions of mind-boggling complexity—financial rabbit trails that sometimes disappeared into offshore bank accounts, trips to Long Island, San Diego and Kansas City, slippery politicians and schools of red herrings. Ultimately the quest led to the Houston business establishment, which, when examined in depth, intersected on many planes with the Mafia and the CIA.

After receiving the anonymous phone call, Seay began researching the deals between Howard Pulver and Mainland and quickly found himself drowning in a sea of records: hundreds of corporations and partnerships in transactions covering thousands and thousands of pages of documents on file in the deed records of Harris County, which encompasses Houston. After Seay reported to his editors the problems he was encountering because of the size of the task, Assistant Managing Editor Tom Nelson asked me to go through the records with Seay to try to make sense of them. That project took the two of us several months, and by the time we analyzed the documents we still weren't sure what we had.

It seemed that Pulver and his three partners, who were apartment syndicators from New York City, had come into Houston in the mid-1970s and bought up more than 35 aging apartment projects. They loaded these buildings up with huge mortgage debt and then immediatly flipped the properties by selling them to limited partnerships that they themselves headed. Then, in late 1984 and early 1985, they sold all the promissory notes securing the enormous mortgage debts on the properties to Mainland Savings. This transaction passed all of the risk from the real estate operators onto the S&L and enabled the speculators to cash in their paper profits. There were 56 of these notes, with a total face value of $333 million. At the time of the sale of the promissory notes to Mainland, the apartment projects were worth about $192 million, according to the county tax assessments. The questions are: How much did Mainland pay for the promissory notes, and thus, how much did it, and ultimately the taxpayers, lose on these vastly overvalued purchases?

Seay and I went to see Raymond Hill for answers. The interview was intended to be a friendly information-gathering and fact-finding one. We believed that Hill had every intention of helping us understand what happened at Mainland Savings, and why it happened.

In our interview, he was initially very friendly and all smiles. However, instead of taking questions from us, he started off with a rambling speech about the history of Mainland Savings and why it failed. The tale is a familiar one by now, and has been used by almost everyone in the industry and its apologists to try to explain what happened. The story has some basis in truth, but is incomplete and inaccurate. It goes like this:

The inflation of the late 1970s put the squeeze on savings and loans by raising the cost (the interest rate) they paid for deposits, compared to the lower interest rates they were receiving on their long-term home loans. Congress and the Reagan Administration tried to solve the industry's problems by removing the cap on interest rates they could pay for deposits and loosening up the restrictions on the types of property they could invest in and make loans on.

So far so good. But then, according to Hill (and others), the problems in the industry arose when the economy turned down and the government regulators began criticizing the loans and investments they had initially approved. It sounded reasonable enough at that time to Seay and myself, but we weren't interested in some vague, general theory; we wanted the hard details on the Pulver deals.

Hill's condescending, holier-than-thou attitude was also starting to grate. At one point he bragged that his "prophecy" about the plight of the S&L industry had come true. "I've been given the curse of a certain amount of foresight," he said. His patina of self-deprecation simply exacerbated his arrogance. "I want you to tell me why it failed. Your judgment may be a lot better than mine."

When Seay and I began asking some pointed questions about the purchase of the Pulver notes and the value of the underlying collateral, Hill started weaseling. "You're asking me to remember the details of actions I didn't personally handle," he said. Next, he tried to hide behind Mainland's accounting firm: "In every case we consulted with Coopers & Lybrand." Then he claimed that he had only met with Pulver "on one occasion." Hill also tried to maintain that he was merely a caretaker owner, and hadn't even served on the loan committee—contrary to Mainland documents on file in a federal lawsuit in Houston. He actually ran his savings and loan with an iron hand, according to former officers and employees, and confirmed and reported by other journalists.

Finally, after repeated questioning, Hill told this reporter, "You're a bastard." This from a man who wears his religion on his sleeve and teaches Sunday School Bible class at St. John the Divine Episcopal Church in River Oaks, the richest enclave in Houston. But Hill was just warming up. He said he had not been subpoenaed to appear before any grand jury investigating Mainland's failure, and, he added, "I can tell you that I don't expect to be subpoenaed to a grand jury." Finally, when asked about rumors of the presence of organized crime at Mainland, Hill accused us of "stumbling in the same direction" as the FBI and the U.S. Attorney's Office.

Hill's statements were obviously calculated to impress and intimidate us, but why deliberately flout and thumb your nose at the FBI and the U.S. Attorney? What gave Raymond Hill the idea that he was untouchable? What kind of power did he think would protect him from the press, from grand juries and from the U.S. Justice Department?

Searching for the answers to those questions led to the discovery of Hill's and Mainland's relationships to the Mafia, the CIA, Iran-Contra, Herman K. Beebe, Walter Mischer, Senator Orrin Hatch (Republican-Utah) and James A. Baker III, this country's former Treasury Secretary and Secretary of State, George Bush's close friend and now White House Chief of Staff.

4

GANGLAND SAVINGS, THE CIA AND JAMES A. BAKER III

The first story about Mainland's failure appeared in the *Houston Post* on June 7, 1987, under the byline of Seay and Brewton. It dealt with Mainland's purchase of the promissory notes from Pulver's group, but did not determine the most important facts; namely, how much Mainland paid for the notes and thus how much it lost on them. No one would say—not the people who had worked at Mainland, not Pulver and his associates, not the FBI, nor even the U.S. Attorney's Office.

But it was obvious that Mainland, and ultimately the taxpayers, ended up losing tens of millions of dollars on the deals. Several of the notes went into default just months after Mainland bought them, and then, before Mainland could foreclose on them, the owners put their companies into bankruptcy, stopping any foreclosure. In some instances, Mainland's federal receiver had to pay millions of dollars just to keep the first mortgages current so that the receiver would not lose its second mortgage investment. And in one transaction found in a Houston bankruptcy court proceeding, the federal receiver for the failed Mainland (in other words, the American taxpayers) sold $21 million of the notes for less than $400,000.

Hill had tried to convince us that the Pulver deals hadn't contributed to Mainland's failure, which he claimed had resulted from Mainland's home mortgage loans. In fact, it was just the opposite. Mainland had made few home loans since 1983. Instead, the S&L had concentrated on loans on commercial property and vacant land.

(Most of the S&Ls in this country that stuck with traditional home mortgage lending survived.)

Seay and I were unable to get the documents or calculate the exact loss, so we turned to find out who Pulver and his group were and who their limited partners were. Perhaps that would shed some light on how they could pull close to $100 million out of Raymond Hill's savings association.

The apartment syndicators from New York consisted of four principals, Pulver, Anthony Pedone, Stuart Goldman and Jerome Gladstein, all from the New York City area. In the late 1960s, Pulver, Pedone and Gladstein had been insurance salesmen at John Hancock, together with their early partner Leonard Malin. They formed a partnership that started out selling computer services to physicians; then Malin dropped out, and Goldman, an attorney, joined up several years later. They began selling limited partnerships in precious metals and mines, oil and gas ventures and apartment complexes, all over the United States.

Malin said most of the money that the group used in order to start up came from him. He said he didn't know where the capital came from after he dropped out, but speculated that it came from Pedone. "Someone told me that Pedone had some independent backing. They kept saying that Pedone knew somebody in the oil business in Texas, but nobody could ever pin this down." Pedone's former wife, Bonnie, said anyone who believes Pedone had oil investments in Texas is "barking up the wrong tree."

Pedone grew up around horse-racing tracks, where his father worked as an agent for jockeys, including Eddie Arcaro. Later, Pedone became a prominent investor in standard-bred trotting horses.

Pulver, considered to be the brains of the organization, grew up in the Bensonhurst neighborhood in Brooklyn. When he was working for John Hancock, he lived in a small house on a tiny lot in Bellerose, a blue-collar town on Long Island. "Before he knew me he was starving. He never made more than $15,000 a year," Malin asserted.

By the end of 1974, even before the group's limited partnership business had really cranked up, Pulver purchased a huge mansion on a three-acre lot in the wealthy Long Island suburb of Kings Point. Three years after that, Pedone bought a mansion in tony Greenwich, Connecticut.

Most of their limited partners, and thus the ones who received a large chunk of the Mainland money, were leading businessmen and lawyers in the New York City area, including former U.S. Attorney General Nicholas DeB. Katzenbach, several senior partners with the New York law firm of Sullivan & Cromwell and executives with IBM and GTE. Other investors were Caesar P. Kimmel, an ex-Warner Communications Corporation officer and former executive of the Pittsburgh Pirates (investigated by the baseball commissioner's office for being a partner in a Caribbean casino), and Charles H. Stein, who was attempting to put a casino in Atlantic City before the FBI's "Abscam" bribery investigation cast a shadow on it.[1]

Jim Foxworth, an investment adviser in New Canaan, Connecticut, who recommended that his clients buy into the limited partnerships, told the *Houston Post* that he was "surprised" that Mainland purchased their promissory notes, because, he said, the projects were about to go into foreclosure.

While trying to determine why Mainland made such a large, obviously bad, purchase from the Pulver group, Seay and I got a big break. An investigator with Congress's General Accounting Office, who was interested in organized crime and knew about the *Houston Post*'s first story on Mainland, discovered an indictment in Brooklyn that mentioned Mainland Savings. The Justice Department's Organized Crime Strike Force in Brooklyn had gotten a federal grand jury there to indict Long Island money brokers Mario Renda and Martin Schwimmer for racketeering and fraud in connection with the deposit of union pension funds in financial institutions across the country. One of those was Mainland Savings.

Mario Renda knew that defrauding a savings and loan before 1980 was like stealing a car that doesn't have an engine: a lot of trouble and hardly worth the effort. But beginning in 1980, Congress and then the Reagan Administration made it a great deal easier by opening the vaults of savings and loans to anyone with the temerity to walk in and take out the money.

The process of opening the vaults has come to be called "deregulation"—not exactly the right word to describe what happened, but the one we're stuck with. Deregulation loosened the restrictions on the kinds of loans and investments S&Ls could make, while it lifted the ceiling on the interest rates S&Ls could pay on their deposits—which

---

[1] *Houston Post*, August 23, 1987.

were used for the loans and investments. This meant that S&Ls could pay just about anything they needed to get money and then do just about anything they wanted with it. This, in combination with federal deposit insurance, in which the federal government and ultimately the taxpayers take responsibility for losses to depositors on loans and investments, was an open invitation to the criminal element.

If deregulation was the engine that made the car easy and worthwhile to steal, then the gasoline was brokered deposits. These are deposits placed in a savings and loan or bank by a middleman (broker) who gathers them together from various individuals and institutions such as pension funds and credit unions.

Large amounts of brokered deposits at an S&L were a dead giveaway that the institution was on a fast track to hell. In their most virulent form, brokered deposits were made contingent on loans going to the broker's chosen borrowers. Those in the industry referred to this as "linked financing." Bribery, extortion and conspiracy would be more accurate.

Mario Renda was the king of brokered deposits and "linked financing." Beginning on a shoestring in 1980, by 1983 Renda and his company, First United Fund of Garden City, Long Island, were pumping $5 billion a year into banks and savings and loans across the country. Renda brokered deposits into some 130 S&Ls, according to California author Stephen Pizzo. Every one of them later failed. Mainland was named in Renda's indictment as one of 18 savings and loans nationwide, and only one of two in Texas, into which Renda and Schwimmer brokered union pension funds and then skimmed the interest off into secret accounts.

Renda had a motley crew around him. One of his sidekicks was Salvatore Piga, a mob enforcer and associate of the Tramunti crime family, whose rap sheet includes charges of grand larceny, assault and robbery, burglary, first-degree assault, carrying a dangerous weapon and criminal possession of stolen property. (Carmine Tramunti was a former boss of the Lucchese Mafia family, one of the Big Five crime families in New York City.)

Renda's partner, Schwimmer, whom Renda later turned state's evidence against after they were indicted together, was accused of laundering money for members of the Lucchese family. And the late-lamented mob lawyer Morris Shenker, lawyer for Jimmy Hoffa and an associate of Mafia families in St. Louis, Chicago and Kansas City, appears a number of times in Renda's business diaries. Also, according to Lawrence Iorizzo, an associate of the Colombo Mafia family, Renda "controlled a lot of money being loaned for the benefit of Paul Castellano," the boss (later murdered) of the Gambino Mafia family.[2]

In 1987, Renda was convicted in Florida with Michael Hellerman, a former Wall Street broker doing stock scams for the Mafia, who turned state's evidence against several Mafia members, got a new last name, Rapp, and wrote a book with Thomas Renner called *Wall Street Swindler*.

Bruce Maffeo, a former Brooklyn organized-crime strike force attorney who prosecuted Renda and Schwimmer, said the two brokered into Mainland several million dollars of pension funds from Sheetmetal Workers' Local 38 in New York and Teamsters Local 810 in New York, the latter of which, Maffeo said, was closely connected to organized crime figures.

Renda's deposits were almost always linked to loans, according to Maffeo. That led the *Houston Post* reporters to wondering what loans at Mainland had been linked to Renda's total deposits there, which were estimated to be a little less than $100 million. The indictment of Renda and Schwimmer lists seven wire transfers of interest earned from Mainland to the money brokers' accounts, beginning in June 1982 and continuing into July 1984. The last date was around the time that Mainland began negotiating with the New York apartment syndicators to buy the promissory notes. Were the payments to Pulver's group linked?

Seay and I traveled to Long Island, looking for answers. The first day there, we went to talk to Pulver. It took some effort to find him. He lived in a three-level stone-and-wood-shingle mansion in a secluded area of Kings Point, New York, an exclusive bedroom community on the North Shore of Long Island. Pulver's house sits on several acres, with a pond in front, a large glass dome over an indoor swimming pool, and is surrounded by hedges so that it can't be seen from the street. There is a NO TRESPASSING sign at the beginning of the road leading to the house, and the mailbox on the street still had the name of a previous owner who hadn't lived there in at least 13 years.

When the two reporters tried to talk to Pulver, who answered the door in his bare feet, he gave us ten seconds to get off his property.

---

[2] Affidavit of Lawrence S. Iorizzo in U.S.A. vs. V. Leslie Winkler, United States District Court of Kansas, No. 87-20049-03.

We had initially been looking for connections between Renda and Pedone or Pulver, in particular whether Renda's deposits into Mainland were linked to the Pulver group's deals with Mainland. When asked by Seay if Pedone was connected to Renda's company, Bruce Maffeo had replied, "No comment. Nice try." However, a document search in the New York area did not turn up any direct connections between the men. (One of the things visitors to Mario Renda's office in Garden City, Long Island, noticed was that he had elevated his desk onto a platform so that they had to look up to him. One of the things visitors to Pulver's office in Houston noticed was that he had elevated his desk onto a platform so that they had to look up to him.) So, several days after trying to talk to Pulver, we decided to find Martin Schwimmer and talk to him.

Schwimmer, a Ph.D. professor and author, lived in Kings Point too. When we were driving down the road where Schwimmer lived, a secluded cul-de-sac, we noticed the back of a large mansion with a glass dome on it. It was Pulver's house. He and Schwimmer were close neighbors in the exclusive area and had been so for 11 years. But when asked about Pulver and Mainland Savings, Schwimmer responded, "Who?" Then when asked about Renda's firm, First United, he said, "You'll have to talk to them. I'm not interested in discussing that." He then slammed the door shut.[3]

So here's the situation: Renda and Schwimmer brokered tens of millions of dollars in deposits into Mainland Savings, a medium-sized S&L in Houston, in a scheme where it is known that loans are linked to the deposits, and then shortly thereafter Schwimmer's Kings Point neighbor, Pulver, sells practically worthless property to Mainland for tens of millions of dollars.

When told of this, Maffeo, the Brooklyn organized-crime strike force prosecutor, said "the government appreciates the *Houston Post*'s information." Assistant U.S. Attorney John Smith, in charge of the fraud division in Houston, said, "Sometimes reporters' investigations can lead other investigators to another direction to look into. You hit a home run."[4]

Maffeo said later that two IRS criminal investigators looked into the matter but couldn't find a money trail between Pulver and Schwimmer. Of course, if Pulver and Schwimmer were both working for a higher

---

[3] *Houston Post*, September 13, 1987.
[4] Ibid.

authority, then there wouldn't likely be any such money trail. In that
case, the money trails would lead from the two men ultimately to the
same place. Could it be the Mafia?

The connections of Renda and Schwimmer to the Mafia were
known, but what about the Pulver group? Aside from the rumors, the
talk and the smoke, we found nothing we could get our hands on. It
wasn't until three years later that I found something:

Pulver and his group first came to Texas in 1973, but they started out
in Corpus Christi, not Houston. They bought one apartment complex
in Corpus Christi and then turned to investing in oil and gas leases in
that area. These leases were apparently duds, and in 1978 they unloaded
their oil and gas investments and leases to a Seymour M. Lazar of Palm
Springs, California.

Seay and I couldn't locate Lazar or find any information on him at
that time. But three years later I was researching Castle Bank & Trust,
the infamous Caribbean bank that was used by the mob and the CIA to
hide and launder money. I was researching Castle at that time because
one of the people involved in a $200 million S&L deal in Florida had
been the bank's in-house counsel. And there, in a list of the privileged
few with accounts at Castle Bank & Trust, was Seymour Lazar.

Lazar, an investor and attorney in Palm Springs, had gotten in
trouble with the Securities & Exchange Commission in 1973, during the
attempted takeover of Armour Corp. by General Host. One of Lazar's
partners in this enterprise was Richard Pistell, a close associate of the
international crook Robert Vesco and a friend and broker of the chief
executive of Resorts International, the mobbed-up (at that time) casino
company with ties to syndicate financier Meyer Lansky and his associates. Lazar had also purchased shares of Resorts' predecessor company,
Mary Carter Paint, in a private placement.[5]

What's more, Lazar was an associate of the mutual-fund swindler
Bernie Cornfeld and a friend of Billy Mellon Hitchcock and part of
Hitchcock's LSD scene in California. (Billy Hitchcock has been called
"an American original." The grandson of the founder of Gulf Oil and
the nephew of Andrew Mellon, he bounced back and forth between the
world of high finance and the world of LSD. Hitchcock became a patron

---

[5] *Masters of Paradise*, by Alan A. Block (Transaction Publishers, 1991), and *Acid
Dreams: The CIA, LSD and the Sixties Rebellion*, by Martin A. Lee and Bruce
Shlain (New York: Grove Press, 1985).

of LSD high priest Timothy Leary, and also owned stock in Resorts International and had accounts at Castle Bank & Trust.) Lazar was called "The Head" by his California LSD friends and described himself as "the world's only hippie arbitrage expert."[6]

Finally, Lazar had worked for Louis Chesler.[7] Louis "Uncle Lou" Chesler was one of the biggest mobsters around; he topped the scales at around 300 pounds. Chesler helped Lansky start up gambling in the Bahamas after the mob was kicked out of Cuba by Fidel Castro. Another of Chesler's casino partners was Wallace Groves, a mobster, convicted felon and Lansky associate who had been on the CIA's payroll as a contract agent from 1965 to 1972.[8] Chesler's phone number was also found in the records of the previously mentioned in-house counsel to Castle Bank & Trust.

Another interesting aspect of the Pulver group was that almost all of the financial transactions they had in Houston were with Mainland. But the few that weren't are also of significance. After Raymond Hill quit as chairman of Mainland in October 1985, Pulver's group immediately turned to Sandia Federal Savings in Albuquerque to finance one of their big Houston deals. Sandia paid off a $9 million promissory note owed to Pulver's group by another New York investment outfit, an affiliate of Cantor Fitzgerald, on a downtown Houston office building. This other New York group then defaulted on the loan from Sandia, which later failed, to the tune of $850 million. So in essence, the deal was a $9 million payment from the American taxpayers to Pulver's group.

Sandia was part of a daisy chain of savings and loans, centered in Texas, that made loans to, and had financial affiliations with, Mafia associates and CIA operatives. The details of these transactions will be set out in a later chapter after more of the characters involved are introduced.

Another Pulver group deal in Houston that cost American taxpayers more than $35 million was a $47.2 million loan that the group got on the Colonial House apartments, a huge complex in southwest Houston aimed at the swinging singles set. The apartment project was notorious

---

[6] *Spooks*, by Jim Hougan (New York: William Morrow, 1978), and *Vesco*, by Robert A. Hutcheson (New York: Praeger, 1974).

[7] Ibid.

[8] *Wall Street Journal*, "IRS vs. CIA," by Jim Drinkhall, April 18, 1980.

in Houston for its tacky television commercials done by Pulver's employee, Michael Pollack, in which a well-endowed woman dove into a swimming pool and emerged holding a dripping VCR, a prize for new renters.

The mortgage on Colonial House was one of the few that Pulver's group didn't sell to Mainland. The $47.2 million loan came from a Washington, D.C., company called DRG, but the loan was guaranteed by the U.S. Department of Housing and Urban Development (HUD). The money was supposed to be for renovation of the apartment project, but government investigators said less than $10 million was so used, and that Pulver's group walked away with $18 million. DRG and the Colonial House loan are still under civil and criminal investigation by HUD and the FBI.

DRG also entered into some financial transactions and negotiations with Dallas-based Southmark, a real estate investment firm, and its Houston S&L subsidiary, San Jacinto Savings. As noted, Southmark was used as a mob dumping ground, to buy the investments of mobsters such as Morris Shenker and Herman K. Beebe when they got into trouble. DRG also lent $15 million on a piece of vacant land southwest of Houston that was purchased by several of the principal characters in this book, including Mischer's former son-in-law. They, and that deal, will be discussed in a later chapter.

Pulver and his partners also served as middlemen in several Houston-area land deals between two close associates of Walter Mischer. In at least a couple of transactions, Pulver and his partners bought a piece of land from Joe McDermott, a former employee and sometime business partner of Mischer, and a little while later they turned around and sold it to Jerry J. Moore, the strip shopping center king and reportedly the richest man in Houston. It is not clear why Pulver and his partners were used to do this, but the end result appeared to be that they made some money from Moore.

After Seay and I had nailed down Renda's and Schwimmer's connections to the Mafia, we started looking for other mob ties to Mainland Savings. The next one we found was Leonard Capaldi. Capaldi is from Detroit but has maintained a home in Houston since the mid-1970s. He is an associate of Detroit Mafia *capo* Tony Tocco, whose brother, Jack Tocco, is the boss of the Detroit Mafia, according to U.S. Justice Department documents.

A private investigator close to the FBI, along with a former prosecutor with the Justice Department's Organized Crime Strike Force, an FBI agent with the strike force, and a journalist and expert on the Detroit Mafia all confirmed Capaldi's relationship to Tony Tocco. The organized-crime strike force in Houston had a thick file on Capaldi.

"Lenny is as close as you can get without being blood," said the late Brian Flanigan, who was a mob expert with the *Detroit Free Press*. In 1988, several years before he died of a heart attack, Flanigan told me that Capaldi and Tony Tocco were good friends, traveling companions and "asshole buddies." Capaldi, who has never been convicted of a crime, has the reputation of being a suave, sophisticated jetsetter who travels frequently to Florida, Las Vegas and Europe. A document filed in a state district court case in Houston reports that he owns homes in Houston, Detroit and Florida, as well as in Europe.

Capaldi is alleged by law enforcement sources to be a major representative of the Houston interests of several Midwest and Eastern mob families. He has had investments in Houston in the construction business, restaurants and real estate development.

Macomb Concrete, a Detroit construction company owned by Capaldi's father, built one of the runways at Houston Intercontinental Airport in the early 1970s. After his father died several years later, Capaldi moved the company from Michigan to Houston and changed its name to Macomb Contracting Corp. (Macomb is a county in Michigan that covers the eastern side of Detroit.)

Macomb Contracting went bankrupt in Houston in 1979, leaving 19 government construction and paving jobs totaling $99 million unfinished. Macomb's bonding company, which had to take over these jobs, paid $35 million to finish the work. These jobs included contracts with the federal government, the state of Texas, Harris County and the city of Houston.

More than 50 lawsuits in federal, state and county courts in Houston have been filed against Capaldi and his companies. Most of these suits allege unpaid debts, and in many of them money judgments were obtained and filed for record. Court records show that Capaldi rarely appeared for scheduled depositions in his court cases. One plaintiff in a lawsuit against Capaldi even alleged that Capaldi pulled a gun on him during a dispute.

On occasion, process servers have found it difficult to locate Capaldi to serve him with legal notices. One stated that he had been unable to serve Capaldi with legal papers because of an armed guard on duty 24 hours a day in front of his River Oaks residence. Capaldi leased this house from oil heiress Camilla Blaffer for $4,000 a month. Capaldi moved into this house after he had purchased a mansion from the ex-wife of noted Houston developer Kenneth Schnitzer and then defaulted on the home loan. Schnitzer, who has allegedly associated with New Orleans mobsters, said he didn't know Capaldi, but that he and his ex-wife lost $1 million on the house sale to Capaldi. The last known Houston address for Capaldi is a house right around the corner from Walter Mischer's residence.

In July 1983, one of Capaldi's Houston real estate development companies, Southbelt Properties, purchased 491 acres south of Houston from a Panamanian corporation, Corporation Financier Europamerica. The purchase was financed with a $4.1 million loan from Mainland Savings. Then, in December 1984, Capaldi himself bought 406 acres of this land from his own company, Southbelt Properties. Mainland lent him $3.5 million for the purchase. Six months later, a Mainland subsidiary bought the property from Capaldi for $4.7 million, the money coming from Mainland. So in six months, Capaldi had made $1.2 million, courtesy of Mainland Savings.

But in a rare case in which Mainland was not left holding the bag, Hill Financial Savings in Red Hill, Pennsylvania, bailed Mainland out of this deal. Hill took over the financing, with a $6.25 million loan. In fact, Hill Financial made several loans to Capaldi, on land in North Harris County and land in the Dallas area. Hill Financial will reappear many times in this book, most notably in its financing of the $200 million Florida land deal.

At one time, Hill Financial was trying to arrange for the purchase of some of its Capaldi land by Mike Adkinson, the purchaser of the Florida land from the du Ponts' St. Joe Paper Company, according to documents that were generated in the transaction.

One of Capaldi's foremen with Macomb Contracting was a man named Charles McGuire. McGuire would later gain fame in Houston as its most noted transvestite. After he came out of the closet, McGuire ran for City Council and was defeated. Then, in 1991, he traveled to England to undergo a sex-change operation and came back to Houston as Kathryn McGuire.

In the early and mid-1980s, McGuire was a big investor, at more than $1 million, in the oil and gas limited partnerships of Houston con man Ed Baker. In one of the most celebrated murder mysteries in Houston, Baker was allegedly torched to death in his late-model Jaguar in a field west of Houston in 1985. His grieving widow claimed that the mob had done him in, allegedly because he had lost a lot of their money. Others believed that he had faked his death and high-tailed it to Latin America.

The *Houston Post* found that Florida mob associate Alvin Malnik, the protegé of the late mob financier Meyer Lanksy, had invested some money with Baker. But it turned out to be less than $20,000 in cash, and one of Baker's accountants claimed that Baker had gotten Malnik more than $1 million in tax write-offs. Some investigators theorized that the mob wouldn't whack anyone over less than $20,000. Others said they might do it just to make a point. But no investigator or reporter knew then about McGuire's relationship to Capaldi and his possible fronting for Capaldi on the Baker investment.

A partner and financial backer of Baker was Houston real estate investor Jack Modesett. Modesett's company had owned land in West Texas on which part of a landing strip near Big Bend National Park used by the CIA was located. This landing strip will be discussed in detail in a later chapter on Walter Mischer's CIA connections. Modesett also did business with Howard Pulver's group, including a promissory note that was later sold to Mainland Savings.

Mischer's Allied Bank lent money to Baker to buy an office building, and also allegedly lent money to some of Baker's limited partners, including a mysterious Paris (France) company called Saudi European. This company, as we shall see, had connections to Charles Keating, the ill-fated owner of Lincoln Savings.

Baker's murder or disappearance was never solved.

Mainland's business was not all just fun-and-games with the Mafia. There was another clientele. For instance, there was the time in August 1985 when Mainland handed at least $12 million in cash to Adnan Khashoggi's company, just a week before Khashoggi paid over the initial $1 million of $5 million to Manucher Ghorbanifar to start a secret arms-for-hostages deal with Iran. It happened this way:

Khashoggi first appeared in Houston in 1974, when an American company controlled by him and his two brothers bought a 22-acre tract of vacant land in West Houston just southwest of the Galleria shopping center. Khashoggi purchased the land for a little more than $5 million from the Dallas financial conglomerate of Lomas & Nettleton, which is controlled by wealthy Democratic fundraiser Jess Hay. Lomas & Nettleton had earlier foreclosed on the property after the owner, John Jamail, had defaulted on his loan.

(Lomas & Nettleton was very close to MBank, the bank that financed many of Herman K. Beebe's deals. The two companies shared several directors. In fact, the original loan to John Jamail was from the Bank of the Southwest (which became MBank Houston), which then assigned it to Lomas & Nettleton.)

Khashoggi had very grandiose, expensive plans for the Galleria tract. There was going to be a $300 million development, with a 40-story hotel, and with 10 or more office buildings and retail stores. But nothing happened for several years, until 1979, when Dallas oilman Clint Murchison, Jr., joined up with Khashoggi to revive the development plans. They borrowed $15 million from Texas Commerce Bank and brought in a man named Richard Knight to head the project. (Knight would later be the beneficiary of the largess of Mischer's and President Bush's buddy, County Judge Jon Lindsay, in a contract for a new county jail.)

There was a lot of sound and fury and grand announcements in the newspapers, but still nothing happened, except that it appeared that Khashoggi had pocketed close to $10 million of the Texas Commerce Bank loan. By 1982, Murchison had dropped out and Khashoggi was looking to sell the land. Three years later, there had been no takers for the property, and the Houston real estate market was starting to sink.

Then, in January 1985, Khashoggi joined up with San Antonio developer John Roberts to buy a big piece of property in Aspen, Colorado, that was planned for a large hotel development. Roberts controlled Commerce Savings and was an associate of several other S&L crooks, including Jarrett Woods and Ed McBirney.

Khashoggi and Roberts borrowed $44 million from Commerce Savings to buy the Aspen property. Khashoggi then lent Roberts $14 million for his part of the investment. This money came from San Jacinto Savings (where Chicago mob associate Joseph Grosz was in charge of lending), which placed a second mortgage on Khashoggi's Galleria tract. It is not known who got this money—whether Roberts put it in his pocket or paid it over to Khashoggi or some third party. A Khashoggi company internal memorandum indicates that Roberts got it.

By the middle of 1985, the wheels were starting to come off Khashoggi's American ventures. The Aspen deal was not working out and he had $30 million in debt against the Galleria tract. Then he got in touch with Mainland Savings—the answer to his prayers—allegedly through Roberts. (But Khashoggi had another connection to Mainland through money broker Mario Renda, his former partner.) Mainland proposed to buy the Galleria tract for $68 million. The bulk of this money would come from a $46 million loan from Lamar Savings in Austin. Mainland would lend the rest, $22 million. And the proceeds would be split this way:

The $30 million in prior loans from Texas Commerce Bank and San Jacinto Savings would be paid off. Khashoggi would buy $10 million in preferred stock at Mainland and use $12 million as a downpayment to buy foreclosed loans and real estate from Mainland (called "cash for trash"), thus boosting its capital and keeping the regulators at bay. That left $16 million for miscellaneous costs and Khashoggi.

Mainland was in a big hurry to close the deal before the end of the second quarter of 1985, which was the end of its fiscal year, so that its books, which would be audited by federal examiners at that time, would reflect the transaction. It went ahead with the purchase of the land from Khashoggi on June 30, even though the loans were not funded until August 1. Then Mainland officials found out they had a big problem. They couldn't get an appraisal of the Galleria tract to come anywhere near their purchase price of $68 million.

Incredibly, Mainland did not get an appraisal until September 11, and it reflected a value for the property of only $55 million. The appraisal itself was a joke. It was only two pages long and had no comparable sales and no economic analysis. At the same time, the county tax appraisal district had the property on its rolls at 100 percent of market value for $41.5 million. Even that was way more than it was worth.

So Mainland had to lower the sales price of the tract. It dropped it to $58 million, which was still $3 million more than the "appraisal." But now it didn't have the $10 million for Khashoggi to use to buy its preferred stock. Mainland officials had to figure out some other way to get Khashoggi $10 million. So they bought John Roberts's $14 million note to Khashoggi, which was a second mortgage on the Aspen hotel property after Commerce Savings' $44 million. The hotel tract was later appraised at $38 million, meaning Mainland's note was basically worthless.

There was more to the deal. Khashoggi had been buying up tracts of land next to the Galleria property. He had funded this through a $5 million loan from Summit Savings in Dallas, which was controlled by Roberts. At the August 1 closing of all the loans, Mainland issued Khashoggi two $10 million lines of credit to use for developing these other tracts. And finally, on the same day, Mainland signed a $5 million letter of credit to Khashoggi.

The last letter of credit was very curious. It provided that it could only be drawn on during the first 12 days of November. Ostensibly, the letter was in exchange for 20 percent of the profits of the development of the tracts next to the Galleria property. This was obviously something just trumped up at the last minute. There are some internal Khashoggi company documents that indicate that the letter may have been a guarantee to Khashoggi that he would get paid something for his $10 million in preferred stock that he bought. That explanation doesn't really wash either, since the $10 million came from Mainland anyway, not Khashoggi.

But the $5 million letter of credit does have all the earmarks of a guarantee. And, according to an investigation by a Houston law firm, Hill and his closest underlings "conspired to conceal the issuance of the letter of credit from the board of directors of Mainland." It could have been a guarantee to Khashoggi that he would get his money back on something else. The $5 million figure equals exactly the $5 million that Khashoggi paid to Ghorbanifar in August and September of 1985 for the first two acknowledged arms shipments to Iran in the Reagan Administration's arms-for-hostages deals.

Khashoggi had to be worried about getting his $5 million from the Iranians. But there is no indication in any of the Iran-Contra documents or reports that he ever complained about it. However, in 1986, there was a huge brouhaha because Khashoggi and his Canadian partners hadn't gotten paid back for a $10 million deal. Khashoggi sent his lawyer, Roy Furmark, to see William Casey, the director of the CIA and Furmark's friend, about this, and it threatened to blow the whole Iran scheme sky high.

The FBI was also curious about the $5 million letter of credit. An internal memorandum dated April 9, 1986, from Emmanuel Floor, one of Khashoggi's top lieutenants, to two other Khashoggi employees is entitled "FBI investigation/Mainland letter of credit." Floor tells the two employees that he spent an hour that day with two FBI agents in Salt Lake City (where Khashoggi's American companies were headquartered). The memo continues: "They [the Salt Lake City FBI agents] have been asked by the Houston FBI office to ask questions regarding the Mainland letter of credit. They were particularly interested in negotiations relating to the letter of credit. They specifically wanted to know who presented the letter of credit to AK Houston Properties [Khashoggi's company] and who was involved and were we present when the letter of credit was signed. I indicated to them that our discussion through late July did not involve the letter of credit and that the letter of credit developed in late July in Houston.

"I have given both of them Tariq's [one of the Khashoggi employees to whom the memo was addressed] name as being the Triad [Khashoggi's umbrella American company] officer involved in receiving the letter of credit from Mainland.

"They were extremely interested in the overall transaction but the focus seemed to be on the letter of credit.

"I explained to them that under our original transaction, Mainland was to find a buyer for the preferred stock and/or lender and that when the transaction was modified in late July the letter of credit was developed as a way to back up Mainland's performance.

"I wanted you both to be advised of this information."

There are several interesting aspects to this memo. First, Floor is obviously trying to coach them as to what to say to the FBI if they are questioned, so they will have their story straight, particularly about the purpose of the letter of credit.

Second, why would the FBI be mostly interested in a measly $5 million letter of credit out of a $72 million transaction that cost taxpayers at least $50 million? The date of the memo is April 9, 1986, which is five days after Mainland was closed down by the feds. But there is no way that such a transaction could have been discovered and investigated in such a short time period. The FBI had to have been working on this for some time before talking to Floor. Why?

It is now known that the FBI knew about and was investigating the first arms shipments to Iran in August and September 1985. Perhaps this was part of that investigation. Or they could have just been following up on a possible criminal referral made to them by examiners at Mainland, because allegedly the letter of credit was not authorized by the Mainland board. But if that were the case, there were many more questionable aspects to this deal than the $5 million letter of credit.

Khashoggi himself, in a press conference in Houston in the summer of 1990, denied that the money for the Iranian arms deal came from Mainland Savings. He said the money came from "overseas funds."

Well, first of all, how many nanoseconds would it take to wire money from Mainland, or any other American financial institution, to anywhere else in the world. And in one sense it can be said that at least some of Mainland's money, and thus the taxpayers', was used in the first publicized Iranian arms-for-hostages deal. Once Mainland's money from the Galleria deal went into Khashoggi's big pot, it became basically indistinguishable from the rest of the money. So when Khashoggi pulled out the $5 million for Ghorbanifar, a certain percentage of that belonged to the American taxpayers.

Mainland, which had taken a $16 million participation in the Lamar loan, and guaranteed the rest, eventually took the whole loan over. So Mainland ended up with an investment in the entire deal of more than $70 million. The tract was later sold by the feds for some $14 million, which equates to a loss for the taxpayers of more than $50 million.

The Houston press conference in the summer of 1990 in which Khashoggi denied that the arms-for-hostages money came from Mainland, was called to announce a new oil and gas joint venture with two Houston men, Jerry D. Allen and Bill Turney. Khashoggi said that he and nine other "friends from the Middle East," whom he would not identify, were investing $100 million in the new company.

Turney was a bankruptcy workout specialist in Houston, and had helped reorganized the businesses of the late-lamented Ed Baker, the same who, it was feared, had been torched in his Jaguar. Allen, on the other hand, was well acquainted with the oil and gas business. In 1983, his energy company, Longhorn Oil and Gas, went bankrupt in Oklahoma, owing more than $317 million in debts. A good chunk of that was to Penn Square Bank, whose demise had been hastened by loans to Allen and his drilling investors, who later sued Allen for fraud after Penn Square's federal receiver came after them for their unpaid promissory notes.[9]

Before the bankruptcy, Allen had been the financial co-chairman of the Republican National Committee and was a member of the Republican Eagles, which took a minimum donation of $10,000.

Allen and Turney told reporters at the Houston press conference

---

[9] *Daily Oklahoman*, February 25, 1983.

that they had been partners with Neil Bush in his Apex oil company, which Neil started up in Denver after his ill-fated JNB Exploration bit the dust. Of course, their new partner, Khashoggi, and Neil's father were well acquainted. Records and testimony in Khashoggi's 1990 trial with Imelda Marcos showed several telephone calls between Khashoggi and Bush's vice-presidential office in 1985 and 1986, during the height of Iran-Contra.

The Khashoggi deal wasn't the only Mainland financing the tracks of which lead back to the netherworld of the CIA and Iran-Contra. In the fall of 1983, Mainland started lending money to a company that also trails back to drug smugglers, money launderers, CIA proprietary airlines and Castle Bank & Trust.

Beginning in August 1983, more than a year before the Khashoggi deal, Mainland lent more than $1 million—possibly as much as $3 million—to a Cayman Islands company called Sara, Ltd. The loans were secured by three tracts of land in Houston, at least one having an apartment complex on it. Then, in the fall of 1984, Mainland refinanced its earlier loans to Sara and bumped the total to more than $3.5 million.

The legal documents on the loans show that the general partner of Sara, Ltd., was another limited partnership named B.C. One, Ltd., whose general partner was a Texas corporation called SGDevco. The president, secretary, treasurer, registered agent and sole director of SGDevco was Houston businessman H. Stephen Grace. (SGDevco presumably stands for Stephen Grace development company.)

Mainland also lent Grace and a partner some $6.7 million and then made a $232,000 personal loan to him to pay the delinquent interest on this loan and keep it off Mainland's delinquent loan report, according to a Houston law firm that investigated Mainland's failure. In addition, Mainland made a loan to a different Grace corporation, Dane Development, and then used the proceeds from a loan to another company to pay the principal and interest on its loan to Dane, which was delinquent, according to the law firm. (Most of these shenanigans were illegal.)

Before Grace formed the companies that got the loans from Mainland, he had been the vice president of finance for Century Corporation, the Houston development company controlled by Mischer's close friend Kenneth Schnitzer, who allegedly hobnobbed with mobsters.

Another principal in Sara, Ltd., is a Lebanese named Salim Saab. Saab, who signed some of the Mainland documents as secretary of Sara, holds Lebanese, Swiss and U.S. passports. He is suspected of laundering money for the mob, according to federal law enforcement sources, who have said he was known to hang out at a restaurant owned by Mischer's former son-in-law, Robert Corson. A Corson associate confirmed that Corson and his gang knew Saab.

Another listed secretary of Sara was Paget-Brown & Company, Ltd., of the Cayman Islands. Both Sara and Paget-Brown & Company have mailing addresses in the Westwind Building on Georgetown in the Caymans. Paget-Brown & Company is controlled by Caymans attorney Ian Paget-Brown, who was born in Torquay, England, and has been admitted to practice law in the Caymans, Colorado and Washington, D.C. He is named in a Florida Department of Law Enforcement investigative report on drug smuggler Jack DeVoe and money launderer Lawrence Freeman, who was involved in the $200 million Florida S&L deal.

The Florida report discusses a July 27, 1981, letter from DeVoe's Bahamas attorney, Anthony McKinny, to Paget-Brown. (The mailing address of Paget-Brown is the same as that listed for Sara some three years later in the Mainland loans.) McKinny's letter is an inquiry about two companies, Carib Holdings Limited in the Caymans, and its subsidiary, Seagreen Air Transport Limited, registered in Antigua. Paget-Brown had some controlling interest in these companies, but neither the letter nor the Florida report indicate why DeVoe was interested in them. McKinny stated to Paget-Brown that he represented a Bahamas company that was negotiating a loan to Carib Holdings.

Although the U.S. Federal Aviation Administration shows no airplanes registered to Seagreen Air Transport from 1984 to 1990, an October 11, 1988, letter from the FAA's Caribbean Flight Standards District Office in Puerto Rico regarding "FAA Certification of Seagreen Air Transport" states that "on August 18, 1988, this office did approve a maintenance program for Seagreen's (sic) Air Transport B707, N14AZ . . ."

Although Seagreen was apparently using this Boeing 707 jet transport, with tail number N14AZ, it was actually owned at the time by an El Paso company called GrecoAir, which is headed by a man named David Tokoph. There is no lease agreement on record with the FAA from GrecoAir to Seagreen. But, on April 30, 1986, Tokoph leased this aircraft to St. Lucia Airways,[10] located in St. Lucia, West Indies.

---

[10] Fixed Wing Lease Agreement, filed with FAA, dated April 30, 1986, between David Tokoph DBA Aviation Consultants and St. Lucia Airways, Ltd.

The *Washington Post* reported in February 1987 that a St. Lucia 707 flew to Teheran on November 25, 1985, carrying Hawk missiles. The Senate Intelligence Committee report on Iran-Contra did not identify this airline, but called it a "CIA proprietary."

The Chronology of the Iran-Contra affair is loaded with references to St. Lucia and its arms trips all over the world. According to the *Washington Post*, St. Lucia flew arms to Angola and Iran and may even have flown Reagan Administration officials to Teheran in May 1986 to negotiate arms for hostages.

The *New York Times* reported in February 1987 that "Santa" Lucia Airways was flying missions for the CIA, delivering arms to guerrillas in Angola in 1986. The newspaper reported that the airline made at least three trips to Zaire for that purpose: between March 20 and April 20, for two weeks between May 15 and May 30, and during one night in October.

These facts, taken together, demonstrate that Paget-Brown's Seagreen was maintaining the Boeing 707 for the CIA.

Finally, Paget-Brown was involved with Chicago attorney Burton Kanter, CIA super-operative Paul Helliwell and their Castle Bank & Trust. Penn State professor Alan A. Block reported in his book *Masters of Paradise* that in 1976, Helliwell contacted the head of Castle Bank's Cayman Islands office to tell him that Kanter was coming down to go through the files. After Kanter inspected them, he instructed the Cayman director to destroy some of them, put some of them back and keep the rest in special security. Helliwell then told the director to buy a secure, fireproof filing cabinet, put the special files in the cabinet, lock it and take it to Ian Paget-Brown.[11]

This is the same Ian Paget-Brown whose company was borrowing money from Mainland Savings.

Mainland Savings failed on April 4, 1986. The way the Federal Savings and Loan Insurance Corporation handled Mainland's failure has made it impossible to tell the exact losses, but they have been estimated at $300 million to $500 million.

Although the FBI has been investigating Mainland since it failed, there have been only two indictments of Mainland officials. Twin brothers from England, Philip and Thomas Noons, who worked at Mainland in mid-level positions, were indicted for using offshore companies to buy

---

[11] *Masters of Paradise,* by Alan A. Block (Transaction Publishers, 1991).

Mainland assets at below fair value. Not only did the Noons brothers have little or nothing to do with the failure of Mainland, their indictments were the result of information dug up by private investigators, not the FBI.

After Mainland failed, the Federal Savings and Loan Insurance Corporation hired the Houston law firm of Andrews & Kurth to investigate the failure, file a lawsuit against the officers and directors and recover all assets that were fraudulently taken from Mainland. Although Andrews & Kurth was paid millions of dollars for its legal work at Mainland, it apparently did not recover any money. Much of the law firm's efforts was spent defending Mainland, and thus several of its officers, including Raymond Hill, from a single lawsuit brought by one borrower who claimed he had been cheated by Mainland.

After the feds and Andrews & Kurth had allowed the statute of limitations to expire for filing a lawsuit for damages against the officers and directors of Mainland, and the newspapers wrote scathing stories about this, a large manila envelope without a return address appeared on my desk. It contained a lawsuit drawn up by Andrews & Kurth against the officers and directors of Mainland, but it had never been filed.

The unfiled lawsuit contained page after page of detailed allegations of wrongdoing, including criminal wrongdoing. When confronted with this, officials with the Federal Savings and Loan Insurance Corporation acknowledged that there had been wrongdoing at Mainland but it wouldn't be worth it to file a lawsuit. They said that the former officers and directors of Mainland did not have enough assets to justify the expense of a lawsuit.

When I took the unfiled lawsuit to the U.S. Attorney's Office in Houston to show prosecutors and FBI agents the details of the alleged criminal wrongdoing, the only question that U.S. Attorney Henry Oncken asked was—you guessed it—how I came into possession of the document.

Oncken was later drummed out of his job after his office was subjected to criticism, including some withering blasts from a congressional committee, for attempting to downplay the extent of fraud in Houston S&Ls and for not cracking down on S&L fraud. It was later discovered that Oncken had several loans from S&Ls that subsequently failed and were connected to alleged fraudulent activity. Before Oncken was named U.S. Attorney he had worked for the Harris County district attorney, and before that for a Houston developer who had been partners with Walter Mischer.

The claim by the feds that Mainland officers and directors didn't have any assets to go after was nonsense, and proven so by the details in the unfiled lawsuit. The attorneys at Andrews & Kurth determined that Raymond Hill received $4.32 million in dividends, salary and legal fees from Mainland in the last four years he was chairman there. Hill not only was the largest stockholder at Mainland and the chairman, his law firm handled property foreclosures at Mainland, which in some cases were overseen by Hill as chairman.

Hill, according to the unfiled lawsuit, "drain[ed] in excess of $4,320,000 from Mainland or its subsidiaries during a period where Mainland's financial condition crumbled. The total compensation which Hill extracted from Mainland between 1982-1985 was outrageous, unreasonable, excessive and not commensurate with the quality of his performance with respect to his duties and responsibilities at Mainland."

Hill, the Episcopalian Sunday School teacher, was typically unrepentant. He said he had done nothing wrong and claimed that the statements in the unfiled lawsuit were "libelous." He also claimed to be broke, although he never disputed the actual dollar figures the unfiled suit alleged that he received at Mainland for his services.

Perhaps Hill had that attitude because Mainland did business with Mafia associates and CIA operatives and because Walter Mischer was his mentor. There has even been speculation that Hill signed a secrecy agreement with the CIA and got a get-out-of-jail-free card for helping the agency at Mainland. But there was something else too:

The junior attorneys at Andrews & Kurth who worked on the lawsuit apparently wanted to file it against Hill and the other Mainland officers and directors. But the lawsuit was stopped at the upper levels of that firm and at the upper levels of the Federal Savings and Loan Insurance Corporation. During this time, the U.S. Treasury Secretary was James A. Baker III, today White House Chief of Staff. Baker was also the former managing partner at Andrews & Kurth and a longtime friend of Raymond Hill. Their families were very close and the two had grown up together, said one longtime Houstonian who knows both men. In fact, in the late 1960s Hill actually represented Baker in a legal matter.

When I called Hill's office for comment about his relationship to

Baker, Ms. Macy (the same Hill employee who when asked about Hill's relationship to Mischer, had called back with the response that Mischer is "considerably older" than Hill) took the question and then called back later with a response. "Mr. Baker is considerably younger than Mr. Hill," she said, simply. In fact, Hill was born in 1925 and Baker was born in 1930.

In an April 2, 1990, letter to FBI Director William Sessions, Houston attorney Ted Walker (who borrowed money from Mainland and later filed a lawsuit against the S&L) told of a chance encounter he had with Raymond Hill:

"On March 15, 1990, I happened to meet Raymond Hill, former chairman of the board and president of MSLA [Mainland Savings], outside the Harris County Courthouse. After seven years of disagreements between us, a friendly atmosphere has developed. During our curbside visit, Raymond Hill discussed his political connections within the Republican party, one of which is James Baker III. Raymond discussed in detail the family relationship and that the Hill family and the Baker family have had Christmas dinner together for decades."

In June 1985, after Mainland Savings had already made its disastrous deals with Howard Pulver's group and was negotiating its deal with Khashoggi, Secretary of the Treasury Baker appeared before a Senate banking subcommittee and testified of the Reagan Administration's optimism about the S&L industry. "I don't think there is any cause for undue concern and I would reject any suggestion that we are in the midst of some sort of a major systemic problem with respect to any element of our financial services industry," Baker told the senators.

In the fall of 1987, while Seay and I were still trying to find more Mafia connections to Mainland, I got a phone call from the same anonymous source who first tipped Seay to Mainland and Howard Pulver. This person, whom Seay had dubbed D.T., for Deep Throat, and whom other *Post* reporters called Darth Vader because in his efforts to disguise his voice over the telephone he sounded like the Lord of the Dark Side of the Force, told me to check out a lawsuit in San Diego that involved Beebe and a man named Charles Bazarian.

My trip to San Diego was the first step in connecting the world of Beebe, the Louisiana mob associate connected to the failure of at least a dozen Texas and Louisiana savings and loans, and the world of Mario Renda, the New York mob associate involved in the failure of financial institutions across the country. Not only did the two show up at Mainland Savings, but they also appeared together in other places and at other failed S&Ls, indicating that Mafia involvement in financial institutions had spread like a virus throughout the nation.

5

HERMAN AND MARIO

In 1981, Herman K. Beebe was looking around for a house to live in while his house in La Costa was being remodeled. He found a 5,000-square-feet beach house overlooking the breakers at Solana Beach, north of San Diego. Beebe brought Vernon Savings' Don Dixon in to do a complicated refinancing and property swap with the house's owner, with Beebe's Bossier Bank & Trust lending $750,000 to the owner. Beebe and Dixon then took possession of the house.

In April 1983, the loan was transferred from Bossier Bank to Beebe's major insurance company, Savings Life, and increased to $1.16 million. Then, in November 1984, Dixon had the loan transferred to Paris Savings. By that time Dixon was staying in the house on frequent trips to Southern California and using it to entertain Vernon Savings board members, customers and at least one Texas savings and loan regulator.

The beach house gained notoriety during the criminal trials of several Vernon S&L executives and customers. Dixon, Vernon president Patrick G. King and senior vice president John V. Hill were all convicted of using Vernon funds to provide prostitutes for Vernon officials and customers at the Solana Beach house. One time, a prostitute was provided for the Texas Savings and Loan Commissioner, Linton Bowman. But apparently nothing dirty was going on, because he claimed later that he was impotent then.

Another time, after a wild three-day party at the beach house, one of the prostitutes was found strangled, her mouth stuffed with gravel and her clothes neatly stacked on top of her nude body. Officials said she had recently become a police informant.

When Dixon started having financial problems in 1985 and was trying to distance himself from Beebe, who was in criminal hot water by that time, he brought in a friend and borrower at Vernon Savings to rent, and possibly buy, the beach house. It was Oklahoma con man and convicted felon Charles Bazarian. Bazarian actually lived in the house for six months and was supposed to buy it. He had been hiding out at the time, but returned to Oklahoma, leaving behind several months of unpaid rent.

The original owner of the house then filed a major lawsuit against Dixon, Beebe and all of their corporate entities involved in the deal, claiming he had been cheated out of his equity in the house. Among those named as a defendant in the second amended petition was Bazarian.

When I was sitting in the clerk's office at the San Diego Courthouse in January 1988, copying this information down, I had no idea who Bazarian was. When I returned to Houston and ran Bazarian's name through the computerized newspaper data bases, I realized I had hit pay dirt.

Not only was Bazarian a friend of Mario Renda, he had actually been convicted with Renda in a banking scam in Florida in 1987. This was Renda's first conviction for bank fraud, in which he got involved in a scam with Michael Rapp, the former mob stockbroker with a new name, and Bazarian. The three cooked up a scheme to get control of Florida Center Bank during a Halloween party at Bazarian's palatial home outside Oklahoma City. It was a complicated scam using bounced checks, brokered deposits and loans. It backfired on them—they all got caught and convicted.

Bazarian was also borrowing big bucks from a California S&L that Renda was brokering deposits into. Furthermore, Bazarian had numerous other connections to Beebe's financial circles. He was a borrower from Dixon's Vernon Savings, and was involved in a small Oklahoma S&L with a Beebe business associate and Houston real estate man named Michael Horne, who had worked at Mainland Savings and before that for Walter Mischer at Allied Bank. Horne also did business at Roy Dailey's First Savings of East Texas, which Dailey, a cousin of Robert Corson and a business partner with Walter Mischer, bought with a loan from Beebe's Bossier Bank and Trust.

(Several years later, the Detroit *Free Press* reported that Bazarian showed up at Bloomfield Savings and Loan, located in a Detroit suburb, along with his associate, mob lawyer Morris Shenker.)

Obviously, something big involving the Mafia was going on in savings and loans all across the country. Seay and I set out to see if we could find other connections between Beebe and Renda. One place where Renda's and Beebe's circles intersected was the San Diego/La Costa area of Southern California. Renda's wife, Antoinette Rizzo Renda, is the daughter of Vincent Rizzo, owner of the Bernardo wineries out of San Diego. In August 1982, Renda and several of his partners met at the La Costa resort to talk over their newly created scam of brokered deposits and linked financing.

Both Renda and Beebe had bank accounts at the tiny San Dieguito National Bank, located outside La Costa. In 1984, Beebe had a bank account there when he guaranteed the previously mentioned $75,000 loan to a travel agency controlled by an associate of Scott Susala. That same year, when the bank had less than $50 million in deposits, some $700,000 of those deposits were union pension funds from the New York City area that had been wired there by Renda and his partner, Martin Schwimmer.

According to the indictment prepared by the Organized Crime Strike Force in the Brooklyn U.S. Attorney's Office, San Dieguito National Bank was one of only six banks across the country where Renda and Schwimmer had "off the books" accounts used in their criminal enterprise. Renda and Schwimmer were convicted of racketeering in skimming union pension funds and bribing union officials in their off-the-books fraud.[1]

The first place officials found Renda and his deposits was the infamous Penn Square Bank in Oklahoma City. Fueled by brokered deposits from Renda and others, Penn Square had engaged in wild and riotous lending in the oil patch before expiring in 1982. Even though it was only a $500 million institution, Penn Square had sold more than $2 billion in oil and gas loan participation to other banks.

Two big banks that were nearly brought down by Penn Square's failure were Continental Illinois in Chicago and Seattle First National (or Seafirst). Continental had to be bailed out in 1984 to the tune of $4.5 billion, while Seafirst had to be sold to avoid a bailout. The Federal Deposit Insurance Corporation paid off $218 million in insured deposits at Penn Square, the largest payoff since 1971, when $80 million was

---

[1] United States of America vs. Martin Schwimmer and Mario Renda, CR 87-423, United States District Court, Eastern District of New York.

required for the failure of Sharpstown State Bank in Houston. That failure was part of the biggest political scandal in Texas history, the previously mentioned Sharpstown scandal.

"The Penn Square experience gave us a rough alert to the damage that can be done by brokered deposits funneled into troubled institutions," said former FDIC Chairman Irvine Sprague in his book *Bailout*.

After Penn Square failed, Renda and others were called to testify before a congressional committee about brokered deposits. But nothing came of it, and apparently no one attempted to determine if any of the bad loans at Penn Square were linked to Renda's brokered deposits. Interestingly, Morris Shenker had a loan at Penn Square that went bad. In addition, Beebe's Bossier Bank and Trust was involved in a complex stock and nursing home deal with Penn Square.

Next, Renda was found at Empire Savings in Mesquite, Texas, which failed in early 1984 at a cost to the federal government of more than $100 million. Empire's failure was the first big one after deregulation and signaled the beginning of the savings-and-loan debacle. Empire busted out because of its loans on large land flips and acres of empty, sometimes incomplete condominiums along Interstate 30 east of Dallas. The small S&L ballooned from $13 million in deposits in 1982 to about $310 million in 1984. More than half of the deposits—approximately $160 million—came from Mario Renda.

Since Empire failed it has been the subject of massive civil and criminal investigations and litigation by federal and state authorities and investigative reporting by both Dallas newspapers. More than 100 convictions have been obtained by prosecutors, although the biggest fish, the owner and major borrowers, escaped in their first trial with a hung jury. The Justice Department kept after them though, and they were convicted in the second trial and sentenced to 20 years in prison. Yet no one has been able to determine, or to the best of my knowledge, even tried to determine, whether any of the loans that took Empire down were linked to Renda's deposits, and thus whether any of the lost money ended up in the hands of the Mafia.

The owner of Empire, Spencer Blain, had been in the savings and loan business in Texas for some time. He was a director of the Federal Home Loan Bank of Little Rock, which oversaw S&Ls in a five-state area, and came to Empire after serving as president of First Federal Savings in Austin. He bought control of Empire from developer Danny Faulkner and his associates with an $800,000 loan from Falkner and his partner, James Toler, a former mayor of Garland, Texas.

In August 1982, Blain paid off his Empire stock loan with a $2.25 million loan from Allied Lakewood Bank. Part of this loan was used to purchase land along the Interstate 30 corridor, which Blain flipped six months later for a profit of $15 million.[2] Allied Lakewood Bank, where Toler was a director, was part of Walter Mischer's Allied Bank empire. Further, it was one of the banks listed in the 1985 Comptroller of the Currency report on Beebe as being controlled by Beebe and his associates or which did significant business with banks controlled by Beebe and his associates.

There were also connections between Beebe and Danny Faulkner, a sixth-grade dropout and former house painter, who said he couldn't read or write. Faulkner and his associates were the main beneficiaries of the largess of Blain and Empire, receiving well over $100 million in loans that later went bad. Dale Anderson, Beebe's former partner, said they didn't do any business directly with Faulkner, but they did meet with him to discuss some business deals. And an associate of Faulkner and Blain, Robert E. Davis, was indicted with Beebe in 1987 for bank fraud.

The indictment alleged that Davis conspired with Beebe and others in misapplying loans from banks controlled or affiliated with Beebe. Davis signed insurance policies as an authorized representative of Lloyd's Texas, Inc., on race horses that were used as collateral for loans to an associate of Beebe and Davis. The indictment alleged that Davis, Beebe and others "submitted false and fraudulent livestock mortality insurance binders pertaining to the collateral securing the loans" at the Beebe banks. The charges against Davis were later separated from Beebe's, and after Beebe pleaded guilty, the charges against Davis were allowed by prosecutors to lapse.

The original indictment states that Davis committed his alleged acts in May and June of 1984. In July 1984, Davis helped incorporate an insurance company called Lloyd's U.S. Corporation, a Texas corporation. Other investors in the company included Faulkner's son-in-law, Kenneth Blanton; Faulkner's concrete supplier, Perry Bodin; Faulkner's insurance agent, George May; one of Faulkner's bank partners, Clyde Vaughn; and Spencer Blain. All of these people, with the possible exception of Vaughn, were involved in Interstate 30 land deals with Empire Savings.

---

[2] *Dallas Times Herald*, February 7, 1985.

(In 1987, Lloyd's of London sued Lloyd's U.S. in federal court in Austin. Lloyd's U.S. countersued, and the two parties settled out of court. The settlement provided that Lloyd's U.S. would change its name to Lloyd's, United States, and would not use any of Lloyd's of London's names.

(In turn, Lloyd's of London agreed not to say anything negative about Lloyd's U.S. nor to interfere in its business. Incredibly, Lloyd's of London, which brought the original action, agreed to pay Lloyd's U.S. $6.4 million. This works out to approximately $300,000 per investor, compared to each one's original investment in 1984 of some $30,000. The agreement was reached on September 30, 1987, just one week before Faulkner and Blain were indicted for fraud at Empire Savings and five months after Blain settled a civil suit against him by the Federal Savings and Loan Insurance Corporation for $100 million. Representing Lloyd's of London was the Houston law firm of Fulbright & Jaworski, while Robert Strauss's Akin, Gump, Strauss, Hauer & Feld was one of the law firms representing Lloyd's U.S.)

The footprints of Renda and Beebe are found side-by-side at several other Texas savings and loans that later failed.

On the flat, high plains of the Texas panhandle, the former music teacher from Queens, New York, and the former central Louisiana farm agent were milking State Savings and Loan of Lubbock. Beebe financed the purchase of this savings and loan by his associate, Tyrell Barker, by having his insurance company, Savings Life, lend Barker $880,000 for the cash portion of the purchase in December 1981.

In exchange, Barker pledged his stock in the S&L as collateral and gave Beebe an option to purchase 50 percent of the shares of State Savings's parent company. In Beebe's bankruptcy case in Florida, the FDIC filed a complaint opposing the discharge of Beebe's debts and alleging, among other things, that Beebe "maintained domination and control of State Savings."

Beebe and his associated companies also borrowed millions from State Savings. In fact, Beebe's guilty plea to bank fraud in 1988 involved a State Savings loan.

Barker, a developer from northern California, had somehow met Don Dixon there and come to Texas with him. They originally intended to buy a savings and loan together, with help from Beebe. But they ultimately decided to get their own S&Ls, with Beebe financing Vernon

Savings for Dixon and State Savings for Barker.

In 1987, Barker was convicted of bank fraud involving State Savings, Brownfield Savings in Brownfield, Texas, and Key Savings in Englewood, Colorado. He was sentenced to five years in prison. Also convicted was Barker's attorney, Lawrence Vineyard, who had purchased Key Savings with an $11 million loan from Vernon Savings.

At the same time Barker and Beebe were controlling the loans made by State Savings, Renda was brokering tens of millions of dollars in deposits into the S&L. He was getting a special interest rate deal on these deposits, meaning he was getting a slightly higher rate than other depositors. Such deals sometimes accompanied kickbacks to S&L officials and/or skims of some of the interest before the depositors, such as pension funds, were paid the interest promised them by Renda.

Another savings and loan where Renda had a special interest rate deal on his brokered deposits was San Jacinto Savings in Houston, which was owned by Southmark, the Dallas-based real estate company and mob dumping ground that had considerable dealings with Beebe. Renda had other business ties to Southmark. He and a partner were developing the Palace Hotel and Casino in Puerto Rico. They fell on hard times and the project went into bankruptcy. The Pratt Hotel Corporation, of which Southmark owned 37 percent, purchased the project out of bankruptcy.[3]

The failure of Empire Savings, which began the great S&L debacle, was preceded in time, by five years, by the failure of a Houston savings and loan, Surety Savings, which was part of the Texas rent-a-bank scandal. It was a dress rehearsal for the S&L scandal to come.

Surety Savings, and the Texas rent-a-bank scandal, had it all: mobsters, CIA operatives, politicians, Ben Barnes, Neil Bush's future business partner and sugar daddy, fraud, one of Michael Milken's biggest future clients, Teamsters Union deposits, a congressional investigation instigated by U.S. Representative Henry B. Gonzalez, a federal regulator named Rosemary Stewart, and Beebe and Mischer.

This earlier scandal shows that the savings-and-loan crisis was not

---

[3] *Inside Job,* by Stephen Pizzo, Mary Fricker and Paul Muolo (New York: McGraw-Hill, 1989).

an isolated, one-time accident. Many of the participants had been up to the same tricks years before. The lesson is: It happened before. And if we do not learn its lessons—who was behind it, how it happened and why it happened—it could happen again.

6

THERE IS NOTHING NEW
UNDER THE SUN

The story begins on January 26, 1972, when Houston Police Chief Herman Short announced the indictment of reputed Mafia associate Raymond Novelli. "The investigation has extended nationwide, and it involves illegal operations dealing with banks, labor unions, construction companies and savings and loan companies," Short stated.

Novelli, a contractor and developer, had been indicted for embezzling a former employer. When asked by journalists about reports of his connections with organized crime, he replied,"Again this is a political thing. Every time something is written, they connect my name to the Mafia. I don't know where they get it or why they want to tag that name on me."

Novelli did acknowledge being connected to some labor unions in Nevada, and later that year an attorney for one of Novelli's associates, Albert Stavitsky, filed an affidavit saying that Novelli told Stavitsky that he (Novelli) was a Mafia member and would have Stavitsky killed if he testified before a grand jury. Stavitsky fled to Spain.

Novelli had come to Houston from Utah four years earlier with nothing but the shirt on his back. When he was indicted, he controlled five banks and had interests in two savings and loans. He owned a 3,500-acre ranch near Dallas and an island off Haiti where he was trying to establish a gambling casino. He also had a Lear jet and an 85-foot yacht.

When he was arrested, Novelli told reporters he had flown some politicians around in his Lear jet, but he refused to identify them. Some

16 years later, I found one of Novelli's pilots, Ronnie Powledge, who revealed that Novelli did business with Ben Barnes and Herman Beebe. Powledge, who was not Novelli's chief pilot, said Barnes "could very well have" flown in Novelli's plane. Novelli's former secretary, Helen Spencer, confirmed that Barnes used the plane on several occasions.

According to a former Pasadena, Texas (a suburb of Houston), police officer who investigated Novelli, Lloyd Bentsen also used Novelli's plane. However, Powledge said Bentsen didn't use the plane, while Spencer said she didn't know if Bentsen used it. "I don't think he and Bentsen had that much to do with each other," she said.

But Powledge did say that Novelli knew Lan Bentsen, one of the senator's sons. And one of Novelli's business partners, Vannie Cook, said Novelli was friends with Jim Bath of Atlantic Aviation, who was Lan Bentsen's partner and an alleged CIA operative. (Chapter 16 is all about Bath.) Cook was on the board of directors with Lloyd Bentsen at a savings and loan in South Texas that eventually ended up in the hands of CIA asset Guillermo Hernandez-Cartaya (to be discussed later).

Then, in January 1973, Novelli and five former Surety Savings officers and directors were indicted for fraud. The charges included Novelli's purchase of stock in five small Texas banks from the officers, using the proceeds of a $2.75 million Surety loan. Novelli jumped bond in 1974 and disappeared. He was found two years later by the FBI living under a false name in California and was sentenced to 15 years in jail. After he got out of prison he went to work for some organizations called the Jesus Jubilee Foundation and Convicts for Christ.

(Art Leiser, the former Texas S&L examiner, said that in the mid-1980s he ran across Novelli's wife as one of the proposed purchasers of a savings and loan. He said he put a stop to it.)

After Novelli was indicted in January 1972, Surety Savings was sold by its owners, who were indicted with Novelli the next year, to Cyril J. Smith, Jr. Smith was the son of the state's leading water district attorney, who had helped Mischer set up some of his utility districts. Smith Jr. was indicted in 1978 for fraud at Surety Savings, along with a former Texas state representative, James C. Day, Jr., who would later become a partner with Leonard Capaldi. They both pleaded guilty and received probated sentences.

Several months before he was indicted in Texas, Day became a target in a bizarre FBI sting that involved fugitive financier Robert Vesco, military planes destined for Libya and former Democratic National Committee chairman John White (the former Texas agriculture secretary).

(The details of this sting operation, which are practically incomprehensible, are contained in the book *Vesco* by Arthur Herzog. Day pleaded guilty to defrauding Vesco and lying about his influence with White and got a two-year prison term. The FBI spent $25,000 trying to bribe White, but the Justice Department refused to appoint a special prosecutor and the charges against White were dropped.)

In late 1975, before he was indicted, Cyril J. Smith, Jr., secretly sold the savings and loan to a man named Larry Parker, who was building a tennis club in Houston. Parker, who had been introduced to Beebe by a local attorney, immediately began wheeling and dealing.

One of the first loans Parker made was to the Enchanted Oaks Joint Venture, which was composed of TMC Funding, a Mischer company, and two Mischer associates, including his son-in-law, Robert Corson. The loan from Surety for the strip shopping center was for $840,000 and refinanced an earlier loan of $475,000 from Allied Spring Bank, a member bank of Mischer's bank holding company.

Teamsters Union deposits began flowing into Surety, which was buying certificates of deposit at Beebe's Bossier Bank and Trust, which in turn bought $1.5 million in San Antonio Ranches municipal utility bonds from Surety.

Surety made a $1.9 million loan to Eagle Pass rancher Richmond C. Harper, who was indicted with drug smuggler Barry Seal and Gambino Mafia family associate Murray Kessler in the sale of explosives to anti-Castro Cubans. The loan was arranged by Ben Barnes, who got $250,000 of the proceeds for a mortgage he held on some of Harper's property. Another $1 million of the loan went to pay Harper's overdraft at a Mexican bank that was threatening to foreclose on Harper's ranch in Mexico. In addition, Navarro Savings and Brazosport Savings, controlled by Carroll Kelly with financing from Beebe, made loans of $180,000 and $125,000 to Harper at the urging of Barnes.

In May 1977, Parker signed a $100,000 promissory note to Denver developer Richard Rossmiller, secured by 8,000 shares of Surety stock. That same day, Rossmiller sold the note to Beebe. Earlier that month Rossmiller signed an $800,000 promissory note to Beebe and Beebe's partner K. C. Hood. This note was secured by seven promissory notes to Surety Savings, including one that involved a George Aubin company and several others signed by a company affiliated with Albert Prevot, Beebe's associate.

(At one time Aubin had a home loan financed at Surety, and his front-man-to-be, J. B. Haralson, went to work for Surety after the rent-a-bank scandal broke.)

It is not clear how the promissory notes to Surety ended up being controlled by Rossmiller—some were assigned to him by Arvada State Bank in Arvada, Colorado, where he was a major stockholder—nor why Beebe was apparently moving close to $1 million to Rossmiller.

Rossmiller showed up a year earlier in the Texas rent-a-bank scandal when he and his two Denver partners bought the Peoples State Bank in Marshall, Texas, from Ben Barnes and associates of Barnes and Beebe.[1] Before they bought this bank, Rossmiller and his partners were seeking help from Beebe in financing their Marketplace Shopping Center in Aurora, Colorado.

To help with this, Beebe brought in his buddy, Donald Luna, a con man and loan broker from Birmingham, Alabama, who claimed to represent labor unions in making loans of union funds. Luna lined up Mile High Savings and Loan in Denver to make the loan to Rossmiller and his partners. In a letter to Beebe and Barnes, Luna stated that "the lender has requested that you keep your young man, Mr. Rossmiller, quiet and away from the lenders in order to complete this deal."

A letter to Luna that was part of the congressional hearing mentions Rossmiller's Marketplace loan along with a loan to something called ICE Forum from Carroll Kelly's Brazosport Savings.

One of Rossmiller's two partners was Denver architect Bill Walters. Walters was brought to national attention in the late 1980s because of his relationship to Neil Bush, the President's son. In 1983, after Neil had worked just a few years for Amoco as a landman (someone who researches property titles and works on oil leases), he and his two partners were set up in the oil business by Bill Walters. Walters contributed $150,000, or half of the initial start-up capital, and received a limited partnership interest of 6.25 percent in the company. One of Walters's banks, Cherry Creek National, opened up a $1.25 million line of credit, later expanded to $1.75 million, for the young company.

In August 1985, Neil Bush was named to the board of directors of Silverado Banking, Savings and Loan Association, and in that capacity voted on a number of loans and other transactions involving Walters and his companies. In 1991, the Office of Thrift Supervision repri-

---

[1] Subcommittee on Financial Institutions of House Committee on Banking, hearings on failure of Citizens State Bank in Carrizo Springs, Texas, 1976.

manded Neil for not revealing his business relationships to Walters when he voted on Walters's loans.

Back in 1976, when Donald Luna, Herman Beebe and Ben Barnes were trying to arrange a loan to Rossmiller and Walters, they went to Mile High Savings in Denver, which agreed to make the loan. Several years later, Mile High changed its name to Silverado.

The director of enforcement for the Office of Thrift Supervision that sought sanctions against Neil Bush in the late 1980s was Rosemary Stewart. This is the same Rosemary Stewart who 13 years earlier as an attorney for the Federal Home Loan Bank Board was the examiner of Surety Savings during the rent-a-bank scandal; who saw the $1.9 million loan to Richmond Harper; who saw the involvement of Ben Barnes and Herman Beebe; and who saw the loan to Walter Mischer's associates. And then she apparently did nothing and said nothing when most of these people got back into the savings and loan industry in the early and mid-1980s.

This is the same Rosemary Stewart who urged regulators to go easy on Charles Keating's Lincoln Savings and then left the Office of Thrift Supervision in 1990 and went to work for the law firm of Jones, Day, Reavis & Pogue, which represented Keating's Lincoln Savings and a number of other dirty S&Ls, such as Vernon.

So . . . ten years after the Surety deals and the rent-a-bank scandal, every one of these people was heavily involved in the savings-and-loan debacle and together responsible for billions of dollars in losses to the taxpayers.

Luna, who got convicted for his union loan brokerage scams, showed up at Flushing Federal Savings, a mob-infested S&L in Queens, New York. Luna was convicted for fraud at Flushing Federal, where he was obtaining and brokering loans. Also convicted at Flushing, where Mario Renda was brokering deposits, were several mob associates who were involved in a scheme that received some financing from Acadia Savings in Louisiana, which had been controlled by Beebe's associate Edmund Reggie.

Rossmiller became, according to a federal regulator pursuing his hidden assets, the biggest debtor in the country to the federal deposit insurance system, owing more than $200 million for loans that went into default. In 1989, Rossmiller filed for personal bankruptcy in Denver, showing debts of about $57 million, which made his one of the biggest personal bankruptcies in Colorado history.

Rossmiller and his affiliated companies borrowed close to $180 million from Hill Financial Savings in Red Hill, Pennsylvania, one of the biggest dirty S&Ls in the country. Hill Financial also lent $80 million to Mike Adkinson in the $200 million Florida land deal in which a savings and loan owned by Mischer's former son-in-law kicked in $20 million.

One of Rossmiller's associates and a partner in borrowing from Hill Financial was Allan Reiver, a reprobate lawyer who had moved to Denver from Houston. Reiver graduated from the University of Houston law school in 1968. The next year he filed a lawsuit against the Houston Police Department, claiming police officers were harassing him by stopping him and searching his car for drugs. His request for an injunction was denied and the next year he moved to Denver. In 1989, Reiver, a known drug user, pleaded guilty to assault. The victim, a woman, claimed Reiver mutilated her genitals during oral sex, allegedly biting off her clitoris.

Sometime in the 1970s, Reiver was introduced to the chairman of Atlantic Richfield, Robert O. Anderson. They formed a partnership for the purposes of real estate development in Denver. One of their most infamous developments was the Broadway Plaza, in which they took an old warehouse-style Montgomery Wards in 1984 and tried to convert it into an upscale shopping center.

Hill Financial, to whom Rossmiller had introduced Reiver, sank more than $80 million into the project before the bottom fell out and Reiver withdrew in 1988. In addition to Reiver and Anderson, one of the limited partners in the project was a limited partnership of Hill Financial and Rossmiller.

During the time Anderson was doing business with Reiver and Rossmiller, he brought in Walter Mischer as a partner in a 250,000-acre ranch in far west Texas near Big Bend National Park. Mischer told me that when he was visiting Anderson in Denver, the oil man showed him Broadway Plaza and introduced him either to Reiver or Rossmiller.

In 1989, Anderson and Mischer sold the ranch to the state of Texas for a park. The eastern edge of this ranch is only a few miles from a CIA landing strip and transshipment point that will be described in a following chapter on Mischer.

By 1978, Surety was brain-dead from all the years of past abuse. Federal and state regulators were scrambling to find something to do with the S&L or someone who would buy it. One person whom Beebe's buddy Larry Parker brought in to try to resuscitate Surety was Charles Hurwitz, the head of Federated Development. Hurwitz and Federated, whose primary bank was Mischer's Allied Bank, were turned down by the regulators because the capital Hurwitz wanted to put into the institution consisted primarily of junk real estate and repossessed real estate, according to Art Leiser, chief examiner for the Texas Savings and Loan Department.

Today Hurwitz is better known as a corporate raider and greenmailer who has drawn the ire of environmentalists with his purchase of Pacific Lumber and his plans to increase the cutting of redwoods the company owns in Northern California. He bought Pacific Lumber in late 1985 with the help of $450 million of Michael Milken's junk bonds.

Hurwitz grew up in Kilgore in East Texas and graduated from the University of Oklahoma in 1962. While there he allegedly rubbed shoulders with Larry Mizel, who graduated in 1964. Mizel would go on to later fame as head of M.D.C. Holdings, a home builder in Denver and one of the biggest players in the Silverado Savings-Lincoln Savings-San Jacinto Savings-Drexel Burnham circle.

Twice during the 1970s Hurwitz's companies got into trouble with federal regulatory authorities. In 1971, Hurwitz's Summit Insurance Company of New York agreed to a permanent injunction with the SEC barring it from violating securities laws. This case also involved convicted felon and securities con man John Peter Galanis and Galanis's associate, Ramon D'Onofrio, who shows up later as a business partner of renegade intelligence operative Richard Brenneke.

Hurwitz also had a number of contacts with Herman Beebe. It was Hurwitz who introduced Beebe to B. G. Wylie, Carroll Kelly's halfbrother, according to Wylie. And Beebe's former partner, Dale Anderson, said they "saw" Hurwitz several times. One time, Anderson said, Hurwitz was trying to do a "big deal" with an insurance company in Chicago. "Jack Freeman made him the loan. We didn't get the play," Anderson related. Freeman was a Dallas insurance man and close business associate of Beebe and Ben Barnes—they owned several banks and insurance companies together.

In 1982, Hurwitz begin to buy stock in United Financial Group, the parent company of United Savings of Texas, one of the largest S&Ls in the state. By 1984 Hurwitz's company was the biggest United Financial shareholder, with 25 percent of the stock, and Hurwitz became chairman of the board and chief executive officer.

By 1988, United Savings was insolvent and Hurwitz stepped down as chief executive officer. Regulators cited "loan-underwriting deficiencies, a failure to maintain appraisal reports, poor maintenance of books and records and insufficient internal controls" in United's failure. The S&L also had a large portfolio of junk bonds from Drexel Burnham, which in turn owned some 10 percent of United's stock. The S&L was sold to fellow corporate raider Lewis Ranieri at an estimated cost to taxpayers of $1.6 billion.

Ironically, in March 1991, Hurwitz's umbrella company, Maxxam, was allowed by federal regulators to buy 32 mortgage loans and 26 commercial properties that were owned by failed savings and loans and were either delinquent or in foreclosure. The Resolution Trust Corporation, which manages the assets of failed S&Ls, sold the property to Maxxam for $130 million. Maxxam officials said they were going to increase the value of the properties and then sell them or hold them as long-term investments. (Maxxam didn't volunteer, and no regulator suggested, that any profits be used to reduce the $1.6 billion debt incurred by taxpayers from the failure of United Savings.)

After Hurwitz was turned down in his attempt to buy Surety Savings, the defunct institution was finally sold in 1979 to Farm & Home Savings, which is headquartered in Nevada, Missouri, but does a great deal of its business in Texas. Farm & Home Savings has a long history of associations with people close to Walter Mischer.

For 30 years, from the mid-1950s to the mid-1980s, Farm & Home was controlled by Charles A. "Sonny" Duncan, Jr., from San Angelo, Texas. Duncan was a good friend and business partner with Howard Terry, Mischer's close associate and colleague. In fact, Terry served on Farm & Home's board of directors and at one time in the 1980s was chairman of the board. In turn, Duncan had been a member of the board of directors of Marathon Manufacturing, which was owned by Mischer and Terry.

In 1982, Duncan's stepson, Dempsey Watson, married Mischer's daughter, Paula. It was their house that President Bush and his wife visited some ten years later.

After Duncan died in 1987, Dan Arnold was brought in to run Farm & Home. Arnold, a former partner at Vinson & Elkins, one of Mischer's law firms, had been the chairman of First City Bank, where Mischer's companies had a number of outstanding loans. Then, in November 1989, Houstonian Joe F. Lynch was named vice chairman of

Farm & Home. The next year the Office of Thrift Supervision forced Lynch's resignation, giving no reasons but indicating concern about conflicts of interest with Lynch's other business endeavors.

At that time, Lynch was chairman of National Asset Bank in Houston, which was set up to sell off all the foreclosed property and non-performing (i.e., bad) loans at Allied Bank when First Interstate Bank in Los Angeles purchased Allied. Lynch was also chairman of First Continental Real Estate Investment Trust, a real estate trust in Houston whose directors included Walter Mischer, Jr.

Robert L. Clarke, the former Comptroller of the Currency, had an investment in First Continental Real Estate Investment Trust, and also a big loan with Farm & Home Savings. The *Washington Post* reported that Clarke was a longtime business associate of Lynch and had taken out a $250,000 loan from Farm & Home in November 1988.[2]

In April 1991, Dan Arnold submitted his resignation as chief executive officer of Farm & Home, while Lynch was allowed back in as vice chairman. No explanations were given for either move.

In a related action, the Office of Thrift Supervision removed Houston certified public accountant Mark J. Brookner as a consultant to Farm & Home because of his previous position as vice chairman and chief financial officer at the failed Gibraltar Savings of Houston, the largest S&L in Texas. Brookner was also banned for life from federally insured financial institutions without the permission of federal regulators. Brookner's boss at Gibraltar Savings was J. Livingston Kosberg, who after he left Gibraltar went into business with his old friend Charles Hurwitz.

One of the loans that Farm & Home inherited when it bought Surety in 1979 was the $840,000 to Mischer's company and his two associates on the Enchanted Oaks shopping center. Mischer's partners were his former son-in-law, Robert Corson, and Corson's first cousin, Roy Dailey. Less than a month after Surety's demise, the joint venture sold the property to Michael Shea and his wife, Cheryl, of San Diego, California, who flipped it the same day to a company called KLP, Inc., whose president was Leilani Jones Pierce of Houston.

In 1986, KLP defaulted on its promissory note to the Enchanted Oaks joint venture, by that time solely Mischer's company, which took

---

[2] *Washington Post*, April 30, 1991.

the property back. Three months later Mischer's company defaulted on its old $840,000 loan from Surety, and Farm & Home foreclosed on the mortgage and took the property.

This foreclosure created an additional tax liability for Mischer and his former partner and son-in-law, and resulted in communications back and forth between their two companies. When the ex-son-in-law, Robert Corson, found out about this he became furious and told an employee never to talk to Mischer's employees again and never to mention Mischer's name in his office again.

This story was told to *Houston Post* reporters Seay and me by Rebecca Sims in the fall of 1988, some 18 months after we started our investigation of Mainland Savings. Sims had been the accountant for Corson's development company and had quit when asked to commit bankruptcy and tax and bank fraud. She then started investigating Corson and his associates, who also owned a savings and loan. Sims called Seay and chewed him out over an S&L story that, she claimed, had missed several important points.

Seay suggested to me that we pay Sims a visit. After she told us about her background and her break with Corson, she said she had found out that Corson was a CIA asset. We were nonplussed. That was not what we wanted to hear. We were looking for something to the effect that Corson was a Mafia associate.

Sims also said she had gone to Houston attorney Marian Rosen to see what her legal rights against Corson were. Rosen, a flashy criminal defense and divorce lawyer, had represented ex-CIA agent Edwin Wilson in his Houston trial for smuggling C-4 explosives to Libya. Sims said Rosen was initially enthusiastic about her case and knowledgeable about nefarious CIA acts and connections.

Sims said she and Rosen began looking for another person to join her in suing Corson, in order to get additional funding for a lawsuit. Then one day Rosen said she was going to be meeting with Senator Lloyd Bentsen and other high-ranking Democrats and would be discussing Sims's case with them. Sims never heard anything further from Rosen, and when she called Rosen's office the next week she was informed that they no longer had time to handle her case. Sims said Rosen did give her one piece of advice. "Marian told me that if I wanted to stay alive I should get with an investigative reporter," she said.

When I returned to the *Houston Post* after meeting with Sims and began thinking about what she had said, her story began ringing some bells. When I had researched the Sunday magazine piece on Mischer, one of the power broker's business rivals said he was convinced Mischer had purchased 700,000 acres in Belize, the small Central American nation, for a CIA project.

And, during our tracking of Mario Renda across the country we encountered an organized crime strike force prosecutor in Kansas City, Lloyd Monroe, who had been after Renda and his mob associates in a Kansas City bank scam. We had been sending Monroe copies of our stories on Mafia involvement in S&L failures. But instead of praising them, as we had hoped, he kept saying that we were missing something important, something big. Maybe Monroe was talking about the same thing Sims was: the CIA.

It was at this point in time that Seay was told by his editors that he could no longer work with me on the story, that his duties as daily banking reporter for the business section took precedence. In fact, *Post* then-Editor-in-Chief Peter O'Sullivan issued an order, only half-joking, that Seay and I were forbidden to speak to each other.

It was also about this time that Seay's original source, D.T., dried up. We had eventually learned his identity. He was a Republican political operative who was trying to embarrass Democratic politicians. The reason he had pointed us to Mainland Savings was that it had lent more than $3 million to a limited partnership full of Houston and Texas Democratic politicians. The partnership went bust and the loan went bad, leaving the taxpayers holding the bag. But when I started working on the CIA, D.T. stopped calling.

After Seay and I met with Sims and Seay was pulled off the story, I wrote a memo to the City Editor, Margaret Downing, asking for two months to check out the CIA allegations. Downing okayed it, and I plunged into the CIA morass. The two months stretched into a year.

The first questions to answer were whether Sims's former boss, Robert Corson, and his former father-in-law, Walter Mischer, were operatives for the CIA.

7

THE CHERRY BUSTERS

Robert Corson glared across the boxing ring at his opponent in the neutral corner. The husky teen-ager was working himself into a fighting frenzy by telling himself over and over that his adversary, classmate Trooper Keeton, had been intimate with his mother, although he wasn't phrasing it in exactly those terms. Of course Keeton hadn't, but that seemed to be the thought that made Corson the maddest.

The two boys strode to the middle of the ring for the traditional touching of gloves before the bout began. But instead of touching gloves, Corson just sucker-punched Keeton with a vicious right cross. "He left a knot on me that's still there. He beat the hell out of me," Keeton recalled. "He was like a professional fighter. If he could have stayed in boxing he could have been the heavyweight champion of the world."

Corson was a good-natured thug who averaged about two fights a week. "He was always talking about how tough he was," said Keeton, who first met Corson when they were registering for classes at Marian Christian High School in Houston. It was in the fall of 1964. They were at the private Roman Catholic school for basically the same reason: they had dropped out of public schools because they were juvenile delinquents.

Even then, Corson showed the ingenious creativity and outrageous behavior that would serve him well when he became involved in the shadowy world of organized crime, the CIA and savings and loans. He was the president of a group of boys who called themselves the cherry busters. The ostensible chief goal of this group was to separate young maidens from their maidenheads. In reality it was a bunch of high school football players who got together to drink and drive and party. By the summer of 1964, they had accumulated a nice communal pot of money with which to live it up. However, their esteemed president, Corson, and his best friend, Ron Bonaguidi, a football player at St. Thomas High School, appropriated the money to their own use, took off for Mexico and blew it in wild and riotous adventures south of the border.

When they returned to Houston, there were accountings demanded and questions asked. Corson answered them all with his fists. Keeton said one reason Corson pummeled him so hard in their boxing match was that he had sharpened his skills fighting irate cherry bustees that summer.

Another reason Corson was a good boxer, according to Keeton, was that his father had instructed him in the fine arts of pugilism at an early age. Beyond that, Corson's father was "a big blank in his life," Keeton said. Some of Corson's later business associates said that Corson was not the name he was born with. It was Boles, they claimed, after his alleged real father, a purported narcotics smuggler currently hiding from the law in the small Central American country of Belize. They also said that Corson took his name from a later step-father, who was a high-ranking military officer. Mischer confirmed this, although he said he didn't know who Corson's natural father was.

But there is little doubt about who is Corson's mother, the most influential and dominant person in his life. Born Billie Jean Banks in the small Northeast Texas town of Gilmer, she was 15 years old when she gave birth to Robert, her first child, in 1946. With a body that would stop a freight train, B.J., as she is called, went through husbands and lovers as if there was no tomorrow. Close friends and associates say she has been married at least eight times: to Boles, Corson, a man named Schumacher, a Las Vegas gambler, a man named Eyden, several others and, finally, to William L. Garman, an Occidental Chemical executive now living in Desert Springs, California, whom she divorced in 1985.

B. J. Garman gained brief national notoriety in October 1989 when she became the first person in this country to be publicly banned for life from the savings and loan industry.[1] (The next year her sister's son, Roy

---

[1] Office of Thrift Supervision, press release, October 19, 1989.

Dailey, became the first owner of a Houston savings and loan to be convicted for fraud.)

B.J. was a director of her son's Vision Banc Savings in Kingsville, Texas, which failed in March 1989. Under the thrift bailout legislation passed that year, the names of all persons sanctioned by the federal regulatory agencies were to be made public. B. J. Garman was the first. But the newspapers and wire services didn't know who they had. Some of the news accounts stated that "he" could not be reached for comment, and that "his" name didn't appear in the Kingsville telephone directory. They would have had better luck looking for her in Las Vegas, where around that time she was laundering tens of thousands of dollars in cash through gambling casinos.

Even though some of the allegations by the feds against her were criminal in nature, B. J. Garman may never see the inside of the jail, because, according to one of her former employees, it is likely that she doesn't know how to read. Thus, it might be impossible to prove that she knew what she was agreeing to, signing or approving.

Anyway, back in 1964 Corson was 17 and chasing after a 16-year-old girl. His mother had found her and was pushing her son toward her. "She was all he could talk about that summer," Trooper Keeton said. Just after he turned 18 and several days before Christmas 1964, Corson dropped out of the twelfth grade and eloped with the girl. At least that's how the girl's father described it later. However, one person close to the girl's father said they may have eloped, but it was a marriage arranged by the girl's father and Corson's father, either his real one or his adopted one, and it had something to do with the mob or the CIA or both.

One of Corson's high school classmates, who would later become a Texas savings and loan examiner, said that to elope Corson had either stolen his mother's $10,000 real estate commission check or forged her name on a $10,000 check and cashed it. Corson took the 16-year-old girl to Rio Bravo, Mexico, a small dive just across the Rio Grande from Mercedes, Texas, in the Rio Grande Valley, where they got married.[2] They moved to Nevada, where the girl's father found them several months later and brought them back to Houston.

The girl's name was Paula. She was the only daughter of Walter Mischer.

[2] Divorce proceedings in state district court in Harris County, Texas, No. 1064994, Paula M. Corson vs. Robert Louis Corson.

After Mischer tracked down Paula and Corson living in Nevada in early 1965, several months after they had eloped to Mexico, he brought them back to Houston, where Corson was put into the real estate business by his mother and Mischer.

There is little in the public record regarding Corson from that time until his divorce from Paula in 1976. One of his friends said he bounced around a bit and at one time even had a job in one of Mischer's banks. In a deposition he gave in 1984 in a lawsuit against him, Corson testified that he had a "high school education" (it is not known if he ever graduated from high school) and then attended "Kerr Naval Academy in Pass Christian, Mississippi."

There is no Kerr Naval Academy in the Gulf Coast town of Pass Christian, Mississippi. There was, however, a Kern School for problem boys there, which took six or eight boys every year. It is no longer in existence, and it could not be confirmed that Corson ever attended the school. Next, Corson testified, he "enrolled there [presumably Pass Christian, Mississippi] at the Baptist college and stayed for about six weeks." There is no Baptist college in Pass Christian, Mississippi.

Then, Corson continued, he "worked in the produce business for a while; I had my own company," although he doesn't say what its name was. Next, he got into the real estate business: "I owned a company called Schumacher and Corson," apparently from 1968 to 1970. Schumacher was one of his mother's married names.

By the early 1970s, Corson was in a real estate partnership with John Adger and Roy Dailey. Dailey is his first cousin, who would later have the distinction of being the first owner of a failed savings and loan in Houston to be convicted of fraud. By the time Corson got divorced, it was just he and Dailey, in a company called Dail-Cor. Their property holdings were not significant, but included 50 percent of the Enchanted Oaks Shopping Center, a little strip center in northern Harris County. The other half was owned by TMC Funding, a subsidiary of the Mischer Corp.[3]

The divorce itself appeared to be bitter and acrimonious. Paula filed on March 3, 1976, alleging that Corson beat her. They were granted a divorce on September 17, 1976. Six weeks later, Paula married Conway O. Cook III, whom she divorced the following year.[4]

---

[3] Divorce proceedings between Paula Corson and Robert Corson, No. 1064994, Harris County District Clerk.
[4] Ibid.

While she was married to Cook, Paula filed two actions against Corson. First, she asked the judge to hold Corson in contempt of court for pushing and shoving her. Then she asked that his parental rights to their three children, born in 1966, 1967 and 1969, be terminated because he smoked marijuana in their presence.[5]

It is difficult to know how seriously to take these allegations since nothing came of them. They, and the divorce, certainly didn't stop Mischer from doing business with Corson, although from that time on, Mischer and Corson both tried to keep their association secret. Perhaps, otherwise, it would have looked too cold, callous and calculating of Mischer in light of the divorce and his own daughter's allegations of violence and drug use. But there was really no reason for a big shot like Mischer to continue dealing with a two-bit operator like Corson. It doesn't make any sense, except that it was at about this time that Mischer reportedly got Corson connected to the CIA.

Mischer's relationships with the CIA and the intelligence community go way back, perhaps as far back as the early 1950s. Two events occurred then that indicate there was a lot more to Walter Mischer than met the eye.

In 1952, Mischer bought his first property around Lajitas, a little hole-in-the-wall on the Rio Grande just west of Big Bend National Park in far west Texas. "Isolated" wouldn't even begin to describe how far away from anything Lajitas is. Mischer started out with 26,000 acres and eventually bought the "town" itself, which was little more than a ramshackle general store, and hundreds of thousands of acres around it.[6]

About the only living things around Lajitas in 1952 were a few ranchers, some prospectors, occasional tourists on their way up the river road from Big Bend to Presidio and smugglers from Mexico. (Lajitas was one of the outposts used by General "Black Jack" Pershing in his pursuit of Pancho Villa earlier in this century.)

Mischer said he wanted to restore the area to an Old West town in hopes of making it the Palm Springs of Texas. He put in a restaurant and hotel, a few other tourist traps with Old West fronts and a pitiful little nine-hole golf course.

But the biggest business in the area today is narcotics trafficking. Some of it comes over the Rio Grande on foot, some on truck and some

---

[5] Ibid.
[6] *Houston Post*, November 22, 1987.

by airplane. One of the landing strips used for the transshipment of drugs is about 12 miles northeast of Lajitas, according to Joaquin Jackson, a Texas Ranger who patrols the area. It's a lot longer—4,000 feet—and a lot wider—200 feet—than the typical narcotics-smuggling landing strip. That's because it had to accommodate C-130 cargo planes bringing in arms and weapons for the CIA for transshipment to Latin America.

Although Mischer doesn't own the land—he owns property to the south and to the west—CIA contract pilots and law enforcement officers have said he controlled the landing strip.

Mischer and former Atlantic Richfield Chairman Robert O. Anderson owned more than 200,000 acres to the west of the landing strip. The eastern boundary of their land was about three miles from the strip.

Anderson's father was a leading oil and gas banker, and one of the first to lend money on oil in the ground, at First National Bank of Chicago, a favorite lending institution of the CIA. In 1986, after Anderson retired from Atlantic Richfield, he joined in an oil and gas partnership with Walter "Tiny" Rowland, the British industrialist who owns Lonrho P.L.C. (Lonrho stands for London-Rhodesian). Rowland is a close associate of Adnan Khashoggi, who approached Rowland to help in the bridge financing of the Iranian arms-for-hostages deal.[7] In an interview with Rev. Moon's *Washington Times*, Khashoggi stated that Rowland "apparently has a special relationship with U.S. intelligence agencies."

In May 1992, the U.S. Treasury Department's Office of Foreign Asset Control began an investigation into late-1991 transactions between Rowland's Lonrho and Libya, including a possible joint venture in the United States, with Khashoggi acting as the middle man in the deal. Since 1986, the U.S. government has barred American companies and individuals from dealing with Libyan-owned or -controlled entities. Lonrho's second biggest shareholder is U.S.-based Fidelity Management.[8]

Rowland's connections to the Reagan Administration are quite impressive. In June 1981, his pilot was arrested in Houston for illegal possession and illegal importation of an AK-47 automatic rifle, while flying Rowland and his wife to Acapulco. Rowland was quick to let the

---

[7] The Tower Commission Report on Iran-Contra.

[8] *Financial Times*, May 1, 1992.

arresting Customs agents know that he was a personal friend of Alexander Haig, then the Secretary of State.

When questioned about the landing strip, Mischer, who knows the area like the back of his hand, disclaimed any knowledge of it. When its exact location and orientation were described to him, he began talking about it as if it were another landing strip that was miles from the one in question.

The actual owner is Eve Nichols, a widow who lives in Florida and who has never set foot on the site and didn't even know the strip had been built on her property until several years ago, when a relative who was hunting in the area saw it and later told her about it. She said whoever built it did so without her knowledge or permission.

Richard Brenneke first told me about the landing strip. Brenneke, a controversial Portland, Oregon, arms dealer and real estate manager who says he worked for the CIA as a contract agent for 18 years, was acquitted in federal court in Portland in 1990 on charges of making false statements about working for the CIA and other statements he had made to a judge.

A West Texas law enforcement officer, a longtime federal agent who patrolled the Rio Grande area for years, former Pentagon criminal investigator Gene Wheaton, and veteran CIA contract pilot Robert "Tosh" Plumlee all have confirmed Brenneke's description of the purpose of the landing strip: a CIA transshipment point for guns and drugs into and out of Latin America. (Both of the law enforcement officials asked that their names not be used, fearing that their jobs would be in jeopardy if they were identified.)

I was able to locate this landing strip using aerial photographs and a map Brenneke drew spontaneously at his desk in his Portland home. The strip, and its location and orientation, coincide almost exactly with Brenneke's rough map. Brenneke could not have obtained the location from a map or from the Federal Aviation Administration as the landing strip is not shown on any U.S. Geological Survey topographic maps and has not been registered with the FAA.

Brenneke's credibility is a controversial matter among reporters and government investigators who have dealt with him. Some say that everything he has told them checks out; others, like Jack Blum, a former congressional investigator, and journalist Mark Hosenball say he is a con man and a liar.

The jurors in Brenneke's trial in Portland believed Brenneke over witnesses from the CIA, the Secret Service and Donald Gregg, a long-time CIA official, who was then Vice President George Bush's national security adviser and is now U.S. Ambassador to South Korea. The jury took a vote on each of the five charges against Brenneke and voted 12-0 each time for acquittal. And it wasn't a question of the jury feeling that the government had simply not proved its case beyond a reasonable doubt. The jury foreman told reporters that the jury believed what Brenneke had said was true.

There is no doubt that Brenneke is frustrating to deal with. In many cases, he can't, or won't, provide documentation for the claims he makes. One day he will answer a question a certain way, and then the next day he will give a different answer to the same question. I spent a week with Brenneke in Portland and left feeling frustrated because Brenneke provided very little corroborating documentary evidence for the things he said.

It was only after I confirmed Brenneke's description of the landing strip outside Lajitas and its use that I gave any credence to what he said. Reporters have to distinguish between what Brenneke knows from his own personal experience and what he knows because someone else told him. Reporters must make this differentiation because Brenneke doesn't.

Brenneke was one of the first people to talk publicly about the so-called "October Surprise"—the trips that members of the Reagan-Bush team allegedly made in October 1980 to cut a deal with the Iranians so that the Iranians would continue holding the American hostages until after the election. In exchange, if the Reagan-Bush team won the election, they would ship military equipment to Iran. Brenneke's indictment for making false statements before a judge was based in part on his statements about this.

October Surprise is a controversial subject and has not been conclusively proved or disproved. The subject got red-hot during the summer of 1991, with a number of people coming out saying they were now convinced that it happened, including Gary Sick, a respected scholar and former member of the Carter Administration's National Security Council.

Then Brenneke was "exposed" in a story in the *Village Voice* as having lied about his presence in Paris during the alleged meetings. Former CIA officer Frank Snepp wrote the story, stating that he had seen credit card receipts that showed Brenneke was in the United States and not Paris during the alleged meetings. Even so, Snepp acknowledged that a lot of Brenneke's past information had been good. Snepp testified on Brenneke's behalf in his perjury trial and then convinced Brenneke not to talk to ABC's "20/20," which was preparing a program on the *Houston Post*'s stories on the CIA and S&Ls. Brenneke's refusal to go on camera was a major factor in "20/20's" decision not to show the story.

So it goes in the world of CIA contract agents, where journalists must cling particularly fast to the first rule of reporting: If your mother tells you she loves you, check it out. In that regard, what I can say about Brenneke is that the things he has told me that I am interested in and that I have been able to check out do check out.

Brenneke said he flew into the Texas landing strip in the early 1980s with some Colombian and Panamanian associates of the Medellín drug cartel. He said they told him the landing strip was Walter Mischer's. "This was in 1982 or '83. It was a straight agency operation. It was straight guns for drugs. There was also paramilitary training there," Brenneke said.

Tosh Plumlee, a former CIA contract pilot now living in California, said he did not know Brenneke but confirmed his claim that the strip near Lajitas was most active in 1982 and 1983. Plumlee said he never flew C-130s into the strip, "but we were familiar with that operation." The paramilitary training there, according to Plumlee, was the "beginning of your mercenary-type training stuff from your Israeli Mossad boys." (Mossad is Israel's intelligence agency.)

Plumlee, who is the subject of a lengthy article in the April 5, 1990, issue of the *San Diego Reader*, flew missions for the CIA and the U.S. military in Latin American from 1979 to 1986. He said he carried men and equipment, sometimes returning to the United States with drugs. Plumlee is named in several books and articles about the Contra affair but is only identified in them as a mysterious pilot named "Tosh." In the 1982 book *The Fish Is Red,* by Warren Hinckle and William W. Turner, he is identified (although only by his name Robert Plumlee and not by his nickname) and quoted as a CIA contract pilot who flew in the CIA's "Operation Mongoose" missions against Fidel Castro in the early 1960s.

Some of the weapons going through the strip were shipped to the Colombian drug cartels as well as to the Contras, Plumlee said. According to Brenneke, "The guns came from the United States and went to the

Martin-McCoy warehouse in Honduras, or to Panama, then God knows where. I suppose some went to the Contras, but most were too sophisticated for them."

Ron Martin, a Miami gun dealer, and James McCoy, the former military attaché at the United States Embassy in Managua, Nicaragua, and friend of the late Nicaraguan dictator, Anastasio Somoza Debayle, were partners in an arms company that supplied weapons to the Contras, first for the CIA and then, after the Boland Amendment, for Oliver North's "Enterprise." They and their so-called "arms supermarket" in Honduras are mentioned frequently in North's White House diaries.

According to Brenneke, from 1983 to 1985 Martin and Robert Corson were partners in a casino in the Canary Islands, off the coast of Morocco and a part of Spain. That could not be confirmed, but it may not be as far-fetched as it sounds. In 1987 divorce proceedings in Miami, Martin's wife alleged that he owned a jai alai *frontón* in Benidorm, Spain.[9]

Brenneke also said that in the mid-1970s Martin borrowed money from Mischer's bank to buy guns for Chile. That could not be confirmed either, but Mischer didn't deny it. Mischer did say it wasn't likely, because loans from his bank were almost always secured by property in the Houston area. However, there are several mortgages filed by Allied Bank in the property records in Miami that are secured by property outside Houston, including some thoroughbred foals in Kentucky and France.

An independent indication that these people run in the same circles lies in Oliver North's White House diaries. In one entry Martin is linked to Miami businessman Sergio Brull in a gun deal. In another entry, Brull, along with Corson's future attorney, S. Cass Weiland, is in the middle of an unidentified White House project in Belize, where Mischer and his partners bought 700,000 acres (more about this later).

Plumlee said the Lajitas area was a good place for a guns-and-drugs transshipment point because it is wide open and remote. "There is good truck transportation and it's easy to get across the Rio Grande." Although the landing strip is in the middle of nowhere and miles from any human habitation, there is a well-maintained county road that goes from the Lajitas-Terlingua highway up to the strip. A large truck, such

---

[9] Judith Martin vs. Ronald J. Martin, Eleventh Circuit Court of Dade County, Florida, 89-36966, August 16, 1989.

as a fuel truck or water truck, could make it easily.

Another important factor, Plumlee said, is that the people in the isolated, conservative Big Bend area, including law enforcement officials, would be cooperative with the CIA, particularly if they thought the operation was in the interests of national security.

Almost all of the people in the area that I contacted either said they knew nothing about the landing strip or gave conflicting stories about when it was constructed, who built it and how it was used. For example, a former Texas Ranger who patrolled the area said that the he knew little about the strip, but that in the early 1980s it was in excellent condition. Several days later, he called back to say that he could "assure" me that there had never been any "activity" at the strip.

A physical inspection of the area indicates otherwise. There are holes, pits, depressions, piles of dirt, cleared areas and little roads on both sides of the strip. Also, on both sides of the strip, running parallel to it for the entire length, are big, deep tire tracks. The tracks are in pairs, closely spaced, closer together than truck tracks. They appear to be tracks formed by the landing gear of a big, heavy airplane. Other experts on such landing strips said they could also be tracks from loading machines or tracks from a portable, pipeline-type fuel system.

A West Texas law enforcement officer, who spoke on the condition that his name not be used, said the pits, depressions and holes with piles of dirt next to them were used to hold 55-gallon drums of aviation fuel. Plumlee said the drums were used to hold drugs as well as fuel. "There was always a DEA [Drug Enforcement Administration] question about what was being put in those drums."

When asked about C-130 flights into the landing strip, several local residents volunteered that it was not long enough to accommodate a C-130. However, a fully loaded Lockheed C-130 Hercules with four propeller engines is rated for take-off at about 3,700 feet. The strip is about 4,000 feet. In addition, there are no obstacles, great rises or mountains off either end of the runway for miles. Further, most of the other dirt landing strips in the area are about 2,000 feet, designed to accommodate small single-engine planes.

Kenneth Clouse, the manager of the airport at Alpine, a nearby town, said the landing strip is in the flight path of a low-level training route for C-130s out of San Antonio, Dallas and Houston. He said that on occasion he would be flying down a canyon taking pictures and suddenly find himself "nose to nose" with a C-130. "During the Contra affair we had lots of C-130 activity. Then it slacked off," Clouse said.

Joaquin Jackson, a local Texas Ranger, acknowledged that the C-130 low-level training route would be "good cover" for contraband smuggling with C-130s. "Every now and then we see C-130s," he said. "They all are an olive drab, so you never know if they are Army or CIA."

Mischer and several area law enforcement officials said they thought the landing strip had been built by the Terlingua Ranch Co. The eastern 200 feet of the strip does lie on land once owned by the Corpus Christi-based real estate development firm, which had been cutting up its ranch into smaller parcels and selling them to investors.[10] However, officials of the company deny having anything to do with the strip, particularly after being told that most of it lies on land owned by a Florida widow who didn't know anything about it.

Houston real estate investor Jack Modesett, who had backed Ed Baker, the con man allegedly burned to death in his Jaguar, and had done business with Howard Pulver, headed the company that owned the Terlingua Ranch. Modesett, who is noted for teaching a popular adult Sunday School class at the First Presbyterian Church in Houston and whose father was in the oil business with Joseph Kennedy,[11] denied any knowledge of the landing strip. "There wasn't any strip around there that I knew anything about, back when we were involved in it, which was in the late '60s," Modesett said. However, Modesett's company didn't buy the property around the landing strip until 1970, according to land records in Brewster County.

"My involvement with the whole company ceased back in the early '70s," Modesett stated. However, in May 1981, as company president, Modesett signed a release of a promissory note from Pulver's group on a Houston condominium. Reminded of this, Modesett replied, "All right, yeah. I was out of Terramar for a while, then I was back into it for a while, and then we were out of it again."

Published reports indicate that Modesett was president of the Terlingua Ranch Company in mid-1974. William McNair, who became president of the company after Modesett left, said Modesett severed his relationship with the company in 1975 and then came back in 1980.

I finally determined that a Big Bend area construction contractor, Sonny Stillwell, actually built the landing strip in 1975. Stillwell said he

---

[10] Brewster County land records.
[11] *Corpus Christi Caller-Times*, July 23, 1973.

built it for a Houston man, but couldn't remember his name. But Stillwell denied that it was Mischer.

Stillwell said the Houston man and his partners were in that area trying to mine low-grade lignite coal to use in making fertilizer. However, a local real estate man who first identified Stillwell as the landing strip builder, said the owners were in that area to get fill material for road construction.

Stillwell also said he never used the strip to fly into. Asked about gun shipments into it, he replied, "Yeah, there was that bunch in there. They set up a kind of a hunting camp. They brought in high-powered guns, machine guns, shooting things up." He said he couldn't remember who these people were.

Gene Wheaton, a former Pentagon criminal investigator, claims the landing strip was part of a nationwide private secret operation that trafficked in guns and drugs and trained Central American mercenaries and hit men.

Wheaton's name comes up a number of times in Oliver North's White House diaries. At one time he was apparently trying to work with North's group and was going to arrange the delivery of some small planes. At a later date in the diaries, he is discussed as having a falling-out with retired Air Force General Richard Secord, who headed up North's resupply efforts to the Nicaraguan Contras.

Wheaton said he was asked by North and Secord to participate in their secret operations. He said he declined when he found out about possible connections to drug smuggling. Later, he worked as a paid investigator for the Roman Catholic Church-connected Christic Institute, which sued a number of CIA-connected people, including Secord, for their alleged involvement in the bombing at La Penca, Nicaragua, where dissident Contra leader Eden Pastora was targeted and several journalists were killed or injured.[12]

(The Christics have lost most of their court fights in this lawsuit. A multi-million-dollar judgment was rendered against the Christics and, most recently, an IRS investigation into the non-profit status of the organization was initiated. It appears that the IRS is trying to place the tax liability of the contributions to Christic on the organization itself rather than on the individuals.)

Wheaton said the landing strip near Lajitas was tied into another

---

[12] Avirgan et al. vs. Hull et al., United States District Court, Southern District of Florida, 86-1146.

landing strip about 60 miles to the northeast on the Iron Mountain Ranch outside Marathon, owned by Midland oilman William Blakemore II, President Bush's close friend and a Contra supporter.

Wheaton said the Iron Mountain Ranch was used as a transshipment point for guns to Latin America and for paramilitary training. A West Texas law enforcement officer who works in that area confirmed the paramilitary training. He said UCLAs—the CIA's term for Unilaterally Controlled Latin Assets—were being trained there.

Blakemore would not confirm the use of his ranch for paramilitary training or transshipment of guns. "I have all kinds of relationships with the Army and the Air Force, but nothing on the illegal side." Asked if he did anything for the CIA, he replied, "If I had, I obviously couldn't tell you. I have been associated with all branches of the military. Some of it is highly confidential."

About the same time Mischer began buying land around Lajitas (1952) he and a partner, a lumber man named Joe E. Younce from North Carolina, bought two paper mills in Honduras, according to Mischer. Mischer said he traded his interest in the mills in 1954 or 1955 to Dallas oilman Clint Murchison, Jr., for some land. The times and place are intriguing. It was in 1952 that the CIA and United Fruit Co. began to discuss seriously the overthrow of the liberal Arbenz government in Guatemala. This included a visit and speech in Houston about Guatemala by a United Fruit representative. CIA training of "rebel" forces was done in Honduras and the CIA-led attack in 1954 came from Honduras.[13]

CIA training for the coup was also done in Nicaragua with the wholehearted approval and support of that country's dictator, Anastasio Somoza García, father of the future dictator Anastasio Somoza Debaye. Mischer acknowledged that he had met with Somoza when he was working in Latin America at that time, and had asked the strongman for some construction work.

Perhaps it is all just coincidence. But what is a small-time thirty-year-old sewer contractor from Houston doing purchasing paper mills in Honduras and hobnobbing with the dictator of Nicaragua at the same time he's buying 26,000 acres on our border with Mexico?

---

[13] *Bitter Fruit*, by Stephen Schlesinger and Stephen Kinzer, (New York: Doubleday, 1982).

At that time in the early 1950s, Mischer had virtually nothing. "He didn't have a pot to piss in," said one Houston businessman who was active in that period. "In 1952, all he had was a tractor and two dump trucks." Another Houston businessman said the only thing Mischer was doing then was paving parking lots. "He had to be fronting for somebody" in the two land deals, this longtime Houstonian said.

In a subsequent interview Mischer altered his story. He said it was not two paper mills, but just a "peckerwood sawmill" in Comayagua, a small town about 40 miles northwest of Tegucigalpa. He also said he was partners with a Houston attorney named Holman in addition to Younce. "I didn't invest much money. I bought two trucks, or gave him two trucks."

When asked about CIA activities in Honduras at that time, he replied, "Oh, yeah. No, I never did get involved with them, but they were down there in Honduras." Mischer also added that in his original investment in Lajitas he was partners with a Houston developer named Lewis Tyra along with three other people. "I think we paid $1.70 an acre," he said.

Mischer then claimed that in 1952 he was doing about $25 million worth of business. When told that other people who knew him then said he had nothing, Mischer asserted, "I was beyond that, I guess, in '52. Well, I might not have been too far beyond that in '52."

Mischer's dealing with Clint Murchison, Jr., in Honduras is also curious. Both Clint Sr. and his son were close to New Orleans Mafia boss Carlos Marcello[14] and the CIA. The father had business interests in Haiti, and one of his employees who looked after these interests was CIA asset George DeMohrenschildt (who will be discussed in more detail in a later chapter). Clint Jr. also had a number of connections to the CIA.

CIA agent Robert Sensi testified in federal court in Washington, D.C., in 1987 that he worked with Clint Jr. on a CIA project in Sierra Leone to try to replace secret satellite-tracking stations in Liberia. The CIA was concerned that it would lose the valuable tracking stations as a result of the military coup in 1980 by Sergeant Samuel Doe.[15] The CIA also used Farhad Azima and his Global International Airways to take Doe on a round-the-world pleasure trip to curry favor with the military

---

[14] *Mafia Kingfish*, by John H. Davis (New York: New American Library, 1991).
[15] *Washington Post*, October 21, 1987.

dictator so it could keep its tracking stations in Liberia. (More on this in a later chapter about Azima.)

Another CIA tie to Murchison was his connection to First Intercontinental Development Corp. in Santa Monica, California. California journalist Mary Fricker said Murchison was a director of the company with Robert Nichols, an arms dealer and CIA operative, and Robert Maheu, a CIA contract agent and former Howard Hughes aide who was the first liaison between the CIA and the Mafia in the spy agency's attempt to use Cosa Nostra members to assassinate Fidel Castro. Fricker and her co-authors, Paul Muolo and Steve Pizzo, reported in their book *Inside Job* that they were told by an informant that First Intercontinental Development was a cover for CIA activities abroad.

And as previously noted, in the early 1980s Murchison Jr. joined forces with Saudi Arabian financier and arms broker Adnan Khashoggi to try to develop a 20-acre tract of vacant land near the Galleria in Houston. That partnership split up and in August 1985, just days before Khashoggi put up $1 million to start the first Iranian arms-for-hostages deal, Khashoggi sold the tract to Mainland Savings, for a profit of some $12 million.

Also in 1986, Vision Banc Savings, owned by Mischer's ex-son-in-law Robert Corson, made a loan to the Belgian-American Investments and Trading Co., a mysterious Dallas-based company with affiliates in the tax haven of Netherlands Antilles, to buy a piece of property in Dallas from Murchison's bankrupt estate.

Herman K. Beebe also had a number of relationships with Clint Jr. Murchison was a big borrower from Beebe-bankrolled institutions. One of Beebe's top employees, Lou Farris, left AMI in 1973, went to work for Clint Jr. and became his "closest and most trusted associate."[16]

Clint Jr. and Farris borrowed $1.7 million from State Savings and Loan in Lubbock, Texas, a thrift purchased by Tyrell Barker with financing from Beebe. (Barker went to the federal penitentiary for fraud at his savings and loan.) Farris, Murchison and their companies also borrowed more than $10 million from Interwest Savings in Fort Worth, which lent money to other Beebe associates and was involved in daisy-chain lending with several Beebe institutions, including one transaction involving Beebe partner Albert Prevot that began with Allied Bank.

Murchison eventually became directly involved in the financial in-

---

[16] *The Murchisons*, by Jane Wolfe (New York: St. Martin's Press, 1989).

dustry. He purchased a bank, the Dallas/Fort Worth Airport Bank, with financing arranged by Beebe from the National Bank of Commerce in Dallas. The *Dallas Morning News* reported that Beebe actually controlled Murchison's bank, and that loans were passed back and forth between the bank and Beebe's Bossier Bank & Trust.

Murchison also borrowed $20 million from First South Savings in Little Rock, Arkansas, a dirty S&L that failed in 1986, and that also lent $16 million to Mike Adkinson, who borrowed hundreds of millions of dollars from institutions connected to Beebe and Mischer, and will be discussed later in a chapter on the $200 million land deal in Florida.

After Mischer finished his business in Honduras, he severed his ties with his first partner, Pat Harris, and established the Mischer Company by himself. He then took up with Houston homebuilder Howard L. Terry, with whom he is still doing business. Mischer and Terry bought their first bank, the First National Bank of San Antonio, for $1 million in 1959. In 1962 they bought Continental Bank, which would be the foundation for Mischer's banking empire, from Houston wildcatter Michel Halbouty. That began a spree of bank buying and land development for Mischer. And sometime in this period he was allowed into the inner sanctum of power in Houston: Suite 8F.[17]

Suite 8F was in the Lamar Hotel in downtown Houston, where the most powerful people in Houston met to play cards, drink, gossip and decide who got what. Mischer was the youngest member of the group and the last to join before old age and death closed its doors. In 8F were the Brown brothers, George and Herman, the financial backers of LBJ who owned the giant construction firm Brown & Root; Gus Wortham, the insurance king of American General Insurance Co.; Jesse Jones, "Mr. Houston," lumber man, banker and publisher of the *Houston Chronicle* who headed the Reconstruction Finance Corp. for Franklin D. Roosevelt; Judge James Elkins, who founded the law firm of Vinson & Elkins and First City Bank in Houston; and, occasionally, Oveta Culp Hobby, who married a Texas governor, William P. Hobby, and published the *Houston Post.*

Mischer was especially close to Judge Elkins. Mischer said he borrowed his first $1 million from Elkins in the 1950s. From then on, Mischer maintained close relations with First City Bank and Vinson &

---

[17] *Houston Post*, November 22, 1987.

Elkins. He borrowed tens of millions of dollars from First City to finance his real estate development activities, and used Vinson & Elkins for legal representation. When the Hermann Hospital Estate scandal broke, with Mischer's only son in the middle, Vinson & Elkins was brought in for damage control.

An interesting sidebar: There is a company outside Washington, D.C., called the Parvus Company, established in 1984 and made up of retired CIA officials and other intelligence and military people. Its stated purpose is to provide its clients with "special response to: information needs at home and abroad; security threats and vulnerabilities; problems involving political, business and security crises; requirements for discreet assistance in protecting business interests overseas."

Parvus's advisory board reads like a Who's Who of the American intelligence community, including the chairman, Richard Helms, former director of the CIA; James Leer, former Director of Security for the National Security Agency; and retired Lieutenant General James Williams, former director of the Defense Intelligence Agency.

Parvus was also named by former Pentagon investigator Gene Wheaton and former CIA officer Bruce Hemmings as being CIA-connected.

There is one advisory director, though, who sticks out like a sore thumb, because there are no ostensible intelligence ties to him. He is Theodore G. Dimitry, who is listed in Parvus's literature as merely an attorney in Houston. In fact, Dimitry is a partner at Vinson & Elkins, specializing in admiralty and maritime law. The only time Dimitry has ever appeared in articles in the *Houston Post* was as an attorney for SEDCO, former Texas Governor Bill Clements's oil company, when it was involved in litigation over a massive oil spill.

Dimitry refused to discuss his connections to Parvus.

Mischer by himself didn't really belong in the 8F group in the 1950s. (Later he would have belonged. In 1985 he was voted into the Texas Business Hall of Fame, along with Gus Wortham and Dallas megadeveloper Trammell Crow.) There were many other men in Houston who were not members who were richer, smarter and more powerful. But Mischer plus the CIA plus the Mafia, that would even get the Lamar Hotel janitor a ticket in.

8

MISCHER AND THE MULE

The connection of Robert Corson to the CIA via Mischer was first told to me by two intelligence operatives, and was confirmed by two Texas law enforcement officials.

According to Will Northrop, Corson rode the CIA mule in with the Republican party. Northrop is a good old boy from North Carolina who graduated from military school and fought in Vietnam. He lives in Israel and holds dual citizenship there and in the United States. He also claims to have been a colonel in Israeli military intelligence.[1]

Northrop was a key liaison between the CIA and Israel in Central America during the early 1980s.[2] He was pushed out after Oliver North's "Enterprise" ostensibly took over the Contra war from the CIA. Northrop hates North with a passion, but liked William Casey, the late CIA head, whom he dealt with directly.[3] Congressional investigators found that Casey's phone logs showed him in frequent contact with Northrop, according to a May 1988 United Press International story about Iran-Contra.

Northrop was indicted by a federal grand jury in New York in April

---

[1] "Bush Aide Linked to Scandal; Documents Detail Arms, Drug Sales," by Brian Barger, United Press International, May 16, 1988; "George Bush, Spymaster General," by Frank Snepp and Jonathan King, *Penthouse*, January 1990; *Israeli Foreign Affairs*, October 1988; "How the Israelis Leaked Irangate to Save Their Own Intelligence Agents," by Richard Ryan, *In These Times*, February 17, 1987.
[2] Ibid.
[3] Ibid., and interview with Northrop.

1986, along with some other Israelis and Sam Evans, an attorney for Saudi Arabian middleman Adnan Khashoggi, for conspiring to sell weapons to Iran.[4] The charges were dropped after one of the key witnesses died and the Reagan Administration's own arms sales to Iran became public. There is some speculation that Israel intelligence agents leaked the United States's secret Iranian arms-for-hostages deals in retaliation for, and protection of, the indicted Israelis.[5]

Asked about Corson, Northrop replied: "I have heard that Corson had very heavy agency connections. Corson has all the moves and all the connections. But I cannot tell you that he has come across my radar screen like Dickie [Brenneke] has, or even some minor players like Oliver North or somebody like that.

"Corson was really sort of a home-grown Republican type of guy. The difference between a guy like Brenneke and a guy like Corson, is that Brenneke was born into this stuff, and Corson sort of rode, or seemingly rode, the mule in with the Republican party.

"I really haven't looked that hard at Corson. I've run across his name and somebody would mention him from time to time, but I can't really say he was a CIA operative in the sense like Brenneke was, you know. I've seen Brenneke in the field. All this is such home cooking. You don't know where the CIA stops and where the Republicans start."

(Corson would one day attach himself to the most influential Republican politician in Houston, who is also a close friend and political operative of George Bush's. That will discussed in the next chapter on how Corson was able to buy a Texas savings and loan.)

According to Brenneke, Corson worked with him in laundering money for the CIA. Brenneke said his group would take cash from organized crime-controlled casinos in Nevada and physically transport it outside the country, to be used for CIA purposes. Corson was one of the mules, or couriers, who transported the money, Brenneke said: "There was no doubt in my mind that Corson was a contract agent. The people in Langley [CIA headquarters in Virginia], the eight-hour types, said Corson was agency, and he spoke about his friends in Washington."

A Texas law enforcement official who has worked with American

---

[4] United States of America vs. Samuel Evans et al., United States District Court, Southern District of New York, 86 Cr. 384.

[5] *In These Times*, op. cit.

intelligence agencies confirmed Corson's work for the CIA. This officer said that Corson also did work for the Israelis but may not have known it because there were several layers of cutouts between Corson and the Israelis.

A former Israeli intelligence officer, Ari Ben-Menashe, who was involved in shipping billions of dollars' worth of weapons to Iran during the Iran-Iraq War, has alleged that Brenneke was used by him and his associates as a stalking horse, or red herring, to divert attention away from the real weapons deals.

Ben-Menashe was indicted in 1989 in a U.S. Customs sting operation for attempting to sell three C-130 cargo planes to Iran. After spending 11 months in jail without bail, he was acquitted by a New York jury. Ben-Menashe claims the Bush Administration went after him because he had leaked information on the earlier American arms-for-hostages deals with Iran. Ben-Menashe has claimed it was he who leaked this information to a Lebanese newspaper, which began the exposure of the Iran side of the Iran-Contra scandal. He said he did this in retaliation for the indictments of the Israelis in the 1986 sting operation that included Northrop. However, Ben-Menashe has said he did this because of the other Israelis involved—not Northrop, who he said, was working with a different group than his.

Ben-Menashe, like Brenneke, was disparaged by some media critics after he emerged from the closet. The Israeli government's official stance on Ben-Menashe since his arrest has been that he was a "low-level translator," but recent revelations that have emerged from inside Israel tell a different story. During an interview with freelance journalist Craig Unger, Moshe Hevrony, former aide-de-camp to the director of Israeli military intelligence revealed: "Ben-Menashe worked directly under me. He had worked for the Foreign Flow desk in External Relations. He had access to very, very sensitive material."[6] Ben-Menashe also served as a source for respected investigative journalist Seymour Hersh in his book about Israel's nuclear arsenal, *The Samson Option.*

(Several of these intelligence sources—Ben-Menashe, Brenneke, and Northrop—have been criticized by some reporters and others, including George Bush, who have tried to debunk the so-called "October Surprise" theory. This book is not about October Surprise and I have no opinion about it. However, there are two points to consider: Criticizing

---

[6] *Village Voice,* July 7, 1992.

a theory by attacking its proponents rather than its substance is a weak and questionable methodology; and these people have greater credibility and a better record of telling the truth than do the CIA and George Bush.)

The company that Brenneke and Corson worked for in laundering Mafia cash for the CIA, according to Brenneke, was called the International Fund for Mergers and Acquisitions, or IFMA for short. It was incorporated by Brenneke in Panama in 1970 and set up to be an offshore mutual fund. That is, it would take money from Americans and invest it offshore so that the income would not be taxable.

The Panamanian incorporation papers show Brenneke was the vice president of IFMA and Ramon d'Onofrio was the president. D'Onofrio, who was mentioned in the previously discussed SEC investigation of Charles Hurwitz, is a notorious con man and stock-fraud artist who has been convicted three times for bankruptcy fraud and stock fraud.[7] He has associated with both organized crime and CIA operatives.

In 1983, the *New York Times* named D'Onofrio as an business associate of Alfred Buhler, a Liechtenstein lawyer, businessman and CIA contract agent and paymaster in Europe. Buhler had been shielded by the CIA from questioning by United States law enforcement officials about his alleged illegal activities, including the use of Swiss banks and Liechtenstein companies by organized crime.[8] D'Onofrio testified under oath before the Securities and Exchange Commission regarding Buhler's activities with Penn Central, which failed in 1971. He revealed that Buhler told him he assisted "manipulators like myself doing illegal things."[9] Furthermore, an unpublished report obtained by this reporter quoted D'Onofrio as having done some work for the CIA in Africa.

Brenneke said there was very little activity with IFMA in the first years of its existence. It was then turned over to the CIA to launder money for use in Central America, including later assistance of the Contras. "That's Richard's contention, or recollection of things of that nature. But I have no recollections of it," D'Onofrio said, not specifically denying Brenneke's CIA claims about IFMA.

A 1988 report by the Washington-based International Center for

---

[7] *Barron's*, May 9, 1988.
[8] *New York Times*, "European Tied to Illegal Acts Is Shielded by CIA," by Jeff Gerth, February 8, 1983.
[9] Ibid.

Development Policy, an anti-Contra organization where Brenneke briefly worked, quotes José Blandón, a former Panamanian intelligence chief, as saying the IFMA was used by Mike Harari for money laundering. Harari, a former Israeli intelligence officer and close associate of former Panamanian military dictator Manuel Noriega, was reportedly arrested by American forces in Panama during the 1989 military action there. Government officials later denied that Harari had been captured, and several days later he showed up in Israel.

"IFMA was a CIA laundry in Panama City," vouches Northrop. "Mike [Harari] was just following orders. IFMA was the agency's little shop."

D'Onofrio has said he doesn't "remember" Corson, but adds that that is not unusual because Brenneke "had other people that he used."

Corson is listed in federal law enforcement records as a "known money launderer," said present and former law enforcement officials who have access to these records. But sometime between 1987 and 1989, information on Corson's airplane trips from the United States to Panama and the Cayman Islands, both well-known money-laundering havens, was erased from federal crime information computers, according to these officials.

It appears that Corson and his attorney, Stephen Cass Weiland, may know this. In a December 21, 1989, letter to me at the *Houston Post*, Weiland stated, "You will recall that you told me on December 20 that you had 'federal law enforcement records which indicated that he [Corson] had made at least eighteen (18) trips to the Cayman Islands and Panama.' You, and your editors, and your lawyers, should understand that information is not correct and further investigation on your part should easily demonstrate the lack of credibility which you for some reason attach to your unnamed, and otherwise unidentified, 'federal law enforcement records.' "

(Weiland never responded to a letter from me six days later asking him how many trips Corson made to the Cayman Islands and Panama, since he categorically stated that 18 was incorrect.)

Brenneke said Corson got into CIA work through Mischer. Corson introduced Brenneke to Mischer in the mid-1970s in the lobby of Allied Bank in the Esperson building in downtown Houston, Brenneke recalled, describing the mural on the wall there. "I met Mischer originally through Corson. I didn't work with Mischer. He was a couple of steps up," Brenneke said, adding that he has no doubts that Mischer has strong connections to the CIA.

Neither does Northrop. "It's my understanding that Corson didn't have the juice that Mischer did." Northrop said he only met Mischer once, at a Republican fundraiser in Texas.

When first questioned about his alleged ties to the CIA, Mischer denied that he has ever done any work for the agency. In a later interview he was more adamant. "I've never had anything to do with the CIA, in any capacity, at all. . . . You're on the wrong track on that CIA deal. I guess I would have felt a little complimented if they had asked me. They never, I never, I guess they didn't ever figure I was of any use to them because they sure as hell never asked me anything."

Mischer then insisted he could prove that he never did any work for the CIA. He said he was arranging for someone to get a letter from the CIA stating that he had never done anything for the agency. When I asked him who was arranging that, he replied, "None of your goddamn business." When I told Mischer I would like to see a copy of the letter and put it in this book, he said, "To hell with you and the letter [I think he meant to say 'book.'] If I get it, it will be because I'm trying to do something to you."

When I told a former Houston law enforcement official and co-author of a book about a Houston CIA agent what Mischer had said, he commented, "About the only thing Walter could use that letter for is to blow his nose."

(As a matter of policy, the CIA does not confirm or deny whether a private citizen has worked for the agency as a contract agent or asset. In one of its rare exceptions, it told the Justice Department that it has never employed Richard Brenneke. The Portland jury in Brenneke's perjury trial didn't believe this.)

Mischer also acted astonished that Corson worked for the CIA. "What in the world would he be doing for the CIA?" he asked. Questioned whether he knows Ramon d'Onofrio, Mischer replied, "No. Is he a CIA guy? The CIA has some strange people from time to time."

In a letter dated February 20, 1990, to the *Houston Post*, Corson stated that he has "never known or been involved with anyone in organized crime or in the CIA." That is not an explicit denial. The question is whether Corson did any *work* for the CIA. If he were a cutout he could have worked for the CIA, yet his statement could have a grain of truth in it.

The CIA, as is its custom, has so far neither confirmed nor denied any relationship to Mischer or Corson.

The lawyer who helped Corson with his letter, and also represents him on his savings-and-loan criminal charges, and who has represented him on some civil matters, is Stephen Cass Weiland, with Jackson & Walker in Dallas. It is unusual for a Dallas lawyer to be representing a native Houston boy like Corson, particularly given the size, strength and depth of the Houston Bar. And Weiland refuses to say how he met Corson and came to represent him. But there are some interesting intersections in the two men's lives.

Before Weiland moved to Dallas and started representing Corson, he was a top aide to U.S. Senator William Roth (Republican-Delaware), and the chief counsel to the powerful Senate Permanent Subcommittee on Investigations, which Roth chaired. While at the committee, Weiland concentrated on and conducted investigations regarding precious-metals fraud, international narcotics trafficking, offshore banks and money laundering.[10] Weiland refused to answer questions about whether he encountered Corson in any of these investigations.

Weiland's former boss, Senator Roth, is related by marriage to the du Ponts, one of this country's oldest and richest families, headquartered in Wilmington, Delaware. Roth is married to the former Jane K. Richards, the daughter of Robert H. Richards, Jr. According to the book *Du Pont Dynasty,* by Gerard Colby, Richards is a director of the Du Pont Company and Wilmington Trust. And, Colby writes, "Jane's grandfather, Robert H. Richards, Sr., was the 'guiding genius' secretary of Pierre du Pont's Christiana Securities, the family holding company." In addition, Roth's brother-in-law, Jane's brother, Robert H. Richards III, is married to Marianna du Pont, the granddaughter of Irenee du Pont, the patriarch who died in 1963.[11]

The du Ponts also connect to Corson through the St. Joe Paper Co., which was founded by family rebel Alfred I. du Pont, who ran away to Florida and made his fortune there. His most valuable holding was the St. Joe, the state's largest private landowner with more than one million acres of timberland in addition to pulp and paper mills.

---

[10] E.g., "Crime and Secrecy: The Use of Offshore Banks and Companies," report by the Permanent Subcommittee on Investigations, 1985.

[11] *Du Pont Dynasty: Behind the Nylon Curtain,* by Gerard Colby, (Lyle Stuart, 1984).

In the summer of 1986, Corson's savings and loan was bankrupted and eventually failed, primarily because it lent $20 million toward the $200 million purchase of 21,000 acres of land in the Florida panhandle from St. Joe Paper Co. (This deal will be analyzed in detail in a later chapter.)

The du Ponts are no strangers to the CIA either. Alfred I. du Pont's son Alfred Victor du Pont, an architect, was recruited by General William "Wild Bill" Donovan to work in the Office of Strategic Services (OSS), the World War II predecessor of the CIA. Du Pont served on the OSS's French desk in Washington.[12]

Also, when William Casey, who headed the CIA under Reagan, was an attorney in private practice in the 1950s, he was hired by two du Pont brothers for tax advice on their inheritance. Casey handled the matter so well for them that they made him a partner in one of their companies that invested in oil leases—which made Casey $771,000 when the company was liquidated.[13]

In 1983, Richard C. du Pont's Summit Aviation retrofitted a Cessna to carry bombs and machine guns that was used by the CIA to bomb Managua, Nicaragua, on September 8, 1983.[14] Summitt also allegedly transported arms for the Contras and retrofitted other Cessnas so that the Contras could use them to fire rockets.[15]

Helping Richard du Pont with Summit Aviation was CIA operative Pat Foley. Rob Owen, Oliver North's messenger boy to Contra operations, wrote a memo to North on February 10, 1986, that said, "No doubt you know the DC-4 Foley got was used at one time to run drugs and part of the group had criminal records. Nice groups the boys chose." The "boys" were the CIA.

When he was chief counsel to the Senate Permanent Subcommittee on Investigations, Weiland made a cameo appearance, along with his boss, Senator Roth, in Oliver North's White House notebooks. On January 6, 1984, North got a phone call from a George Woodworth regarding Weiland. North butchered Weiland's name, writing down "S. Kass Wyland, counsel, Perm Sub Committee on Invest. of SSCI (Sen. Roth)."

[12] OSS: The Secret History of America's First Central Intelligence Agency, by R. Harris Smith (University of California Press, 1972).
[13] Casey: From the OSS to the CIA, by Joseph E. Persico (New York: Viking Penguin, 1990).
[14] Colby, op. cit.
[15] The Chronology, by the National Security Archive.

North then wrote that Weiland "wants Woodworth to proceed" with a meeting with Sergio Brull in Miami. The next line was set off in quote marks by North: "White House [underlined twice by North] is interested in moving on project in Belize." Then he has in parentheses, "said by Wyland to Tazwell." The next entry in North's diary shows his schedule for the coming Tuesday, on which he has a meeting with Roth and Weiland set up for 12:30. Then he wrote, "Sergio knows Vesco's ex-bodyguard (who is in Spain)."

Brull, who is mentioned in North's notebooks later in association with CIA-connected gun dealer Ron Martin, is a Cuban businessman who reportedly fought at the Bay of Pigs. In a May 13, 1986, conversation recorded in North's notebook between North and his liaison to the Contras, Rob Owen, there is a discussion of Brull. They talk about him in connection with the purchase of an airplane and having contact with John Molina, a banker for Ron Martin, who was gunned down in the street in Panama City in 1987.

On July 29, 1986, North had a meeting with retired Air Force Major General Richard Secord, who was running the Contra resupply effort as well as handling arms shipments to Iran. They discussed Ron Martin and Sergio Brull, along with Miami gun dealer David Duncan and the use of an East German ship that Panamanian dictator Manuel Noriega was holding.

Brull was also named by Secord in an interview he had with the FBI in July 1986. Secord said Brull was an associate of Jack Terrell, who had been involved in efforts to resupply the Contras.[16]

In 1989, Brull was sued by a bank in Haiti for allegedly absconding with the proceeds of a $1.4 million letter of credit that was to buy 5,000 tons of Brazilian sugar for Haiti. The bank couldn't locate Brull to serve him with the lawsuit and alleged that he had fled the country. The bank was able to track the $1.4 million that Brull took to a bank in Madrid, Spain.[17]

Another member of this circle who was in Belize around this time was Carl Jenkins, an old CIA agent whose previous claim to fame was his role as Rafael "Chi Chi" Quintero's case officer during the Bay of Pigs fiasco.[18] (Quintero, an infamous CIA operative who worked with

---

[16] Iran-Contra Affair, Congressional Report, Appendix A, Vol. 1.
[17] Banque de L'Union Haïtienne, S.A., vs. International Basic Economic Corp. and Sergio D. Brull, 89-21843 in the 11th Circuit Court of Dade County, Florida.
[18] *Manhunt*, by Peter Maas (New York: Random House, 1986).

Thomas Clines and Edwin Wilson, among others, was brought in by Secord and Clines to help with the Contra resupply effort.)[19] Jenkins is mentioned in a number of places in North's notebooks, including one memorable list by North that reads "Gene Wheaton, Carl Jenkins, [John] Hull, [Rob] Owen, [Oliver] North." This list was compiled by North on April 18, 1986, apparently during a telephone conversation with Alan Fiers, director of the CIA's Central American Task Force, who would later plead guilty to misleading Congress on the Contra affair.

Almost every time Jenkins appears in North's notebooks, he is in the company of Wheaton, the former Pentagon criminal investigator. Wheaton said Jenkins was using the tiny nation of Belize as a training area for Latin Americans and Laotians to fight in Nicaragua against the Sandinistas.

One of Jenkins's first assignments with the CIA was in the 1954 coup in Guatemala. Jenkins and his helicopter company in Guatemala were also customers of Commercial Helicopters in Baton Rouge, Louisiana.[20] (This company got most of its financing from Louisiana mobster and savings-and-loan looter Herman K. Beebe, and one of its principals was a close friend of drug dealer and CIA asset Barry Seal. More on this later.)

On January 11, 1984, the day after North had scheduled a meeting with S. Cass Weiland and Senator Roth regarding Belize, North got another phone call from George Woodworth. He wrote in his notebook that it was about Weiland, who "wants to contact [the next word is illegible] people in Belize camps." The word that is illegible appears to be a four-letter word that begins with "dr" and ends with a "g." However, it doesn't appear to be the word "drug."

About the same time that Jenkins was training anti-Sandinistas in Belize and Corson's future attorney was saying the White House was interested in moving on a project in Belize, a friend of George Bush's, and Ronald Reagan's biggest campaign fundraiser in 1980— i.e., Walter Mischer—was getting involved in small English-speaking Belize. He started out in 1984 in a shrimp business with his close friend, the late Houston developer Kieth Jackson. Then, in the fall of 1985, he and his partners purchased 700,000 acres in the interior northwest corner abutting Guatemala and Mexico.

---

[19] *The Crimes of Patriots*, by Jonathan Kwitny (New York: Norton, 1987).
[20] Commercial Helicopters bankruptcy filings in Baton Rouge.

It was a curious purchase, to say the least. First of all, it was in the interior, where roads are bad or nonexistent, with no access to the Caribbean Sea. It was also strange to buy 12 percent of a country like Belize and not even get access to the ocean.

Second, the partners were an incongruous bunch. One was from among the original owners of the land, Barry Bowen, whose family was forced to sell because the Panamanian bank that held the mortgage was threatening to foreclose, or so the buyers said.[21]

Among the partners was Coca-Cola Foods, the soft-drink company subsidiary in Houston that makes orange juice. This company, headed then by Eugene Amoroso, claimed that it was looking for land in South America to grow oranges because of the recent freeze in Florida. But that explanation seemed flimsy. The freeze had occurred in December 1983. This purchase was almost two years later—and then it turns out the company apparently didn't do soil testing until after they bought it. The soil tests, the company said later, showed that only 25,000 to 30,000 acres were suitable for citrus. By 1990 the company had sold much of its land and placed on indefinite hold any plans to grow citrus.[22]

The remaining partners were Walter Mischer and Paul Howell, a Houston oilman who had been an admiral in the U.S. Navy and a former director of the Houston branch of the Dallas Federal Reserve Bank. Mischer, who was a member of the board of directors of the Howell Corp., has given several different answers on how he and Howell came to buy the land.

In an interview on November 6, 1989, Mischer claimed that Coca-Cola "found the land," but in an interview on July 30, 1990, he said, "Paul Howell found that property." Asked if Coca-Cola found the land, he replied, "No." Asked to explain the contradiction in his two answers, he said, "Coca-Cola came to us because we had already looked at the property."

Mischer and his partners paid cash for the land, approximately $2 million to $3 million each.[23] Mischer said he couldn't remember the name of the Panamanian bank holding Barry Bowen's note, but said the partners paid their money through the Bank of Nova Scotia. Mischer and Howell spent another $1.5 million clearing some of the land, and

---

[21] *Washington Post*, October 9, 1989.
[22] Letter from Coca-Cola Foods, October 19, 1990.
[23] *Forbes*, May 4, 1987.

they were logging some trees and planting some citrus, Mischer said in a November 1989 interview.

Mischer has denied that the land was intended for use by the CIA as a transshipment point for weapons and material into Latin America and as a paramilitary training area. "That's far-fetched," he said.

Is it? Here is what is known: Oliver North quotes the chief counsel of a powerful Senate subcommittee that the White House is interested in a project in Belize. This counsel later shows up as Robert Corson's attorney. Also, regarding this Belize project, North discussed a Cuban-American, Sergio Brull, who is associated with CIA-connected Contra gun dealer Ron Martin, who in turn has reported business dealings with Corson.

Next, a CIA agent, Carl Jenkins, who had worked in the agency's 1954 Guatemala coup, is using Belize to train Contras. Jenkins later appears in the bankruptcy filings of a Louisiana helicopter company whose principals have close business and personal associations with Herman K. Beebe, the Louisiana mobster doing business with Mischer's Allied Bank as well as with Barry Seal, assassinated drug smuggler, DEA informant and CIA asset who was training Contra pilots in Arkansas.

Belize was also a favorite transshipment point for a narcotics trafficking group smuggling cocaine from Colombia to the United States. One of the leaders of this group was Jack DeVoe, a pilot with CIA connections. A money launderer for DeVoe was Lawrence Freeman, a Miami attorney who was an associate of the late CIA mastermind Paul Helliwell. Freeman was also involved in the $200 million Florida land deal with the du Ponts' St. Joe Paper Co. and Corson.(More on all this in later chapters.)

Also, in the mid-1970s, Cuban-Mexican drug trafficker Alberto Silicia-Falcón, who had alleged ties to the CIA, talked with his lieutenants about taking over the entire country of Belize, according to *The Underground Empire*, by James Mills. By all accounts, Belize has been a hotbed of narcotics smuggling and marijuana growing.

Then, Corson's ex-father-in-law buys into 700,000 acres in Belize. The vague plans for this land later vanish into smoke. Some say because they were disrupted by the October 1986 downing of Barry Seal's old C-123K on a resupply run to the Contras with Eugene Hasenfus the only survivor. One of Corson's former employees said that their office went into an uproar when the news of this crash came out. "That's the airline we use" (referring to Southern Air Transport, the former CIA proprietary connected to the C-123), said either B. J. Garman or Corson, according to the employee.

Southern Air Transport was a CIA proprietary until 1973, when it was sold to the man who had been fronting the ownership for the CIA. The airline company was later sold to James Bastian, who had been an officer in Air America's parent company and Southern Air Transport's in-house lawyer.

When Southern Air's role in the Iran-Contra scandal was exposed— it had been the airline of choice to haul arms to Iran and to the Con- tras—Bastian denied any connections to the CIA. What he couldn't deny were connections to the CIA's Iran-Contra cutout, Oliver North, who went to his old buddy Oliver "Buck" Revell, then Assistant FBI Director (and now special agent in charge of the FBI's Dallas office), to try to stop an FBI investigation into Southern Air Transport's suspicious activities.

Corson was no stranger to Belize either. One of the few trips outside the United States he admits to taking was to Belize with his partner Sandy Aron. His mother, B.J., and infamous Houston developer Mel Powers took trips down to Belize around New Year's 1987 and May 1987 to discuss a business deal with some New York insurance people. At least one eyewitness, and officials who have seen Customs' records, state that Mischer accompanied them. Mischer vehemently denies this, and the Customs records that would answer the question were denied to me when I requested them under the Freedom of Information Act.

In 1991, with the FBI, the IRS and the Arizona Department of Public Safety after him, Corson skipped the country. He first went to Teguci- galpa, Honduras, and then to Belize, according to law enforcement officials. Belize has no extradition treaty with the United States.

Despite considerable evidence to the contrary, Mischer adamantly maintains that he has had nothing to do with Corson since the latter's divorce from his daughter.

But one deal between the two that was continued after the divorce was the Enchanted Oaks Shopping Center, a small strip shopping center north of Houston. This was a joint venture between a Mischer com- pany, Corson and his cousin Roy Dailey. A mortgage on the property filed by Surety Savings in Houston in January 1976 showed the owners to be the Mischer company and Roy Dailey, trustee. However, Corson's divorce papers revealed that Dailey was fronting for him and that he,

Corson, actually owned 25 percent of the shopping center. Documents filed in 1978 and 1979 indicate that the joint venture continued to be the Mischer company and Roy Dailey as trustee for himself and Corson.

It was not until 1985 that the Mischer company filed papers showing it to be the sole owner of the shopping center. When Farm & Home Savings foreclosed on the property in November 1986, there were the previously mentioned communications between employees at Corson's company and employees at Mischer's regarding how to handle the tax liability incurred by the foreclosure. Sims, Corson's former accountant, said it was obvious Corson was trying to keep his relationship with Mischer a secret and that he was scared others would find out about it.

Following the divorce, Corson participated in deals, such as borrowing money and receiving money, with at least three of Mischer's Allied Bancshares member banks. For example, in February 1978 one of Corson's and Dailey's companies, Chateau Realty & Building Corp., borrowed money from Allied American Bank. Some of the security put up by Corson and Dailey for this loan was 2,130 shares of stock they owned in Cypress Bank. In 1980, Allied Bank acquired all the stock of Cypress and changed its name to Allied Cypress Bank.

In February 1983, Corson sold a piece of land he owned north of Houston to Stop 'n Serve, which borrowed $426,000 from Allied Humble Bank to pay Corson. And in October 1983, Corson borrowed $350,000 from Allied Champions Bank to purchase land for a strip shopping center. In addition, his October 1984 financial statement shows a $37,500 loan from Allied Champions bank secured by 7.7 acres in Magnolia, Texas.

Mischer tried to distance himself from the Allied Bank deals with Corson after the divorce, saying, "I didn't have anything to do with the bank after 1977, after the heart attack and bypass. I was a passive investor."

This is contradicted by a story on Mischer in *Forbes* magazine on April 8, 1984, which states that Mischer "wasn't even slowed down by triple-bypass surgery in 1977. When he's not cooking up other deals as chairman of $92 million [sales] Mischer Corp., a real estate firm, or working at one of his six ranches or playing Texas politics (he was a big money backer of LBJ in the old days), he's downtown at Allied's greenglass, 71-story headquarters, courting customers. He visits three or four prospects a week and refers a dozen or so contacts a month to loan officers."

After Mischer's daughter divorced Corson, he went to work for Houston real estate appraiser and developer Paul A. Lewis. An April 9, 1978, story in the *Houston Post* stated, "Robert Carson (sic), local developer, who has built and sold 100 shopping centers in Houston, joins the Lewis brothers in the ownership and management of Reatta," which was the development company of Paul Lewis and his brother, David.

At the same time Corson joined the company, Lewis started to borrow money from Allied Bank for shopping centers and day-care centers. His first loan from Allied Bank was in February 1977, for $300,000. In June of that year, Lewis borrowed $144,000 from Allied, and then $975,000 the next month. His final Allied loan was $370,000 in September 1979.

The first public document that showed Lewis and Corson in a land deal together is dated October 5, 1977, when Corson's mother served as the middle man in a land flip: On that date, about half an acre of land in Harris County was deeded to B. J. Eyden, trustee, who was Corson's mother, by the Breakfast Club, Ltd. Two weeks later, B.J. deeded the land to Paul Lewis, trustee. Both deeds were filed for record the same day.

One of the general partners of the Breakfast Club was the Johnson-Loggins Company, which is owned by Glenn Loggins, a business partner and former employee of Mischer. Two months later, a similar flip involving B.J., Lewis and Johnson-Loggins took place.

Corson's closest business associate in his company with his mother was Bill Chester, who also functioned as Corson's bodyguard. Chester had worked for Mischer at Allied Bank before joining Corson, according to one person close to Corson, and had apparently been sent over by Mischer to watch out for and keep an eye on Corson. Mischer denied knowing Chester.

One of Corson's former chauffeurs and bodyguards in 1986, Tom Sturdivant, told a private investigator that Corson and Mischer were close to each other. Sturdivant said that Mischer backed Corson financially in several business deals in the mid-1980s.

Corson has claimed in a letter that Sturdivant is not credible because he fired him for theft. But Sturdivant made his comments during an investigation of a Corson associate by Houston attorney Tom Alexander, who is Mischer's attorney and close personal friend. Alexander allowed me, while working for the *Houston Post,* to examine his files on

Corson, which included the interview with Sturdivant. Alexander, who would give his right arm to protect Mischer, did nothing to keep the Sturdivant interview secret, and in fact turned over his files containing the Sturdivant interview to the United States Attorney's Office in Houston. However, this was more than a year before I began asking questions about Corson's connections to Mischer and the CIA, and thus long before Mischer began publicly denying any connections.

When told about this, Mischer replied, "Well, it might have been some stuff that Paula got involved with, where she signed a note and I bailed her out. But I never done business with him or had any business with him. But he convinced her at one point to get on some notes, and I bailed her out, and if you're talking about that, that was after they had divorced."

When I told Mischer I was not talking about that, but about all the Allied loans, including those with Paul Lewis, he replied, "Well, I, I, I, I know that Paul and David Lewis were customers of the bank, and that Robert and Paul were kinda buddies. Yes, I did know that. And I think that Paul got the same treatment that I did from Robert—lost his money."

There were other intersections between the Mischer circle and Corson after the divorce. There was the loan from Corson's savings and loan to Joe McDermott, a friend, business associate and former Mischer employee, who was given his start in the Houston development community by Mischer. In 1986, Corson's S&L lent McDermott several million dollars secured by Splashtown U.S.A., a water entertainment and amusement park north of Houston.

Mischer at first denied that any of his associates were involved with Corson. When he was told that McDermott had dealt with Corson, he said he called McDermott up to question him about it.

And there was Catbird's.

There were always strange characters hanging around Catbird's, an upscale honky-tonk and bar in west Houston.

First, there was John Hull from Costa Rica, whose ranch near the Nicaraguan border was a jumping-off spot for private and CIA aid to the Contras. Hull would occasionally come to Houston to meet with Contra supporters, including Oliver North and Rob Owen. In 1990, Hull was charged with drug trafficking by the Costa Rican government and then indicted for murder there in the La Penca bombing in which seven people were killed in the attempted assassination of Eden Pastora, a Contra leader who had fallen out of favor with the CIA. Hull jumped bond in Costa Rica and returned to his native Indiana.

There was also John Riddle, a Houston lawyer and developer, whose companies had borrowed more than $300 million from some of the most infamous and corrupt failed Texas savings and loans, including Vernon, Western and Continental.

There was Ken Qualls, too, a pilot who worked for a CIA-related airline company. In 1979, Qualls was a pilot for American Continental Corporation, which was controlled by Charles Keating, who would later go down in history in his attempt, as the head of Lincoln Savings and Loan, to buy some U.S. senators. It was also Qualls who allegedly flew a BAC 1-11 to Paris in October 1980, carrying members of the Reagan-Bush Republican candidacy team to meet with Iranians to negotiate the alleged October Surprise deal.

The only time Catbird's appeared in a story in the *Houston Post* was in a gossip column in July 1987, when it was the site of a birthday party for Houston restaurateur Tilman Fertitta. Fertitta, who said he knew Corson, is a member of a Galveston family that is related to the old Maceo family, a Mafia family that ran the rackets and gambling in Galveston from the 1930s to the 1950s.

Although the Maceos were under the authority of the New Orleans Cosa Nostra, their patriarch, Sam, was a Mafia figure of some importance. He played a key role in getting mobster Moe Dalitz a license from the Nevada Tax Commission for his Desert Inn hotel and casino in Las Vegas.[24]

The Fertittas also control a hotel/casino in Las Vegas that they have advertised in a package vacation deal with their Key Largo Hotel in Galveston.

In *War of the Godfathers*, former FBI agent William F. Roemer, Jr., described how the Chicago Mafia was trying to kill Moe Dalitz in Las Vegas because he had defected to the New York Bonanno family: "[Joe] Ferriola [acting Chicago Mafia boss] rented a home in west Las Vegas, a couple blocks off I-15 not too far from the Palace Station, which is Frank Fertitta's hotel/casino. Fertitta had friends in Chicago, too. He had been associated with Carl Thomas at the Tropicana when it was being skimmed for [the] Kansas City and Chicago [Mafia families]."

---

[24] *The Green Felt Jungle,* by Ed Reid & Ovid Demaris (New York: Pocket Books, 1964).

Frank Fertitta is Tilman Fertitta's first cousin, once removed. Tilman is the head of a company in Houston that owns several noted restaurants, including Landry's and Willie G.'s. When asked about the statements in Roemer's book, Tilman replied: "Carl Thomas was Frank's partner. He thought he was going to be hot shit and show the mob in Kansas City how to skim money. Carl Thomas was barred from Las Vegas. He can't even come into the city. That was when it [the Palace Station] was the Bingo Palace, though. It opened up as a little five-and-dime, little tin slot-machine joint. It just grew and grew and grew. But since it's ever had any success and any size, Frank's been in it by himself for the last ten years. Carl was just in it from the begining. But he was bought out as soon as he got in trouble."

Fertitta said that Sam Maceo was his great-uncle, but when asked about Maceo's Mafia ties, he replied, "I don't know. What's the Mafia? I never . . . What is that? I've never seen the word Mafia used, though. That's the first I've ever heard the word 'Mafia' used. They were in the gambling business." Fertitta said he had read *The Green Felt Jungle*, a 1963 book by Ed Reid and Ovid Demaris about the Mafia control of Las Vegas. The book describes Maceo as a "mafioso" and "Galveston's underworld chieftain."

Fertitta also denied that the Maceo family was under the aegis of the New Orleans Mafia. However, Aaron Kohn, the late head of the New Orleans Metroplitan Crime Commission, said there were close ties between the two. In 1937, Sam Maceo was indicted in a massive narcotics investigation that had been led by famed special Customs agent Walter Craig. Indicted along with Maceo were Houston restaurant owner Vincent Vallone and Biaggio Angelica, who, according to Kohn, was one of the New Orleans Mafia's key representatives in Southeast Texas.

Vincent Vallone, the grandfather of noted Houston restaurateur Tony Vallone, was shotgunned to death in a mob hit outside his Houston restaurant in 1949. There were allegations that Carlos Marcello had ordered the hit. Evidence was presented before a Congressional Crime Committee that Marcello had spoken to Vallone on the phone before the hit. Marcello's phone records also show that the Mafia boss had spoken to Houston oilman Lenoir Josey before the Vallone hit.

Attending the Tilman Fertitta birthday bash at Catbird's was Archie Bennett, at that time a commissioner on the Port of Houston Authority and head of the Mariner Hotel Corporation, a Houston-based hotel company. Shortly thereafter, Southmark, the Dallas-based real estate company and mob dumping ground, bought Mariner. Bennett moved to Dallas to work for Southmark and filed for bankruptcy there.

Bennett's bankruptcy filing shows millions of dollars of debt to banks and savings and loans that later failed. MBank foreclosed on 2,000 shares of stock Bennett owned of the National Bank of Texas, a failed Houston bank whose directors included Tilman Fertitta. Also listed in Bennett's bankruptcy papers is a $500,000 unsecured loan from his good friend Walter Mischer.

At the front of Catbird's, inside near the bar, was a chair that was called the "catbird's seat." Not only was it a symbol for the restaurant, it stood for something more significant. It was a rare public expression of the relationship between Catbird's owner, Robert Corson, and Walter Mischer.

Catbird's was named by Corson for the expression "sitting in the catbird's seat," a favorite Mischer adage. In fact, Mischer's best friend, the late Kieth Jackson, told me in 1987 that "sitting in the catbird's seat" is Mischer's favorite expression. (Mischer seemed to have an affinity toward names that expressed success. The name of the club in his Carrousel Motel was the Brass Ring Club.) Mischer said it was "bullshit, rumor shit" that Catbird's was a secret symbol of his relationship to Corson.

As for Catbird's, after opening with great fanfare in May 1987, it went broke and closed its doors before the end of the year. The $40,000 borrowed to fix it up—a loan from Westside National Bank, where Corson and his mother owned the largest block of stock—was never paid back. Today the site of Catbird's is occupied by a Pig'n Whistle bar.

When Corson bought Kleberg County Savings and Loan in 1986, he borrowed $6 million from MBank Houston for the purchase. After a year, his savings and loan was insolvent and he couldn't make the payments on the MBank loan. MBank renewed the loan, with a large participation by Allied Bank. After the refinancing, which included an additional $2 million in cash, Corson's mother and partner, B.J., was heard to remark that "Papa [Mischer] came through."

When told this, Mischer said, "I never had anything to do with her, ever. I don't know why she said that. She could have said anything." In a later interview, Mischer called B.J. Garman "the sorriest piece of humanity I know." And, Mischer added, "I don't know how he [Corson] got the money [to buy Vision Banc Savings]. I don't know how he could have gotten approval [to buy an S&L]. Corson had a terrible reputation. He owed everybody in the country. It didn't make any sense."

On the contrary, it made a lot of sense when Corson's relationships to Mischer and Jon Lindsay were considered.

9

THE MULE GETS VISION

The story of Harris County Judge Jon Lindsay is a classic tale of the corruption of a politician—a naive nobody who lucks into an election victory and then is gradually corrupted by the privileges and perks of political power.

Lindsay is called the County Judge, but he's not a judge at all. He is head of the Harris County Commissioners Court, the governing body of Harris County, which includes Houston. The position is called County Judge because that person used to make quasi-judicial decisions on such things as mental competency and liquor licenses.

Lindsay is the most powerful politician in the Houston area, not just because of his elected position (the mayor of Houston may have more sheer governmental power than the county judge), but because of his influence and position in the Republican party. A good friend of President George Bush, Lindsay headed Bush's presidential campaign in Harris County in 1988. And one of his first, and closest, aides was Chase Untermeyer, who went on to work in the Reagan-Bush Administration and then became White House Director of Personnel when Bush was elected President.

Among the government services the Harris County Commissioners Court is responsible for, and which bestow power on its members, are: flood control, medical care for the poor, roads and parks in unincorporated areas, and the county's criminal justice system. Because of the Commissioners Court's control of flood control and roads in undeveloped areas, its members are courted extensively by, and get large campaign contributions from, contractors, engineers and developers.

Back in the early 1970s, a small-time civil engineer named Jon Lindsay had a little construction company that built things like swimming pools. Lindsay came to Houston from New Mexico—he had grown up in Santa Fe and gone to college at New Mexico State University—and lived in the rural area of North Harris County. In trying, almost begging, to get construction contracts from the city of Houston he probably realized that politicians have a surer thing, and easier job, than he did. So he ran for state representative, as a Democrat, and lost.

By then, politics was in his blood, so he decided to take another shot—this time as a Republican, and against County Judge Bill Elliott, a powerful, keen, straight-talking, tough, liberal Democrat. Under normal circumstances, Lindsay would never have had a chance against Elliott, but something very rare happened before the 1974 election. Both Houston newspapers decided to take after Elliott, conducting investigations and writing expose's, and Lindsay won in a major upset.

When Lindsay first took over as County Judge, he found himself almost immediately in a power struggle with County Commissioner Bob Eckels, a mean, arrogant, sanctimonious, greedy, corrupt SOB, who was firmly ensconced in the hip pocket of Houston developers, including Walter Mischer.

For example, one time there was a vote before Commissioners Court on a proposed toll road from near downtown Houston up through northern Harris County. This road was going by some of Mischer's land and he was strongly supporting it. Somehow that word didn't get to Eckels, or, if it did, it didn't sink in. After the commissioner in whose precinct the road would run said he opposed it, Eckels voted against it, saying he would follow the practice of Commissioners Court and acquiesce to the wishes of the affected commissioner. When Mischer found out what happened, he called up Eckels and blistered his butt. When the next vote on the proposed toll road was taken, Eckels voted in favor of it.

Mischer later acknowledged calling Eckels about the vote, but said, "I didn't eat him out. I don't think I've chewed *anybody* out." He also denied controlling Eckels: "I'd like to see the guy who has Eckels in his hip pocket."[1]

Eckels had been indicted five times before he was finally run out of

---

[1] *Houston Post*, November 22, 1987.

office after being convicted of accepting an illegal gift, equivalent to Al Capone's conviction on income tax evasion. Eckels later died of a heart attack.

Anyway, compared to Eckels, Lindsay seemed like Abraham Lincoln. Open, frank and accessible, Lindsay got good press coverage, including some I wrote in the *Houston Chronicle*; in particular, favorable stories on his park system on flood-prone Cypress Creek. One of his first moves after getting elected was to initiate a program to purchase vacant land along Cypress Creek to keep the flood-plain land from being developed and to provide much- needed park and green space for county residents.

Lindsay also got better press than the city politicians, primarily because he was so much more accessible than they were, particularly Mayor Kathy Whitmire. Lindsay not only gave reporters his home phone number, he gave them his car phone number too, and if he couldn't be reached immediately, he would always quickly return phone calls—perhaps because he remembered that he owed his political career to reporters.

But something started happening to Lindsay around the time he was re-elected to his third term in 1982. Perhaps it was just the inevitable outcome of that simple axiom "Power corrupts." Perhaps he started believing all the fawning sycophants and yes-men and -women he had surrounded himself with. Perhaps he liked all the side-bar business deals the boys were now cutting him in on. Or perhaps it was the easy availability of female companionship.

(An inveterate skirt chaser, Lindsay is married to an attorney, Toni Lindsay, who went to law school after their children were grown. After law school, Toni got a job with the Houston City Attorney's Office, and then with only a few years of experience and negligible trial practice, she was appointed to a state district judgeship by Governor Bill Clements.)

More can be learned about politics in America by comparing Lindsay's list of campaign contributors in 1974 to his current list, and by comparing his 1980 financial statement to his 1985 statement, than by reading a dozen political science textbooks.

There are few big names or big contributions on the 1974 list: mostly $50 and $100 from farmers, small businessmen and country folk from little north Harris County communities like Tomball, Spring, Hufsmith and Klein. The Republican party was the biggest donor to Lindsay, who had also lent himself $8,000. Seven days before the 1974 election, Lindsay had only raised $29,000 in contributions. Lindsay's current contribution list, on the contrary, is dominated by big Houston law firms, banks, construction contractors, architects, engineers and developers.

In 1980, Lindsay listed total assets of $447,123.12 on his financial statement. But some $367,000 of this was his house and the surrounding 54 acres. The only stocks, bonds and securities he owned were 500 shares of Alief Alamo Bank, valued at $7,500, and $18,802 in U.S. Treasury bills. And this was after he had been in office for five years. But by 1985, Lindsay listed stock ownership in 12 companies, including Harris County Bank and West Houston National Bank. He also had bonds in three public entities, as well as CDs at Harris County Bank with a value between $50,000 and $100,000. And he was involved in partnerships that owned 70 acres in north Harris County and an apartment project.

Lindsay's total investments outside his house and surrounding acreage were somewhere between $241,000 and $500,000, based on the broad categories used—and this does not include the value of the stock Lindsay owned in the 12 companies (something he neglected to include in his report). This compares to about $80,000 in 1980.

In 1985, Lindsay showed his borrowed funds to be somewhere between $30,000 and $150,000. This compares to $23,300 in 1980. Subtracting his debt from his total assets (again factoring out his house and surrounding acreage) shows a net worth of about $57,000 in 1980 and somewhere between $181,000 and $350,000 in 1985. At the same time, Lindsay was supporting a wife and three children, all of whom he was putting through college. This on a annual salary that started at about $55,000 in 1980 and rose to about $75,000 in 1985.

In 1984, Lindsay got his first bad press when he admitted that he hires his friends and campaign contributors to do work for the county. Lucrative county contracts for architects and engineers, and other "professional" services, are not awarded on a best- (or lowest-) bid basis, as are construction contracts. "I pick my friends," Lindsay said, quickly adding, "as long as they are qualified."

Shortly after saying that, Lindsay appeared before the Harris County Hospital District, which runs the county's tax-supported charity hospitals, to defend the district's decision to build a new hospital in the middle of a federally designated 100-year flood plain. Although building in the flood plain flew in the face of Lindsay's professed philosophy, he strongly supported construction of the new hospital in its planned location.

The factors that apparently outweighed his flood-plain position, not to mention endangering the lives of poor people needing emergency medical care who might be prevented access because of floodwaters, were these:

(1) The land in the flood plain was owned by Dallas businessman H. R. "Bum" Bright, a rich, powerful, prominent Republican and owner of the Dallas Cowboys football team. The hospital district paid Bright $3.8 million for the land, which was about $2 million more than it was valued on the county's tax rolls.[2]

(2) The architects picked to design the new hospital were longtime "friends" and campaign supporters of Lindsay. Bernard Johnson, Inc., and 3D/International were chosen—for a fee of $2.47 million. Principals of Bernard Johnson began donating to Lindsay in 1976 and by 1984 had contributed about $18,000 to his campaign coffers. Principals in 3D/International, including Jack Rains, who would later be named Texas secretary of state by Governor Clements, started contributing to Lindsay in 1980, and by 1984 had kicked in about $4,000. (As the saying goes, it doesn't take much to buy a Texas politician; but once they're bought, they stay bought.)

Asked if he influenced the hospital district in its selection of architects, Lindsay replied, "I attempted to. I contacted the board members and told them I wanted qualified local architects selected. I told them to give our local people more consideration, and I think they did. I told them that Bernard Johnson and 3D/International are local firms."[3]

In addition to the hospital in the flood plain, the county was also building a new hospital in the Texas Medical Center. One of the architects chosen was CRS Sirrine, a Houston-based engineering firm. At that time, the largest stockholder in CRS was Gaith Pharoan, a Saudi Arabian who would get caught up in negative publicity in 1991 as one of the principals in BCCI, the Middle East bank convicted of drug-money laundering in Florida. Pharoan, an alleged front man for BCCI in America, was indicted for his role.

When Lindsay appeared before the hospital district board, which is

[2] *Houston Post*, October 7, 1984.
[3] *Houston Post*, December 23, 1984.

appointed by Commissioners Court, he threatened the members with ouster if they didn't get with the building program and start pouring concrete. Critics of the new buildings said that the district should spend more money on services, not buildings, particularly when there were more than 6,000 empty beds in the city's private hospitals. The chickens came home to roost in 1991 for the district and Commissioners Court when the expense of constructing and operating the new hospitals contributed to a severe budget crunch that led to the closing of beds in them and other cuts in their services.

In 1977, one year after Bernard Johnson officers starting contributing to Lindsay, the company was awarded, at Lindsay's urging, a $3.8 million contract to design the county's new jail. Experts in a later federal court hearing said the jail's design was fatally flawed because guards would have difficulty viewing inmates in their individual cells.

In addition, in 1983, 3D/International won, upon Lindsay's recommendation, the contract to design the county's new psychiatric hospital.

(3) One of the strongest proponents for the construction of the new hospital, as well as another new one in the Texas Medical Center, was the Baylor College of Medicine, which supplied the doctors and residents who treat the indigent patients—at an annual fee of more than $20 million. Baylor is one of the most powerful institutions in Houston, because of the big shots on its board and because of the influence and prestige of its chancellor, heart surgeon Dr. Michael DeBakey.

In answering some of the critics who argued against building new hospitals, Lindsay said privately that Baylor was simply too important to be turned down and he didn't want to jeopardize its relationship with the hospital district. What he didn't tell anyone, and what didn't come out until more than five years later, was that he was a partner in an apartment complex with DeBakey and several other Baylor doctors.

In October 1983, Lindsay purchased a 3 percent interest in the Green Meadows Apartments in northern Harris County for $10,773 in cash and promissory notes totaling $72,919. His partners included DeBakey, Stanley Appel, chairman of the Department of Neurology at Baylor, and E. Stanley Crawford, one of Baylor's top surgery professors.

The next month, the partnership borrowed $5 million from First City National Bank of Houston to buy the apartment project. First City was headed by James Elkins, Jr., the son of the man who lent Walter Mischer his first $1 million. When it made the $5 million loan, First City had a contract with Harris County to serve as the depository for the county's money, which Lindsay had voted to approve eight months earlier. Such contracts, which are awarded on a bid basis usually determined by which bank offers the highest interest rate, can be quite profitable for a bank and are the subject of competition.

The bank foreclosed on its $5 million mortgage in July 1986 after the partnership defaulted on its loan. Lindsay said he never paid off his promissory notes and the bank never sued him for the unpaid balance.

Gene Green, a stockbroker at Underwood Neuhaus, which put the limited-partnership deal together, said, "As I recall, the bank said it would just take the property" and not sue the limited partners. Green said he is "sure" that First City didn't get back all the money it loaned to the partnership. "The bank just let [the limited partners] walk."[4]

Lindsay bought his limited partnership through Underwood Neuhaus, which at that time was Harris County's financial adviser on bond issues. Underwood Neuhaus, whose municipal bond partner was one of Lindsay's best friends, was chosen on a non-bid basis on Lindsay's recommendation.

Asked about the conflicts of interest he had in the deal with Baylor doctors, First City and Underwood Neuhaus, Lindsay replied that he was unaware that DeBakey and other Baylor doctors were his partners; he said he didn't remember being aware that the partnership borrowed money from First City; and he said there was nothing wrong with his relationship to Underwood Neuhaus, since the stockbroker he used was not in the same department that the county dealt with. When first asked about using Underwood Neuhaus as his stockbroker when it was the county's financial adviser, Lindsay replied, "Shit, can't I buy stock from somebody."

Lindsay had now come full circle. The conflicts of interest he was engaged in were the same kinds of things that he had criticized Bob Eckels for. One difference, though: The two-year statute of limitations for criminal prosecution had long since run on Lindsay's wrongdoings.

The property that Lindsay and his partners bought has an interesting history. On June 11, 1982, it was sold by an affiliate of American General Corporation to Robert Corson's stepfather, William L. Garman, who was acting as a trustee for unknown beneficiaries, presumably Corson and his mother. American General is a giant insurance company

---

[4] *Houston Post*, February 16, 1990.

in Houston that was controlled for years by Gus Wortham, one of the original members of the Lamar Hotel Suite 8F group that included Walter Mischer. Among other business dealings together, American General and Mischer's company were partners in a giant residential development west of Houston called Cinco Ranch.

Four days after the first sale, Garman flipped the property to a man named Monzer Adeeb Hourani, acting as a trustee for unknown beneficiaries. It appeared that there was a gain of almost $400,000 for Garman: Hourani signed a promissory note to Garman for $1 million, while Garman had signed a note to American General for $612,000. (The difference between these two notes is only a guess as to the profit Garman made in four days. It is not known what amounts, if any, were the cash downpayments in the sales.) Hourani also said that when he bought the property from Corson's stepfather, Garman, that he dealt exclusively with American General and did not know who Garman was, even though he signed a deed of trust to Garman.

Hourani is a wealthy investor from Lebanon, who keeps a very low profile in Houston. He married a Mormon woman from Utah and joined the Mormon Church. Hourani is close to U.S. Senator Orrin Hatch (Republican-Utah) and also, reportedly, to U.S. Senator Jesse Helms (Republican-North Carolina). He said he is "friends" with the two senators—"very clean," he termed the relationships.

However, documents turned up in the BCCI investigation showed that Hatch wrote a July 31, 1986, letter to the Office of the Director of the Federal Savings and Loan Insurance Corporation, leaning on them not to pursue legal action against Hourani regarding his deals with our old friend Mainland Savings (more about this to come). Hatch also apparently tried to arrange a loan from BCCI to Hourani, and at one time wanted to make Hourani the trustee of his blind trust.

A former employee of Hourani said that he is in constant communication with former Houston mayor Louie Welch, who served as the go-between for Hourani and the downtown Houston business establishment, including Mischer. Hourani said Welch is a "consultant" for him.

Hourani's former employee also said that Hourani would brag about his "intelligence" connections. A former high-ranking officer at Lamar Savings in Austin, where Hourani did business, said that Hourani claimed to have ties to the Mossad, Israel's intelligence agency. Hourani denied having any relationship to the CIA or any other intelligence agency.

Hourani's Houston offices are located in the building where the DGI offices of Corson's associate, Mike Adkinson, were located before Adkinson moved to Mel Powers's Arena Tower. And one of Hourani's companies is named the DI Group. But Hourani denied having any connections to Adkinson and denied being involved in any gun deals to the Middle East.

In May 1983, about a year after he purchased his residential development property, Hourani divided it in two and deeded both tracts to a partnership that included a Hourani company. In October, this partnership carved a 1.42-acre tract out of one of the halves and sold it to Robert Corson, acting as a trustee. Corson borrowed $350,000 from Allied Champions Bank, an affiliate of Mischer's Allied Bank, to buy the land and then built a strip shopping center on it. Hourani said he only met Corson one or two times. He said he couldn't believe that Corson worked for the CIA. "He looks like a country bum," Hourani said.

When a *Houston Post* story about this land deal was published in 1990, Hourani called me and threatened to file a $10 million libel suit. He said his attorney, Bob Brill of Brill & Brooks, was preparing the suit as we spoke. When told that Brill was also an attorney for Corson, Hourani denied knowing that. After he was asked questions about his connections to the CIA, Adkinson, gun deals to the Middle East, Hatch, Helms, Welch, and loans from Mainland Savings, Hourani said he was going to forget about the lawsuit.

(Between March 1987 and April 1988, the Brill & Brooks attorneys, along with business associates of Hourani, including Louie Welch, contributed more than $17,000 to Senator Hatch's campaign war chest.)

More than 18 months later, when Hourani had been drawn into the BCCI scandal, NBC News producer Mark Hosenball reported in the *New Republic* that Hourani told him he and a BCCI shareholder named Mohammed Hammoud "over several years worked with their mutual friend, Senator Hatch, on various private schemes to free U.S. hostages held by terrorists in Lebanon."

Meanwhile, less than a month after Corson bought his land from Hourani in 1983, a Hourani partnership sold the adjacent tract to Lindsay's partnership. There were denials all around, of course. Hourani denied knowing that Lindsay was part of the partnership (although he knew DeBakey was), and Lindsay denied knowing that Corson owned the adjacent tract of land.

The first direct public connection between Corson and Lindsay appeared on March 5, 1985, when Corson contributed $100 to Lindsay's campaign fund. Corson's mother, B.J. Garman, also contributed $100. On April 24, Lindsay wrote a general letter of recommendation on his Harris County stationery for Corson, which stated:

"To whom it may concern:

"Robert Corson is a person well known to me to be of the highest character. I have been personally acquainted with him for many years and know he enjoys an excellent reputation as a good family man and businessman. He is a native Houstonian and takes an active interest in his community.

"Mr. Corson has my unreserved recommendation as a person who will be diligent in any endeavor he pursues. Thank you.

"Sincerely, Jon Lindsay, County Judge."

Corson then used this letter of recommendation in his efforts to buy Kleberg County Savings Association in Kingsville and to get state and federal regulatory approval for the purchase. In a May 30, 1985, letter to Nelson Sharpe, the chairman of Kleberg County Savings, Corson stated that he was "enclosing recommendations from banks and other companies that I have dealt with over a period of years." One of the seven letters of recommendation was Lindsay's. His was the only letter from a public official.

In July 1985, Corson signed a stock purchase agreement with the shareholders of Kleberg County Savings to buy all of the outstanding stock of the association for $5.5 million. Then in September he filed a change-of-control application for the S&L with the Texas Savings and Loan Department and with the Federal Home Loan Bank Board. On December 23, the feds gave their approval to Corson's purchase and then "approval was received from the Texas Savings and Loan Commission on or about January 16, 1986," according to a lawsuit Corson later filed against the former owners.

The approval from the Texas S&L Commission was received one day after Corson made a $10,000 contribution to Lindsay's re-election campaign. This was the largest single campaign contribution from an individual that Lindsay had ever received.

(The only other campaign contributions Corson made in 1986 were $500 to U.S. Congressman Jack Fields (Republican-Texas), $2,000 to U.S. Congressman Jack Kemp (Republican-New York), $8,000 to Texas Republican gubernatorial candidate Bill Clements, and $500 to Jimmy

Hayes, a Louisiana congressman who is a close associate of Louisiana Governor Edwin Edwards.)

Lindsay said he doesn't remember Corson's $10,000 contribution. He acknowledged that it was a "rather large campaign contribution. But I think I've had other $10,000 contributions." (The only other $10,000 contribution Lindsay had received was listed as a contribution from Houston engineer James Dannenbaum and his wife.)

Then in September 1986, about two months before the County Judge's election, Corson hosted a party at his home for Lindsay. Lindsay's campaign records show a $600 contribution from Corson for the party, but Corson's own financial records show that he spent $3,209.60 on the party, including $1,500 paid to his wife, Randi Corson, for food, $549 for limousine service, $445.29 for liquor, $225 for valet service and $340.31 for the photographer. It would have been a violation of Texas election laws if Lindsay knew that Corson spent more than $3,000 on the party and then reported it as a $600 contribution. Lindsay claimed the receipts that Corson provided showed the party cost $600. "It was not that big a reception. There were only about 25 people there," Lindsay said.

In June 1986, after the $200 million Florida land deal with St. Joe Paper Co. was closed, Corson chartered a business jet and took Lindsay to Las Vegas to see a boxing match, charging this to his savings and loan. When asked if he had ever gone with Corson on any out-of-town trips, Lindsay said: "He was on, one time that we went on. I forgot who the host was—some title company, probably doing business with him at one time. I don't remember where we went." Asked if it was Las Vegas, Lindsay replied, "I don't think I've been to Vegas with him. I've been to Vegas a few times."[5]

When Lindsay was told that Corson charged his savings and loan to take him to Las Vegas to see some fights, Lindsay replied, "Well, I went with a . . . I went to that boxing match out there. I don't think it was with Corson. Well, maybe it was with Corson. Well, it could have been with Corson."[6] Lindsay denied that Corson had provided female companionship for him in Las Vegas. "That's a bunch of crap."

Lindsay conceded that he went on hunting trips to Mexico with Corson. And: "Maybe we went duck hunting around here a time of two," he added.

[5] *Houston Post*, February 11, 1990.
[6] Ibid.

When I first questioned him about his relationship with Corson, Lindsay denied being well acquainted with him. "Where is he at?" Lindsay asked. "Is he in jail yet?" When Lindsay was asked if he ever did any favors for Corson, he replied, "No. Hell no. We were just friends."[7]

Asked if he remembered writing the letter of recommendation for Corson in which he stated that Corson "is a person well known to me to be of the highest character. I have been personally acquainted with him for many years . . ." Lindsay replied, "No, I don't. Did I? I don't recall doing it. It could have happened. I do a lot of things like that for people I know."

In addition to recommending Corson as a person of the "highest character," Lindsay also wrote that Corson "enjoys an excellent reputation as a good family man . . ." In that regard, Corson's first wife, Paula Mischer, accused him in their 1977 divorce proceedings of beating her and smoking marijuana in front of their children. His second wife, Randi, who sued him for divorce in 1982, alleged that he beat her.

When he was asked about allegations of Corson's drug use, including cocaine, Lindsay replied, "No. Actually, I didn't know him that well. I had dinner with him a couple of times, and he introduced me to friends."

(When Mischer was asked about Corson's relationship to Lindsay, he replied, "I doubt very seriously if he ever really knew Lindsay well." Mischer said he got a call from Lindsay after a *Houston Post* story was published about the involvement of CIA operatives in failed savings and loans that mentioned Mischer's name in connection with Corson.)

Asked why Corson would contribute so much to his campaign, Lindsay replied, "Well, I guess he was trying to butter me up, think that I would be able to help him in some way. I thought he was a safe individual for campaign purposes because I didn't have any business affiliations with him. He was not an engineer or a contractor or anything like that."

There are several interesting points about that statement. First, Lindsay implies that there might be something wrong with his taking contributions from engineers and contractors. Second, Corson was a real estate developer, and thus very dependent on Commissioners Court for favorable decisions on roads and flood control. And, most impor-

---

[7] Ibid.

tant, Lindsay seems to have forgotten that he wrote a letter of recommendation some nine months earlier that Corson used to buy a savings and loan and get regulatory approval for it. In fact, final approval for his purchase came one day after Corson made his $10,000 donation to Lindsay.

Art Leiser, who was chief examiner for the Texas Savings and Loan Department at the time Corson got approval to buy his S&L, said he believes Lindsay's letter helped persuade the Texas Savings and Loan Commissioner, at that time L. Linton Bowman, to approve the sale to Corson.

Leiser also said that after Corson took over Vision Banc Savings, Leiser's examiners would get "veiled threats" from Corson's people when they went to Kingsville to check out the S&L. "They let it be known that they were good friends of Judge Jon Lindsay," Leiser said. When told this, Lindsay said, "I'm sorry I ever got to know that guy."

Corson's former chauffeur, Tom Sturdivant, told Houston private investigator P. M. Clinton, who worked for private investigator Clyde Wilson, that Corson claimed to have Lindsay in his back pocket. When Sturdivant wanted to return to his native Tennessee, Corson threatened him by saying that Judge Lindsay could have him put in jail if he talked about anything Corson was involved with, Sturdivant told Clinton. (Lindsay doesn't have the authority to jail anyone, but Sturdivant may not have known that.)

In addition to the letter of recommendation from Lindsay, Corson used six others in his quest for Vision. One was from Carl Stockholm, president of South Main Bank in Houston, who stated that he had "personally known and dealt with Robert Corson for approximately three years, both at South Main Bank and some dealings while president of Allied Champions Bank."

Another letter was from Ford Hubbard, Jr., who was president of Westside National Bank, where Corson and his mother were the largest stockholders. Hubbard stated: "It has been my pleasure to be associated with Mr. Robert Corson, both professionally and personally, for the past three years. Mr. Corson has always handled his financial affairs with us in a professional and timely manner. In my opinion, he is an outstanding businessman and will honor his commitments. Mr. Corson is a respected citizen with impecable (sic) character."

And there was a letter from S. H. Yager, Jr., executive vice president of General Homes, which stated that "General Homes Corporation has been doing business with Robert Corson for a period of approximately two years. During that time we have sold him roughly a dozen tracts of land worth approximately 60 to 70 million dollars."

To help shepherd his application for change in ownership of Kleberg County Savings through the regulatory process, Corson hired Alvis Vandygriff, the former Texas Savings and Loan Commissioner, the same one who did not object to Herman K. Beebe's renewed involvement in Texas S&Ls.

Vandygriff had stepped down as commissioner in 1983 and became counsel to the law firm of Phillips, King, Smith & Wright in Houston. The Phillips was Charles T. Phillips, who controlled First South Savings in Houston, a problem-plagued S&L that later failed. The King was Bill E. King, who controlled Columbia Savings and Caprock Savings, two fraud-riddled S&Ls that later failed. King also owned a title insurance company that he bought with a $20 million loan from San Jacinto Savings, brokered by Herman K. Beebe. The Smith was E. Ashley Smith, a Texas state representative.

Another member of the firm, David Blunk, said Vandygriff was sought out by many people wanting to enter the S&L business. "He [Vandygriff] received a call from Robert Corson, who indicated he wanted to acquire an S&L. A meeting was convened. Vandygriff and the firm were retained to represent Robert, and I was called in," Blunk said.

"It became known," Blunk continued, "that Corson was a former son-in-law of Walter Mischer. I heard him mention the name Walter Mischer—it came up one time in a fairly early meeting—that he [Corson] had not had to work very hard, that his former father-in-law was Walter Mischer, which helped ease his financial concerns."

A federal official said that during an investigation of Vision Banc Savings, Blunk stated that part of Corson's credibility, qualifications and assets was that he was Walter Mischer's former son-in-law, and that Corson made the representation that he had a close relationship with Mischer. "Blunk readily accepted that. He came back to it several times—this guy [Corson] was dear friends with Mischer and that was good enough for anyone in Houston," the federal official added.

(Blunk was placed on the board of directors at Vision Banc and at Westside National Bank. During his tenure on the board of both institutions, he was concurrently legal counsel for Albert Bel Fay, President Bush's political mentor and Mischer's good friend.)

After Corson obtained his stock purchase contract and received state and federal regulatory approval for the purchase, the next order of business was to get the $5.5 million to complete the deal. Like every other purchaser of a savings and loan in the go-go days, Corson borrowed the money from another financial institution. In this case, Corson turned to a big Houston bank he had used in previous land deals, MBank Houston.

On March 7, 1986, the day Corson bought Kleberg County Savings, he signed a $3.7 million promissory note to MBank. One week later he signed an additional note to MBank for $2.3 million. Collateral for the notes also included some promissory notes on land Corson had purchased south of Houston from General Homes. Corson then sold the property to a partnership including John Riddle.

The next year, when the notes were due and Corson was having financial difficulties, MBank refinanced the loans, adding another $2 million on top, secured by Corson's beachfront property in Florida. Federal investigators said that Mischer's Allied Bank took a large participation in the new loan.

MBank was not only used by Corson to finance some of his land deals, it was also the lead bank for General Homes, which signed a $316 million promissory note to MBank Houston on February 8, 1985. And, according to Herman K. Beebe's former partner, Dale Anderson, Beebe actually used MBank more often than Allied Bank to finance his deals.

MBank Houston was a wholly owned affiliate of MCorp, a Dallas-based bank holding company. MCorp was formed in October 1984 by the merger of Mercantile Bank in Dallas and Bank of the Southwest in Houston. Bank of the Southwest worked very closely with the law firm Fulbright & Jaworski, in the same way that First City National Bank was connected to Vinson & Elkins.

The same month that MCorp was formed, Bank of the Southwest gobbled up Capital National Bank in Houston in the largest bank merger in Texas history to that date. Capital National Bank had been formed in 1965 in Houston, and in 1969 joined a Swiss bank, Paravicini Bank, to start a new Swiss bank called Bank for Investment and Credit Berne.

The chairman of the new Swiss bank was J. F. Paravicini, the head of Paravicini Bank, while the vice chairman became L. F. McCollum, Sr., chairman of Capital National. Other investors in the new bank included Boeing in Seattle, Seagrams in Montreal, Minute Maid in Zurich (an affiliate of Coca-Cola), the London subsidiary of Brown &

Root and the Schlesinger Organization of London and Johannesburg. One of the directors of Capital National Bank was George Bush's close friend and trustee of his blind trust, William Stamps Farish III, then an officer with Underwood Neuhaus.

Another director of Capital National at the time the Swiss affiliate was formed was J. Hugh Liedtke, who was Bush's original partner in Zapata Petroleum back in the 1950s and later chairman of Pennzoil.

Shortly after the union of Capital National Bank and Paravicini Bank, Paravicini's owner was caught helping Billy Mellon Hitchcock (the oil heir, LSD freak and associate of Seymour Lazar) hide and launder some $67 million of Hitchcock's money, which included proceeds from the manufacture and sale of LSD.[8] Paravicini was also involved in fraudulent stock transactions with Hitchcock and was eventually forced to sell Paravicini Bank.[9] After Paravicini got into trouble with Hitchcock, Capital National Bank continued on in the Swiss bank, and Paravicini's travails were never mentioned in the Houston press.

After Corson bought Kleberg County Savings with MBank's money and changed its name to Vision Banc (the new logo was a peregrine falcon, the animal and symbol of choice for CIA types), he really began to live it up. That year he spent more than $250,000 on automobiles, including $120,000 for an Astin Martin; he bought a high-speed cigarette boat—the drug smugglers boat of choice—for $150,000; and he spent around $100,000 for thoroughbred racehorses. In addition, he rolled up more than $150,000 in gambling debts at Las Vegas casinos. His favorite casinos were Caesar's Palace and the Golden Nugget. Once, after he had frequented the Dunes casino, he got a call from the FBI, and decided thereafter to stay away from Morris Shenker's old gambling house.

Corson was reportedly paranoid about his security and was always carrying guns with him. He also had a special Mercedes stretch limousine, which he sent to Chicago to be armor-plated. Once one of his employees was found dead, floating in Corson's backyard swimming pool; Corson and his associates showed up at their office the next day toting guns. Corson told his employees the dead man was a Filipino gardener in his fifties who had a heart attack. The dead man was actually a Jamaican in his late thirties.

---

[8] *Acid Dreams: The CIA, LSD and the Sixties Rebellion,* by Martin A. Lee and Bruce Shlain (New York: Grove Press, 1985).
[9] Ibid.

During this time, Corson continued to make flights carrying money south of the border, according to law enforcement sources who have seen the federal records on the flights. And he also had a huge steel walk-in safe installed in his $1 million-plus house in west Houston. The man who installed the safe said he was instructed by Corson to do all his work at night in order to avoid observation, and to place mirrors in front of it. On one side of the safe were gun racks, on the other side were drawers from top to bottom, made to be just the right size to hold bearer bonds.

Although it was the St. Joe Paper Co. land deal that bankrupted Vision, there were other deals that helped sink the S&L. There were the government securities swaps that allegedly lost more than $3 million. There was the loan to Joe McDermott, Mischer's former employee and longtime business associate. There was the $7 million loan to Belgian American Investments and Trading Company to buy land in Dallas that was in the Clint Murchison, Jr., bankruptcy. There were the loans involving Robert Ferguson, who fronted for Corson in the purchase of one tract of the Florida land deal, and the strange stock loans to John Riddle for a Canadian company.

Riddle and Ferguson had something else in common. So before we continue to explore CIA connections to other S&L looters such as Herman K. Beebe and Mario Renda, let's consider the curious case of a fraternity at the University of Texas and its alumni, who were involved in the savings-and-loan debacle.

10

THE BOYS OF KAPPA SIGMA

The Mexicans advanced upon the Texans, who were holed up, surrounded and cut off. With their sombreros, bandannas, ponchos and long rifles, the Mexicans were a particularly fearsome bunch of cutthroats, looking to wreak mayhem on the freedom-seeking Texans. As they unleashed blood-curdling shrieks, from behind their lines came the sounds that meant no surrender and no prisoners.

At the Alamo in 1836? No, it was 130 years later during the annual re-creation of the Texas War of Independence on the campus of the University of Texas at Austin. Playing the Mexicans were members of the Kappa Sigma fraternity. Legend has it that one year during the traditional War of Independence re-creation, cannon fire from the celebration awoke a nameless Kappa Sig. In a hung-over stupor from the previous night's drunken brawl, he grabbed a white towel, leaned out the window and waved it around, yelling, "Me no Alamo." Thus began the tradition.

It was just like the Kappa Sigs to play the Mexican enemy. They were an I-don't-care, go-to-hell bunch—waspy wannabes, semi-thugs, frat rats and con men on the make, who drove Corvettes and tried to screw cheerleaders. Kappa Swigs, they were sometimes called. One of their favorite initiation tricks was to take the freshmen down to the whorehouses on the Mexican side of Laredo and Del Rio. (Of course, that could probably be said of every fraternity in the state of Texas.)

Some famous, influential Texans passed through Kappa Sigma, including noted Houston heart surgeon Dr. Denton Cooley, who was the fraternity's grand master of ceremonies in 1941. That same year, Frank Erwin was the grand treasurer.

Erwin would later be appointed by Governor John Connally as chairman of the Board of Regents of the University of Texas, where he reigned with an iron hand, fighting every reform movement and liberal professor as if they were the communist devil incarnate. Erwin was also a banking attorney whose expertise lay in getting his clients' bank charter applications approved by the Texas Banking Commission.

Erwin was close to Ben Barnes too, close enough to be called Barnes's "chief political strategist."[1] Barnes said it was Erwin who introduced him to Eagle Pass rancher Richmond Harper, the same man caught in the 1972 explosives scheme with Barry Seal and a Gambino associate.

Another infamous Kappa Sigma alumnus is oilman Nelson Bunker Hunt, the son of H. L. Hunt, who tried, and failed, to corner the silver market. Hunt dropped out of UT, but he did stay long enough to get his picture in the 1944 yearbook as a freshman pledge to Kappa Sigma. Forty-one years later, Oliver North and Spitz Channell were hitting him up for a big donation to the Contras. He contributed $237,500.

Former Houston City Councilman Jim Westmoreland, who was ousted by voters from office in 1990 for making a racist remark, was a Kappa Sigma at UT. After Congressman Mickey Leland was killed in an airplane crash in Africa, there was a move to rename a Houston airport after him. Westmoreland suggested to a reporter that Houston Intercontinental Airport be renamed "Nigger International." He later said he was just joking—ha, ha, ha, just like a Kappa Sig.

In the early 1980s, Westmoreland narrowly escaped indictment in the FBI's Brilab (bribery-labor) sting operation. Two Houston men were indicted and convicted for giving him a bribe in a sting operation that netted New Orleans Mafia boss Carlos Marcello. Westmoreland later said he didn't know it was a bribe—ha, ha, ha. (The attorney who pulled Westmoreland's chestnuts out of the fire was a Kappa Sigma brother, Tom McDade, then of Fulbright & Jaworski.)

Another well-known Kappa Sigma is Richard Rainwater, the Fort Worth dealmaker and leveraged buyout artist who cut his teeth in high finance with the Bass brothers. In 1965, Rainwater was the grand trea-

---

[1] *Shadow on the Alamo,* by Harvey Katz.

surer of Kappa Sigma. The grand master that year was Nick Krajl from Galveston.

Krajl has made a small fortune lobbying for pari-mutuel gambling in Texas and representing dog-racing interests who have been competing for pari-mutuel licenses in Texas. In October 1990, the *Houston Post* reported that Krajl had received at least $2.4 million from dog-racing interests. At one time Krajl was an aide to Texas politician and Mischer minion Ben Barnes, and he operated the Quorum Club in Austin, a famous watering hole for politicos.

In 1965, when Krajl and Rainwater were running Kappa Sigma, there was a freshman pledge named George Aubin, from the tiny South Texas town of Stockdale, just 14 miles up the road from Walter Mischer's home town of Gillett. Aubin embraced Kappa Sigma and its *Weltanschauung* with all his body and soul. Twenty years later, the names of his companies showed the measure of his devotion: Kappa Properties, Inc., Kappa Development Company, Sigma Capital Corporation and Sigma Realty Corporation.

It is difficult to know where to begin in describing Aubin's shenanigans since he left the Kappa Sigma womb.

Within five years, he was up to his eyeballs in the Texas rent-a-bank scandal. During the early and mid-1970s, Aubin was a co-owner of 12 small Texas banks that were part of a circle of more than 20 such banks whose control was swapped around among the same groups and which made loans to each other. Aubin's main partner was Bill Haley, an uncle of one of his Kappa Sigma brothers, Walter Beard.

It was during this period that Aubin met up with Herman K. Beebe, another prime player in the rent-a-bank scandal. Aubin said a Houston banker, whose name he couldn't recall, introduced him to Beebe. By 1975, Aubin and his longtime childhood friend from Stockdale, Jarrett Woods, had borrowed $30,000 from Beebe. In his 1979 personal bankruptcy filing, Aubin declared a $25,000 debt to Beebe.

In a 1988 interview, Aubin said it had been ten years since he had anything to do with Beebe, and since that time, he said, he had only seen the man in passing. However, Dale Anderson, who joined Beebe's empire in 1975, said Aubin and Beebe may not have done much business directly with each other, but Aubin was "always hanging around" Beebe's entourage.

Aubin also knew who the power in Louisiana was. When he sent one of his employees to Louisiana to try to drum up some mobile home loan business, he told the employee that first he had to go to New Orleans and "check in with Carlos," referring to Marcello.

While his Kappa Sigma mate Krajl was pursuing dog racing, Aubin was making a name for himself in horse-racing circles. In 1985, he paid a near-record $5.5 million for the racehorse Princess Rooney. His champion quarter horse, Brigand Silk, which he bought for about $50,000, won the big All-American Futurity race at Ruidoso Downs, New Mexico, one year and then died mysteriously. Aubin collected approximately $6 million in insurance and later filed a slander suit against KPRC-TV (Ch. 2), the NBC affiliate in Houston, for a story it did on the horse's death.

In 1984, Aubin bought the 567-acre Murty horse farm near Lexington, Kentucky, next to the famous Calumet Farm. According to a $120 million lawsuit filed against Aubin in 1990 by Sunbelt Savings, Aubin fraudulently used $14.2 million of a loan from Western Savings in Dallas, owned by his old buddy Jarrett Woods, to buy the farm.

Aubin had earlier dodged a $48 million bullet fired at him by E. F. Hutton. By wild, speculative trading in U.S. Treasury notes, options and commodities, Aubin had run up a $48 million deficit at Hutton.[2] To try to cover his losses, Aubin wrote more than $46 million in worthless checks at—where else?—Western Savings. A federal judge in Houston awarded E. F. Hutton $48 million in damages from an Aubin-related company, but did not hold Aubin personally liable for the debt. The judge chided Hutton: "That Aubin was an obfuscating liar is no excuse not to examine corporate records before assuming an obligation."

The corporate records the judge was talking about were those of a shell company that had guaranteed Aubin's debt. Its assets, and the assets Hutton would have to look to in repayment of Aubin's $48 million, were two worthless Texas savings and loans: Mercury Savings in Wichita Falls and Ben Milam Savings in Cameron.

These two S&Ls were bought in 1983 by Aubin's partner, J. B. Haralson, but everyone, including federal regulators, E. F. Hutton and anybody else familiar with the situation knew that Haralson was fronting for Aubin, who had been hired as a $15,000-per-month consultant. Aubin needed a front man because he had been banned from the industry after the rent-a-bank scandal.

The two savings and loans were operated out of Aubin and Haral-

---

[2] *Burning Down the House,* by James Sterngold (New York: Summit Books, 1990).

son's office on Richmond Avenue in Houston. One reason Aubin borrowed from Western Savings to buy the horse farm in Kentucky was that he had been forbidden from borrowing any more money from Haralson's savings and loans. The two institutions were closed down by the feds in 1986 at a cost to the taxpayers of more than $70 million.

Haralson was one of Aubin's partners during the rent-a-bank scandal, as was Jarrett Woods, but only as minor investors. Before that, in the late 1960s, Haralson was a partner with B. G. Wylie and Wylie's half-brother, W. Carroll Kelly, Jr., and others, in the purchase of Brazosport Savings and Loan from Lloyd Bentsen, who entered the Senate several years later.

Haralson took over as president of Brazosport Savings, but Wylie, as majority stockholder, eventually let him go, according to Wylie, because of certain improprieties.

Wylie, a blunt-talking good old boy, was a partner with Richmond Harper in a meat-packing plant in Eagle Pass that was the beneficiary of the largess of Ben Barnes and Herman K. Beebe. Wylie said that Houstonian Charles Hurwitz, who would gain notoriety in the mid-1980s as one of Michael Milken's leveraged buy-out buddies, introduced him to Beebe.

(Haralson claimed he only met Beebe "one time," and had never done any business with him. When told this, Dale Anderson, Beebe's former right-hand man, laughed and said that they handled the insurance policy for Haralson's wife.)

Carroll Kelly, Wylie's half-brother, was the same savings and loan executive who told state regulators that he was Beebe's man in Texas. Ben Barnes, who went to law school at UT with Kelly, first introduced Kelly to Beebe. Kelly was also a Kappa Sigma.

In the early 1970s, Kelly bought Haralson's and Wylie's stock in Brazosport Savings and then consolidated it with several other Texas S&Ls that he purchased with financing from Beebe. A stockholder in one of those S&Ls in the Texas panhandle was Billy Clayton, a former speaker of the Texas House of Representatives who got indicted in the FBI's Brilab sting operation and then was acquitted after the FBI made a crucial mistake in tracking the cash allegedly given to Clayton.

Kelly, along with his minority partner, B. G. Wylie's son David, renamed the consolidated savings and loan Continental Savings, and then got a loan on its stock at Walter Mischer's Allied Bank, with a guarantee from Beebe. This raises the question of whether any of

Beebe's money ended up in the pockets of Brazosport's original owner, Lloyd Bentsen. During the 1988 presidential campaign, Bentsen told the *Houston Post* that he didn't know what happened to Brazosport Savings after he sold it. "If Beebe was financing Kelly, we had no knowledge of it," Jack DeVore, Bentsen's spokesman, told the *Post*.

After Continental Savings started going downhill, the Allied Bank loan was transferred to San Jacinto Savings in Houston, owned by Southmark. When Continental failed in 1988, San Jacinto got stuck with the $17 million bad loan. Then when San Jacinto failed itself the next year, the taxpayers got stuck with it.

A big borrower at Continental Savings was one of Kelly's Kappa Sigma brothers, Harry Blake Terry, who was used by Kelly and Beebe as a front man and straw borrower from Continental. Terry borrowed $19 million from Continental to purchase several hundred acres of land surrounding a polo ground in San Antonio that Beebe wanted to develop as a pari-mutuel horse-racing track.

But the plan fell apart when Beebe's bank, Bossier Bank & Trust, which had the loan on the polo ground itself, failed in the summer of 1986. Before that happened, Continental was having trouble keeping Terry's $19 million loan from going into default. So it had one of its other borrowers, Robert Corson's associate Mike Adkinson, transfer $1 million to Terry from a Continental loan Adkinson got.

(Terry was also one of the purchasers, with B. G. Wylie and Carroll Kelly, of Brazosport Savings from Lloyd Bentsen.)

Kelly's character as a Kappa Sigma is demonstrated by the following:

One day, Kelly was out eating in a Houston restaurant with his partner in Continental Savings, David Wylie, along with Wylie's wife and her sister. After the meal, Kelly lighted up a cigarette. As he took a deep drag, one of the sisters chided him for this and told him it was ruining his health. Kelly denied it, and a fierce argument ensued, the sister claiming that she was in better physical condition than Kelly.

The two ended up challenging each other to a contest to see who was in better shape. They finally decided to have a mile race. To make it interesting, they bet each other $1,000; Wylie and his wife placed their bets on the sister.

The entire party left the restaurant to find a place where the two could race. They located a deserted road and measured off a mile. The cars were parked at the end of a mile and they flashed their headlights to start the race. The sister pulled out in front, and by the time they were 100 yards from the finish it was obvious she would win. Kelly suddenly grabbed his chest, fell to the ground moaning and groaning and flopping around. He was having a heart attack and needed help, he yelled in apparent pain. The sister stopped and came back to assist him. As she bent over him, he jumped up, grabbed her, threw her into the nearby bar ditch, and ran on ahead, winning the race.

As she walked slowly back to the car, Kelly demanded that she pay him the $1,000. She refused and he became loud and belligerent and accused her of welshing on the bet.

Kappa Sigma. *Semper fidelis.*

This is a man whom the state and federal regulatory authorities allowed to be in charge of more than $300 million of taxpayer-guaranteed deposits at Continental Savings.

(The two women in the story are sisters of Joseph P. DeLorenzo, who sold Navarro Savings and Loan in East Texas to Kelly and Wylie with financing from Beebe. DeLorenzo went to jail in 1977 for fraud he committed at Central National Bank in Houston, which had lent some money to Kelly when he was buying out purchasers of Brazosport Savings from Lloyd Bentsen. DeLorenzo, the president of Central National Bank in the mid-1970s, was convicted for misapplying almost $2 million in bank funds. The money was lent to two professional football players and then funneled to Saratoga Development Corp. in San Diego. Saratoga's co-owner was Allen R. Glick, who as a front for the mob borrowed more than $100 million from the Teamsters Union pension fund to buy two Las Vegas casinos. Glick was booted out by Nevada gaming authorities after they discovered that the mob was skimming about $12 million a year from his casinos. Glick was also doing business at the time with Beebe's partner, Lance Alworth, a former San Diego football player.)

In 1956, the year before Carroll Kelly joined Kappa Sigma as a freshman pledge, the grand master of the fraternity was Joe Russo from Houston. Russo went on to become a Houston businessman, noted for development of the Lyric Center office building downtown, one-time minority ownership of United Press International, and ownership of the Houstonian Hotel and Conference Center on the West Side, President Bush's much-criticized legal residency.

Houston Post gossip columnist Betsy Parish once ran an item on Bush and Russo, saying that Russo was waiting at the Houstonian to

greet Bush when he arrived for the economic summit in July 1990.
"Donning his elephant-emblazoned Hermés tie for the occasion, Joe
[Russo] waited on the front steps to welcome his old chum, the President. When Bush exited the limo, they both immediately smiled in
recognition. They both were wearing the 'same' cravat. Talk about your
close ties."

Russo is also a personal friend of Senator Lloyd Bentsen. "Joe's a
fellow that puts things together. He is a gutsy, gutsy man, a fast learner
with a high degree of enthusiasm," Bentsen told the *Houston Post*.[3]

Asked to characterize his relationship to George Bush, Russo replied, "Oh God! I'd say to you the relationship would be just like any
other American—that we're very proud to have a man like George Bush
be our president, who's from our community. But I have no relationship
that's very unique, except he lives here at the Houstonian, and we
happen to manage the Houstonian for a partnership that is owned by
a group of investors."

Further asked to characterize his relationship to Lloyd Bentsen,
Russo said, "Same way. I mean, just glad to have a Texan like that on
the team. But I have no relationship with him, just like the president; it
would be the same."

One of the few times that I saw Walter Mischer in a public political
gathering was at the Houstonian at an election-night party of a Houston
City Council candidate whom he and Russo were backing against Kathy
Whitmire's favored candidate. The Mischer-Russo candidate lost. That
same night, Mischer's lieutenant, Jim Box, appeared at Whitmire's
victory party to offer his congratulations, along with the women, blacks
and gays who had sealed Whitmire's triumph.

Russo ran into financial problems in the late 1980s and filed for
bankruptcy, coming in for criticism for transferring assets to his children, including his stake in the Houstonian.

Russo also owned a savings and loan in Houston, called Ameriway
Savings, which failed in May 1990, just two months before President
Bush was seen greeting him warmly at the Houstonian. The Resolution
Trust Corporation, set up to dispose of the assets of failed S&Ls,
assumed $137 million of its assets. Savings and loan regulators who
examined Ameriway filed two criminal referrals on Russo to the Department of Justice. This means that the regulators believed that Russo may

---

[3] *Houston Post*, November 25, 1987.

have committed crimes at his S&L. But nothing ever came of these criminal referrals.

Russo said he didn't know about the criminal referrals. "But let me say this," he added, "I assume that there are probably many, many of those filed on any group that failed, from banks to thrifts to borrowers. But that wouldn't surprise me." Then, asked if he had ever been interviewed by the FBI or appeared before a grand jury, Russo replied, "No. No. Does that give you some help, I hope?"

In 1990, Russo tried to buy a piece of property near the Houstonian from the Resolution Trust Corp., which is supposed to have a policy prohibiting it from selling foreclosed real estate to anyone who had been involved in a failed S&L. After a story about this was published in the *Houston Post*, Russo dropped his attempt to purchase the property.

Russo and his affiliated entities also borrowed tens of millions of dollars from five exceedingly dirty Texas S&Ls: Lamar, Sunbelt, First South, Champions and San Jacinto. When Russo was asked in 1992 how much he and his affiliated companies had borrowed from failed savings and loans, he replied, "Gee, I have no idea. I really don't. That was so many years ago I have no idea what it would be."

Joe Russo and Carroll Kelly may have controlled more federally insured S&L deposits than any other of their fraternity brothers, but none of them, perhaps no one else in the country, borrowed more, and paid back less, from fraud-riddled S&Ls than Kappa Sigma John Riddle.

Riddle, who was grand scribe of Kappa Sigma in 1971, was two years behind his idol there. Some college boys want to be the President of the United States, some others want to be the National League batting champion, a few might even want to be the Pope. John Riddle wanted to be like George Aubin. And he just might have exceeded his master and mentor.

Riddle earned a law degree after graduating from UT and started out working for David Bolton, a real estate appraiser in Houston. But before too long he went into law practice with Wade Kilpatrick and Victor J. Rogers II. Kilpatrick, a Kappa Sigma brother, was grand master of the fraternity in 1970. Rogers is the scion of the Rogers family from Beaumont, who will be discussed in a following chapter. (Rogers attended UT at the same time as Riddle and Kilpatrick, but was a little too aristocratic for Kappa Sigma.)

Riddle, Kilpatrick and Rogers also owned a title insurance company together, Investors Title, which showed up in the middle of a number of dirty Texas S&L deals.

By the mid-1980s, the law firm had essentially split up and Riddle was into real estate development in a big way. He was doing projects, mostly strip shopping centers and apartment complexes, in Florida, Texas, Arizona and California. He and his companies had borrowed more than $300 million from at least eight different savings and loans in five states. These loans included:

(1) More than $30 million from Kappa Sigma Carroll Kelly's Continental Savings. Some of these bad Riddle loans were later foisted upon Mike Adkinson in a classic cash-for-trash deal. This means the borrower gets the cash (loan) in exchange for taking some trash (bad loan or foreclosed real estate) off the S&L's books.

(2) Some $30 million to $40 million from Sunrise Savings in Boynton Beach, Florida, where then-Vice President Bush personally interfered in the federal regulatory process. (This will be described in a later chapter on Sunrise.)

(3) More than $30 million from Peoples Heritage Federal Savings and Loan in Salina, Kansas.

(4) Some $40 million to $50 million from Vernon Savings. In possible exchange for these loans, a Riddle-controlled bank in Houston, Texas National Bank-Westheimer, purchased $9 million in loans from Vernon. These loans, which amounted to about 35 percent of Texas National Bank-Westheimer's total assets, went bad and led to the failure of the bank.

(The president of Riddle's Texas National Bank-Post Oak was Riddle's Kappa Sigma brother Walter Beard.)

(5) More than $2 million from Mercury and Ben Milam Savings, controlled by Kappa Sig George Aubin.

(6) Some $5 million from Liberty Savings in Leesville, Louisiana, controlled by San Antonio developer and former UT athlete James Hague.

(7) And, finally, a whopping $195 million from Western Savings in Dallas, controlled by Aubin's childhood friend Jarrett Woods. One of these loans was for the purchase by Riddle from James Hague of some property around Austin that was partly based on the appraisal of a building that didn't even exist.

(The actual total amount of money lent to Riddle and his companies may be less than the total listed above because some of the Western loans may have bought out or wrapped around some of the loans from Vernon, Continental and Peoples Heritage.)

In 1990, Sunbelt Savings, which took over Western Savings, was awarded $284 million in damages in a federal lawsuit against Riddle and his partner, Richard E. Dover, for defrauding Western Savings. Riddle had already filed for bankruptcy, though. He owed the federal receivers for all the failed banks and savings and loans so much money that he merely showed it on his bankruptcy filing as $1.

Riddle's bankruptcy papers also showed a debt of $22,500 to M&R Investment, which was Morris Shenker's company that owned the Dunes Hotel and Casino in Las Vegas.

Richard Dover was convicted for income-tax fraud in federal court in Houston in 1990. But as of the writing of this book, Riddle, like his Kappa Sigma idol, Aubin, has escaped criminal indictment. One federal regulator refers to Riddle as the "teflon John."

In one case, Riddle was found in the middle of a Ponzi-like scheme involving savings and loans in Illinois, Mississippi, Louisiana and Kansas that resulted in the indictment of several S&L officers in Illinois. A federal regulator familiar with the case said that Illinois federal prosecutors were ready to indict Riddle when their counterparts in Dallas contacted them and asked them, for reasons unknown, not to do so.

One business partner and friend of Riddle who has been indicted is Robert Corson, the CIA mule. Riddle and Corson did a number of business deals together, including the purchase of 1,312 acres west of Houston next to Cinco Ranch, the 5,416-acre development acquired in 1984 by Walter Mischer's company and American General Insurance Company from Josephine Abercrombie and Robert Mosbacher, Secretary of Commerce in the Bush Administration and later Bush campaign chairman.

Riddle also had an airline company, First Western Aviation. Federal Aviation Administration records show only one plane was ever registered to this company, a twin-engine Beech with tail registration number N85CC. This plane was registered to Riddle in 1984, and then in 1985 he transferred its registration to First Western Aviation. Federal law enforcement sources who have seen the records said that Corson took some of his money-laundering trips to Latin America in N85CC.

Former Israeli intelligence officer Ari Ben-Menashe has alleged that First Western Aviation was used as a cutout by the Israelis and the CIA to transport American arms to the Middle East. One of Corson's former partners said he got the impression that Riddle was just fronting First Western Aviation for Walter Mischer.

First Western Aviation obtained bank financing from UnitedBank-Houston,[4] which was controlled by Vincent Kickerillo, a very close and longtime business associate and friend of Walter Mischer's.

"I know him," was all Mischer said when asked about Riddle.

Another Kappa Sigma brother of Riddle and Kilpatrick was Steve Adger, whose brother John was a partner with Corson and Roy Dailey in the early 1970s in a real estate company called Adger, Corson and Dailey. John Adger testified in Dailey's fraud trial in 1990 that he took $300,000 in cash to Dailey as a kickback for a loan to a Dailey associate from Dailey's First Savings of East Texas.

There were several other Kappa Sigmas in Corson's operations. One was the previously mentioned Robert Ferguson, who was a member of the fraternity at the same time with George Aubin and Walter Beard. Ferguson was a straw borrower for Corson on a small tract of land in the Florida panhandle that was part of the $200 million, 21,000-acre purchase by Mike Adkinson from St. Joe Paper Co. Ferguson got $98,000 for fronting the deal and then letting the property go into foreclosure.[5]

Ferguson also received a home loan from Corson's savings and loan. Corson's S&L then forced Ferguson's estranged wife out by foreclosing on the loan. It subsequently let Ferguson rent the house for a nominal sum, according to several law enforcement officers and Lesley Ferguson, his estranged wife.

Another Kappa Sigma in business with Corson was Ford Hubbard, Jr., a fraternity member back in the early 1950s. Hubbard was president of Westside National Bank, whose controlling stock was owned by Corson and his mother. Hubbard wrote a letter of recommendation on Westside National Bank stationery for Corson when he was trying to acquire a savings and loan in 1985. (Riddle listed a debt of $293,360 to Westside in his bankruptcy filing.)

---

[4] Financing Statement on file with the Texas Secretary of State, November 20, 1985, #334051.

[5] In the matter of the marriage of Lesley Ferguson and Robert B. Ferguson. Deposition of Robert B. Ferguson, June 2, 1987, Fort Bend County District Court, No. 53,674.

When a group of about 30 savings and loan executives from across Texas met secretly in Houston in June 1985 to discuss ways to foil federal regulators and allow them to continue to make deals even as they were insolvent and headed for massive taxpayer bailouts, they were called together by Kappa Sigma Carroll Kelly. Kappa Sig Joe Russo also attended the meeting.

The June 11 meeting was called by Kelly and David Wylie in a May 22, 1985, letter written on Continental Savings stationery. The list of savings and loans represented at the meeting is a Who's Who of the biggest failed S&Ls in Texas, including Vernon Savings, Mainland Savings, Lamar Savings, Paris Savings, First South Savings, Western Savings, Continental Savings, State Savings of Lubbock, Ameriway Savings and Universal Savings.

Topics discussed at the meetings were: evasion of loan limits to one borrower; evasion of growth limits by the sale of participation between savings and loans and the use of front men and straw borrowers; removal of delinquent loans and foreclosed real estate from S&L books by selling them to other S&Ls (known in the industry as "trading a deal horse for a dead cow").

The letter from Kelly and Wylie stated that "as savings and loan association stockholders and/or managers, we have experienced a great deal of change in our industry and, as of late, most of the changes have been caused by regulators and their response to the Empire Savings failure." (Empire failed in early 1984 and, as previously discussed, was the first big S&L to fail in the nation.)

Wylie and Kelly, the letter continued, "have always recognized the need for cooperation among our fellow savings and loan competitors and now, more than ever, we need an accurate understanding of our competitors' lending philosophies.

"Consequently, we think it is important that we meet to discuss the future of our industry and anything we might do collectively to better posture our institutions in the present economic and regulatory environment.

"We would like very much for you to attend. However, if this is not possible, we think it mandatory that a high-level executive from your organization serve as your substitute."

Leonard Thomas of Colonial Savings in Kansas, the only S&L outside Texas represented, said that he thought the meeting was a "secret meeting. I'm surprised someone found out about it," Thomas told me when a story on the meeting was being prepared for the *Houston Post*.[6]

Having a secret meeting to plan naughty things was nothing new, of course, to the boys of Kappa Sigma who called and attended the meeting.

Finally, consider the person who headed the fraternity in 1972. A small, quiet, shy boy, who probably never ever got drunk and chased women, he didn't fit the stereotype for Kappa Sigma. In fact, if anyone was the opposite of George Aubin, it was he. Yet there he was, Walter M. Mischer, Jr., who was probably admitted into Kappa Sigma and elevated to the top simply on the basis of who his father was.

Asked about all the numerous and curious connections of Kappa Sigmas to the S&L debacle, Walt Mischer, Jr., just laughed and said there was nothing to it—ha, ha, ha.

Now, with the Kappa Sigma boys in place, taking their roles in the S&L debacle alongside the Mafia, we consider again the question of CIA involvement. We know about Corson and Mischer, but what about the Mafia-connected Typhoid Marys of the S&L industry: What about Mario Renda and Herman K. Beebe?

---

[6] *Houston Post*, February 12, 1989.

11

H.K. AND THE CIA

There was something more to Herman K. Beebe than just the drinking, the skirt chasing, the business wheeling and dealing, the La Costa hangout, the Teamsters, Carlos Marcello and the Mafia.

There were the helicopters for the CIA agent in Guatemala who was training Contras in Belize; there was Gilbert Dozier, the former Louisiana agriculture commissioner serving time for extortion and bribery, who was going to turn state's evidence against Beebe until President Reagan pardoned him at the request of CIA Director William Casey;[1] there was Beebe's financing the establishment of Palmer National Bank in Washington, D.C., which was helping funnel money to the Contras three blocks from the White House; and there was E. Trine Starnes, Jr., one of the biggest borrowers at Beebe-controlled S&Ls and one of the biggest private donors to the Contras.

But first there was Barry Seal and the C-4 explosives in a Shreveport warehouse destined for anti-Castro Cubans in Mexico.

Adler Berriman "Barry" Seal—"El Gordo"—the fat man, also known as "Thunder Thighs," was from Baton Rouge, Louisiana. Called the world's greatest pilot, he was at least the youngest ever to captain a Boeing 747, at the age of twenty-six. But several years later he turned to the Dark Side of the Force: He was caught dealing with Mafia

---

[1] Dan Moldea reported in *Dark Victory* that a Casey partner in a company called Multiponics was Carl Biehl, an associate of the Marcello New Orleans Mafia family.

associates and CIA operatives in one of the most bizarre and inexplicable criminal cases on record.

It went down this way:

On July 1, 1972, Seal was taking some sick leave from his job as a captain flying 707s and 747s out of New York to Europe for Trans World Airlines. As he walked out of his motel room near the New Orleans International Airport, he was arrested by federal agents and charged with violating the Mutual Security Act of 1954, which prohibited the exportation of weapons without the permission of the U.S. State Department.

Also involved in the plot and arrested that day were eight other individuals in Shreveport, Louisiana, New Orleans and Eagle Pass, Texas. A DC-4 that Seal had recently purchased in Miami was seized at the Shreveport Regional Airport. On board were 13,500 pounds of C-4 explosives, 7,000 feet of explosive primer cord, 2,600 electric blasting caps and 25 electrical detonators. The explosives, according to the U.S. Attorney's Office in Louisiana, were destined for Cuban exiles in Mexico, who were going to use them in an effort to overthrow the government of Fidel Castro.

Arrested in New Orleans along with Seal was a man from Brooklyn, New York, named Murray Morris Kessler. Kessler was the key middle man in the deal. He was the one who agreed to sell the explosives to the Cubans and then arranged for the transportation.

Kessler, who had six previous criminal convictions and was awaiting trial in New York on income-tax fraud when he was arrested, was well known to the Brooklyn Organized Crime Strike Force. He was a friend and business associate of Emmanuel "Mannie" Gambino, a member of the Gambino Mafia crime family and nephew of Carlo Gambino, the boss of the Gambino family.

Kessler and Mannie Gambino were partners in Neptune's Nuggets, a Long Island frozen stuffed-seafood packaging firm that had been criticized in *Newsday* articles for having a product that was extremely low in seafood and extremely high in bacteria. About a month before Kessler was arrested in the explosives scheme, Mannie Gambino dropped out of sight. Gambino, reported by Jonathan Kwitny in *Vicious Circles* to be a loan shark, had been murdered.

The man who brought Kessler into the scheme was just as interesting as the mob associate from Brooklyn. He was Richmond C. Harper, a millionaire banker and meat-packing plant owner from Eagle Pass,

Texas, a small town on the Rio Grande between Laredo and Del Rio. After he was charged in the conspiracy, Harper told reporters, "I do know Murray Kessler. He is a friend of mine. And I have loaned him my airplane occasionally when he is down in this part of the world. I don't know what business he is in. To be truthful, I really don't."

In a statement Seal made after the trial, he said that the "request for arms and ammunition was brought across the border to a rancher/banker by the name of Mr. Richmond Harper in Eagle Pass, Texas, who had very deep ties right into the White House." One of those people in Washington close to Harper was Myles J. Ambrose, the U.S. Customs Commissioner, who at that time was also in charge of the Federal Narcotics Bureau, the predecessor of the Drug Enforcement Administration. Ambrose would come to visit Harper and go hunting with him on his ranch in Mexico, according to a former Customs official under Ambrose: "We tried to warn him [Ambrose]. Tell him that this guy [Harper] is bad. He wouldn't listen." Ambrose's visits to Harper were also discovered in 1976 by the House banking subcommittee investigating the Texas rent-a-bank scandal.

Ambrose resigned his position in November 1972, apparently after learning that Harper was going to be indicted in the case. Harper was indicted the next month.

(One of Ambrose's running buddies was Jack Caulfield, a White House undercover spy and aide to John Ehrlichman, and one of the conceptual fathers of Richard Nixon's White House Plumbers, the leak-pluggers who turned to perpetrating dirty campaign tricks.)

In addition to the scheme to sell explosives to anti-Castro Cubans, Harper had also been observed by Customs agents flying arms and ammunition to Shreveport, and earlier to Alexandria, Louisiana. It may be just a coincidence, but Herman K. Beebe moved from Alexandria to Shreveport in 1971.

In a written statement after the trial, Seal said that "Flores [one of the defendants] contacted Richmond Harper, who contacted alleged Mafia connections in New York, who contacted a representative of theirs in Louisiana, who contacted me, Adler B. Seal, for the contract for the flying."

This statement is important because it shows Seal—for the first time that I am aware of—admitting to a connection to the Mafia. Was it Beebe's doing?

The possibility that it was increases with three additional pieces of information. One, the warehouse where the explosives were stored in Shreveport was owned by Beebe, according to a private investigator and a Customs official who is familiar with the case. Two, with the help of Beebe's partner, Ben Barnes, Harper obtained a $1.9 million loan from Surety Savings in Houston—where Beebe was doing business and brokering deposits. And three, one of the principals of a helicopter company that Beebe financed was a longtime, childhood friend of Seal's.

Seal, Harper, Kessler and the other defendants were not brought to trial until the summer of 1974. The trial seemed to be proceeding in a normal fashion until the fifth day, when Seal's attorney requested a mistrial and the judge granted it.

It seems that the government prosecutors couldn't produce two key witnesses against the defendants. One, Jaime Fernandez, was involved in the explosives scheme when the government began its investigation and later became a government informant, according to prosecutors. Jimmy Tallant, the lead prosecutor from the Organized Crime Strike Force, told the judge that Fernandez was a co-conspirator until he went to Mexican authorities with the scheme. Tallant stated that he went to Mexico to try to get Fernandez to come to Louisiana to testify, but Fernandez refused.

The second witness, Francisco "Paco" Flores, was a defendant, but federal agents couldn't find him. The judge declared a mistrial and the charges were later dismissed by an appeals court. End of story, or so it seemed.

However, after the trial, Seal wrote out a four-page statement, apparently because he felt he was being unjustly harassed by the Customs Service in his subsequent travels into and out of the United States. In this statement, Seal spins a fantastic story about how the whole scheme was a government sting operation set up to ingratiate our government with Fidel Castro so that he would sign an anti-hijacking agreement. In the proposed agreement Castro would let American planes hijacked to Cuba return without having to pay stiff fines.

The Customs Service undercover agent who carried out the sting was Cesario Diosdado, according to Seal, who "through records I have obtained from a private investigative agency in Denver, Colorado, has been proved to have been an ex-CIA agent who worked in the Bay of Pigs invasion and had been working both sides of the fence in the Miami/Cuban area."

Diosdado testified in the trial that his investigation began with Jaime

Fernandez, but earlier stories indicated that Diosdado had either started the ball rolling or picked it up and ran with it, even traveling to New York to show Kessler some letters of credit with which to buy the explosives.

But much later, ten years after the trial, Seal changed his story about the purpose of the operation. In sworn testimony in a trial in Las Vegas in which he was a government witness, after he had turned informant, he testified that the explosives were for CIA-trained anti-Castro Cubans.[2]

Several law enforcement officials familiar with the case said that regardless of whether the scheme was a Customs sting or a CIA operation for or against Castro, the CIA pulled the plug on it during the middle of the trial. The agency did so because some of the key participants and witnesses worked for the CIA and it didn't want to compromise their identities as CIA assets.

Russell Welch, an officer with the Arkansas State Police who has spent years investigating Barry Seal, said the case was dismissed because "Seal and others were protected, because the informant was protected, the CIA didn't want to burn him."

Richard Gregorie, a former assistant U.S. Attorney in Miami, who used Seal as a drug informant in 1984, told Rodney Bowers of the *Arkansas Democrat* that the case was dismissed because of "government misconduct."

"Although Gregorie said he had no knowledge of prior undercover work," Rodney Bowers reported in December 1989, "he told the *Democrat* in a recent interview that the 1972 incident gave an 'indication' that Seal might have been involved in a government operation at that time."

After the charges were dismissed, Seal, who had been fired by TWA, began to work full-time as a CIA asset and a drug smuggler. His activities between the explosives case and his murder on the parking lot of a halfway house in Baton Rouge in February 1986—allegedly by associates of the Colombian Medellín drug cartel—have been well reported by journalists Kwitny, Bowers, John Cummings, John Camp and Jerry Bohnen, who revealed that:

After the explosives case was dismissed, Seal began working full-time for the CIA, traveling back and forth from the United States to Latin America. By 1977 he had turned to narcotics trafficking, and

---

[2] *Wall Street Journal*, April 22, 1987.

became one of the most proficient, if not THE most proficient, drug smuggler in this country. But in 1983 he was turned in by an informant in Florida, convicted and sentenced to a long jail term. Desperate, he tried to make a deal with the DEA to turn informant, but no one would listen to him until he spoke to George Bush's Vice Presidential Task Force on Drugs.

Seal told Bush's Task Force that the Sandinistas in Nicaragua were involved in drug smuggling. Even though there was not one shred of evidence for it, and still isn't, this "revelation" thrilled the task force to bits, and Seal was basically forced onto the DEA as an informant.

One of his first tasks was to catch the Sandinistas in the act. So he took his C-123K cargo plane to the CIA, which installed a hidden camera in it. Seals flew the wired plane to Nicaragua and allegedly took some pictures—he said the camera malfunctioned and he had to operate it by hand—of a purported Sandinista official loading cocaine onto the plane. The CIA and Oliver North decided to blow Seal's cover and use the pictures as anti-Sandinista propaganda. The story appeared in the Moonie paper, the *Washington Times*, and President Reagan displayed the picture on national television in an attempt to get Congress to restore aid to the Contras.

Several journalists later blew the story out of the water as a setup, and there has been no evidence before or since then that the Colombian cartels have transshipped narcotics through Nicaragua. There has been, however, much evidence that some Contras and their supporters were trafficking in drugs.

Meanwhile, Seal had been busy training Contras at his new base of operations in Mena, Arkansas. At least seven pilots have told reporters of Seal's work with the Contras. The last one to go public, Terry Reed, said he was introduced to Seal by Oliver North. Reed said that North wanted him to turn over a light plane he owned to North's Enterprise and then report it as stolen and collect the insurance. Reed declined to do so, but the plane was later stolen, and Reed collected on his insurance. The plane turned up in Seal's Contra resupply operation and Reed was charged with fraud.

After Reed began talking about Seal, North and the Contras, and subpoenaed North for his trial, the government, after going after Reed with everything it had, dropped the case against him— but not before requiring the local prosecutor to get a security clearance and requiring Reed not to comment on the case for 30 days afterwards.

The federal government also went after Bill Duncan, an agent with the Internal Revenue Service Criminal Investigation Division, who was investigating the flow of drug money through Barry Seal's operations. When Duncan was called to testify before the House Subcommittee on Crime regarding federal interference in Arkansas and Louisiana police investigations of Seal, he was ordered by one of his IRS superiors to perjure himself if he were asked questions about Seal's relationship to then-Attorney General Ed Meese and whether Meese had ordered evidence withheld from a federal grand jury investigating activities at Mena, Arkansas.

Duncan resigned over the matter, after 17 years with the IRS. He then went to work for the House Subcommittee on Crime in an investigation of Seal's operation, but eventually got stymied there as well. He was arrested when he took a gun inside a House office building, even though he was authorized to carry a weapon. The House subcommittee cut his travel funds, and once again he resigned in frustration.

Another investigator probing into Seal's operations was Gene Wheaton, the former Pentagon criminal investigator who went to work for the Christic Institute after parting company with Oliver North and Richard Secord. Wheaton said he tracked Seal's C-123K cargo plane flying from Mena to William Blakemore's Iron Mountain Ranch in West Texas. (There is also an Iron Mountain in Arkansas near Seal's Contra training grounds.)

Blakemore said he had no knowledge of this.

Seal's C-123K, which he called the Fat Lady, would go down in history after its "Fat Man" was murdered. This was the C-123K that was shot down in October 1986 by the Sandinistas as it was making a resupply run to the Contras. The resulting crash blew the lid off the White House's secret support of the Contras, as the plane and its occupants were tracked to the CIA-connected Southern Air Transport in Miami and to Oliver North.

While Wheaton was tracking Seal and other CIA assets, he ran into a helicopter company in Lafayette, Louisiana, called Commercial Helicopters. The president and majority stockholder was a timber man named Charles F. Haynes, Jr. The other principal in the company was Vaughn R. "Bobby" Ross, who started out as the pilot for the company's first helicopter. Ross, from Baton Rouge, was a longtime close friend of Barry Seal. "We grew up together," Ross said.

"It was the same crowd around Ed Wilson that introduced me to Bobby Ross," said Wheaton.

(Ed Wilson is the ex-CIA agent who is now in prison for selling more than 20 tons of C-4 explosives to Libya, among other felonies. Some of Wilson's closest associates were ex-CIA officials Thomas Clines and Theodore Shackley. In the late 1970s, Wilson put up $500,000 to front Clines to half-ownership of the Egypt American Transport Services, or EATSCO, which won the contract to transport billions of dollars' worth of American arms to Egypt under the Camp David Accords. Other silent partners, according to Wilson, included Shackley and Richard Secord.[3] The company was later convicted of overbilling the Pentagon for $8 million. In 1990, Clines was convicted of income-tax fraud involving payments received for arms shipments to the Contras. Clines had been brought in by Secord to handle arms procurement. Shackley left the CIA in 1979 after having Wilson hung around his neck like an albatross. "The Blond Ghost" had been deputy to the director of operations—the spy agency's covert action arm—under CIA director George Bush, and was even mentioned as a possible future candidate for CIA director. In 1984, Shackley participated in some meetings with Iranians regarding release of terrorist hostages that paved the way for the later arms-for-hostages deals.)

Commercial Helicopters was started by Haynes and Ross in 1979 with one helicopter to ferry supplies to offshore oil rigs. But it grew rapidly, and at its height boasted a fleet of 35 helicopters. But the company fell on hard times and filed for bankruptcy in the summer of 1984. At that time, it had 26 helicopters and left numerous creditors and financial institutions holding the bag for millions of dollars.[4]

Ross, however, landed on his feet. He was appointed to a top position in the Louisiana Department of Transportation by Governor Edwin Edwards. Commercial Helicopters had provided helicopter service for Edwards during his 1983 campaign to regain the Governor's Mansion, and claimed in an adversary proceeding in its bankruptcy case that Edwards owed it $85,351 for such services. The two "adversaries" eventually settled out of court for $17,000. But there was more to Commercial Helicopters than just offshore oil work and ferrying Edwards around Louisiana.

---

[3] *Manhunt*, by Peter Maas (New York: Random House, 1986).
[4] United States Bankruptcy Court, Middle District of Louisiana, Case #84-523.

Ross, while denying that the company ever did business with his childhood buddy, Barry Seal, or the CIA, volunteered: "We used to lease helicopters from Flying Tiger Airlines." This airline company was established by General Claire Chennault in the 1950s as a cargo company, and became one of the largest private cargo companies in the world. It was not a CIA proprietary, but it did work for the CIA. It took its name from the group of pilots organized by Chennault during World War II to fly supplies to Chiang Kai-shek's nationalist Chinese. This group formed the foundation for the CIA's proprietary airline, Civil Air Transport, a branch of which became the infamous Air America.

Commercial Helicopters also negotiated the sale of helicopters to Saudi Arabia for use as medical ambulances, and provided parts and services to a helicopter company in Guatemala. This company, Helicopteros de Guatemala, was run by Wheaton's buddy Carl Jenkins, the old CIA agent from Louisiana who was living in Guatemala and training Contras in Belize. At the time Commercial Helicopters filed for bankruptcy, it was holding for repair about $150,000 worth of helicopter parts belonging to Jenkins's company.

A letter filed with the bankruptcy court on April 11, 1985, from Gary Villiard, the general manager of Commercial Helicopters, states that on May 30, 1984, Jenkins and Ricardo Moratoya from Helicopteros de Guatemala instructed him to transport a helicopter owned by the company from New Orleans to Commercial Helicopters' facilities in Lafayette, and then to ship it to Guatemala along with an engine belonging to them. Villiard said in the letter that he complied.

Jenkins had other connections to the Ed Wilson/Tom Clines/Ted Shackley/Dick Secord group. As previously noted, he was Chi Chi Quintero's CIA case officer during the Bay of Pigs, after which Tom Clines became Quintero's case officer. (Shackley was Clines's boss and headed up the CIA's Miami station after the Bay of Pigs disaster; he was also involved in the CIA's use of the Mafia to try to assassinate Fidel Castro.)

Jenkins also headed a large CIA base in Laos from 1970 to 1973, during which time Shackley, Secord and Clines were all involved in CIA operations in that area. Also working with these individuals in that theater were General John Singlaub and a Marine officer named Oliver North.

Wheaton claimed that Haynes and Ross told him that Commercial Helicopters had purchased API Distributors, the Houston-based com-

pany set up in 1978 by Wilson and Clines, and employing Quintero and
Shackley, to sell oil-drilling equipment to Pemex, the Mexican oil company. Ross said he had never heard of API Distributors, but that Haynes
had started a company called API Oil Tools & Supply, which leased
power tongs, a oil-drilling tool—mostly to companies around Houston,
Ross said.

Haynes incorporated API Oil Tools & Supply in February 1981,
according to Louisiana incorporation records. This is around the time
that Wilson's criminal activities began to be exposed.

And who financed the start-up of API Oil Tools for Haynes? The
same man who was financing Haynes's Commercial Helicopters operations: Herman K. Beebe, Sr. "Beebe loaned him tons of money —millions of dollars," U.S. Attorney Joe Cage said of Haynes.

Commercial Helicopters' bankruptcy records show that when the
company filed for bankruptcy it owed Beebe-controlled companies more
than $2 million. It would have owed them more than $3 million, except
that Edmund Reggie's Acadia Savings took out more than $1 million of
the company's debt to Beebe's Bossier Bank & Trust. In addition, one
of Beebe's insurance companies, Consolidated Bankers Life Insurance
Co., had the reinsurance on Commercial Helicopters' employee benefit
plan.

Beebe also brought Haynes into a venture that borrowed $4 million
from the Beebe-bankrolled State Savings and Loan in Lubbock, Texas,
to buy the Amaliah Lumber Company in northern New Mexico from
Pennzoil. "That deal stunk to high hell," Cage said.

Two other people who got money out of the Amaliah purchase were
Don Dixon, who owned Vernon Savings and Loan, and a character
named Bernie Souza. Souza, from the Fresno, California, area, had been
in the real estate business in Fresno, where he apparently did business
with Southmark, the mob-infested Dallas real estate company. He then
moved to Houma, Louisiana, where he teamed up with Leon Toups.
Among other things, the two borrowed close to $14 million from Ver-
non Savings, secured by a second mortgage on a ranch in Colorado,
took the money and immediately defaulted on the note.

(Dale Anderson, Beebe's former right-hand man, said that in 1989,
while working out of Beebe's former headquarters building in Shreveport [which had been foreclosed on and taken over by Southmark], he
saw Souza walking down the hall. Anderson asked the people operating
the building what Souza was doing there and they responded that he was

interested in buying the building from Southmark.)

Bobby Ross claimed that Beebe cheated Haynes in the New Mexico lumber deal: "Haynes bought a big sawmill from Beebe in New Mexico, but he didn't get the timber rights. That's like having a snow cone stand in the desert."

At the same time Beebe was financing Commercial Helicopters, he also financed the start of a very peculiar bank in Washington D.C.

12

THE MOBSTERS, THE SPOOKS AND GEORGE BUSH: THE PALMER NATIONAL BANK STORY

Palmer National Bank is located in a busy business district of the nation's capital, just three blocks north of the White House. But it is much closer to the Presidency than that in terms of its politics and the people who organized it and control it.

When Palmer opened its doors in June 1983, the founding chairman of its board was Stefan Halper, a conservative Republican political operative who had absolutely no banking experience, but was an old hand at governmental wheeling and dealing and political espionage.

After Halper graduated from Stanford University and attended Oxford, he joined the Nixon White House in 1971 as a domestic policy adviser. He stayed there during Watergate and through the Ford Administration, holding positions in the Office of Management and Budget, the Office of Communications and the Office of the Chief of Staff.[1]

When Halper first began working for the White House, his father-in-law, Ray S. Cline, was head of the State Department's Intelligence Bureau. Cline is a leading member of the CIA's old-boy network. He had joined the CIA's predecessor, the OSS, during World War II, serving at one point in China. Other OSS veterans of the China front included E. Howard Hunt, John Singlaub, Mitch WerBell and Paul Helliwell. (Many of this country's fiascos that touched the CIA, including the Bay of Pigs, Watergate and Iran-Contra have involved one or more of these

---

[1] Application to the Comptroller of the Currency to organize Palmer National Bank.

China OSS veterans.) Cline, who was a Harvard fellow when he joined the OSS, later served as chief of CIA stations in Taiwan and Germany, and worked his way up to Deputy Director of Intelligence before joining the State Department. Exiting the department in 1973, he joined the conservative think-tank/lecture circuit group as an expert on anti-terrorism.

After the Democrats took over the White House in 1977, Stefan Halper went to work as a legislative aide to U.S. Senator William Roth, the earlier-mentioned Republican from Delaware with ties to the du Pont family. (Another Roth aide was Stephen Cass Weiland, the future attorney of Robert Corson.) Then, in 1980, Halper was named policy director of the presidential campaign of George Bush, and when Reagan won the nomination, he joined the Reagan-Bush team as a policy coordinator.

Cline, too, worked in the Bush campaign as a top foreign policy and defense adviser. "Cline boasted during the primaries that he intended to 'organize something like one of my old CIA staff' to help Bush win," said a 1988 article in the *Village Voice*.

During the 1980 campaign, Halper worked in a select group that was trying to find out what the Carter campaign was doing. In a July 7, 1983, story by Leslie Gelb, the *New York Times* reported that Halper had been in charge of an operation to gather inside information on Carter's foreign policy. Halper concentrated in particular, according to the *Times*, on whether Carter's people might be able to pull off an "October Surprise," in getting the American hostages in Teheran released before the election, possibly thereby securing a victory for the Democrats.

The *Times* quoted an unnamed source as saying, "There was some CIA stuff coming from Halper, and some agency guys were hired." One former CIA official working for Halper during the campaign was Robert Gambino, who had headed the CIA's super-sensitive Office of Security. Other ex-CIA officers worked under Gambino.

In May 1984, a House subcommittee came out with a report implicating Halper in the so-called "Debategate" scandal in which inside information from the Carter Administration ended up in the Reagan campaign for use in the debates between the candidates. The report stated that Halper, as Director of Policy Coordination, either received or circulated non-public information from inside the Carter campaign.

"I may have seen a few pages of it, but I can't confirm any particular subject or format," Halper told the *New York Times*.

The subcommittee report concluded that James A. Baker III, who was in charge of the Reagan debate group, had obtained the Carter materials from Republican campaign manager William J. Casey, who went on to become Director of Central Intelligence. Casey denied that he had provided Baker with any Carter materials, but the subcommittee believed Baker because of corroboration by Baker aide Margaret Tutwiler.[2]

The *Times* reported that Baker and David Gergen, who both served in the Bush campaign during the primaries, brought Halper on board the Reagan campaign staff after the Republican National Convention. When the *Times* attempted to contact Gergen for comment about its story on Halper's gathering Carter inside information, Gergen didn't return their phone calls. Gergen, currently an editor with *U.S. News & World Report*, instead called Cline, who then called the *Times* to deny any CIA connection with the Reagan-Bush campaign.

After Reagan won the 1980 election, Halper was named to a newly created position of deputy director for the State Department's Bureau of Politico-Military Affairs. "State Department officials said the White House, and Mr. Gergen in particular, had applied a great deal of pressure to create this position for Mr. Halper," the *Times* reported.

Less than two years later, Halper resigned his position to help organize Palmer National Bank.

One of the five other organizers of the bank was Frederic V. Malek, another veteran on the Nixon White House. As Nixon's White House personnel chief, Malek compiled figures for Nixon on the number of Jews among top officials of the Bureau of Labor Statistics. Several of these people were later transferred out of their top positions. This came back to haunt Malek in September 1988, after George Bush named him deputy chairman of the Republican National Committee. He resigned this position after the *Washington Post* published a story about his early services for Nixon. He has, however, remained in favor with Bush, who picked him to manage the Republican National Convention in 1988, and then named him to direct the economic summit of world leaders in Houston during the summer of 1990. Malek is now the Bush-Quayle campaign manager.

---

[2] Subcommittee on Human Resources of the House Committee on Post Office and Civil Service, "Unauthorized Transfers of Nonpublic Information During the 1980 Presidential Election," May 1984.

Also in 1982, the same year Malek began organizing Palmer National Bank with Halper and others, President Reagan named Malek, a West Point graduate, Green Beret and Harvard MBA to the U.S. Postal Service's board of governors.

Other organizers of the bank included John Barnum, an attorney who was general counsel of the U.S. Department of Transportation from 1971 to 1973 and Deputy Secretary of the department from 1974 to 1977; William Kilberg, an attorney who was the solicitor of the Department of Labor from 1973 to 1977 and a member of the Reagan-Bush transition team on labor; and John A. Knebel, an attorney who had been Secretary of Agriculture under President Ford.[3]

The only organizer not from the Washington, D.C., area was Harvey McLean, Jr., a real estate developer from Shreveport, Louisiana. McLean's father was in the oil business in Shreveport, and at one time had worked with George Bush in Zapata Offshore Oil Co., according to a former top official at Palmer. McLean went to prep school in Lawrenceville, New Jersey, and then on to Harvard. He earned an MBA from the University of Virginia and then returned to Shreveport in 1966.

McLean and Halper met while they were both working on Bush's 1980 run for the Presidency. McLean was a full-time unpaid volunteer on Bush's team in Alabama, said Glen Parker, a friend of McLean's from Shreveport who was also doing volunteer work for Bush in Birmingham, Alabama. "Harvey told me that there was a mutual friend in Houston who introduced him to George Bush," Parker told me.

One time, Parker said, he and McLean spent two days driving Neil Bush, the candidate's son, around Birmingham. "He had just gotten out of Tulane," Parker remarked about Neil. Also working on Bush's Alabama team was Margaret Tutwiler, said Parker. Tutwiler is currently James Baker's spokesperson.

McLean may have also been on Bush's finance committee, according to Fred Bush, finance director of the campaign (who is not related to the President). And the *Dallas Morning News* reported: "When George Bush was just another Republican looking for his party's 1980 nomination, he spent several hours talking politics with Harvey McLean at a New Orleans fundraising dinner."[4]

---

[3] Application to the Comptroller of the Currency to organize Palmer National Bank.

[4] *Dallas Morning News*, "After the Fall," by Bill Minutaglio, August 4, 1991.

The full-time paid staffer for Bush during the Alabama primary was Peter Monk, who had worked in the Peace Corps for Nixon, Parker pointed out. "This guy was real strange. He used to talk about Nicaragua all the time. He and Harvey became good friends." Halper, too, remembers Monk and McLean being friends: "Monk was a highly partisan Republican, a real attack-dog Republican," Halper said, adding that Monk married a du Pont.

After the 1980 election, McLean moved to Dallas and Halper went to work for the State Department. The following year, Halper was going to a foreign trade conference in China, and "there was an opportunity to bring someone along with me,' said Halper, "who might have an interest in the area, who was sort of a friend and so on, and so I asked Harvey if he might like to go.

"Somewhere over the Pacific we got into a conversation about banking. Now mind you, I had never been a banker. I was one of those guys who had a checking account with $71.38 in it, and banks frightened me a little bit. But Harvey said, 'Well, got to have a good bank in Washington.' He was sort of bemoaning the fact that banks were not as strong or responsive as they should be. And as the conversation unfolded, he basically said, 'Look, if you'll create the bank, I'll put up the money.' "

So McLean put up the money to start the bank: $2.85 million, or 95 percent, of the bank's $3 million initial capitalization. But McLean didn't pull this money out of his own pocket. It really came from McLean's good friend and financier Herman K. Beebe, who arranged for his bank, Bossier Bank & Trust, to lend the money to McLean.

McLean—patrician, high-strung, an absent-minded professor type who was interested in foreign affairs—seemed an odd match for Beebe, the outgoing, get-drunk-and-chase women, wheeling-dealing mob associate. But, "they were tight, real close," prosecutor Joe Cage said. "He was Beebe's boy all the way," Art Leiser, the Texas savings and loan chief examiner, has said of McLean.

(As of the writing of this book, McLean's ex-wives number three, while Beebe only had one. In the early 1980s a Dallas magazine named McLean one of the "ten most eligible bachelors" in the city.)

One thing Beebe and McLean did share was a penchant for secrecy. Halper, of all people—who locked his door at the Reagan-Bush campaign offices, where his own boss didn't know what he was doing half the time—said of McLean, "He practiced a form of information control more carefully and secretly than anyone I ever met."

Dale Anderson, Beebe's former right-hand man, remembers the Palmer loan as being unusual. "We didn't have a piece of the action," he said, meaning that Beebe didn't retain some ownership of the bank or profit participation or option to buy some of the bank. "I don't know why we didn't have a piece. I don't know why McLean went to Washington, either. It was curious to me why anyone would go that far to own that small a bank. There is some real hidden agenda there."

Cage believes that Beebe had a hidden interest in Palmer National Bank. "H.K. didn't do any business where he wasn't a partner or didn't have a profit participation. I heard that he did on Palmer. There had to be some connection with Herman. Or he may have told Harvey, 'I've got a bank I want to buy in Washington, D.C., and we're going to use your name.'" (McLean did use the name of his grandmother and one of his daughters, "Palmer," for the bank.)

The 1985 Comptroller of the Currency report on Beebe lists Palmer National Bank as one of 12 national banks which ". . . may in some way be controlled or influenced by Beebe."

Beebe's loans to McLean for developments in Shreveport—for residential homes, apartment complexes and commercial developments—made McLean one of the biggest, if not THE biggest, developer in Shreveport. When McLean moved to Dallas, Beebe introduced him to his own business partner, Don Dixon. "Dixon and McLean made instant love," said Dale Anderson.

The same year Palmer National Bank opened its doors, 1983, Dixon had his Vernon Savings and Loan lend several million dollars to McLean to buy Paris Savings and Loan in little (pop. 27,000) Paris, Texas, near the Oklahoma border in the northeastern part of the state.

One of Dixon's attorneys was quoted in a San Diego lawsuit as saying that Dixon called Paris S&L his "junk bank." Paris Savings lent Dixon more than $3.5 million on an $8 million mansion Dixon was building in Rancho Santa Fe in Southern California. But Vernon came crashing down on Dixon, failing spectacularly with 96 percent of its loans in default, before he could finish his mansion.

All told, McLean and his companies borrowed more than $34 million from Vernon Savings. One of his companies, Iona Development, borrowed $17 million from the Beebe-bankrolled Continental Savings, which was owned by Beebe's "man" Carroll Kelly. In addition, McLean borrowed millions of dollars from the following savings and loans that had connections to Beebe and his circle and later failed: Independent

American Savings in Dallas, Hiawatha Savings in Kansas, First South Savings in Arkansas, Sandia Savings in New Mexico and San Jacinto Savings in Houston.

In 1989, the federal receivers for Vernon Savings, Independent American Savings and Hiawatha Savings placed McLean in involuntary bankruptcy because of some $28 million he owed them on defaulted loans on Texas real estate developments. The bankruptcy filings also showed that McLean owed Continental Savings $11.7 million in unpaid loans.

All in all, it appears that the federal taxpayers had to absorb more than $40 million in bad loans taken out by Beebe's buddy McLean at savings and loans bankrolled by Beebe. In addition, Paris Savings and Loan failed in 1988 and was merged with 11 other insolvent Texas S&Ls at a total cost to American taxpayers of $1.3 billion.

Meanwhile, back at Palmer National Bank, officials were making various loans to conservative Republican political-action committees, including $400,000 to the National Conservative Political Action Committee, or NCPAC. Other Palmer borrowers were political action committees for U.S. Senator Robert Dole, Republican from Kansas, and for U.S. Representative Jack Kemp, Republican from New York and now George Bush's Secretary of Housing.

Another customer at Palmer was conservative fundraiser Carl R. "Spitz" Channell, who was brought to the bank, according to a former top officer at Palmer, by Halper. But Halper said he couldn't remember whether he brought Channell to Palmer. He did say he "never met Spitz Channell in my life. I wouldn't know him if I fell over him."

In February 1985, Channell established an account at Palmer for one of his foundations, the National Endowment for the Preservation of Liberty (NEPL). This foundation used White House briefings and private meetings with President Reagan to raise about $10 million for the Nicaraguan Contras when Congress had banned military aid to the rebel forces. Channell was the first person to plead guilty to illegal activities in the Iran-Contra scandal. He was placed on two years' probation for using NEPL to help Oliver North raise donations for military weapons for the Contras. His actual conviction was based on telling donors that their contributions to NEPL were tax-deductible when they weren't.

These private donations were channeled from NEPL's accounts at

Palmer to an account in Switzerland used by North for Contra funding and for arms deals with Iran. The money would go from an NEPL account at Palmer to an account in another Washington bank controlled by Richard Miller's IBC consulting firm, to a company called I.C. in the Cayman Islands, and then on to the Lake Resources account at Crédit Suisse Bank in Geneva controlled by North and Richard Secord.

For instance, in March 1986, NEPL transferred $725,000 from its account at Palmer to an IBC account at another Washington bank. On April 9, IBC wired $740,000 to I.C. in the Caymans, which then wired $650,000 to Lake Resources in Geneva. This followed a note North wrote on April 3 to remind Secord to send $650,000 to Lake Resources. On April 16, Secord reported: "650K received today as reported by the banker."[5]

The *Washington Post* also reported that I.C. sent $21,182 to the Gulf and Caribbean Foundation, which was headed by Midland oilman William Blakemore the previously described friend of Walter Mischer and George Bush.

(One of the unsolved mysteries of the Iran-Contra scandal involved I.C., which is drawn in the middle of North's chart— found in his White House safe—outlining the Contra operation and its funding. The *Washington Post* named some of the I.C. principals as residents of George Town on Grand Cayman, but no other information was ever turned up on them or the company, which later changed its name to Intel Co-Operation.

(Several of the principals of I.C. were principals of a company headed by Houston airplane operator Jim Bath, who once told a partner he worked for the CIA. Bath is close to Jack Trotter, a Mischer associate, as well as to sons of George Bush and Lloyd Bentsen. One of Bath's partners was named as a supplier of aircraft to Contra-connected operations (more on this in a later chapter).

In addition to holding deposit accounts for NEPL, Palmer also made a loan to NEPL to buy office furniture at its Washington, D.C., office near the White House. After Channell was implicated in Iran-Contra, his foundations fell on hard times and moved out of their fancy offices. Tags on furniture in the abandoned reception room there read: "Subject to a lien of the Palmer National Bank."[6]

---

[5] *The Chronology*, by the National Security Archive; *Washington Post*, March 3, 1987.
[6] *The New York Times*, August 7, 1987.

NEPL documents obtained by the National Security Archive show that it had four bank accounts at Palmer at the end of April 1986. Total deposits in these four accounts at that time were about $377,000. NEPL also had a $10,000 certificate of deposit at Palmer then.

In a June 14, 1990, letter to the *Houston Post*, Webb C. Hayes IV, Palmer's chief executive officer, claimed, in an effort to downplay the close connections between Palmer and NEPL, that "Palmer was one of several Washington banks that maintained bank accounts for the National Endowment for the Preservation of Liberty." This statement is contradicted by NEPL's own documents on file with the National Security Archive. They state that on April 30, 1986, the only other bank NEPL had an account with—for $5,000—was Irving Trust, a New York bank. These documents also show large accounts with E. F. Hutton, the stock brokerage firm.

After his guilty plea, Channell testified in Oliver North's trial on charges of obstructing Congress, destroying government documents and receiving an illegal gratuity. Channell, a well-known homosexual, died in May 1990 from pneumonia while recovering from cancer treatment and a car accident. He had been struck by an automobile while walking near his office.

Palmer CEO Webb Hayes claimed in his letter that "Palmer has never made loans to or for the benefit of the Contra rebels." Besides the question of how Hayes could know the ultimate destination or benefit of every dollar lent by Palmer, the loan to NEPL certainly benefitted that foundation and thus, indirectly, the Contras.

(A former top official at Palmer said he was there when a loan to Ecuador for military trucks was being discussed. After he raised the question of the legality of such a loan, he never heard anything more about it.)

Halper, who was eased out of Palmer in late 1984 after the Debategate scandal hit, said he did not know the bank was used by Channell to funnel money to the Contras. But he did say he knew Oliver North: "Ollie is a friend of mine. His daughter and my daughter are in the same pony classes, stuff like that."

In fact, Halper is featured in the very last entry in North's White House notebooks. The entry is the last one North wrote on November 25, 1986, the day he was fired by President Reagan for his part in diverting profits from Iranian arms sales to the Contras. North entitled the entry "Legal Defense Fund." Underneath this heading North wrote Halper's name, along with the name of a mutual associate, Chris Lehman, the brother of the former Secretary of the Navy.

About this, Halper said: "We at that time thought we might be able to help him [North] in the development of a legal defense fund. The fund got off the ground. He did develop a legal defense fund. We got trustees and put it in place."

After Halper left the board of Palmer, he was installed as chairman of the National Bank of Northern Virginia, a bank Palmer expressed interest in purchasing at one time. An attorney for this bank was J. Curtis Herge, who was also an attorney for the National Conservative Political Action Committee, which borrowed more than $400,000 from Palmer when Halper was chairman.

In addition, Herge was an attorney for the Nicaraguan Resistance Education Foundation, an organization that supported the Contras. And, when Channell and NEPL got into trouble with its donations to the Contras, Herge represented the organization and made statements on its behalf.

At the same time that NEPL was sending money through Palmer to the Contras, Halper's father-in-law, Ray Cline, was advising GeoMili-Tech, a firm associated with retired Major General John Singlaub, one of the principal leaders of private efforts to resupply the Contras. Cline told the joint Congressional Iran-Contra committee that the fee for his advice to GeoMiliTech went to his company, SIFT Inc., whose stockholders were members of his family, including a daughter who was married to Halper at that time.

Cline told the committee that he was advising GeoMiliTech on selling arms to the CIA and to foreign countries. Singlaub, a consultant to GeoMiliTech, and Barbara Studley, the head of GeoMiliTech and former Miami radio talk-show host, had earlier arranged for the sale of $5 million in weapons to the Contras.

One Palmer loan that benefitted Beebe and some other savings-and-loan crooks, including Don Dixon, was a $250,000 participation Palmer purchased from Beebe's life insurance company, Savings Life. The loan was on the 5,000-square-feet beach party house overlooking the breakers at Solana Beach, north of San Diego—the very same one that involved the lawsuit that named both Beebe and Charles Bazarian as defendants.

As previously noted, Don Dixon wanted to put some distance between himself and his mentor, Beebe. So Dixon had most of the Bossier

Bank loan on the beach house transferred to McLean's Paris Savings. In a deposition in the lawsuit over the beach house and the loans, McLean testified that Paris bought a 71 percent interest in the Savings Life loan. An affidavit by an attorney for the beach house's owner stated that Palmer National Bank bought $250,000 of the loan from Savings Life.[7]

In his letter to the *Houston Post*, Palmer CEO Hayes stated, in an obvious attempt to try to distance his bank from Beebe: "In August 1983, when Palmer had recently opened and was seeking loans, Palmer purchased a $250,000 participation in a well-secured mortgage loan from Savings Life Insurance Company. The transaction was handled exclusively by Mr. Waters, the president of Savings Life. Savings Life agreed to repurchase the participation from Palmer on demand. In October 1984, Palmer was paid in full as agreed."

Of course, Savings Life was totally controlled by Beebe. The "Mr. Waters" referred to by Hayes is John Bennet Waters, who was also at one time the president of Beebe's umbrella holding company, AMI. According to the 1985 Comptroller of the Currency report on Beebe, Waters had large, troubled loans at several Beebe-controlled banks.

At this time at Palmer National Bank—the spring of 1985— McLean's Palmer stock loan at Bossier Bank and Trust was sold to San Jacinto Savings and Loan in Beaumont, Texas. This was just months after Beebe had been convicted of defrauding the Small Business Administration on a nursing home loan. When Art Leiser, the chief examiner for the Texas Savings and Loan Department, found out about the Palmer stock loan at San Jacinto, he blew up: "I called them up and chewed their ass out. What do they think they are doing? I asked them. They don't make those kinds of loans. They only make true-blue home loans."

Leiser said he couldn't figure out why San Jacinto—which is different from the San Jacinto Savings in Houston owned by Southmark— made the loan. But an examination of the board of directors around this time showed two familiar names. They were Ben J. Rogers and Victor J. Rogers. (This Victor J. Rogers is the uncle of the Victor J. Rogers II who was John Riddle's law partner.)

Ben and Victor are two members of the Rogers clan in Beaumont, which founded the Texas State Optical chain. The Rogerses emigrated

---

[7] Walter J. Van Boxtel vs. Harvey McLean et al., San Diego Superior Court, No. 581506.

from Chicago to Beaumont in the 1920s and changed their name from Rubenstein. And their business interests extended far beyond optical shops in small Texas towns:

When the Caesar's Palace casino in Las Vegas opened its doors in 1966, the biggest stockholder was Jay Sarno, who was identified in federal reports as a front man for the Chicago mob. Not surprisingly, Jimmy Hoffa arranged a $10.5 million Teamsters loan for Caesar's. Convicted mob bookie Jerry Zarowitz was brought in to run the casino, while the host was Elliot Paul Price, identified in Senate hearings as an associate of New England Mafia boss Ray Patriarca.[8]

In *The Boardwalk Jungle*, Ovid Demaris states that "the FBI and the IRS were convinced that Zarowitz and Price had been planted in Las Vegas to protect the hidden interest of the real owners of Caesars Palace. Evidence would show that the hidden owners included Tony Accardo and Sam Giancana of the Chicago family; Ray Patriarca, Joseph Anselmo, Jerry Anguilo and Joseph Palermo of the New England family; and Jerry Catena, Vincent Alo, Tony Salerno and Jimmy Napoli of the Genovese family. Together they skimmed millions from the casino."

The largest stockholder in Caesar's Palace was Sarno, with 1,400 shares, the second largest was Nathan Jacobson, with 650 shares, and the third largest stockholders were four members of the Rogers family from Beaumont, Texas—Ben, Victor, Nathan and Sol—who together owned 600 shares.[9]

In 1969, Lum's, a fast food chain out of Miami, bought out the controlling interest of Caesar's Palace. Lum's, headed by Clifford Perlman, paid $48 million in cash, including $12 million in Lum's common stock, and assumed $24 million in Teamsters Union pension fund loans. In 1971 the SEC tried to stop Lum's from completing its purchase of Caesar's Palace, alleging fraud and deceit. Some of the executives charged in the SEC action were Zarowitz, Sarno, Jacobson, Harry Wald (then secretary-treasurer) and Albert Faccinto.

(The defendants signed a consent order, neither admitting nor denying guilt but agreeing not to violate SEC laws in the future.)

Also in 1971, a Zarowitz aide, Jerry Gordon, was indicted along with the mob's high potentate of finance, Meyer Lansky, for illegally skimming gambling proceeds from the Flamingo Hotel in Las Vegas.

[8] *The Boardwalk Jungle*, by Ovid Demaris (New York: Bantam Books, 1986), and *The Teamsters*, by Steven Brill (New York: Simon and Schuster, 1978).
[9] *The Grim Reapers*, by Ed Reid (New York: Bantam Books, 1969).

The charges against Gordon were dropped when he turned state's evidence, and he continued to work for Zarowitz at Caesar's.

Caesar's and Perlman then got into a great deal of hot water because of their business dealings with Alvin Malnik, the earlier-mentioned Miami attorney and close associate of Lansky. In 1979, when Caesar's applied for a license to operate a casino in Atlantic City, the New Jersey Division of Gaming Enforcement found that Perlman, William McElnea and Jay Leshaw were unsuitable for licensing because, among other things, of their business dealings with Malnik. McElnea resigned from Caesar's and sold his stock to Perlman, who, after much appeals, discussion and fighting, sold his stock back to Caesar's.[10]

All during the time that Sarno first, then Perlman, allegedly controlled Caesar's Palace, the Rogerses apparently maintained a presence and position in the casino company. Records at the Nevada State Gaming Control Board show that Victor J. Rogers was licensed as a director of Caesar's from 1970 to 1983. Incorporation records on file with the Texas Secretary of State in 1985 show that Victor Rogers was a director of Caesar's Palace. Some of his fellow officers and directors included Harry Wald and Albert Faccinto, who were charged with SEC violations along with Sarno and Zarowitz, and William McElnea. The records also showed Jerry Gordon, who was indicted with Meyer Lanksy, as a vice president.

I could not determine whether the Victor J. Rogers listed as a Caesar's Palace director is the uncle or the nephew, Victor J. Rogers II. Although the uncle was likely the original investor in the casino company, an article in the *Beaumont Enterprise* in the mid-1970s identified the nephew as an officer in the company.

Victor J. Rogers, the uncle, did not answer written questions I submitted to him about his stock ownership and board membership in Caesar's Palace or any other casino company. A letter to me from his lawyer, George Michael Jamail, stated that the questions "have no bearing upon S&L matters," and "we see no reason to respond to questions which are totally unrelated to any savings and loan associations matters . . ."

In the 1972 book *Shadow on the Alamo*, about the Sharpstown scandal in Texas politics and banking, author Harvey Katz described the 1969 swearing-in ceremony of Ben Barnes as Texas Lieutenant

---

[10] Demaris, op. cit.

Governor. After listing all of Barnes's supporters who were there, including Walter Mischer and Robert Strauss, he then stated:

"Neither John E. Gray nor Morris Jaffe were present. Both granted extraordinary favors to Barnes in his two campaigns, such as free use of their private airplanes. Jaffe is one of the biggest construction magnates in the state. Gray is a banker from Beaumont who has had intimate dealings with Walter Mischer. Among Gray's business associates are the infamous Rogers brothers, owners of Caesar's Palace and Circus Circus in Las Vegas and the Texas State Optical Company back home."

A letter to me from Victor J. Rogers's lawyer, George Michael Jamail, states that "Victor Rogers has met Walter Mischer, Sr., who he understands is associated with Allied Bank. He has never met Walter Mischer, Jr. He has never socialized with them. Victor Rogers has done some banking with Allied Bank."

Caesar's Palace was Robert Corson's favorite place to gamble in Las Vegas. In fact, he apparently overdid it there because the casino filed a lawsuit against him for past-due gambling debts, and won a judgment of $92,000 in 1989. Caesar's was also Corson's mother's favorite place to launder cash, according to U.S. Customs Service officials.

After Victor J. Rogers II, the nephew, graduated from the University of Texas and got a law degree from the University of Michigan, he moved to Houston and began practicing law with Wade Kilpatrick and John Riddle. This is the same John Riddle, the Kappa Sigma who was a business partner with Corson and borrowed hundreds of millions of dollars from dirty savings and loans, including Don Dixon's Vernon.

In fact, Dixon tried to get Riddle to buy the Solana Beach house to pay off the Paris Savings loan. Riddle had agreed to do so, but a land deal he was planning in the San Diego area—which would have provided him with the necessary cash—fell through. Dixon then brought in Charles Bazarian to buy the house.

In 1985, Victor Rogers II, the nephew, was half-owner of Equitable Savings and Loan in Austin with J. Scott Mann, a former University of Texas football player from Baytown, who married a daughter of Judge Roy Hofheinz, the father of the Astrodome. Mann bought out Rogers for $6.7 million in August 1985, just before everything hit the fan. Several years later Rogers's investment would have been worthless.

Mann had participated in the 1982 purchase of Jefferson Savings and Loan in McAllen by a group of his Austin business associates, who bought the S&L from Guillermo Hernandez-Cartaya, one of the all-time bad boys of the Western Hemisphere. Hernandez-Cartaya, a Cuban exile, Bay of Pigs veteran and CIA asset, had purchased the S&L from Lloyd Bentsen's father. (This will be discussed in more detail in the next chapter.)

After he bought out Victor Rogers II, Mann merged Equitable Savings with the successor to Jefferson Savings to form CreditBanc Savings, which went on a lending spree to such people as Ben Barnes and John Connally and to former Mischer employee and business associate Joe McDermott. By the end of 1986, CreditBanc Savings was in deep doo-doo and the regulatory hounds were baying.

Mann and Barnes then went to House Speaker Jim Wright to complain about the attitude of regulators in examining CreditBanc. Wright wrote a strong letter to Ed Gray, the chairman of the Federal Home Loan Bank Board. This apparently slowed the regulators down a bit. But CreditBanc was eventually declared insolvent and taken over by the feds in 1988. Two years later, the FDIC filed a $76 million lawsuit against Mann and the law firm of Jones, Day, Reavis & Pogue, alleging fraud and self-dealing.[11]

Back to San Jacinto Savings in Beaumont, where Ben and Victor J. Rogers, the uncle, sat on the board of directors. When Harvey McLean transferred his Palmer National Bank stock loan from Bossier Bank & Trust to San Jacinto Savings, he picked up an extra $200,000 in cash after paying off Beebe's bank.

A letter from Victor J. Rogers's attorney stated: "Victor Rogers does not know who made the loan to Harvey McLean. He had nothing to do with it. He does not know who arranged or approved it. Neither Victor Rogers nor his brother, Ben, owned any stock in the S&L. He was not on any committee." The letter continued: "Victor Rogers does not know Harvey McLean nor has he had any dealing with him. Victor Rogers does not know Herman K. Beebe. He did not know Herman K. Beebe owned Bossier Bank & Trust. Victor Rogers has never done any business with Mr. Beebe."

The San Jacinto loan was made in April 1985 and was for one year. Shortly after it was due, the other Palmer stockholders bought McLean's stock. Some four months later, Barry Seal's old C-123K was shot down

---

[11] *The American Lawyer*, March 1991.

over Nicaragua, a newspaper in Lebanon wrote a story about American arms deals with Iran and Oliver North got help from Stefan Halper for a legal defense fund.

But McLean didn't completely abandon his business with Palmer after he sold his stock. His 1989 bankruptcy filings reveal that he has two accounts at Palmer and had interest income from them of $4,452 for 1987 and 1988.

Now is the time to dig back to the 1970s and another corrupt S&L that was giving regulators fits along with Surety Savings: Jefferson Savings and Loan. Surety had its Mafia connections, while Jefferson had ties to Lloyd Bentsen and the CIA.

13

JEFFERSON SAVINGS: THE CIA AND THE SENATOR

Before the so-called "deregulation" of the savings and loan industry was even a gleam in Ronald Reagan's eye, there was another savings and loan in Texas besides Surety that was giving regulators and prosecutors problems in the late 1970s. This institution was Jefferson Savings and Loan in McAllen, way down south in the Rio Grande Valley of Texas, the land of political machines, political bosses, political patronage and the *patrón*.

Jefferson S&L was chartered in 1956 with six directors, including future U.S. senator Lloyd M. Bentsen, Jr., his brother, Donald, and his father, Lloyd M. Bentsen Sr., *el patrón*. Another director was Vannie Cook, who would one day be a business partner of reputed mob associate and Surety S&L looter Raymond Novelli. Lloyd Jr. stepped down as a director the next year, but continued as a large stockholder with 15.5 percent of the shares. Donald also held 15.5 percent of the shares, while Lloyd Sr. was the biggest shareholder, with 18 percent of the stock.

By 1974, two new names had appeared on Jefferson's board of directors. They were Guillermo Hernandez-Cartaya and his father, Marcelo Hernandez. Hernandez-Cartaya is a Cuban exile who fought in the abortive CIA-backed Bay of Pigs invasion, was captured and then was ransomed by the U.S. government. He went to work for Citizens & Southern Bank in Atlanta and then in 1970 formed World Finance Corporation in Miami.

By 1977, Hernandez-Cartaya and World Finance were the focus

of intense and extensive state and federal investigations into drug smuggling, money laundering, gun running, political corruption and terrorist activities. But the case fizzled out in 1978 and only resulted in one income-tax indictment of Hernandez-Cartaya, in 1981. The CIA was partly, if not totally, responsible for pulling the plug on the investigation.[1]

At least 12 World Finance employees had past associations with the CIA[2]. When Assistant U.S. Attorney R. Jerome Sanford, who resigned in frustration and disgust over the failed investigation, tried to obtain from the FBI its CIA files on World Finance, he was denied access on the grounds of national security. But the CIA did acknowledge that it had 24 documents relating to World Finance that were generated in 1976 and 1977.

One of the six founding directors and stockholders of World Finance, along with Hernandez-Cartaya, was Washington lawyer Walter Sterling Surrey, described by journalist John Cummings as "a charter member of the old boy network of U.S. intelligence." Surrey had served in the OSS (the CIA's predecessor) in World War II, and after the war went to work for the State Department as head of the Division of Economic Security Controls. He resigned his position with World Finance in 1976 and has denied any knowledge of intelligence or illegal activities at the company.[3]

In 1985, Surrey's Washington law firm, which concentrated on international law and represented a number of foreign countries and multinational companies, merged with the nation's biggest savings-and-loan law firm, Jones, Day, Reavis & Pogue. This was the same law firm that hired Rosemary Stewart, the former head of the Office of Enforcement for the Federal Home Loan Bank Board, and the same firm that represented Vernon Savings and Lincoln Savings. It was also the same firm being sued by the feds over alleged misconduct at CreditBanc Savings in Austin, the successor to Jefferson Savings.

(After Hernandez-Cartaya was convicted of bank fraud in 1982, he sold Jefferson Savings to a group of Austin investors. They later changed its name to Franklin Savings, which was merged by Scott Mann with

---

[1] "Miami Confidential," by John Cummings, in *Inquiry*, August 1981; *Newsday* article by Knut Royce, October 3, 1988.
[2] *Endless Enemies*, by Jonathan Kwitny (Congdon & Weed, 1984).
[3] Kwitny, op. cit.

Walter M. Mischer, Sr., Houston developer, banker and political power broker who is a friend and campaign supporter of both George Bush and Lloyd Bentsen. *(The Houston Post)*

Walter Mischer, Sr. (middle), with his close friend and business partner, Vincent Kicherillo, and Kicherillo's wife. *(The Houston Post)*

George Bush and Lloyd Bentsen when they were campaign opponents in 1970. Bush and Bentsen are part of, and answer to, the same circle of Houston businessmen, led by Walter Mischer. *(AP/Wide World Photos)*

Herman K. Beebe, Louisiana Mafia associate and godfather of failed Texas S&Ls. *(Shreveport Times)*

Mario Renda, New York mob associate and money broker to more than 100 failed S&Ls. (Courtesy Byron Harris, WFAA TV, Dallas)

Raymond Hill (right) and his wife at a party in Houston in 1968. Hill is the former chairman of Mainland Savings, which was looted both by mobsters and CIA operatives. (*The Houston Post*)

John Connally, former Governor of Texas, and his S&L borrowing partner Ben Barnes, former Lieutenant Governor of Texas. Barnes is a business partner of Walter Mischer and Herman K. Beebe. *(The Houston Post)*

The thrill of victory: Robert L. Corson, CIA mule, in the spring of 1986 after purchasing Kleburg County Savings and Loan...

The agony of defeat: Corson after getting busted for illegal promotion of gambling in 1990. (Courtesy of Arizona Department of Public Safety)

Harris County Judge Jon Lindsay (center) with his wife, Toni, and the late Republican operative Lee Atwater. Lindsay helped his biggest single campaign contributor, Robert Corson, acquire an S&L. *(The Houston Post)*

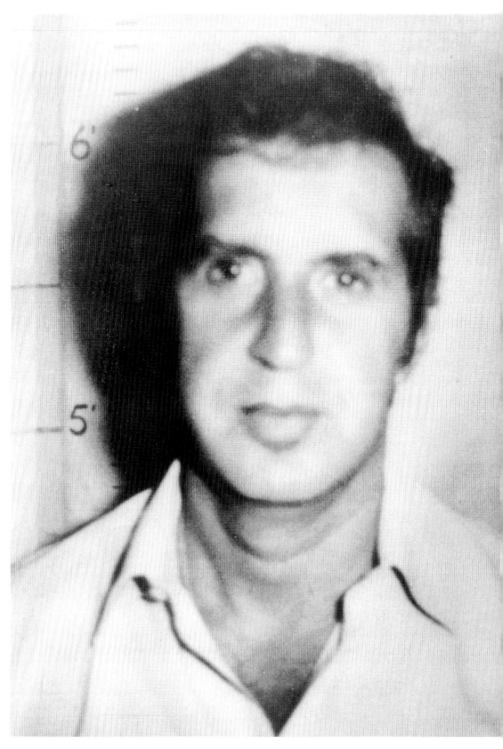

Fernando Birbragher, convicted drug-money launderer and owner of a Miami airplane equipment company. *(Miami Herald)*

Farhad Azima, Iranian native and CIA contract agent who borrowed from
Indian Springs State Bank; this bank was subsequently looted by mobsters.
(Kansas City Star)

Leonard Pelullo, Miami developer and Philadelphia Mafia associate who borrowed
from Sunshine State Bank and American Savings and Loan in California.
(Miami Herald)

Ray Corona, former president of Sunshine State Bank, associate of both mobsters and CIA operatives; Corona is a convicted bank-fraud felon.

Jim R. Bath, Houston airplane company owner, CIA operative, and friend of both Lloyd Bentsen and George Bush. Bath was a notable S&L borrower.

Mike Adkinson, Florida redneck, Houston homebuilder, and associate of both mobsters and CIA agents; he borrowed more than $200 million from fraud-riddled S&Ls. *(The Houston Post)*

George Bush waves goodbye to reporters and sightseers as he takes off for a second day of fishing from the Ocean Reef Club on Key Largo. Ocean Reef is owned by Bush's friend and major campaign doner Carl Lindner. CIA gun runner Jack DeVoe smuggled his Colombian cocaine into this prestigious club.
(Miami Herald)

Equitable Savings to form CreditBanc Savings.

In the spring of 1992, Jones, Day, Reavis & Pogue anted up to the losers' table when it settled with the bondholders of Charles Keating's A.C.C. But Jones Day was not the first or the last to make amends for its wayward ways; 90 of the 95 original co-defendants settled with the plaintiffs.)

In addition to CIA connections to World Finance, there was also evidence of Mafia ties. The DEA and congressional investigators found links to Santo Trafficante, the Mafia boss in Florida, including a World Finance employee who was a Trafficante associate.[4] An Interpol report identifies Juan Romanach, a World Finance director, as the Trafficante associate.

An affiliated company, Dominion Mortgage Corporation, which shared the same Coral Gables address and borrowed $2 million from World Finance to buy an office building there, worked with the Trafficante family to supply drugs to Las Vegas. Dominion Mortgage was also trying to buy the Caesar's Palace casino in Las Vegas.[5]

In 1976, Hernandez-Cartaya bought Jefferson Savings from Lloyd Bentsen, Sr. "I remember old man Bentsen called me out of the blue and said they decided to sell the savings and loan," said Art Leiser, at that time the chief examiner of the Texas Savings and Loan Department. "I said I understood, and hoped they would sell it to someone who would take as good care of it as they did. The next thing I know, they had sold it to Cartaya."

When I was a reporter for the *Houston Post* and first discovered Hernandez-Cartaya's purchase of Jefferson Savings from the Bentsens, I called Senator Bentsen's office to ask about his involvement. His press secretary, Jack DeVore, returned the call and I told him my questions for the senator. DeVore replied that the senator was at a conference on a island off the coast of Spain, but he would try to get some answers to my questions.

DeVore called back shortly thereafter, apparently having spoken to Bentsen and also to Bentsen's attorney in the city of McAllen. DeVore stated categorically that the "senator has never owned any interest in Jefferson Savings and Loan." He then said he had "satisfied" himself that "Senator Bentsen doesn't know Cartaya and has never had any

---

[4] *In Banks We Trust*, by Penny Lernoux (Penguin Books, 1986).
[5] Ibid.

dealing with him." I then asked DeVore if Bentsen ever owned any stock in Jefferson. He replied, "He didn't recall owning any."

Then I told DeVore that I had documents that were filed with the Texas Savings and Loan Department that were signed by Bentsen, and notarized, that showed him to be an original director and stockholder, owning 116.25 shares out of 750. DeVore said he would get back to me.

Less than 30 minutes later, Bentsen called me from the island off the coast of Spain. Yes, he had been one of the original organizers of Jefferson, he said, but then "I sold my interest in Jefferson and bought Brazosport Savings and Loan." He insisted that he sold his stock "long before" the sale to Hernandez-Cartaya. "I had no part of that deal," he said.

Asked about Hernandez-Cartaya, he said, "I don't know who the man is." And in reply to a question whether he knew about CIA intervention in the criminal prosecution of Hernandez-Cartaya for fraud at Jefferson, he stated, "No, and I sure would if that was the case."

It *was* the case, in fact:

A federal prosecutor who worked on the Jefferson Savings prosecution of Hernandez-Cartaya told me the following story with the stipulation that his name not be used: "I got a call from an FBI agent in Laredo, who said the SAC [special agent in charge] in San Antonio needed to talk to me. We met in a McAllen hotel at 9 p.m.

"There was a person from the CIA with him. He [the CIA officer] told me that Cartaya had done a bunch of things that the government was indebted to him for, and he asked me to drop the charges against him. I said, 'I'm not giving you any promises,' and that I would think about it." The prosecutor then told me, "The CIA guy said in the room there that Cartaya had scammed Saudi Arabia out of $30 million and that the CIA approved it."

(This is probably in reference to an incident in 1978 in Ajman, one of the United Arab Emirates. According to author Penny Lernoux, some Arabs in Ajman invested $37 million in one of Hernandez-Cartaya's loan schemes and then, when they discovered the money was gone, confiscated his passport and threatened to cut off his hand. John Cummings, in his account for *Inquiry*, simply states that Ajman authorities discovered vast shortages of cash in the Ajman bank. . . . A confidential report prepared in early 1987 by a former law enforcement official in Europe, for a prospective business partner of Adnan Khashoggi, demonstrated Khashoggi's long-term relationship with Hernandez-Cartaya. According to the report, "In early 1978, whilst in Ajman, Hernandez-Cartaya got into difficulties when the authorities there discovered that he had systematically milked their joint venture, Ajman Arab Bank. He managed to evade arrest by using a false passport previously supplied to him by his associate Aldereguia-Ors. Both men were subsequently arrested in Miami on charges relating exclusively to the false passport . . ." Hernandez-Cartaya and his associate were found innocent of the passport charges by a Miami jury. The confidential report goes on to state: "It should be noted that the Ajman Arab Bank was subsequently saved from collapse when it was bought by Bank of Credit and Commerce International." BCCI is, of course, the notorious Arab bank that was convicted in Florida on money-laundering charges and banned from the United States.[6])

The federal prosecutor informed me that he told his boss in the U.S. Attorney's Office in Houston of the request by the CIA officer. "My boss said to do whatever you think best. So I decided to go ahead and prosecute him."

Hernandez-Cartaya was convicted in 1982 of defrauding Jefferson Savings. His sentence was combined with his 1981 income-tax fraud sentence of five years. He was indicted again in 1982 for defrauding Jefferson Savings, along with his father and his friend and business partner, Camilo Padreda. This time prosecutors did drop the charges the next year, saying the investigation was "flawed." The judge in the case also allegedly urged the prosecutors to drop the indictment.

Padreda, a Cuban exile living in Miami, is a prominent and influential Republican fundraiser and developer in Dade County. In 1990, he pleaded guilty to falsifying U.S. Department of Housing and Urban Development documents in getting a HUD guarantee of a $17.8 million loan to build an apartment complex. And, in 1986, he was in a business deal with another prominent Dade County Republican, John Ellis "Jeb" Bush, one of the President's sons.

In the October 3, 1988, issue of *Newsday*, reporters Knut Royce and Gaylord Shaw reported that Padreda was once a counter-intelligence

---

[6] Corporate records on file in the Texas Secretary of State's Office show that Rinaldo J. Cartaya, a relative of Hernandez-Cartaya, is an executive vice president and director of a company called BCCI, registered in Texas. This BCCI apparently stands for Brownsville Country Club, which the Cartayas invested in.

office for former Cuban dictator Fulgencio Batista. When Castro came to power, Padreda fled to the Miami area and became a candy salesman.

Newsday reported that in 1986 Jeb Bush's real estate company, Bush Realty, Inc., became the exclusive leasing agent for a nine-story Miami office building constructed by a Padreda partnership with the aid of a $1.4 million HUD grant. Jeb told *Newsday* that he did "not believe" he had called federal officials to help Padreda get housing funds. "I am a very honest person, and I hate to categorically say something. I do not recall. I do not believe I've called anybody on Camilo's behalf."

Newsday also reported that in February 1988 Padreda went to Washington as one of 127 "Distinguished Presidential Appointees" to the White House's Conference for a Drug Free America. *Newsday* said Padreda's office is "adorned with autographed pictures of Ronald Reagan and George Bush. Padreda told *Newsday* reporters that he met George and Jeb Bush in 1980, when George was seeking the presidential nomination. Regarding his relationship to Jeb Bush, Padreda said, 'Believe me, believe me, you're not going to find anything wrong.' "

Before Hernandez-Cartaya was indicted in 1981, he pretty much had his run of Jefferson Savings. After he bought control of the S&L, "the first thing he did was make a $7 million loan on an office building he had in Florida," Art Leiser confirmed. "I came down there and told him, 'You can't do that. Get that loan out of here.' "

Leiser said he found out that "big bags of cash" were going out of Jefferson Savings to a bank in St. Louis. Law enforcement sources said Hernandez-Cartaya was using the S&L to launder drug money.

Leiser also said he was looking for any way he could to stop the Cuban exile and get him out of Jefferson S&L. "I knew that he was a tennis player, so I challenged him to a tennis match. I told him that if he won, we'd stop investigating him, but that if I won, he would leave. He laughed and said, 'Art, you don't think you would win, do you?' " Leiser said he interpreted that to mean that Hernandez-Cartaya would do anything it took to win, including physical action. Leiser said that he wasn't afraid of Cartaya but some of his examiners were.

One day, Leiser was having a drink at a bar in McAllen with an FBI agent who was working undercover trying to expose a fraudulent home loan application scam at Jefferson. Leiser said he was commiserating with the agent about how Hernandez-Cartaya seemed to be untouchable: "I said, what is it with Cartaya? He's so bad, yet he's getting away with it. And the FBI agent looked at me and said, 'Did you ever think about the CIA?' "

All of this occurred before deregulation and the beginning of the savings-and-loan debacle in the mid- and late 1980s. The two most egregious cases of savings and loan fraud in Texas before deregulation—Surety Savings and Jefferson Savings—were crawling with mobsters and CIA operatives. Therefore, it should come as no big surprise that mobsters and CIA operatives were at the head of the pack *after* deregulation.

We have seen Herman K. Beebe's connections to the intelligence world, but what about the first mobster out of the chute after deregulation, Mario Renda?

14

MARIO AND FRIENDS

Mario Renda started out inauspiciously on his life of crime. After majoring in music education at Queens College, he opened up a summer music camp in Massachusetts in 1963, which he ran for more than ten years. But he had big dreams, expensive tastes—and an expensive wife. In 1975, Renda gave up his summer music camp business to become chairman of an international construction company called International Planners and Developers (IPAD). Suddenly he was involved in business deals in Haiti, Saudi Arabia, Ivory Coast and Jamaica, and was talking deals with Adnan Khashoggi.

No investigator, prosecutor or reporter has come up with how Renda was able to make such a transition and entrance into the world of international finance and business. Perhaps it was through the good graces of his father-in-law, who was involved in a bank called the Bank of Sicily. But it is unlikely that his overseas activities would have escaped the attention and interest of the CIA, particularly given some of the countries he was dealing with.

For instance, in 1976 Renda brokered the construction of the National Guard headquarters in Riyadh, Saudi Arabia, to a Long Island construction company. Renda related to Bruce Maffeo, the Brooklyn organized crime prosecutor, that he "was told by a member of the Saudi Arabian royal family that the construction bid would be awarded in exchange for a 10 percent kickback."[1]

---

[1] October 3, 1988, letter from Maffeo to Robert Fink, attorney for Martin Schwimmer, Renda's indicted partner in First United Fund.

Also in 1976, Renda arranged the financing for construction of a hotel in Ivory Coast, a country on the west coast of Africa and a neighbor to Liberia. Renda told Maffeo that a government official "demanded and received a concealed interest in the project in exchange for government support."[2]

In 1977, Renda entered into a joint venture with Khashoggi on a $5 million deal to build precast concrete homes in Saudi Arabia. That agreement allegedly fell through later, apparently as did several other Renda-arranged deals including the proposed construction of a cement plant in Haiti. Renda was negotiating the cement plant in 1978, and agreed, he told Maffeo, to pay a Haitian official a "concealed interest in the plant in exchange for government support of the proposal."[3] Renda said the plant was never built because he couldn't arrange for financing.

By this time, Renda had quit his job at IPAD, and was the treasurer of the Arab International Bank of Saudi Arabia, an offshore bank where he cut his teeth on banking and certificates of deposit. Also around this time he was negotiating to purchase and operate a casino in Jamaica. Renda agreed to cut in a Jamaican official for a piece of the action in order to get a license, he told Maffeo, but the official reneged and Renda never got his casino.[4]

Renda was at Arab International for about a year when he left and formed his own company, Arabras, which was set up under the vague rubric of international trade and finance. In 1980, after Congress lifted the ceiling on interest rates on savings deposits, Renda changed the name of his firm to First United Fund. He was off and running with brokered deposits.

As previously noted, Adnan Khashoggi, a Renda associate, made more than $12 million in profits out of a land deal with Mainland Savings, where Renda was brokering deposits. This occurred just days before Khashoggi began wiring money to Iranian middle man Manucher Ghorbanifar to start a U.S.-Iran arms-for-hostages deal (described in detail in Chapter 4).

Khashoggi's relationship with Renda is discussed in an affidavit by Lawrence Iorizzo filed in federal court in Kansas. Iorizzo, a mob associate, was in the gasoline business in New York, and was charged with bootlegging gasoline (pocketing the taxes) along with Michael Franzese,

---

[2] Ibid.
[3] Ibid.
[4] Ibid.

a captain in the Colombo Mafia family. Iorizzo fled to Panama, but later returned to testify against Franzese, and was then placed in the federal witness protection program.

In his affidavit, Iorizzo tells about being introduced to Renda in late 1981 by a mutual friend and business partner, V. Leslie Winkler. Winkler, an international con man, was in the veal-feeding business with Iorizzo and was participating in linked financing scams with Renda.

Winkler, Iorizzo stated in his affidavit, "told me that Renda was very close to Adnan Khashoggi, an Arab oil magnate, and that Renda might be able to assist me in obtaining a Kuwaiti oil contract. Renda explained that Khashoggi owned property in the town where I lived and wanted to build a helicopter pad on his estate but had encountered resistance from local authorities. Renda told me that I could ingratiate myself with Khashoggi if I could assist in obtaining the necessary permits for the helicopter pad."

(In a press conference in Houston in the summer of 1990, after Khashoggi had been acquitted along with Imelda Marcos for helping her and her late husband hide Philippine assets, Khashoggi denied even knowing Renda.)

Another person with connections to the intelligence community also appears in Iorizzo's affidavit. Iorizzo discusses how he and Renda planned a linked financing scam with a New York bank, using an Iorizzo company called Houston Holdings (HH). "I explained to Renda that HH was a Panamanian 'shelf' corporation inasmuch as I had literally purchased the company's papers from a lawyer in Panama who maintained them, along with other entities, on the shelf of a bookcase in his office in Panama. This lawyer's last name was Samos, and I believe that I had been introduced to him by V. Leslie Winkler or our mutual acquaintance Eric D'Antin.

"Renda, V. Leslie Winkler and I discussed that HH was a company which had been originally created and used as an off-shore 'cash laundry' by its previous owner. I explained that HH had been used in prior years by its previous owner to hold several millions of dollars in Panamanian banks and financial institutions. I had purchased the financial statements of this company from Samos for prior years along with the stock of the company for approximately $10,000."

Samos is Steven Sandor Samos, a Hungarian refugee who at one time was a director of the Free Trade Zone Corporation in Miami. Samos moved to Panama, married Alma Robles Chiari (a relative of Panama's last freely elected President), and began selling off-the-shelf Panamanian shell corporations to anyone who needed one.

In the late 1970s, Samos helped Tony Fernandez, a narcotics trafficker and CIA contract agent, and Ray Corona, a drug-money launderer, buy Sunshine State Bank in Miami.[5] They were caught in the mid-1980s, and Samos turned state's evidence against Corona while receiving immunity from prosecution for his admission of laundering drug money.

(Corona got a $3 million loan in 1984 from Peoples Savings and Loan in Llano, Texas, which he used to shore up the capital of Sunshine State Bank in order to try to keep the federal regulators from closing down his bank. There will be more about this in a later chapter on Sunshine State Bank and Peoples Savings.)

Samos also appeared in the Iran-Contra scandal in connection with an off-the-shelf Panamanian company called Amalgamated Commercial Enterprises (ACE). This company was set up in 1984 and then sold the next year to Southern Air Transport, a former CIA proprietary that was shipping weapons to Iran and to the Contras. ACE appears on the diagram of the Contra aid operation found in Oliver North's hite House safe. It was used by Southern Air Transport and North's "Enterprise" to funnel money for the Contra war. According to the *Wall Street Journal*, ACE was used to buy two planes for the Contra resupply operation and provided maintenance and fuel for the aircraft. In a November 16, 1985, entry in North's White House diaries, he writes: "Tell Alan [Fiers—the head of the CIA's Central American Task Force] that ACE is OK."

All of ACE's employees apparently worked for a Panamanian company, International Management & Trust Corporation, which had been owned by Samos, the *Wall Street Journal* reported. It is not known whether Samos retained control of that company after he sold it in 1983, nor what his role may have been in setting up ACE, the *Journal* said.

Miami attorney John Mattes, who defended a man charged with violating this country's neutrality act by helping the Contras and was later hired by Ray Corona after Corona went to jail, related that Oliver North gave Samos's name to Southern Air Transport. A Southern Air vice president then flew to Panama to meet with Samos and set up ACE, said Mattes.

---

[5] *The Big Fix*, by James Ring Adams (John Wiley & Sons, 1990).

ACE's bank accounts for the Contra operation were at Banco de Iberoamérica, a Panama bank principally owned by the Arab Banking Corporation, which received money from North's accounts in Switzerland. This bank was also used by Samos in transactions with Sunshine State Bank.

Somehow, in all of Renda's ramblings and business dealings, he hooked up with a lawyer from Omaha, Nebraska, named Jack Chapman. Chapman had worked for the CIA during the 1960s as a contract agent, apparently in the Caribbean and Haiti. Chapman indeed told federal investigators that he worked for the CIA. And one official of the CIA confirmed to the FBI that Chapman "had been some sort of contract employee, but the CIA felt that he had gone off the reservation."

Chapman said he first met Renda when "at one time I was in New York and he was introduced to me. We filed three lawsuits on his behalf, on behalf of his attorneys, in California and New York. They were breaches of contract with various people. At the time, we were trying to help him do some activities, and we weren't earning any money out of it and on that basis there we kind of gave up association."

According to officials familiar with the case, another service Chapman performed for Renda was to take more than $500,000 in cash to Renda's partner, Joseph DeCarlo, Sr. (who later turned state's evidence against Renda). DeCarlo then took the cash to another Renda partner, Martin Schwimmer, who used it to bribe Teamsters Union officials. These officials, in exchange, would hand over their pension funds for Renda to deposit into savings and loans.

Officials familiar with the case, who spoke on the condition that they not be identified, said this cash started out in one of Renda's "off the books" bank accounts where he and Schwimmer put their money skimmed from union pension fund deposits. The money was then wire-transferred to a bank in New York and next wired to a man named Clemard Joseph Charles. Charles is a Haitian exile who had been in contact with the CIA since the early 1960s. Charles laundered the money for Renda; that is, he turned it into cash so it couldn't be traced back to Renda. Charles washed the money by first wiring it to bank accounts in Switzerland. After that, investigators lost track of it, but when it came back into the United States to Chapman, it was in cash.

Most books on Haiti describe Clemard Joseph Charles as François "Papa Doc" Duvalier's personal banker, business partner, financial adviser—and bagman (an agent who delivers a bribe or payoff money). It seems that Charles first gained Papa Doc's favor in 1964 when he was able to smuggle two aircraft into Haiti from the United States, which had an embargo on aircraft and arms shipments to Haiti.

Duvalier rewarded Charles with a private bank, Banque Commerciale, along with the monopoly on compulsory car and old-age insurance and the control of Port-au-Prince's main wharf.[6] Charles was also placed on the board of directors of 14 major companies and became the exclusive agent for General Electric U.K., Siemens Schuckerwerke and Toyota Motors. He received numerous commendations from Papa Doc, including Commander of the Order of Civil Merit, the Order of Work and the Order of Agricultural Merit.[7]

Suddenly, in 1967, Duvalier had Charles thrown in jail. Charles languished for ten years until he was released by Papa Doc's son, Jean-Claude "Baby Doc" Duvalier, and exiled. All the books say that Papa Doc threw his banker and bagman in jail because Charles had gotten too big and too rich and too cocky. Maybe so, but there was something else involved that the books don't mention: the United States Central Intelligence Agency.

Charles was recruited by the CIA in 1963, the same year the agency was sponsoring and paying exile and rebel groups to try to overthrow Papa Doc. We know Charles was recruited by the CIA then because of the findings in the late 1970s of the House Select Committee on Assassinations.

The committee was investigating the assassination of John F. Kennedy and tracking a man named George DeMohrenschildt, a White Russian count with extensive ties to the CIA. DeMohrenschildt had moved to Texas, worked in the oil business and befriended Lee Harvey Oswald. In fact, there is some evidence that DeMohrenschildt was used by the CIA to keep an eye on Oswald.[8] DeMohrenschildt had met Charles in Haiti, where he had business interests, including a share in the government sisal hemp operation. DeMohrenschildt was also keeping an eye on Clint Murchison's meat-packing business and cattle

---

[6] *Haiti: The Politics of Squalor,* by Robert I. Rotberg with Christopher K. Clague (Boston: Houghton Mifflin, 1971).

[7] *Haiti: The Duvaliers and Their Legacy,* by Elizabeth Abbott (New York: McGraw-Hill, 1989).

[8] *Conspiracy,* by Anthony Summers (Paragon House, 1989), and *High Treason,* by Robert J. Groden and Harrison Edward Livingston (Berkley Books, 1990).

ranches there. At one time he had worked for Three States Oil and Gas, one of Murchison's oil companies.

DeMohrenschildt was also on close, friendly terms with Houston oilman John Mecom, Sr., according to a Houston private eye familiar with the Russian count. And the count and George Bush apparently knew each other. Bush's name and his Midland, Texas, address were in DeMohrenschildt's address book.

One CIA contract agent, Herbert Atkin, has reported that DeMohrenschildt's real job in Haiti in 1963 was to supervise a CIA-sponsored plan to overthrow Duvalier.[9]

In May 1963, DeMohrenschildt arranged a meeting between Clemard Charles and Dorothy Matlack, who was Assistant Director of the Army Office of Intelligence, the U.S. Army's liaison with the CIA. According to DeMohrenschildt's CIA files, which the assassination committee obtained, the purpose of the meeting with Matlack was to arrange a rendezvous between Charles and a CIA representative. DeMohrenschildt attended the meeting with the CIA, to Matlack's surprise. "She did not know what role DeMohrenschildt was serving, but felt he 'dominated' Charles in some way," reads the committee's CIA memo, which then reported that Matlack stated, "I knew the Texan [DeMohrenschildt] wasn't there to sell hemp."

Finally, the kicker in the CIA memo: "Because of the potential political information Charles could give about the current situation in Haiti, the CIA became the primary contact with Charles."

That puts Charles's ability to obtain two aircraft from the United States in 1964 during an embargo and his subsequent 1967 jailing by Duvalier in a whole new light. For it was in 1967 that Mitch WerBell, along with some Haitians and Cuban exiles, were caught planning an invasion of Haiti from Florida.[10]

WerBell was a veteran of the OSS office in China during World War II along with E. Howard Hunt, Paul Helliwell and John Singlaub. He told author Jonathan Kwitny that he did not work "for" the CIA, but "with" the CIA. He said the distinction was that he got paid by private groups and not by the CIA.

Anyway, the charges against WerBell for planning the invasion of

---

[9] *The Fish Is Red,* by Warren Hinckle and William W. Turner (New York: Harper and Row, 1981).
[10] *The Crimes of Patriots,* by Jonathan Kwitny (New York: Norton, 1987).

Haiti were later dropped—which proved, he claimed, that the operation was sanctioned by the U.S. government.[11] After Charles got out of jail in Haiti in the late 1970s, he hooked up with WerBell on another Haiti operation. This indicates that WerBell and Charles (and the CIA) may have been working together to get rid of Duvalier in 1967. Papa Doc found out about it and clapped Charles in jail.

After Charles got out of jail in Haiti, he apparently put his experiences there and with the CIA to good use. A federal agent with the Organized Crime Strike Force said that in addition to his dealings with Renda, Charles was involved in laundering money for the mob in Nevada and was doing business in Florida with a member of the Bonanno Mafia family. (Family boss Joe Bonanno got the first casino license in Haiti from Papa Doc in 1963. And Bonanno associates may have helped Charles get the aircraft from the United States in 1964.)

Also in Florida, Charles shows up as a director of a company called St. Charles Pacific Peace Organization, a non-profit company which filed to do business in the state in 1988. One of the officers in this organization is Watergate burglar Frank Sturgis, who has strong, long-time ties to both the Mafia and the CIA. Sturgis, who was originally Frank Fiorini from Philadelphia, helped the mob run their casinos in Cuba before Castro kicked them out, and then he helped the CIA in their anti-Castro plots.

After Charles left Haiti, he went to Miami and became president of a company called C.I.C. Enterprises, which filed to do business in Florida in 1977. The registered agent and secretary of this company was a Miami attorney, Albert Krieger.

Krieger will show up later in this book as a close friend and attorney for Miami lawyer Lawrence Freeman, who pleaded guilty to laundering drug money. Freeman had previously worked for CIA super-agent Paul Helliwell and served as in-house counsel for Castle Bank & Trust in Nassau, Bahamas, which had been used by the CIA and mobsters to funnel and launder money. Freeman also was involved in the $200 million land deal in the Florida panhandle with St. Joe Paper Co., Mike Adkinson and Robert Corson.

As for Charles's longtime and constant desire to be President of Haiti, it too came to naught. After Baby Doc Duvalier abdicated in 1986, the country finally got around to holding elections in early 1988. Charles

---

[11] Ibid.

was one of the candidates for president, but three days before the election the Haiti Supreme Court tossed his name off the ballot along with four other candidates'.

The first place Mario Renda got caught with his brokered deposits-linked financing scam was a tiny bank in a strip shopping center in Kansas City, Kansas. Not surprisingly, it was crawling with mobsters and at least one very interesting CIA asset, an Iranian native named Farhad Azima.

15

Nobody Hands You a Contract

On July 22, 1983, someone drove William Lemaster's Lincoln Continental across a bridge in the small town of Lexington, Missouri, about 25 miles east of Kansas City, then made a U-turn and came back across the bridge, gaining speed until the car crashed into the concrete foundation of a war memorial. There was an explosion and fire, and the driver's body was burned beyond recognition.

No autopsy was performed on the remains, which were quickly cremated. The body was identified as that of Lemaster, who had been seen leaving a family party in his Lincoln shortly before the crash. One of the primary items used to identify him was his golf bag in the trunk. Many questions remained unanswered, but whether his demise was an accident, suicide, homicide or even faked, Lemaster had been in big trouble, caught in a vise between federal investigators, the Mafia and perhaps even the CIA.

Lemaster was not a bookie for the mob or a double-agent for the CIA, he was a banker, a well-respected banker who was brought in to run the tiny ($8 million in assets) Indian Springs State Bank. The bank had been languishing in a strip shopping center between Wig City and the Athlete's Foot, on the Kansas side of the border. In early 1980, the bank's owners hired Lemaster from his banking job in Lexington to try to make something of Indian Springs State.

What he needed, Lemaster decided after he took over the bank, was a "rainmaker," someone who could bring big deposits and big borrowers into the bank. So, in 1981, he hired Anthony Russo. And Russo, a former lawyer in Kansas City, did just that. He brought in depositors; he brought in borrowers. He also brought in a CIA asset and the Mafia.

For example, one of the borrowers at Indian Springs was Carmen Civella, the son of Kansas City's Mafia boss, Carl Civella. The $300,000 Carmen borrowed on an Italian restaurant in Kansas City was still owed to Indian Springs when the bank failed.[1] Another mob borrower was Carl Caruso, a bagman for the Civella family who carried the cash skimmed from the Tropicana casino in Las Vegas to Mafia families in Kansas City and Chicago. The two Carls were convicted in 1983 for their skimming operations.

Morris Shenker, the mob lawyer from St. Louis, guaranteed a $200,-000 loan from Indian Springs to his Dunes Hotel and Casino in Las Vegas. And a Shenker associate from Las Vegas, Jay Fihn, was also a borrower at Indian Springs.

On the deposit side, at least 12 people with reputed ties to organized crime had accounts at Indian Springs, including Joseph "Joey Doves" Aiuppa, the boss of the Chicago Mafia family, who had been brought in by Anthony Russo.[2]

Mario Renda and his brokered deposits were also brought in by Russo. Renda brokered more than $6 million into the little bank, in exchange for loans to his straw borrowers of more than $5 million. These loans were not repaid and, more than any others, contributed to the failure of Indian Springs State Bank in January 1984.

No one seems to know how Lemaster got together with Russo or why he brought the mob associate into Indian Springs, but Lemaster had to know about one thing in Russo's past: In 1974, Russo was convicted for conspiracy to promote bribery and interstate prostitution. He spent 16 months in prison for this conviction, and surrendered his law license the day before he entered the penitentiary. Before he stopped practicing law, he had represented members of the Civella family in some of their criminal tribulations.

(Incredibly, the Federal Deposit Insurance Corporation's board of review in Washington approved Russo's employment by the bank, despite his felony conviction, mob associations and a recommendation by the FDIC regional office not to approve it.)

The second biggest borrowers at Indian Springs, next to Renda's

---

[1] *American Banker*, "Linked Financing," November 1984.
[2] Ibid.

linked financing strawmen, were also brought in by Russo: Farhad Azima and his companies, including Global International Airways. The affairs and fates of these people and institutions became inexorably intertwined.

When Global filed for bankruptcy in late 1983, Azima and his companies had almost $600,000 in unpaid loans at Indian Springs, which failed three months later. Although the final, unpaid debt by Global was eventually whittled down to about $60,000 after offsets and adjustments, Azima and Global "certainly did contribute to the failure" of Indian Springs State Bank, to quote Michael Manning, a private Kansas City attorney hired by the FDIC to investigate Indian Springs's failure.

(Manning was one of a few investigators and prosecutors most responsible for bringing Renda to justice, or purported justice.)

Between 1981 and 1984, Azima and his affiliated companies borrowed close to $2 million from Indian Springs, a gross violation of the bank's lending limit to one borrower, which at Indian Springs was less than $500,000. Also, Azima and Global racked up large unsecured overdrafts on their accounts at the bank. From April 1982 to March 1983, these overdrafts averaged about $150,000 a day. Federal examiners expressed concern about both the overdrafts and loan limits to one borrower.[3]

These problems were compounded by the connections and conflicts of interest that existed among Azima, Global and Indian Springs. For example, Azima was elected a member of Indian Springs's board of directors in 1982 when he became the fourth largest shareholder, with almost 10 percent of the stock. He claimed later that he lost all of his $400,000 investment in the bank's stock when it failed, but it is likely that he borrowed this money from another financial institution and suffered little loss from his own pocket.

When Azima was asked about the large overdrafts that Global had at Indian Springs, he replied, "I don't get involved in the details of the operations. I have no idea about that. The company had credit lines and obviously was authorized overdrafts." Then, asked whether he should have known about them because of his position as board member of Indian Springs, he answered, "Outside directors don't get involved in the operations of the bank."

That statement is contradicted by Azima's claim that as an Indian

---

[3] FDIC examination reports on Indian Springs State Bank, 1982 and 1983.

Springs board member he opposed large loans to Renda's straw borrowers on property in Hawaii. He claimed he "warned" the bank "against being involved in that type of thing. But I was a minority stockholder and nobody would pay any attention to what I would say."

It's hard to believe that William Lemaster wouldn't heed Azima, a director, big stockholder and borrower at his bank. In addition, Lemaster was an advisory director of Global International Airways and had borrowed more than $55,000 from Indian Springs to buy stock in Global. Also, in 1982, Lemaster borrowed $50,000 from Azima personally, and never repaid it.[4]

Anthony Russo, too, was an advisory director of Global in addition to being a financial consultant for the company. One of his recommendations was that Global buy gasoline from Morris Shenker's associate, Jay Fihn. Russo testified in one of his tax fraud trials that he received a commission for every gallon of gas Fihn sold Global, which, in turn, had a contract to fly junkets of gamblers to Shenker's Dunes Hotel and Casino. Russo also borrowed more than $55,000 from Indian Springs to buy stock in Global. He said he bought the stock in the name of his children and later sold it back to Azima.[5]

Other connections: Anthony Russo's brother-in-law worked for Global, and an attorney for Azima and Global, Howard Lay, was brought in as an attorney for the bank. He withdrew when Global filed for bankruptcy in October 1983, owing $280,000 in unsecured loans to Indian Springs. At that time, Global had $145,000 in certificates of deposit at Indian Springs and was later allowed to offset those deposits against the loans owed.

After Indian Springs failed, in January 1984, Azima and some of his fellow board members filed a lawsuit against Renda and his linked-financing cohorts for defrauding Indian Springs. The FDIC got an injunction against that lawsuit and then sued Azima, Russo and other directors for fraud and negligence in the failure of the bank. This lawsuit was settled out of court with unknown payments from the directors. One source familiar with the suit said Azima was reportedly required to pay cash in addition to the coverage of his director's liability insurance.

---

[4] *Kansas City Star*, "The Indian Springs Connection; Azima Was Failed Bank's 'Best Customer,' " June 10, 1984.
[5] Ibid.

Farhad Azima was born in 1942 in Rezaiyeh, Iran, to a prominent, wealthy, landlord family that had close ties to the ruling Pahlavi family. His father, Yusef, was a lawyer and Iranian Supreme Court justice. In 1959, Azima traveled to the United States to attend school, beginning at a junior college in Chanute, Kansas, because it didn't have an English-language proficiency requirement, and eventually graduating from William Jewell College in Liberty, Missouri, in 1968.

After college, Azima became involved in various businesses in Kansas City with family members, including a restaurant, an export-import company, a travel agency and a rug company. Among other ventures, he had been arranging the shipment of live cattle to Iran. He decided to go into the cattle-shipping business for himself and on December 30, 1977, he incorporated Global International Airways, starting with a multi-million-dollar loan from Commercial Credit Corporation and one Boeing 707.

But his business ran into unexpected trouble in 1979 when the Shah was deposed. Shipping cattle to Iran was out, so he took an Iranian banker, Mansour Rasnavad, as his partner and tried to break into the charter business. At its apex in the early 1980s, Global was one of the largest private air carriers in the world, with seventeen 707s, two 727s and one 747.

This, like many successes chronicled in this book, was helped along by the United States government. One of Global's first big contracts was hauling military equipment to Egypt for the Egyptian American Transport and Services Corporation (EATSCO), as a result of the Camp David Accords between the Carter Administration, Israel and Egypt. Azima told the *Kansas City Star* that the EATSCO contract accounted for about half of his company's cargo division revenues.

EATSCO, as previously noted in Chapter 11 on Herman K. Beebe's connections to Commercial Helicopters, was the company owned by former CIA officer Thomas Clines and Hussein Salem, an Egyptian. Ex-CIA operative Edwin Wilson put up Clines's half, $500,000, of the initial capital of EATSCO. Former CIA Associate Deputy Director of Operations Theodore Shackley, according to his Iran-Contra testimony, acknowledged that he did "consulting work" for EATSCO and during that time he dealt specifically with Clines and Salem. Shackley, along with Salem's brother, an oil geologist, were also contemplating an oil venture, but according to Shackley, nothing came of it. Azima has said that Salem, a former Egyptian intelligence officer, was his friend.

Salem was also a friend of Edwin Wilson's, but Azima said he didn't know Wilson and had never done business with Wilson. Azima added that Global International Airways was not implicated in any of the criminal activities of EATSCO, which was fined $3 million for overbilling the Pentagon $8 million in freight costs. Also fined was Air Freight International, the Baltimore freight-forwarding company used by EATSCO. AFI hired Global for the air shipping.

Another big Global customer was the U.S. Department of Defense, which contracted with Azima's company to provide Military Airlift Command (MAC) transportation of military passengers. One such contract for $2.7 million began on October 1, 1983, just days before Global filed for bankruptcy, and continued through September 1984. And Global stated in its bankruptcy papers that it anticipated an additional $9 million in MAC business.

Another Azima company, Capitol Air, Inc., of Smyrna, Tennessee, won a $5.5 million MAC contract for long-range international air transportation services in August 1982. Azima placed Capitol Air into bankruptcy in New York in 1984.

Global's bankruptcy papers show that the Department of Defense owed Global $100,000 at the time the company filed for Chapter 11. But they also show that Global owed the Department of Defense $367,000. The papers do not indicate the nature of this debt.

A June 5, 1986, letter from the U.S. Air Force's accounting division to Global states that Global might have to pay $18,797, which "represents an invoice from the German Federal Ministry of Defense for aviation fuel issued to Global in support of an Air Force exercise." The letter doesn't indicate the nature of this Air Force exercise, which took place in the summer of 1984, after Global filed for bankruptcy.

Several people who knew Azima said he had good connections with the Reagan Administration. Frank Van Geyso, who flew 707s for Global for four years, said, "Any time we had a little problem with the feds [Federal Aviation Administration], Azima would jump on a plane to Washington and straighten it out. The feds would be mad as hell, but there was nothing they could do."

Azima has refused to say how much money he has contributed to Republican party candidates: "That is not information I prefer to discuss. I would not say it is a lot." Azima made his first campaign contribution to the Republican party in October 1983, just three days before Global filed for bankruptcy. Federal Election Commission records show that from 1983 through 1988, he contributed $54,196 to

Republican candidates and $15,500 to Democratic candidates.

Furthermore, from 1984 to 1986 Azima contributed $27,000 to the President's Dinner Committee, which was also called the Republican Senate-House Dinner Committee. This dinner is an annual event in Washington in which the President speaks. Gary Koops, a spokesman for the National Republican Congressional Committee, told the *Houston Post:* "It's a fairly large event, one of our major fundraising events of the year. Those invited are people that have long supported the Republican party, or for that case, President Reagan, major donors, people like that."

Koops said he "is sure that President Reagan attended" the 1986 dinner. Vice President George Bush probably attended too, Koops indicated. Azima's 1986 contribution to this dinner was recorded on May 8, according to Federal Election Commission records. This date was just before Azima's scheduled testimony in Anthony Russo's tax fraud case, which had to be taken out of order because, Azima told prosecutors, he had to attend a White House function.

In the first week of July that year, a Boeing 707 owned by Azima and his wife, Lynda, was used to ship 23 tons of arms to Iran as part of the secret Reagan Administration arms-for-hostages deal. The 707, which had previously been owned by Global, was leased to Race Aviation, owned by Azima's brother, Farzin. Azima denied having anything to do with Race or the shipment of arms to Iran. However, in a March 7, 1986, letter he received from Farzin regarding the lease of the 707, Azima was told: "Your continuous support is of utmost importance to this company as well as the undersigned." Global's bankruptcy filings also show that Farzin was a Global employee and on March 15, 1985, Race Aviation paid $400 to Global for office rent.

"Farhad hides behind his brother a lot," one federal prosecutor familiar with Azima remarked dryly, when told of Azima's denials of any connection to Race Aviation.

When the Iran-Contra scandal broke in November 1986, Farzin Azima was mentioned specifically by Iranian Parliament Speaker Ali Akbar Hashemi Rafsanjani as an arms dealer who the Reagan Administration knew was selling arms to Iran. Farzin was referred to by Rafsanjani as "this counterrevolutionary who is now a fugitive . . . [and who] has been helping us with arms deals and on occasion . . . has traveled to Iran."[6]

---

[6] *Washington Post*, November 20, 1986.

Azima denied any connection to the Iran-Contra scandal, saying he had been thoroughly investigated and "cleared." But when he was asked if he knew William Casey, the director of central intelligence during Iran-Contra, he replied, "He is dead. It's academic." Asked if he was denying that he knew Casey, he replied, "Next case."

(An interesting sidebar: Global International Airways and Aviation Leasing Group—Azima's main company after Global went bankrupt—borrowed about $8 million between 1984 and 1988 from Utica National Bank and Trust in Tulsa, Oklahoma, using several airplanes as collateral. The head of Utica National Bank was Victor Thompson, the father of Robert Thompson, an aide to then-Vice President George Bush.[7] Robert Thompson gained brief notoriety in the summer of 1990 as the lobbyist who helped James Fail buy Bluebonnet Savings, a combination of 15 failed Texas savings and loans, in the Southwest bailout plan. Fail, whose insurance company pleaded guilty to fraud in Alabama in 1976, put up $1,000 of his own money and borrowed $70 million to buy the S&Ls and get $1.85 billion in federal subsidies. About $35 million of Fail's borrowed money came from I.C.H. Corporation, a Kentucky insurance company that at one time tried to buy Southmark and which appeared on Southmark's bankruptcy as a $35 million creditor.)

Azima had other connections to the Reagan-Bush Administration, and they lead to more interesting characters. During Anthony Russo's trial for income-tax fraud in the summer of 1986, Russo testified that in 1982 he received $25,000 from Global for accompanying the dictator of Liberia, Samuel Doe, on a trip: "Well, you all met Farhad Azima, he was the chairman of the board of Global Airlines. He also came into Indian Springs Bank as a shareholder. His airline was hired by the United States government to fly the President of Liberia, which was a new government, and its cabinet, around the world on a good will tour.

"Liberia is a little country in Africa that I studied about as a result and learned a little bit about. After the War Against the States [I guess this is the way the Kansas City mob refers to the Civil War; in Texas we call it the War of Northern Aggression.] Lincoln, our President, sent some slaves to Liberia to live. And they lived on the, I believe, the west coast of Africa. Yes, the west coast of Africa. And formed this little country called Liberia.

---

[7] Jerry Bohnen, KTOK Radio, Oklahoma City; and *Money Laundering Alert*, "CIA Ties Revealed in Bank Failures," by Anthony Kimery, July 1990.

"The United States has supported that country over the years. And about in 1981 [actually 1980] they had a coup. Sergeant Doe, who was a sergeant in the Liberian Army, overthrew the government. The government was backed by the, our CIA and our government. And when the revolution or coup occurred, the United States then wanted to become friendly with the new government, wanted to continue to have ties between the United States and Liberia—not Libya, Liberia—and wanted us to continue our relationship with them.

"So they hired Farhad's airline, Global, to take Sergeant Doe, his entire cabinet, around the world on a goodwill tour. Farhad asked me if I would go as the, quote, host, to the president and the cabinet, to escort them from country to country.

"It was at that time that, of course, I was an officer of the bank and I had to check with Mr. Lemaster, who was the president, and he covered for me and I took that trip around the world and we went all around the world with the president and his cabinet, and the president and I became friends and I would introduce them and kind of act like an ambassador."

The CIA was, of course, extremely interested in maintaining its secret satellite-tracking stations in Liberia after Doe's coup. As reported in an earlier chapter, CIA agent Robert Sensi testified that he worked with Clint Murchison, Jr., on a CIA project to try to replace the Liberian stations.

When I asked Anthony Russo if the Doe trip was sponsored by the CIA, Russo replied, "Your guess is as good as mine." (Well, in that case, my guess is that the CIA knew about it and approved it and probably helped instigate and plan it.)

When I worked for the *Houston Post* and asked Azima during a telephone conversation to London on September 22, 1989, whether Global ever did any work for the CIA, he replied, and I quote:

"I don't recall such a . . . duh . . . I don't recall such a . . . duh . . . Nobody came on, walked with a contract and handed you, carried a card and do business. No, each, every company does business with, you know, the Military Airlift Command or any other branch of the government, you do transportation, troop transportation, or [it sounds like] NGMC, it's all part of the requirement, if you are in any military program, to do the work, you do it."

I tried again, and asked him specifically if Global ever did any contract work for the CIA. "As a matter of policy, we don't comment on questions like this," he replied, parroting the CIA's standard response to any question it doesn't feel like answering.

One more time I tried, asking him if he could deny working for the CIA. "As a matter of policy we make no comment," he answered. That was the same answer Azima gave to the *Kansas City Star* when it published a lengthy article on June 10, 1984, by James Kindall entitled "The CIA, Arms & Global Airlines." The story contained numerous allegations by former Global pilots about connections to the CIA and mysterious weapons trips.

On one such trip in 1979, Global was ostensibly flying a load of lettuce from Tunisia to Nicaraguan refugees in Costa Rica. The plane was diverted from its scheduled stop at a commercial airport to a military field. The pilot became suspicious and asked to check the cargo of lettuce. He found three double-barreled 57-millimeter machine guns and 150 cases of ammunition with Chinese writing on them. That incident led to a standing joke among Global pilots that, when asked what kind of cargo they were hauling, they responded, "Cabbages . . . and cabbage launchers."

At least one Global pilot had previously worked for Air America, the CIA proprietary that flew in the Far East, and Global did business with several companies that had past, and perhaps present, CIA connections. One, Southern Air Transport in Miami, showed up as a creditor in Global's bankruptcy.

Azima said he doesn't recall any work that Southern Air Transport did for Global. But Southern Air claimed in Global's bankruptcy that Global owed it more than $13,000 for services rendered. And former Global pilot Frank Van Geyso said Southern Air performed maintenance work on Global's planes when they were in Miami. Global also did business with Evergreen International Airlines, a company that was formed from the assets of a CIA proprietary, Intermountain Aviation, after its cover was blown in the mid-1970s. In fact, Evergreen is listed on Global's creditor list directly after Southern Air Transport.

Evergreen operates the giant air base at Marana, Arizona, northwest of Tucson, which Intermountain Aviation had owned. Evergreen's founder and principal owner, Delford Smith, told the *Portland Oregonian* that his company had one contract with the CIA to assist foreign nationals that the CIA wanted removed from other countries or brought to the United States. Smith told the *Oregonian* that he believes in the CIA's cause. "And we don't know when we supported them and when we didn't as a contract carrier," he said.

News reports in July 1984 stated that the CIA was using Southern Air Transport and the Du Ponts' Summit Aviation, as well as Evergreen Air, to transport weapons to the Contras.

(When Walter Mischer, Sr., was a board member of Hermann Hospital in Houston, Evergreen Air was hired by the board to operate its helicopter ambulance service.)

There are some investigators who believe that Global was started in the mid-1970s as an off-the-shelf CIA company that was handed over to Azima to do agency work under commercial cover. One, Gene Wheaton, the former Pentagon criminal investigator, said Global was the "aviation arm of EATSCO—they owned it through cutouts." Another, a private investigator in Houston who does work for federal agencies and has looked into Global and EATSCO, agreed: "Wilson, Clines and Secord incorporated Global." Azima has denied this, pointing out that he incorporated Global in Missouri in 1977. But there is a possible connection between Global and Heinrich Rupp that goes back to 1975. Rupp, a Denver precious-metals dealer, was a former CIA contract pilot sentenced to prison in 1988 for a bank fraud scam involving several mob associates.

Rupp's friend and partner, Richard Brenneke, testified after Rupp's trial and conviction that he and Rupp worked for the CIA and that Rupp was one of the pilots who allegedly ferried Reagan-Bush campaign team members to Paris in October 1980 as part of "October Surprise." After Brenneke's testimony and Rupp's psychological evaluation, the judge reduced Rupp's sentence from 42 years in prison to two years. The U.S. Attorney's Office in Denver then asked the CIA whether Rupp and Brenneke had ever been employed by the agency.

In a November 18, 1988, letter to Assistant U.S. Attorney C. Jeffrey Kinder, CIA Associate General Counsel W. George Jameson stated: "After a diligent search, no record or information of any kind was found that indicates that either Heinrich Rupp or Richard Brenneke ever had a staff or contract relationship with CIA, or otherwise worked for CIA in any capacity."

The Denver U.S. Attorney's Office then brought an indictment against Brenneke for making false statements before a U.S. judge. Almost a year later, Thomas M. O'Rourke, an assistant U.S. attorney in Denver, wrote a letter to Brenneke's attorney, Mike Scott (brother of U.S. Representative Patricia Schroeder, Democrat-Colorado), stating, "I received a telephone call from Bob Caudle of the Central Intelligence Agency. Mr. Caudle told me that CIA files showed that in 1966 Heinrich Rupp received flying lessons at Intermountain Aviation Inc. in Arizona. He said Intermountain had been a CIA 'proprietary.' "

In a December 1990 interview with Dave Armstrong, then Editor of *Texas Observer*, Rupp said he was involved in starting Global, which he said was owned by the CIA. Asked by Armstrong if EATSCO owned Global, Rupp replied, "That's about 95 percent true." An ID card issued to Rupp by a Global International Airlines in Dallas on November 1, 1975, shows Rupp to be employee number A-002. That same year, Rupp was issued an ID card as a pilot for Continental Air Services, a branch of Continental Airlines that was used for contract work by the CIA.

Although Rupp's Global in Dallas is Global International Airlines, while Azima's is Global International Airways, there is one interesting intersection between Rupp and Azima's Global, involving TWA and Saudi Arabian Airlines.

Rupp had worked for TWA on assignment to Saudi Arabian Airlines as a captain and pilot instructor. And, when Global was awarded a worldwide charter in 1980, three of its top eight managers had previously worked for TWA or Saudi Arabian. For example, David Gann, Global's vice president for operations, was a captain and check pilot for Saudi Arabian Airlines from 1973 until he joined Global. And Robert J. Rose, Global's director of marketing, spent three years on a TWA team training Saudi nationals to manage Saudi Arabian Airlines before he joined Global.[8]

George Selman, a flight engineer who worked at Global after three years at Saudi Arabian Airlines, later transferred to CIA-connected Buffalo Airways, which Azima purchased in 1989. Next, Selman went to work at Skyways Aircraft Leasing, operated by CIA agent Jim Bath. (More on this in the next chapter.)

All this, of course, doesn't mean that Rupp is not an unsavory character, a con man, a crook and a liar. His interview with Armstrong is laced with racist, anti-Semitic invective. And he's not above whining that he was convicted for bank fraud because he got hoodwinked by his mob associates.

---

[8] Recommended decision of Chief Administrative Law Judge Joseph J. Saunders, Civil Aeronautics Board, Certificate of Public Convenience and Necessity for Charter Air Transportation, Global International Airways, November 1980.

When Rupp was in Leavenworth Prison he wrote a letter to President Bush dated August 1, 1989, to which he attached a copy of his membership card in the Association of Former Intelligence Officers. The letter contains several blatant factual errors. For example, he stated, "My Agency tenure began in 1957 with the OSS." The OSS was disbanded after World War II. He also stated in the letter that he had investigated the "Imhausen/Libya affair and its connection with Ghorbanifar's I.B.I. in Frankfurt." In fact, I.B.I. was controlled by a man named Barbouti, not the Iranian middle man Ghorbanifar.

Rupp closed his letter thusly: "For the protection of this country and the ideals which I have been sworn to uphold, my lips have been and will be sealed, and I remain, Yours in Faithful Service, Heinrich F. Rupp, Scorpio 688."

Just your typical CIA contract agent.

Global was also named as a CIA front by a retired CIA Middle East expert. In December 1990, Bruce Hemmings, a retired CIA senior operations officer who worked on the Iran desk in 1985, issued several written statements criticizing the CIA's role and cover-up in the Iran-Contra scandal and other misdeeds. In part of his statement entitled "CIA Gun Running to Iran Goes Back to 1981," Hemmings stated:

"Since at least 1981, a worldwide network of 'free-standing' [i.e., no direct U.S. government ties] companies, including airlines, aviation and military spare parts suppliers, and trading companies, has been utilized by the CIA and the U.S. government to illegally ship arms and military spare parts to Iran and to the Contras. These companies were set up with the approval and knowledge of senior CIA officials and other senior U.S. government officials and staffed primarily by ex-CIA, ex-FBI and ex-military officers.

"The companies include Aero Systems, Inc., of Miami, Arrow Air, Aero Systems Pvt. Ltd of Singapore, Hierax of Hong Kong, Pan Aviation in Miami, Merex in North Carolina, Sur International, St. Lucia Airways, Global International Airways, International Air Tours of Nigeria, Continental Shelf Explorations, Inc., Jupiter, Florida, Varicon, Inc., Dane Aviation Supply of Miami, and others, such as Parvus, Safir, International Trading and Investment Guaranty Corp., Ltd., and Information Security International Inc.

"Through these mechanisms, staffed by ex-intelligence and military officers, the administration and the CIA have been able to circumvent and ignore the legal intelligence mechanisms and Congressional oversight. C-130, F-4, TOWs and Hawk missile parts were shipped to Iran in violation of the arms embargo and a variety of mechanisms were used, including International Air Tours of Nigeria in August and September 1985, Arrow Air in November 1985, and Global International and Pan Aviation and others going back in 1981."

In another document, entitled "Corruption Within CIA: A Cast of Characters," Hemmings severely criticizes Thomas Twetten, the deputy director of operations for the CIA and Hemmings's former boss. In one section Hemmings discusses weapons sales to Iran and how Twetten deliberately undermined the case of a foreign official who had information on such sales by turning the matter over to the British:

"Twetten's decision and that of London station is highly suspect and negligent, as they knew, as I did, that the British government was, along with the British arms industry, Tiny Rowland, Ashraf Marwan and Adnan Khashoggi, his partner, deeply involved in such trafficking. Obviously, Twetten also knew that North, Shackley, Clines, Hakim, Robert Sensi, and Cyrus Hashemi, and Farhad Azima were also involved in such trafficking, as all these individuals were part of the same network as him."

Hemmings, who won the CIA's intelligence commendation medallion in 1985, is extremely bitter about the way he was treated by the CIA in its attempts to cover up its role in Iran-Contra.

In his position on the Iran desk in Washington, Hemmings became aware of the senior CIA officials' role in the secret arms- for-hostages transaction with Iran and the subsequent cover up by the CIA. His knowledge of this came up in April 1987 during the confirmation hearings for William Webster as Director of Central Intelligence. Hemmings was ordered by his superiors to prepare a memo on what he knew, but to leave out certain things.

"My refusal to alter my testimony to fit the cover story then, and later in 1989 as a Senate witness, brought me under intense pressure to remain silent or else!! Death, unemployment and loss of access to my children were all used as weapons and threats," Hemmings wrote in a December 1990 statement mailed to me.

All of Azima's wheeling and dealing, his companies' bankruptcies and his associations with mobsters brought him into the gunsights of a very talented and persistent investigator with the Internal Revenue Service's Criminal Investigations Division in Kansas City. After this investigator discovered Azima's connections to the failed Indian Springs State Bank, he went to the Justice Department's Organized Crime Strike Force in Kansas City, which was investigating Mario Renda's linked financing deals with Indian Springs.

The IRS's CID official met with Lloyd Monroe, a veteran attorney with the strike force who had previously prosecuted narcotics cases in Indiana. After the IRS criminal investigator gave Monroe his information on the Azima/Indian Springs connection, Monroe assigned the FBI agents investigating Indian Springs to look into it.

Several days later, the agents met with Monroe and gave him some shocking news. Azima, they said, had a "get-out-of-jail-free card" because of his work for the CIA.

One of the FBI agents involved told me later: "The problem is the fact that this guy had a 'get-out-of-jail-free card.' His association with Global involved contract flying for the CIA."

Some Global flights, the FBI agent added, had munitions and arms going out and narcotics coming in. Van Geyso, a former Global pilot, said that on one of his cargo flights to Bogotá, Colombia, he returned with a shipment of flowers. "I heard there may have been some poppy seeds underneath the flowers," he said.

Azima denied any knowledge of Global airplanes transporting narcotics.

Monroe said that he argued for an investigation of Azima despite his connections to the CIA, but his boss, a former military intelligence man, vetoed it.

Asked if he knew about an FBI investigation being stopped because of his connections to the CIA, Azima replied, "I think you are mixing two different companies. I am totally unfamiliar with this." In a later, written statement issued by Azima's attorneys, Monroe's statements were attributed to sour grapes "after his double defeat by Anthony Russo in the tax cases."

Russo's first trial on tax fraud charges resulted in a hung jury, as did the second trial. The judge then dismissed the charges against the previously convicted felon and mob associate. Azima told the *Houston Post* in 1989 that he had "no idea" about Russo's connections to organized crime. But he told the *Kansas City Star* in 1984 that Russo's connections to organized crime figures did not deter him from doing business with Russo.

Meanwhile, the IRS investigator continued prodding the Justice

Department to prosecute Azima. After the organized crime strike force turned him down, he went to the U.S. Attorney's Office in Kansas City, Missouri, which sat on the information and did nothing. Azima, in the interim, had moved to London, where he headquartered his airplane-leasing business. The United States doesn't have extradition from England for income-tax violations, Monroe noted.

Among Global's creditors in its bankruptcy case was a mysterious Southern California aircraft company that defaulted on a multi-million-dollar loan from one of the biggest failed savings and loans in the country.

Although Response Air had its headquarters in Laguna Hills, California, its principal place of business in 1983 was a hangar at Richards-Gebaur Air Force Base, south of Kansas City, Missouri. Response's principal business was the sale of aircraft parts and supplies, according to incorporation papers it filed in 1984 in Miami. In October 1984, a year after Global declared bankruptcy, Response Air submitted a claim to Global for $155,055 in parts, for which it had not been paid. Global's bankruptcy attorneys responded with a lawsuit to recover $93,962 Global paid to Response in the 90-day period preceding its bankruptcy filing.

However, no officers of Response could be located to serve the lawsuit on, and the Global bankruptcy attorneys filed papers stating that Response had forfeited its California charter for nonpayment of taxes and "is the subject of an investigation by the IRS."

The chief executive officer of Response Air was John M. Campbell, a very common name. But the registered agent of Response was a Joseph Ventresca. When I reached the only Joseph Ventresca listed in phone directories in the Southern California area where Response was head-quartered, he claimed there was another Joseph Ventresca in the area who was the person I was seeking.

Response Air was closely connected to a Texas company called Ransom Aircraft, controlled by Louis T. "Bill" Ransom of Dallas. In 1983, Ransom Aircraft consigned $19.5 million of aircraft parts to Response to sell, Response getting one-third of the profits. In 1984, when Bill Ranson signed a lease in Miami for Ransom Aircraft, his signature was witnessed by Response's representative and registered agent in Miami, Vernon R. Craig.

In the late 1970s, Ransom was at the center of an airplane scandal in Australia, where his companies Global Jet Sales and Parmax of Fort

Worth were trying to buy 12 Lockheed C-130 cargo aircraft owned by the Australian Air Force. A scandal erupted when it was discovered that Ransom's companies intended on selling the cargo planes to Libya. And, although Ransom apparently did not buy the planes because of the publicity, he registered them with the U.S. Federal Aviation Administration.

Most of the C-130s were eventually brought to the United States under the control of a San Francisco law firm, Ford & Vlahos. Two of the cargo planes were destined for a Colombian airline when federal authorities stopped the transfer, fearing the planes would be used by the Medellín cartel for narcotics trafficking. One of the C-130s, according to former Pentagon investigator Gene Wheaton, ended up in Mena, Arkansas, where Barry Seal had his drug-smuggling and Contra assistance operations. The aircraft arrived in Mena after Seal was murdered, Wheaton told me.

(Ransom's partner in the abortive Australian C-130 purchase was Max Park. Park has also been associated with Ian "Dr. Doom" Smalley, a notorious British arms dealer and Ph.D. economist. Smalley was arrested in Texas in 1982 in a government sting operation for conspiring to buy tanks and antitank missiles in the United States for illegal sale to Iran and Iraq. Smalley was acquitted after his attorney, Richard "Racehorse" Haynes, convinced the jury that his client had been entrapped and had believed that the sales were covertly approved by the U.S. government.)

In the fall of 1983, Sunbelt Savings Association of Dallas made a loan to Ransom Aircraft secured by $19.5 million of new and used DC-8 parts, according to a lien filed with the Texas secretary of state. The very next lien filed in the state records was a consignment of these parts to Response Air at Richards-Gebaur Air Force Base by a joint venture of Ransom and Sunbelt Savings.

Less than two years later, Sunbelt filed a lawsuit against Ransom and Response for defaulting on the loan. Documents in the lawsuit state that the DC-8 parts, which included 21 Pratt & Whitney jet engines, were purchased from Delta Airlines. The parts were listed on Delta's books at a value of $23 million, according to lawsuit records, which also stated that Sunbelt lent Ransom $1.5 million in August 1983 and $1 million in September, using the DC-8 parts as collateral. Sunbelt ultimately received a court judgment against Response Air for $1.5 million, but was unable to collect on it.

However, a federal regulator familiar with Sunbelt said the S&L

actually lent the $19.5 million that was recorded in the Texas lien records. None of the money lent on the aircraft parts was repaid to Sunbelt, which finally failed in October 1986, under the weight of defaulted, delinquent and worthless loans. Two years later, Sunbelt was merged with seven other insolvent Texas S&LS, including Jarrett Wood's Western Savings, at a bailout cost to the federal government of $2 to $3 billion.

Sunbelt Savings, known in the industry as "Gunbelt Savings," was controlled by Ed McBirney, a young (mid-thirties) wheeler-dealer nick-named "Fast Eddie." McBirney's beginnings in the thrift industry go back to George Aubin and Jarrett Woods, with many connections to Herman K. Beebe's friends and financial institutions.

Before McBirney consolidated several smaller Texas S&Ls into Sunbelt, he was the president of Texoma Savings in a small town in North Texas. Through McBirney and Aubin, a mutual associate of theirs named John Roberts, a San Antonio developer, purchased Commerce Savings in Angleton, Texas, from Jarrett Woods and Woods's brother-in-law, Thomas Perry. McBirney and Aubin split a $300,000 commission on this sale, and McBirney helped Woods get rid of some bad loans on Commerce's books to facilitate sale of the S&L to Roberts.[9]

(Roberts, as noted earlier, was involved in huge deals in Houston and Colorado with Adnan Khashoggi.)

By 1983, McBirney had control of Sunbelt Savings and Woods had control of Western Savings, and the two began making multi-million-dollar deals between them. Other big borrowers at Sunbelt included Thomas Gaubert, owner of Independent American Savings Association; Joe Russo, Kappa Sigma alumnus and head of Ameriway Savings; K.C. Hood, who had been president of Beebe's umbrella company AMI before he went to work at Western Savings; and Joseph Grosz, the Chicago mob associate who ran San Jacinto Savings.

McBirney also had several direct dealings with Beebe, according to Beebe's former right-hand man, Dale Anderson. One was just a straight loan to McBirney on an apartment project in Dallas. Another was worthy of note:

McBirney wanted Sunbelt to buy an airplane for his use, so he went to Beebe to get a loan from Beebe's Bossier Bank & Trust. Beebe told him that Bossier didn't have the cash in hand to make the loan, but that

---

[9] *Dallas Morning News*, March 31, 1989.

that was not a problem. Bossier got the cash by selling participations in a few loans on its books to Carroll Kelly's Continental Savings in Houston.

And where did Continental get its cash? Why from Sunbelt, of course, which bought certificates of deposit from Continental. Thus, the money to buy Sunbelt's plane for McBirney ultimately came from Sunbelt itself. This is a good example of the way S&Ls operated—and serves as a warning to investigators that unless they track the money to its ultimate source and destination, they don't have the whole story. (One federal investigator who was trying to track the loans Richard Rossmiller got from Hill Financial Savings said he had previously worked on the Butcher brothers' bank scandal in Tennessee, and in one instance had discovered money leaving a Butcher bank and being routed through six different entities before coming back to the Butchers.)

But the most curious loan Sunbelt made has to be the one to Ransom Aircraft and Response Air for the $19.5 million in aircraft parts. Savings and loans in Texas during the 1980s made a lot of unusual loans, but the Sunbelt loan on new and used DC-8 parts appears unique. The DC-8, like the 707, was a dinosaur. Beginning in 1985, the two aircraft couldn't operate in the United States without special, and expensive, noise-limitation equipment. So the parts were probably headed overseas. Although Azima's Global International Airways was apparently Response Air's biggest customer, it doesn't seem likely that the parts were destined for Global, which used 707s, not DC-8s.

After Global declared bankruptcy in late 1983 and Capitol Air declared bankruptcy in late 1984, and the IRS began investigating Azima and the FAA stopped 707s from operating here, the Iranian native moved himself and his businesses to London. He started a company called Aviation Leasing Group, which owned planes and leased them to other companies rather than operating them. He built his fleet up to around 50 planes and vowed never again to own an operating airline company in the United States.

This vow wasn't surprising, given his IRS investigation and the two previous bankruptcies here, which left creditors holding the bag for millions in unpaid bills. Nevertheless, in February 1989 he snuck quietly back into this country and without any fanfare bought a small cargo airline company in Waco, Texas, called Buffalo Airways.

Buffalo Airways was incorporated in Texas in December 1982 by

Wordy Jack Thompson, Jr., a Dallas attorney then. Thompson was also an incorporator, along with Bill Ransom, of Global Jet Sales, the Fort Worth company that was involved in Ransom's attempt to sell the 12 Australian Air Force C-130s to Libya.

In 1986, Thompson was convicted of lying on loan application papers for a condominium loan from Empire Savings in Mesquite, Texas. (Empire's was the first big S&L failure in Texas, discussed in Chapter 5.) Thompson was sentenced to four years in prison and fined $10,000. Shortly before he was convicted, he was disbarred for refusing to give clients money they had won in civil lawsuit settlements.

Thompson was convicted on four counts of falsifying documents, including overvaluing a condominium he owned in Mazatlán, Mexico, on a loan application he made to Empire Savings in November 1982, just one month before he incorporated Buffalo Airways.

Dewayne Sheehy, executive vice president of Buffalo, said he didn't know who Thompson was, and that Thompson now has no relationship to Buffalo. In a written statement to reporters, Azima's attorneys said, "The fact that Mr. Thompson incorporated the organization is of no significance."

Sheehy said Buffalo did not start operations until 1984, when it began with two 707s. At first, he said, Buffalo operated passenger charters, then it went to work for Burlington Air Express, flying night freight. Buffalo had five aircraft then and sold a couple of them to Burlington. "Then we were the unsuccessful bidder for the second contract with Burlington. We went back into the ad hoc freight business from 1984 to 1988," said Sheehy.

(The company that got a great deal of the Burlington work was Southern Air Transport.)

Asked whether Buffalo did business with the CIA, Sheehy replied, "Absolutely not." There is an entry, however, in Oliver North's White House notebooks that indicates otherwise. On March 21, 1985, North received a telephone call from Alan Fiers, the director of the CIA's Central American Task Force, who would later plead guilty to withholding information from Congress during its Iran-Contra investigation. Fiers reported that a pilot for a Buffalo Airways 707 flying from Poland to Guatemala was "on ground in London." The next entry states: "friend in Seattle," and then underneath that, "arms" and either an ampersand or a dollar sign.

So it appears that Buffalo Airways was flying arms from Poland to

Guatemala for the CIA and North, when they ran into some trouble in London and had to call the CIA.

But Buffalo allegedly fell on hard times, and by February 1989, when Azima bought Buffalo, it only had one airplane, Sheehy stated. However, Azima quickly poured the money in, and by the end of 1989 the company had six 707s and was continuing to expand, with bases in Madrid, Spain and Stanstead, England.

Azima said he bought Buffalo as an "insurance policy" for his leasing business in the event any company stopped leasing some of his planes: "We knew their company did exist. We've done business with them before. I knew Larry Walston, president and chief executive of the company. He runs it. It was purely a financial transaction."

After Azima bought Buffalo, a number of its high-ranking employees moved on to a small aircraft company in Houston run by a mysterious aircraft operator with friends in high places.

16

The CIA Takes a Bath

When Jim Bath arrived in Houston in 1965, he was twenty-nine years old and looking for a job. In the next 20 years, Bath would:

(1) become good friends and do business with George W. Bush, the President's son;

(2) go into the real estate business with Lan Bentsen, the senator's son;

(3) work for Edward du Pont's Atlantic Aviation;

(4) take as a partner a former Atlantic Aviation executive who was a board member of an organization that provided aircraft for relief help to the Contras;

(5) become trustee for two of the richest families in Saudi Arabia, including one which owned a Saudi bank that provided financing to Adnan Khashoggi around the time of the Khashoggi-Ghorbanifar arms-for-hostages transactions with the Iranians and whose highest-profile member was indicted in the summer of 1992 on fraud charges relating to the collapse of BCCI;

(6) form a Cayman Islands company whose other principals were also in a Cayman company that was a key intermediary in Oliver North's "Enterprise" in moving private donations to the Contras (which company, Skyways Aircraft Leasing, would hire a number of former employees of Buffalo Airways, including one who had worked at Azima's Global);

(7) become an asset of the CIA, reportedly recruited by George Bush himself;

(8) provide office space for Reza Pahlavi, the late Shah of Iran's son (who, known as the Baby Shah, was in contact with the CIA, which was providing some support to his backers);

(9) form a company with a former Air America pilot;

(10) own stock in Charter Bank, whose directors included E. Trine Starnes, Jr., a big Contra supporter and large borrower from Silverado Savings and several Beebe-backed S&Ls (more on Starnes later);

(11) do business with Jack Trotter, Walter Mischer's close associate, who was a trustee for Senator Lloyd Bentsen's blind trust;

(12) get a sweetheart gasoline contract at Houston's Ellington Field from the Department of Defense; and

(13) borrow money from Lamar Savings and Mainland Savings.

Bath was born in 1936 in Natchitoches, Louisiana. In a deposition in a lawsuit in Houston, he stated that he had "attended three small colleges in Louisiana, basically going to a school where I could find work, which was in radio, TV, and finished my last two years at LSU in Baton Rouge with a degree in publishing management."[1]

He then joined the Air Force, where he was a fighter pilot for five years. His service included three years stationed at Richards-Gebaur Air Force Base south of Kansas City. When he left the Air Force in 1965, he moved to Houston. "I immediately began flying and pulling alert almost full-time at the National Guard. They have a fighter squadron at Ellington just like the one I had come from. So that, in effect, was my first job in Houston," he stated in the Houston deposition.

It was at the Air National Guard that Bath met George W. Bush. They became good friends, but, according to Bush, never did any business together. However, records filed in a lawsuit in Houston involving Bath contradict the President's son: they show Bath was an investor in a Bush oil and gas enterprise. Bush did say that Bath "is a lot of fun."[2] Bath also met Lloyd Bentsen III, one of the senator's sons, at the Air National Guard at Ellington.

Bath first got a job in Houston selling aircraft for a Dallas-based company, Brown Aero Corporation. Brown Aero opened a Houston office, where Bath worked for about three years. Then "in 1968 I was hired by Atlantic Aviation Corporation to open an office in Houston,

---

[1] James R. Bath vs. Charles W. White, 281st Judicial District, Harris County, Texas, No. 86-42551.
[2] *Houston Post*, December 9, 1990.

Texas. In the early 70s—I'll say 1970 because I really don't remember—I was promoted to vice president of the aircraft divisions of Atlantic and basically commuted between Houston and Wilmington for the next several years," Bath stated.

Atlantic Aviation is headquartered in Wilmington, Delaware, and is reportedly the largest business-aircraft sales and service company in the world. It is owned by one of the wealthiest du Ponts, Edward. Active in Republican party politics in Delaware and cousin to former Delaware governor Pierre du Pont, Edward was an officer of the $2 billion family holding company, Christiana Securities, and he and his immediate family owned or controlled more than $72 million in E. I. Du Pont common stock.[3] Richard C. du Pont, who owned the CIA-connected Summit Aviation, also served on the board of Atlantic Aviation.[4]

When Bath was working for Atlantic, he negotiated a distributorship agreement with Israel Aircraft Industries. This company was founded by Adolf "Al" Schwimmer, an American-born Israeli arms dealer and special adviser to then-Israeli Prime Minister Shimon Peres. Schwimmer, along with Yaacov Nimrodi (arms merchant and former Israeli Defense Attaché to Teheran), Ghorbanifar, Amiram Nir (adviser to Peres on counter-terrorism) and Khashoggi, began devising ways to gain the release of hostages held in Lebanon and open dialogue with Iran. Through this group came the TOW missile shipments in the fall of 1985 that coincided with Khashoggi's profits from Mainland Savings.

In 1973, Bath quit Atlantic Aviation and joined with Lan Bentsen to form Bath/Bentsen Interests. They developed an apartment complex outside Houston, some airport hangars and a few other odds and ends of real estate in a county south of Houston. Although they parted company in 1976, according to Bentsen and Bath's deposition, Bath continued to use the Bath/Bentsen letterhead. In July 1990, Bath wrote a letter on Bath/Bentsen letterhead to the Federal Aviation Administration, asking for information about the registration of two airplanes.[5]

Bentsen told the *Houston Post* in a written statement that he and Bath are "periodically involved in the disposition of the properties acquired" from 1972 to 1976. Bath also stated in his 1987 deposition that "Lan Bentsen and I still had ongoing partnerships from when we were

---

[3] *Du Pont Dynasty: Behind the Nylon Curtain,* by Gerard Colby (Lyle Stuart, 1984).
[4] Ibid.
[5] *Houston Post,* December 9, 1990.

actively doing partnerships and deals, but in fact we do them even until today."

The year Bath and Bentsen purportedly separated, 1976, was a banner one for Bath. In March he started an airplane company, Jim Bath and Associates, with Johnson M. "Jack" Taylor, a pilot with 27 years of military service. Taylor had also worked for Atlantic Aviation.

A March 7, 1986, ground-breaking story in the *Texas Observer* on private assistance to the Contras identified Taylor as being a board member and supporter of a St. Louis-based group called Wings of Hope. The story stated that Wings of Hope provided a plane to another group, Mercy Flight, which was bringing wounded Contras out of Honduras.

Another Wings of Hope board member, George Haddaway of Lindale, Texas, told the *Texas Observer* that "crucial support" for their organization came from Taylor. "Every time he sold a big airplane, he sent us 10 percent, so we latched onto him pretty quick. He's a marcher," Haddaway told the magazine. Haddaway went on to say, "I must admit my whole life has been spent concerned with the containment of Marxist-Leninism on this continent."

The author of the *Observer* piece, Dave Denison, said that Wings of Hope was also involved in a government health program in Belize.

Several months after Bath and Taylor started Jim Bath and Associates, Bath got a huge break. He was named as a trustee for Sheikh Salem bin Laden of Saudi Arabia, a member of the family that owns the largest construction company in the Middle East. Bath's job was to handle all of bin Laden's North American investments and operations.[6]

(Bin Laden's father, Muhammad bin Laden, was a patient of Adnan Khashoggi's physician father, and got Khashoggi involved in his first deal as a middle man. This was a truck sale that Khashoggi engineered in the 1950s just after he returned from college in America. Khashoggi sent the $25,000 commission to bin Laden, who returned it to Khashoggi.[7])

According to federal law enforcement sources, bin Laden also did business with Salim Saab, the Lebanese who was a partner with Cayman attorney Ian Paget-Brown in Sara, Ltd., which borrowed money from

---

[6] Resumé of Jim R. Bath.
[7] *The Kingdom: Arabia & The House of Sa'ud*, by Robert Lacey (New York: Harcourt Brace Jovanovich, 1981).

Mainland. These sources said Saab listed on his resumé a contract he had with bin Laden that was secured by a November 1984 letter of credit for $86,000.

Several months after Bath was named as trustee for bin Laden, he became the trustee for Sheikh Abdullah Baroom, who owned a large Saudi Arabian cement and steel company. Then sometime later he began working for Sheikh Khalid bin Mahfouz, the former chief executive officer of his family's National Commercial Bank, Saudi Arabia's biggest and most closely related to the royal family bank.

Sheikh Khalid remained in his position at NCB until one week after he and his London-based associate, Haroon Kahloon, were indicted in New York in 1992 on charges that they had schemed to defraud depositors, regulators and auditors of the insolvent BCCI. At the same time, the Federal Reserve Board announced that it found Sheikh Khalid and NCB had violated American banking laws in trying to acquire Washington-based First American Bancshares in concert with BCCI. Shortly thereafter, a federal judge signed an order freezing Sheikh Khalid's U.S. assets, including a luxury penthouse apartment on Fifth Avenue in New York and stock in MCorp.

It was the National Commercial Bank that lent some $35 million to Khashoggi in the summer of 1985, around the same time Khashoggi was getting more than $12 million in cash from Mainland Savings.

Sheikh Khalid was an investor in Main Bank in Houston along with Bath, former Texas governor John Connally and Gaith Pharoan, another Saudi indicted in the BCCI scandal. In February 1992, Pharoan, David L. Paul and William C. Berry were indicted in Miami federal court on charges relating to the collapse of CenTrust Savings, the largest failed S&L in Florida. Pharoan, who was named in two counts of the 22-count indictment, had good company in the shenanigans perpetrated against CenTrust, and ultimately the American taxpayers: Charles Keating's ACC, BCCI and Michael Milken's Drexel Brunham Lambert. But none of these entities were indicted.

(BCCI was one of the international banks of choice for the CIA's covert operations around the world. From the running of surveillance of the Abu Nidal terrorist network organization out of the Sloan Street branch in London, to the bank account opened by Oilver North in BCCI's Paris branch during North's covert haydays, BCCI operated above the law. Adnan Khashoggi also found the bank's Monte Carlo branch accommodating—he used it in his arms transactions with Iran.)

Sheikh Khalid bought into Main Bank with Bath, Connally and Pharoan in 1976. Connally sold his investment in 1980 to make a futile run for the Republican presidential nomination. Then in 1981, Mercantile Texas Corporation, Capital Bank's holding company and soon to be MCorp., bought Main Bank from Sheikh Khalid.

In 1979, Sheikh Khalid purchased the River Oaks mansion of Chester Reed, the father-in-law of John Ballis, who pleaded guilty to S&L fraud and turned state's evidence against Roy Dailey, Robert Corson's first cousin. The Saudi sheikh purchased the house for $4.25 million through an attorney with the Houston law firm of Baker & Botts, which was also handling his Houston land deals through Bath.

One of Bath's closest business associates was Charles W. "Bill" White, who graduated from the Naval Academy in Oliver North's class and then went on to be a fighter pilot with the Navy, flying off aircraft carriers. White earned an M.B.A. from Harvard and then was recruited in 1978 by Lan Bentsen to work with Bath. In 1980, White and Bath formed a real estate development company together. White and Bath split up in 1986 and began a fierce legal battle over a $550,000 certificate of deposit from a Cayman Islands company that Bath headed. Bath asked White to help him meet the note payments by taking funds from other partnerships with no liability in the note. White refused. White has lost most of the legal fights and is bitter at Bath and his associates, who, he claims, have railroaded him to keep him from exposing Bath's CIA and Saudi connections.

White said Bath told him in 1982 that he worked for the CIA. (That Bath had some connections to the CIA has been independently verified by this reporter and by John Mecklin, an investigative reporter for the *Houston Post*.) White stated that Bath said he was recruited in 1976 by George Bush, the future President and then CIA Director, and given the assignment of monitoring the activities of his Saudi Arabian investors. White said that one time in 1982 he and Bath were at the Ramada Club in Houston when Vice President Bush walked in. Bush waved at Bath and said, "Hi, Jim," according to White.

Another Houstonian who knows Bath on a first-name basis is Walter Mischer, White said. White met Mischer when he and Bath were visiting the insurance giant American General, which was Mischer's partner in the Cinco Ranch development. Bath and Mischer obviously knew each other fairly well, White insisted. Bath's companies borrowed

$800,000 from Allied Bank Pasadena and $200,000 from Allied Bank Deer Park.

Mischer has said he knows Bath, but "just to shake hands with him."

One of Mischer's business partners, Jack Trotter, is listed as a reference on Bath's resumé. A source close to Bath said that Trotter was one of the Houstonians most responsible for introducing Bath around Houston and getting him wired into the right business circles. Bath and Lan Bentsen brokered a number of multi-thousand-acre tracts to syndications formed by Trotter, who was trustee for Senator Lloyd Bentsen's blind trust.

Another reference on Bath's resumé is Sidney A. Adger, the father of John Adger, Robert Corson's former partner, and of Stephen Adger, Kappa Sigma brother of Walt Mischer, Jr.

A small Houston accounting firm, Weatherford Kinton & Associates, which allegedly did work for a Mischer company, also did the accounting, according to White, for Bath's most interesting company, Skyways Aircraft Leasing. However, when Mischer was asked about Weatherford Kinton, which offices itself in the headquarters building of Mischer's umbrella corporation, he replied, "I don't know them."

Skyways Aircraft Leasing began on July 2, 1980, as a company called Cotopax Investments, registered in the Cayman Islands. Then, 29 days later, Cotopax changed its name to Skyways Aircraft Leasing Limited. On July 24, 1980, the directors of Skyways Aircraft Leasing met in George Town, Grand Cayman Island. (Interestingly, the meeting was a week before the name change was registered with the Cayman Islands authorities.) The directors named Bath as president and director and then resigned. All of the stock was made into bearer stock, which meant that it belonged to whoever possessed it. In his sworn deposition in the lawsuit against White, Bath refused to name the owners of the Skyways stock. (Documents filed in another lawsuit indicate that Sheikh Khalid owned Skyways. White said Skyways had at least one airplane, a Gulf-stream, that was on a long-term lease to an Abu Dhabi oil company.)

The original subscribers to Cotopax, who then turned Skyways Aircraft Leasing over to Bath, were Cayhaven Corporate Services, Ltd., of George Town, Grand Cayman; David G. Bird of George Town; and Grant J. R. Stein of George Town. Bird and Stein are both directors of Cayhaven Corporate Services and attorneys with W. S. Walker & Company, a law firm in George Town headed by William S. Walker.

Cayhaven Corporate Services and Bird were two of the three sub-scribers to a Cayman Islands company called I.C., Inc., which was incorporated April 26, 1985. I.C. sits right in the middle of a chart drawn by Oliver North, and found by investigators in North's White House safe, that shows the private network that provided support and money to the Contras. Here's how it worked:

The money started with donations to Spitz Channell's National Endowment for the Preservation of Liberty (NEPL). Then it was wired from NEPL's account at Palmer National Bank to the account of IBC, a Washington, D.C., public relations company formed by Republican operative Richard Miller at another Washington bank. Next, IBC wired the money to I.C. in the Cayman Islands, which then transferred a majority of it to the Swiss bank account used by North's "Enterprise" to fund the Contras.

On March 7, 1987, the *Washington Post* published the only account of these transactions. It called the flow of money a "circuitous route" and then stated: "It is not clear from the documents who is behind I.C., Inc., the Cayman Islands company, or why it was needed to transfer the money." Apparently no investigator with the Tower Commission probe of Iran-Contra or the congressional Iran-Contra committees was able, or even tried, to get to the bottom of I.C. either.

One person behind Cayhaven Corporate Services and the original subscribers to I.C. and Skyways Aircraft Leasing is Cayman Islands attorney William S. Walker. A man in his sixties, Walker has been an attorney in the Caymans for more than 30 years. Sources in George Town said he is from an old family from Guyana.

Cayhaven Corporate Services was ostensibly what is called a "captive manager." This is a company that handles self-insurance plans for companies that want to take advantage of the tax-free environment of the offshore Cayman Islands. A 1988 news story from the Caymans said Cayhaven primarily provides accounting services, and quoted Cayhaven manager Malcolm S. Davies that Cayhaven is "not actively seeking new captive clients and expects to keep a low profile. Premium volume for the captives under Cayhaven's management totals less than $14 million." Sources in George Town said Cayhaven is not one of the island's major captive managers.

In 1986, Cayhaven was replaced as the agent for Skyways by Caledonian Bank and Trust, a small local George Town bank, which is controlled by William S. Walker. From all appearances, Walker is just a nominee or front for the actual owners of I.C. and Skyways. In the case of I.C. and its successor company, Intel Co-operation, they both vanished after they were exposed in the *Washington Post*. After Skyways became embroiled in the Bath/White dispute, it registered in Texas and changed its name to Skyways International. But it apparently continues to be owned by Saudi Arabians.

Of the $3.6 million sent out by NEPL through IBC and I.C., about $1.7 million ended up in the Swiss bank account designated for the Contras. IBC kept about $400,000, while I.C. apparently kept about $1.5 million. Of this, some $452,000 went to another Cayman Islands company with Cayhaven as its registered agent, World Affairs Counselors, Inc. Another $21,182 went from I.C. to the Gulf and Caribbean Foundation.

As previously discussed, Gulf and Caribbean was controlled by Midland, Texas, oilman and a friend of President Bush, William Blakemore. There are at least two other people who are connected to both Blakemore and Skyways Aircraft Leasing, through Jim Bath and others: Jack Trotter and Walter Mischer. Skyways had deposits at Mischer's Allied Humble Bank and Allied Deer Park Bank, according to Bill White, Bath's former partner.

In May 1984, Bath borrowed $550,000 from InterFirst Bank in Houston, ostensibly, according to the bank records at that time, to "facilitate aircraft purchase." As collateral, Bath pledged a $500,000 certificate of deposit in the name of Skyways Aircraft Leasing. However, when the note became due and Bath was having trouble paying it off, a bank document dated May 1986 stated that the purpose of the loan was to make a downpayment on a 25-acre tract of land on Lake Houston. (One of the previous owners of this tract had been Jack Trotter.)

That was when Bath asked White to help him meet the note payments, and White refused. Bath then sued White and was able to get a judge to order that the property White owned be turned over to pay off the note. White said he believes that Bath was using Skyways's money, which may have belonged to the CIA, to speculate in Houston real estate. When the real estate went down, Bath turned on White for the money rather than tell Skyways's owners that he had lost it, White claimed.

Four of the top officers at Skyways came to Bath's company from Farhad Azima's Buffalo Airways. The earlier-mentioned George Selman was Director of Maintenance at Skyways. He had worked for Buffalo for five years before joining Skyways in August 1989, six months after Azima took over Buffalo. Before working at Buffalo, he worked for Azima's Global and before that for Saudi Arabian Airlines.

Selman resigned from Skyways in March 1991, just a few months after the *Houston Post*'s John Mecklin began writing stories about Bath. Skyways's former president and director of operations, William E. Crocker, resigned four months later, in July. Crocker worked at Buffalo Airways for four years before leaving in May 1989 for Skyways. Before Buffalo, Crocker had worked for Arrow Air, a Miami-based company that has allegedly transported weapons for the CIA.

Finally, George Lovell, Skyways's Director of Operations, joined Bath's company in 1987, after working for Buffalo Airways for two years. Back in the mid-1970s, Lovell worked for Saudi Arabian Airlines.

In October 1990, *Houston Post* investigative reporter John Mecklin reported that the Department of Defense was paying millions of dollars more than necessary by buying aviation fuel from a Bath company at Ellington Field. The *Post* reported that Bath's company, Southwest Airport Services, was charging government military aircraft anywhere from 22 cents a gallon to over 40 cents a gallon more than the price the Air National Guard base at Ellington was paying to buy its jet fuel from the Defense Fuel Supply Center, the government agency that wholesales fuel to military agencies.

In December 1990, Mecklin reported in the *Post* that the Department of Defense had paid Bath's company more than $12 million in contract overruns for the aviation fuel. From November 1985 through November 1989, the government paid Southwest Airport Services more than $16.2 million for fuel under contracts that estimated the company would be paid about $3.6 million, according to Mecklin's story.

Southwest Airport Services also has a sweetheart lease at Ellington from the city of Houston, under which it pays $650 a month. Bath's company won the lease in April 1985 under a lottery, but the lease has not been offered to any other fuel firms since that time, even though the lease was supposed to be a temporary measure.[8]

The first building project that Bath and White did together was a 162-unit apartment project in the small town of Humble, north of

---

[8] *Houston Post*, December 9, 1990.

Houston. To get the money to buy the land, Bath put White in touch with Sergio Luciani, White revealed.

Luciani was a loan broker who had his office at Mainland Savings. A Ph.D. economist from Italy, Luciani was brought into Mainland by Raymond Hill's right-hand man, Ron Bearden. Luciani's name appeared in the news in Houston regarding two sensational events. The first was a mysterious one-car accident resulting in the death of Houston businessman Ernest Allred. Luciani had brokered a Mainland loan to Allred and received a Porsche for his payment. The loan had gone bad and Allred was in trouble when he met with his unfortunate accident.

The second event was the arrest and conviction of Martha Marie Preston, dubbed the "crack queen," for her alleged control of crack cocaine distribution in Houston. Luciani sold a convenience store in Houston's Third Ward to Preston, which she turned into a narcotics distribution outlet.

One Mainland borrower said that when he was at Mainland Savings one day, Luciani introduced him to Leonard Capaldi, the reputed Detroit Mafia associate. After Mainland Savings hit the skids, Luciani returned to his native Italy. But in early 1982, when White went to see him at the urging of Bath, Luciani was going strong.

White said he put together a mortgage package for financing of the apartment project. Then Luciani introduced him to Laddie Howard, who was at Drew Mortgage in Houston. Drew Mortgage was a subsidiary of Lamar Savings in Austin, and Howard arranged a 100-percent-financed loan from Lamar, which means that White and Bath did not have to put any money down. (Howard had originally worked at Mainland Savings before joining Lamar. He later headed up the Houston office of Sunrise Savings out of Boynton Beach, Florida.)

After the loan application was submitted to Lamar, Luciani informed White that it had been rejected by the Austin S&L. White told Bath, and "the next thing I know it is back on," White said. So on December 13, 1982, White and Bath signed a $5.2 million promissory note to Lamar to buy the land and build the apartment project.

By December 1983, the project was finished, and the units were leased out. In June 1984, Bath and White renewed the $5.2 million note to Lamar. But even though the complex was completely leased out, the cash flow was not enough to retire the debt. By the summer of 1985, White said, they were more than $200,000 behind in their payments, so Lamar arranged for them to borrow $260,000 from Mainland to cover their payments. The papers were drawn up by Raymond Hill's law firm and Mainland got a second mortgage on the apartment property.

By the spring of 1986, however, Bath and White were in default of both loans. "Lamar wanted us to sell to Monzer Hourani," White said, but that would have left Bath and White still owing the $260,000 to Mainland. So instead, Lamar took the property back and Mainland forgave its note. Lamar then conveyed the property to Hourani, the Lebanese investor who had done business with Robert Corson and who is good friends with Senator Orrin Hatch.

A former high-ranking officer at Lamar said Hourani gave them an "in" with the Reagan Administration. Before Lamar was taken down by the feds, "we and Hourani had a conference call with Hatch and talked about our bailout proposal." Before that, "Hourani flew copies of the REO [real estate owned, or, that is, foreclosed on by Lamar] list, and got to [Danny] Wall [chairman of the Federal Home Loan Bank Board], Hatch, [U.S. Senator Jake] Garn [Republican-Utah] and the White House."

Meanwhile, across Houston another CIA asset was struggling for his financial life. By the middle of 1987, Vision Banc Savings's money had run out and Robert Corson was having financial problems. But one land deal that he was able to get a little walking money from was the purchase of 283 acres south of Houston. Corson bought the land in late 1985 with a real estate company out of Albuquerque, New Mexico, called Bellamah.

Who was behind Bellamah? The search begins in Chicago.

17

CHICAGO

The Gouletas family gets around. The two brothers and their sister were born in Greece, where their father, who had emigrated to America, got caught by World War II on a visit. But the family returned to Chicago in 1946, where they lived in a single hotel room while the parents took odd jobs.

The oldest brother, Nicholas, went to junior college for one year before becoming a door-to-door encyclopedia salesman. At one time a wrestling champion, he excelled especially as a salesman and worked his way up to vice president of North American sales for Collier's Encyclopedia.

The sister, Evangeline, two years older than Nicholas, earned a bachelor's degree in math and a master's degree in education and became a schoolteacher. She also worked for a time as a data analyst on the Minuteman missile program for North American Aviation. In 1981, Evangeline married then-New York Governor Hugh Carey. She had claimed, to the press, to be a widow, but a little research turned up three previous husbands—all still alive.

The youngest brother, Victor, elected to shorten his last name by dropping the last two letters, becoming Victor Goulet. After college he worked briefly at Martin Marietta on a prototype of the space shuttle and then returned to Chicago to attend law school and become a lawyer.

In 1969, the three decided to go into the real estate business together, and opened a storefront office on Chicago's North Side. In the next ten years they became the country's largest converter of apartments to condominiums and were dubbed "Condomania's First Family."[1] By 1981, their company, American Invsco (pronounced "invesco") had bought 79 apartment buildings in 33 cities and had sold more than 18,000 units for a total of $667 million.

The Gouletases were also noted for their byzantine corporate structure and massive bank borrowing to finance their purchases and expansion. And there were persistent stories of connections and financing from organized crime.

In 1978 the Los Angeles District Attorney issued a confidential intelligence bulletin that cited an "information source" who connected American Invsco to the Briar Management Company—"a vehicle for organized crime infiltration of Chicago real estate." (The Los Angeles Mafia crime family was under the dominion of the Chicago family.) Further, in 1980, Congressman Benjamin Rosenthal, chairman of the House Subcommittee on Commerce, Consumer and Monetary Affairs, who was conducting an investigation of condominium conversions, received an anonymous report alleging that the Gouletases' original financing came from Greek mobsters in Chicago.

By 1982, the family had much more to worry about than reports of mob ties. Their creditors were starting to close in on them as the condo market plummeted. Their banks, including the lead financier, Continental Illinois Bank, began taking back their real estate holdings in repayment of some $500 million in debt.

Even though American Invsco went down the tube, the Gouletases still owned other considerable holdings, including Electronic Realty Associates (ERA), the second largest real estate brokerage franchise system in the country. ERA was purchased in 1985 for $35 million by Tamco, the family's other major holding company.

Tamco had been formed in 1977 by Victor Goulet, who put $25 million into the company, while Nicholas and Evangeline, through loans secured by American Invsco properties, injected $50 million in non-voting capital into Tamco, thus insulating the money from American Invsco's creditors. In 1979, Victor took Lyman Hamilton for his partner and made him the chief executive officer of Tamco. Hamilton was the former $700,000-a-year president and CEO of International Telephone & Telegraph Company, one of the largest conglomerates in the world. Hamilton had been treasurer of ITT in the early 1970s when

---

[1] *Fortune*, August 10, 1981.

it was implicated in CIA plots in Chile and investigated for possible bribery in the Nixon Administration. Hamilton himself was never charged with any wrongdoing.

After graduating from Harvard with a master's degree, Hamilton worked on international and intelligence programs for the Federal Bureau of the Budget from 1950 to 1956. Then, from 1956 to 1960, he worked in Okinawa for the civil affairs and military government section of the Army. He joined ITT in 1962.

In 1974, the nomination of William Casey—who would later lead the CIA—to head the Export-Import Bank was temporarily blocked because of his possible role in the ITT bribery affair. Casey was investigated for alleged perjury and obstruction of justice in turning files of the Securities Exchange Commission, which he had headed, over to the Justice Department. But Casey was never charged in the matter and was confirmed as head of the Ex-Im Bank.

Another close associate of the Gouletas family is Allan J. Tessler, an attorney with the New York law firm of Shea & Gould, whose name partner, Milton Gould, was a close friend, attorney and confidant of Casey. Tessler served on the board of several Gouletas-affiliated companies, including Imperial Savings and Loan in California. Tessler is also a business partner and attorney for Dr. Earl Brian, a California physician and businessman who served from 1970 to 1975 as Secretary of Health in then-California Governor Ronald Reagan's cabinet. After Reagan was elected President, he named Brian chairman of a White House task force, the health care cost reduction task force that reported to Ed Meese.

Brian, a close, longtime friend of former Attorney General Meese, was in the middle of a nasty legal dispute between the Department of Justice and William A. Hamilton, the owner of a computer software company that contracted with the department to provide computer services (no relation to Lyman Hamilton). In a lawsuit against the department, Hamilton claimed that Brian tried to force him to sell his software company to the former physician/businessman, and when that failed, Meese and other Justice Department officials conspired to steal the software.

In a letter to Attorney General Richard Thornburgh, William Hamilton's attorney, former Attorney General Elliot Richardson, stated: "In December 1984, Daniel Tessler of 53rd Street Ventures, which had invested in INSLAW [Hamilton's software company] and was one of the companies contacted by Brian in September 1983, demanded that the Hamiltons sign over to him the voting rights of their controlling interest in INSLAW common stock. Tessler is a cousin of Allan Tessler, the Shea & Gould partner who handled M&A [mergers and acquisitions] work for Brian."

Hamilton won his case in bankruptcy court and federal district court, but lost on appeal.

Hamilton has said he had been told by several different people that Brian had connections to the CIA. Former Israeli intelligence officer Ari Ben-Menashe stated in an April 4, 1991, affidavit in the INSLAW case that Rafi Eitan told him that at Eitan's initiative and active encouragement, Brian had sold INSLAW's PROMIS software to Jordan's military intelligence organization. Eitan, according to the *Wall Street Journal*, was in charge of a secret Israeli intelligence unit in its Defense Ministry that was used to steal U.S. technology.

Several problem-plagued Brian companies that Tessler was brought in to head in late 1990 were Infotechnology and Financial News Network.[2] United Press International, the troubled news wire service, is owned by Infotechnology, which purchased it in 1988. The minority owner of UPI at the time Brian purchased it was Joe Russo, the Houston developer, S&L owner and borrower, friend of George Bush and Lloyd Bentsen and Kappa Sigma alum.

"Earl Brian headed one of the other entities trying to acquire UPI in 1986," Russo told the *Houston Post*. "He knows what he is doing. The future involvement by the Russo Group of Houston will be one of an adviser. We look forward to working together with World NewsWire [Brian's company]."[3]

(At the same time Russo was a minority owner of UPI, the wire service's management was contemplating moving its banking business to BCCI and First American Bank in Washington, D.C., which BCCI secretly owned.)

In addition to Lyman Hamilton (no relation to William), other members of Tamco's board of advisers included former Treasury Secretary William Simon; Andrew Brimmer, a former governor of the Federal Reserve Board; William Karnes, retired chairman of Beatrice Foods; and Christian Friedrich Karsten, Dutch banker and chairman of Holland America Lines.

When Lyman Hamilton began running Tamco, he and Goulet com-

[2] *Barron's*, November 19, 1990.
[3] *Houston Post*, February 22, 1988.

menced looking around for companies to buy. They first fixed on City Investing Company, a multi-billion-dollar New York conglomerate that owned General Development Corporation, a Florida home builder. In 1980, Tamco bought 12 percent of City Investing's stock, for about $80 million, with the intention of taking it over. City Investing rejected the offer, and instead agreed to allow corporate raider Victor Posner, who owned about 10 percent of the company's stock, to increase his holdings to 21 percent.

After Goulet founded Tamco in 1977, its only asset was the Dale Bellamah Company in Albuquerque, New Mexico. This company was formed in 1947 by Abdul Hamid "Dale" Bellamah, who claimed to be descended from the royal family of Lebanon. By 1958, Bellamah was reportedly the sixth largest home builder in the world. In 1973, a year after Dale Bellamah died, the company was sold to Ernest W. Hahn, Inc., a shopping-center developer from California. Then in 1978, Tamco bought Bellamah. The purchase was negotiated by a Tamco vice president, Robert J. Bobb, who was married to the daughter of former New Mexico Governor Jack Campbell. Through Campbell and his trips to New Mexico, Bobb, a native of Chicago and graduate of the University of Notre Dame law school, learned of the availability of Bellamah. After Tamco bought Bellamah, Bobb became the chief executive officer of the company.

In 1982, when the Gouletases were having financial problems, Tamco sold Bellamah to Bobb, Douglas Crocker II and some other investors, mostly Bellamah executives. Crocker, a Harvard graduate, had been president of American Invsco, and had written an angry letter to *Fortune* after its story on the Gouletas family was published in 1981. Crocker was particularly incensed about the allegations of organized crime ties.

When Bobb and Crocker, who owned 60 percent of Bellamah, took over the New Mexico company, it was already in a joint venture with the largest utility in New Mexico, Public Service Company of New Mexico. This 50-50 joint venture—Bellamah Community Development—began buying land in New Mexico and four adjoining states.

There were several unanswered questions about the purchase of Bellamah from the Gouletas family: What was the purchase price and where did Bobb and Crocker get the money? Did the Gouletases finance it for them and retain an interest in the company?

Among the first things Bobb and Crocker did after taking control of

Bellamah was to raise cash by selling 20 percent of their interest in the company to an Albuquerque savings and loan, ABQ Bank, for $6 million. Then, one year later, Bobb and Crocker sold another 10 percent of their interest in Bellamah to Key Savings and Loan in Englewood, Colorado, for $9 million.

Key Savings was part of the Herman K. Beebe chain of rotten savings and loans, and was listed in the 1985 Comptroller of the Currency report on Beebe as being controlled by him or his associates. In 1983, Key was purchased by Dallas attorney Larry Vineyard, who had earlier represented Don Dixon in his purchase of Vernon Savings and Tyrell Barker in his purchase of State Savings of Lubbock. Beebe helped finance both of those purchases.

Vineyard took an active role in the operations of State Savings and then helped Barker acquire Brownfield Savings, some 30 miles southwest of Lubbock. Of course Vineyard hungered for a savings and loan of his own, and in the middle of 1983 conspired with Barker and one of their associates to buy Key Savings.

Vineyard first approached Clint Murchison, Jr., for financing the purchase of Key. To help induce such financing, State Savings made an $867,000 unsecured loan to Murchison and a similar unsecured loan to Murchison's partner and Beebe's former employee Louis A. Farris, Jr. Murchison never came through with the financing for Key and defaulted on his unsecured loan.

Vineyard then got a $6 million loan from First City National Bank of Albuquerque to buy Key Savings, in a complex deal that included loans from Brownfield Savings. Vineyard and Barker were later convicted for this scheme and got five years in prison. Before that happened, however, Vineyard secured a $17 million loan from Vernon Savings to refinance his Key Savings purchase. Vineyard converted $2.6 million of that loan for his own use, including the purchase of a $1.2 million house in Dallas and the establishment of trust funds for his children. He was also convicted for that and received an additional five years in prison.

Immediately after Vineyard took control of Key Savings, he had had Key purchase 10 percent of Bellamah, which equaled 5 percent of Bellamah Community Development, for $9 million. Bellamah executive Larry Stroup told the *Albuquerque Tribune* that he'd met Vineyard in 1983 when Vineyard was representing a Houston buyer of some of Bellamah's property.

In November 1985, Bellamah formed a joint venture with Robert

Corson, called Parkwyck, to buy 283 acres in Brazoria County, about nine miles south of the Astrodome. Bellamah put up the entire $4.4 million purchase price. Then, in October 1986, amid talk of grandiose development plans, MBank Houston lent the joint venture $11 million on the property.

The property was never developed: Bellamah defaulted on the loan and declared bankruptcy. But prior to that, Bellamah bought out Corson's interest for $33,000 in cash in the summer of 1987, even though Corson never put up any of his own money. Bellamah executive Larry Stroup, who signed all the Parkwyck Joint Venture documents with Corson, claimed that Bellamah's man in Dallas, Dan Dennison, arranged the deal with Corson. (Dennison never returned my phone calls to him.)

Bellamah's only other Houston-area land deal got its partner, M.D.C. Holdings, into trouble with the Securities and Exchange Commission. M.D.C. Holdings is a large Denver-based home builder and residential developer headed by Larry Mizel. It has gained notoriety in the savings-and-loan debacle for its dealings with Michael Milken, Charles Keating's Lincoln Savings, San Jacinto Savings and, most of all, Silverado Savings, the Denver S&L where Neil Bush, the President's son sat on the board of directors.

The Houston deal occurred like this: In January 1986, M.D.C. bought Wood Brothers Homes, a home builder that had been spun off by City Investing, the New York company that Victor Goulet and Lyman Hamilton tried to buy. Wood Brothers owned some 300 undeveloped, residential lots in Houston that it had acquired when it took over Raldon, a home-building company formerly owned by Vernon Savings's Don Dixon.

In 1986, the home market in Houston was terrible, and M.D.C. wanted to unload its lots and book a profit. At the same time, Bellamah owned a large undeveloped residential property in Castle Rock, Colorado, south of Denver, to which it was trying to attract home builders. Somehow, the two companies got together (not surprising, given their mutual acquaintances in the Beebe/Corson circles and their Chicago connections) and decided to swap property. Bellamah would get the Houston lots and M.D.C. would get 60 acres in the Castle Rock development.

Although Bellamah booked the deal as a straight swap, and thus recorded no profit or loss, M.D.C. apparently booked a profit and was

called on the carpet by the SEC. An examination of the Houston transaction shows that the parties involved tried to hide the fact that the deal
was part of a swap—by using Silverado Savings as a middle man.

On June 24, 1986, M.D.C. sold the Houston lots to Silverado Elektra
Venture, Ltd., a joint venture between Silverado Savings and some other
Denver investors. The deed from M.D.C. to Silverado showed that
Silverado paid $737,707 in cash and signed a promissory note for $2.96
million. M.D.C. didn't file a deed of trust in the Harris County records,
which would have made it much more difficult to foreclose on the
property if Silverado defaulted on the note. That omission indicated
there was something else going on.

That something else happened two days later, when Silverado sold
the lots to Bellamah Community Development. In the deed filed for
record there was no purchase price given, no promissory note refer-
enced, nor was a deed of trust filed. In addition, the vendor's lien (a
mortgage) in the deed was marked out, and there was no reference to
the prior $2.96 million mortgage, which had not been released in the
records.

M.D.C. officials admitted to the SEC that they did not sell the
Houston lots directly to Bellamah because they would be prohibited
from booking a profit because of the related Castle Rock deal. However,
they did not admit that the sale to Silverado and its subsequent sale to
Bellamah were part of a swap.[4] Bellamah officials, nevertheless, told
Albuquerque reporters that the deal was a straight swap.[5]

According to SEC attorneys, Silverado officials said they would not
have taken part in the deal and done M.D.C. the favor if Bellamah had
not bought the lots.

Eighteen months later, Silverado participated in a similar swap with
Bellamah that allowed Bellamah to book a $3 million profit. Bellamah
sold 127 acres of undeveloped residential property near Thornton, north
of Denver, to Silverado for $7.9 million, while Silverado sold a develop-
ment of about 330 acres in Scottsdale, Arizona, to Bellamah for $11.5
million. It is not known how much Bellamah and Silverado originally
paid for their properties or what underlying debt was on them, but the

---

[4] United States Securities and Exchange Commission, In the matter of: MDC
Holdings Corporation, et al., No. HO-2056.
[5] *Albuquerque Journal*, September 30, 1990; *Albuquerque Tribune*, October 5,
1990.

transaction allowed Bellamah to book a $3 million profit, while Silverado recorded an equity investment of $3 million.

This proposed transaction caught the attention of an agent at the Federal Home Loan Bank Board in Topeka, Kansas, who wrote Silverado a letter on January 15, 1988. The letter requested the following information: who the principals of Bellamah were; what Bellamah paid for its Colorado property; what the value of the appraisal of Silverado's Arizona property was; and whether Silverado had a commitment to retire the outstanding debt on its property.

There is no record in the Silverado file released to the public on whether Silverado answered any of these questions, except to provide an appraisal of the Colorado property. What *is* known is that exactly one week after the first query letter went out from the Topeka board, the principal supervisory agent of Silverado for the board, Kermit Mowbray, approved the transaction. It was Mowbray who later that year held off seizing deeply insolvent Silverado until the day after George Bush was elected President!

It was also around the end of 1988 that Bellamah began plans to buy a troubled Albuquerque S&L: Sandia Federal Savings and Loan.[6] Bellamah was going bankrupt too, and was hoping that a purchase of Sandia would help them both survive. Sandia was owned by a group of savings and loan executives from Dallas, who purchased the Albuquerque institution in May 1984 with $16 million borrowed from Vernon Savings. Shortly before this purchase, Sandia bought more than $80 million in loan participations from Vernon.

The owners of Sandia included Delwin Morton, the chairman of NorthPark Savings in Richardson, Texas, and Charles J. Wilson, a director of NorthPark Savings and large stockholder and borrower at the fraud-riddled First South Savings in Little Rock, Arkansas. Morton and Wilson borrowed more than $5 million each from Vernon to buy Sandia Savings stock. Other Sandia shareholders included Thomas Gaubert, a big Democratic fundraiser who controlled Independent American Savings in Dallas, and Dan Wipff, president of Telecom, a Houston-based financial services and industrial manufacturing company. Gaubert and Wipff borrowed a little less than $1 million each from Vernon to buy Sandia Savings stock.

[6] *Albuquerque Tribune*, October 5, 1990.

In 1985, Gaubert bought control of Telecom with a $6 million loan from Sunbelt Savings. He moved the company to Dallas and placed Delwin Morton on its board along with Joseph Grosz, the San Jacinto Savings executive who had worked for the Gouletases. In 1988, Gaubert was acquitted on charges of defrauding an Iowa savings and loan on a Dallas apartment deal that also involved the ubiquitous John Riddle. The $16 million in Vernon loans for Sandia stock were later refinanced at Sunbelt Savings, which bumped them up to $19 million, apparently giving the shareholders a $3 million windfall.

Sandia was heavily involved in deals and lending to Texas companies connected to Corson and Mischer, in addition to the $9 million loan to bail out Howard Pulver's group, discussed in Chapter 4. In February 1985, for example, Sandia purchased three promissory notes from Allied Bank of Dallas signed by Independence Mortgage, Inc. The face value of the 1983 notes totaled $9 million, with the unpaid principal and interest coming to $2.1 million at the time of their sale from Allied to Sandia.

One month after this deal, Sandia lent $15 million on a large tract of land west of Houston to a Houston developer John Ballis. Sandia's money went straight to Allied Bank in Houston, to pay down a $35 million loan Allied made to Ballis to buy the tract and an adjacent piece of land.

Ballis was a former dentist in Beaumont, who moved to Houston and married the daughter of Chester Reed, a wealthy, influential developer and investor who started out as a veterinarian. Ballis was a close associate of John Riddle and had gotten into thoroughbred horses in a big way. A Houston private investigator reported that Riddle had introduced Ballis to George Aubin at the 1985 Kentucky Derby, and one of Ballis' horses, Groovy, raced in the 1986 Kentucky Derby.

In 1990, Ballis pleaded guilty to lying on documents for a loan from First Savings of East Texas and turned state's evidence against First Savings's owner, Roy Dailey, Robert Corson's first cousin. (Herman K. Beebe's bank financed Dailey's purchase of this S&L.) Ballis received a two-year probated sentence for his plea, while Dailey was convicted and sentenced to 12 years in prison.

The land on which Ballis got the Sandia loan had been sold back and forth six times between Ballis and Reed in a period of 13 months, with the debt increasing from the original $13 million Allied loan to $35 million in the last Allied loan. Not only did Mischer's bank make these loans, but his real estate company was working with Ballis to develop the land.

The development loan came in June 1985, three months after the first $15 million Sandia loan. It was a $48.1 million loan from Sandia and included $15 million for refinancing the first Sandia loan. That left more than $30 million for development, but there is little on the ground to show for it. The only visible development is an intersection of two four-lane divided roads, curbed and guttered, which intersect and then go for several hundred yards and just stop. Ballis said some money was also spent on a drainage ditch because the property lies in the 100-year-old flood plain.[7]

Then, in December 1985, Ballis bought about 1,500 acres to the northwest of his property from John Riddle and his partner, Richard Dover. This is the property that Corson and Riddle had contracted to buy from General Homes. Riddle bought out Corson's interest for about $2 million, and when Riddle purchased the land a Corson company received $1.3 million in real estate commissions.

Riddle and Dover borrowed $40 million from Continental Savings when they purchased the land in October 1984. In addition, DRG, the Washington, D.C., company under investigation for HUD fraud, lent $15 million on the property. Next, in July 1985, the two bought an additional 238 acres with a $16.1 million loan from Vernon Savings. Then, when all the land was sold to Ballis in December of that year, Western Savings purchased the promissory notes to Vernon and Continental, and Sandia Savings lent another $15 million. In addition, Peoples Heritage Federal Saving and Loan in Salina, Kansas, had a mortgage on some of the property because it lent more than $40 million on a tract of land that Riddle swapped with Ballis as part of the whole deal.

When the smoke cleared, five savings and loans, which later failed, along with Allied Bank and DRG, had made loans totaling $140 million on about 2,700 acres of land that were valued by the tax district at $25 million. All there is to show for the $140 million, almost half of it from Sandia, are a few underground utilities, some drainage work and the intersection of two four-lane divided streets that go nowhere. General Homes foreclosed and got most of its land back; Western Savings and Sandia foreclosed on their loans and got a few hundred acres back. Almost everyone else walked away.

---

[7] *Houston Post*, December 20, 1988.

One consequence of the land flips and inflated lending was to drive up the apparent value of adjacent land, including the 5,400-acre Cinco Ranch. The Mischer Corporation and American General had purchased this property in early 1984 for $83 million from Robert Mosbacher and others. After Continental Savings made its $40 million loan to Riddle and Allied lent $35 million to Ballis, Mischer and American General sold 800 acres inside Cinco Ranch for $70 million, almost getting their original purchase price back for 15 percent of the land.

Sandia was eventually seized by the feds in February 1989, after the planned Bellamah purchase fell through. Six months later, Bellamah filed for bankruptcy—with $290 million in debts, it was the largest bankruptcy in New Mexico history—but not before Public Service Company of New Mexico bought out its Bellamah partners for $8 million, of which Robert Bobb and Douglas Crocker II got $5 million.[8]

They both returned to the Chicago area, where Bobb became chairman of Chicago Steel and Tinplate, Inc., of Gary, Indiana, and Crocker became chief executive officer of Republic Savings Bank, a Chicago S&L that was owned by Public Service Company of New Mexico.

In 1983, before their former employees bought into Republic Savings Bank, the Gouletases got into the savings and loan business in a big way. Tamco bought 25 percent of Imperial Corp. of America, which owned Imperial Savings in San Diego, from corporate raider and Michael Milken client Saul Steinberg.

Steinberg had split Imperial Corp.'s S&L operations into two entities, Imperial Savings in San Diego and Gibraltar Savings in Texas. Imperial Savings remained with Imperial Corp. whereas Gibraltar Savings was purchased by Houston businessman J. Livingston Kosberg, now a partner with corporate raider Charles Hurwitz. (Kosberg later merged Gibraltar with First Savings to form the biggest S&L in Texas; it became insolvent and was sold to Ronald Perelman in 1988. Other shareholders in First Texas were Kosberg's good friend Robert Strauss, the former chairman of the Democratic National Committee and, under George Bush, U.S. Ambassador to Moscow, and Strauss's son, Richard.)

After Tamco bought into Imperial Corp., Victor Goulet took over as chairman, and put his associates, Lyman Hamilton and Allan Tessler,

---

[8] *Albuquerque Tribune*, October 1, 1990.

on the board of directors. Goulet then financed a big chunk of his Imperial stock with First Executive Corp., a California insurance company controlled by Michael Milken's close associate Fred Carr. Some two years later, Imperial began buying junk bonds, eventually accumulating $1.5 billion, about half of it from Drexel Burnham. This made its junk bond holdings the second largest of S&Ls in the country—next to Columbia Savings, which was controlled by another Milken minion, Thomas Spiegel.

Imperial also got caught in huge organized crime scam run by Filipinos out of a Los Angeles Chevrolet dealership named Grand Wilshire.[9] As described by journalist Benjamin Stein in *Barron's*, Imperial lent $170 million to Grand Wilshire secured by car loans. It was later discovered that many of these loans were bogus or had been pledged to other financiers. But Imperial kept lending to Grand Wilshire up until two days before the company filed for bankruptcy.

In what is probably the best magazine article written on a bad savings and loan, Stein in the October 9, 1989, issue of *Barron's* laid it on the line about the Gouletases' Imperial Savings in the second paragraph:

"Imperial's story is about mismanagement, inadequate regulation, organized crime and questionable accounting. It's also about the astounding power of Michael Milken and Drexel Burnham Lambert and their acolytes to thwart the rational working of the market and defeat the expectations of the ordinary investor. It's about the business practices that may well have cost a major $11 billion thrift its solvency—and about how the taxpayers may well end up holding a very big and very empty bag that leads straight to an office building on South Rodeo Drive, Beverly Hills, with a discreet sign that reads 'Drexel Burnham Lambert.' "

Imperial Savings did fail later—in February 1990—at an estimated cost to the American citizens of a cool $1.6 billion. But before the savings and loan went down the tube, in July 1989 Allan Tessler was named CEO in an attempt to stop the bleeding. Six months later, he stepped down, only to be replaced by Lyman Hamilton. Then, less than a fortnight after Hamilton took over, the Office of Thrift Supervision ordered Imperial to cease all lending and investment operations.

Another fascinating series of events occurred at Imperial in late 1987

---

[9] *Barron's*, October 9, 1989.

and early 1988 that brought in an old familiar face. In August 1987, Victor Goulet defaulted on his Imperial stock loan from First Executive, which took back some 1.4 million Imperial shares as security. That left First Executive as the largest stockholder of Imperial Corp., with a little more than 10 percent. Tamco, too, still owned approximately 10 percent. Then, in October the stock market crashed, sending Imperial's price to $7.50 a share, compared to $15 before the crash. Things weren't looking too good for First Executive's profit position. But who should come to the rescue—none other than Larry Mizel's M.D.C. Holdings, another of Milken's big clients. (M.D.C. raised more than $700 million from Drexel Burnham junk bonds.)

On November 9, 1987, M.D.C. announced that it had purchased a little more than 1 million shares of Imperial, or about 7 percent of the total. Imperial's stock price jumped 15 percent at the news.[10] On February 5, 1988, M.D.C. disclosed that it had bought another 200,000, and finally, on February 18, it announced that it had upped its share of Imperial to 9.6 percent and had petitioned the SEC for approval to buy 24.9 percent of Imperial. The stock price climbed to $12.50 a share.

However, in June M.D.C. withdrew its request to the SEC to purchase 24.9 percent of Imperial stock. Finally, sometime between July and September 1988, M.D.C. sold its entire holdings of Imperial stock for a "nominal gain," it said in an SEC filing, without listing the dollar amount. The speculation was that M.D.C. had been brought in as a strawman to jack the stock price up.

It is not surprising that M.D.C. would become involved in the Gouletases' Imperial, given the Mizel company's previously noted connections to Michael Milken and to Bellamah. And there is another important link between the two, a Denver attorney named Norman Brownstein.

Brownstein, one of the most influential political fundraisers in Colorado, has been called the country's 101st senator by his friend Senator Edward Kennedy (Democrat-Massachusetts), who would occasionally spend the night at the Brownsteins' when he visited Denver. Brownstein, who will be discussed in more detail in the next chapter, on Silverado Savings, was a member of the board of directors of M.D.C. Holdings from 1980 to 1989. And Brownstein's Denver law firm, Brownstein Hyatt Farber & Madden, performed legal work for M.D.C., for which

---

[10] Ibid.

it was paid $492,000 in 1986 and $280,000 in 1987.

Brownstein also represented several Gouletas companies, including American Invsco and Acquest, a company which located apartment buildings for conversion to condominiums. In the late 1970s, when the Gouletases purchased the Denver firm of Fuller and Co., one of the largest full-service real estate brokerage companies in the western United States, the principals on both sides were brought together by Brownstein. Brownstein actually took the owner of Fuller and Co. out to Chicago to meet the Gouletases. (Several years afterwards, the Gouletases sold Fuller and Co. to a Canadian firm.)

As a lobbyist, Brownstein has worked for the junk bond industry, including many companies that issued bonds through Drexel Burnham, and he has also lobbied for savings and loans, including Imperial, that had large junk-bond portfolios.

Another junk-bond S&L Brownstein lobbied for was Lincoln Savings, controlled by Charles Keating, who raised the money to buy Lincoln from Milken. Brownstein first met Keating in the 1970s, and his name appears in Keating's diaries when Keating was wheeling and dealing with Lincoln and the politicians in the mid-1980s. M.D.C. was also involved in several deals with Lincoln, including the sale of junk bonds to Lincoln and the borrowing of money from the S&L in an Arizona land transaction reminiscent of the M.D.C./Silverado/Bellamah deal in Houston. According to news reports, Silverado, which bought some of the Arizona land from M.D.C., may have taken a $2.6 million loss on the sale.

Brownstein also served as co-trustee on some of the Larry Mizel trusts. These are funds controlled by Brownstein and others for the benefit of Mizel and some of his family members. It was Brownstein who introduced Mizel to the Chicago attorney who set up several of the trusts for Mizel. This attorney, Calvin Eisenberg, was a partner of Burton Kanter, the infamous tax attorney who associated with CIA middle man Paul Helliwell and Miami attorney Lawrence Freeman. (As previously noted, Kanter helped set up and control Castle Bank & Trust in the Bahamas, which was used by the Mafia and the CIA to hide and launder money.)

Eisenberg, who worked for the IRS before joining Kanter's firm, was convicted of income-tax fraud in 1982 for diverting two clients' money to a secret trust at Castle Bank & Trust to avoid income taxes.

When questioned about the relationship between Mizel and Kanter,

Mizel spokesman Bill Kostka said that Kanter's law firm prepared wills for the Mizel family in the 1970s. However, one of Kanter's law partners at the time said the firm's primary business was the formation of trusts, particularly offshore trusts, and that the preparation of wills would have been incidental to that.

The relationship between Eisenberg and Mizel shows Mizel operating in a circle of associates that includes Kanter and the Gouletases—all of whom are from Chicago and have alleged organized crime ties.

There are other relationships among people already mentioned that show the Gouletas family and Kanter were operating in the same circles. For instance, there is Sam Zell, the so-called "grave dancer" from Chicago, who buys up distressed properties. Zell bought into Freedom Savings in Tampa, where Marvin Warner and Charles Bazarian were found. In a lengthy profile on Zell in April 1986, the *Chicago Tribune* began the story with a quote by Douglas Crocker, the Bellamah executive who had been president of the Gouletases' umbrella company: "Sam is driven by the game. His checkbook only serves as a measure of whether he's winning or losing. He made enough to retire a long time ago."

The *Tribune* identified Crocker as an "early business associate" of Zell. Then several paragraphs later in the Zell profile, there is a quote from Burton Kanter, who is identified as "an attorney and partner in some of those early ventures." The *Tribune* quoted Kanter: "There were all kinds of deals. We had one business where we bought refrigerators and rented them to college students. But in the main, Sam had a good nose for property. If you viewed us as a group we were the biggest landlords in Reno."

Zell, Kanter, Roger Baskes (one of Kanter's law partners) and another man were indicted in 1976 for using Castle Bank & Trust to conceal profits in a Reno building and parking garage. Kanter was acquitted, and the charges against Zell were dropped after he turned state's evidence against Baskes, his brother-in-law, who was convicted.

Robert Corson is another connecting link between Kanter and his associates and the Gouletases and theirs. The Florida St. Joe Paper Co. land deal brought Lawrence Freeman together with Corson and his associate Mike Adkinson, around the same time that Corson was in a joint venture with Bellamah.

What does all this mean? It indicates, but does not conclusively prove, of course, that these events are related and part of a scheme by people with connections to organized crime and the CIA to relieve some savings and loans of their tax-supported deposits.

These associations are important. Consider, for example, the case of Lake Point Tower in Chicago. The 70-story building, called the world's tallest apartment building, was the "Mona Lisa" and the "crown jewel" of the Gouletas family. American Invsco bought the building in 1977 for $36 million, and then in June 1983 it was transferred to trusts benefitting Nicholas Gouletas and his sister, Evangeline. The Gouletases borrowed $100 million, with the building as collateral, from Continental Illinois Bank, and then defaulted on the loan in 1984.

The Gouletases had brought in their associate, Allan Tessler, to head a group to buy the building. Continental Illinois rejected the Tessler group, claiming that the Gouletases would still have an interest in the building. The Gouletases sued and a federal district judge ruled against them, saying that Nicholas had deliberately misled the bank. Then, according to a May 1986 story in the *Chicago Tribune*, "after Continental [Illinois Bank] rejected Tessler . . . Gouletas returned to the original buyer, a syndicate headed by Douglas Crocker . . ." Although the attempted purchase by Crocker's group fell through, there was apparently no mention or knowledge that Crocker had been the Gouletases' top officer in American Invsco.

About a year later, as the Gouletases continued to fight with Continental Illinois over Lake Point Tower, a new buyer appeared on the scene: Southmark, the Dallas-based real estate concern that had previously helped rescue mob associates Morris Shenker and Herman K. Beebe from financial difficulties. Representing Southmark in the proposed transaction was a man named Joseph Grosz.

Grosz was president of Southmark Funding, a real estate acquisitions subsidiary of Southmark. He was also senior vice president of Southmark's savings and loan, San Jacinto Savings. And, apparently unbeknownst to Continental Illinois and the Chicago press, Grosz was from Chicago, where he had worked for VMS Realty and, before that, American Invsco under Douglas Crocker.

In fact, Grosz was an officer and director of two Florida companies with Bellamah's Robert Bobb and Crocker. Florida corporate records show that Grosz was the president and a director of Florida Bay Club Management. Bobb was the secretary, treasurer and a director of this company, incorporated in January 1983 and involuntarily dissolved in November 1984, by which time Grosz was already working for Southmark. Grosz was also the president and a director of One-O-Three Marker Corporation, which was incorporated in Florida in August 1981 and was still active in 1990. Bobb was the treasurer and a director of this company, while Crocker was a vice president and director.

When I reached Grosz by telephone at his Chicago home in 1989, he initially denied being a business partner with Bobb and Crocker. When asked about the two Florida corporations and the fact that he denied being partners with the two, Grosz replied, "So?" Then, when I began questioning Grosz about his relationship to the Gouletas family, he hung up the telephone.

When the *Chicago Tribune* asked Grosz if the Gouletases would be participating in Lake Point Towers if Southmark purchased the building, Grosz replied, "How can they be calling the shots if Southmark is the owner? . . . They will not be our agent."[11] (And the Chicago press apparently bought this deception.)

Although Grosz was listed in San Jacinto's corporate records as a senior vice president, he was really the chief loan officer and was essentially determining who got major loans from the S&L, according to a confidential federal examination report of San Jacinto.

The examination report was dated September 23, 1985, but its findings extended into 1986. Its summary stated: "All of the major loans are originated out of Southmark Funding (also known as the Dallas loan production office), Dallas, Texas, by Joseph Grosz." The report quoted from minutes of the March 22, 1985, meeting of the San Jacinto board of directors stating that Grosz "be designated an officer of the association with the title of senior vice president and be designated the administrative head of the Dallas loan production office. . . . Be it further resolved that Joseph Grosz be designated as compliance officer for and on behalf of the association in the operation of the Dallas loan production office and in such capacity be charged with the responsibility for full and complete compliance with all state and federal regulation laws . . ."

The report further stated that "Southmark Funding (Joseph Grosz) initiates all major loans which the association subsequently funds. The majority of appraisal concerns pertain to these loans originated in Dallas in Southmark offices." The report goes on to quote Grosz as stating that "the association does not regard the appraisal report as a useful

---

[11] *Chicago Tribune*, July 11, 1987.

tool in the underwriting process and that the appraisal report is obtained only to fulfill regulatory requirements." This explains why, the report states, the appraisal reports received by the association to support the value of the real estate securing a loan do not meet federal regulatory requirements.

If there was any remaining doubt as to who was in charge, the salaries removed it. In 1985, Grosz received $732,973 in salaries and bonuses from Southmark and San Jacinto. In comparison, San Jacinto's chief executive officer got $175,000, while the chief operating officer received $130,000.

Finally, the report concludes, "San Jacinto is an institution which is out of control and at the mercy of Southmark."

San Jacinto had grown rapidly after Southmark bought it in October 1983, in part because of the brokered deposits it solicited. Some of these deposits came from Mario Renda, who had a special arrangement with San Jacinto to pay premium interest rates on the deposits he brought to the S&L.

San Jacinto, with assets of more than $3 billion, was ultimately taken over by the feds in December 1990, at an estimated cost to American taxpayers of $1.6 billion. San Jacinto failed primarily because of the $1 billion or so in loans and investments that Southmark made, through Grosz, according to the regulators and to bankruptcy filings in Southmark's bankruptcy. Among the investments was $50 million to purchase Herman K. Beebe's nursing homes in 1984 and 1985, while Beebe was under criminal indictment. Part of this deal involved issuing Southmark preferred stock to Beebe's holding company. Dale Anderson, Beebe's former right-hand man, said that he and Beebe dealt primarily with Grosz on the details of their transactions with Southmark and San Jacinto.

Not only did Southmark deal with Beebe and the late mob lawyer Morris Shenker, but testimony before the Nevada Gaming Control Board revealed that Grosz was involved in negotiating a $5 million Southmark loan for the purchase of a Nevada casino by Harry Wood, a reputed organized crime associate from Shreveport, Louisiana. Wood worked as a gofer for Shenker and would arrange junkets to Shenker's Dunes Hotel and Casino in Las Vegas. Grosz also reportedly arranged Las Vegas junkets for San Jacinto customers.

In a January 11, 1985, memo to Grosz, Southmark chairman Gene

Phillips told Grosz to process a $475,000 loan through San Jacinto for four individuals: Bobby Lutz, William C. Kennedy, Jr., David E. Wise and Charles V. Ristagno. According to the federal examination report, this loan was reportedly for chartering a new bank, but instead was used to pay off an overdraft at another financial institution for the "purpose of avoiding criminal liability." The report also noted that the loan documents had been altered.

Wise was an associate of Beebe and is named several times in the 1985 Comptroller of the Currency report on Beebe. Kennedy is also named in the report, which states that "in 1975, Kennedy was barred from the securities business by the SEC because of his participation in a stock manipulation scheme."

Other loans from San Jacinto that were outstanding while Grosz was working at Southmark included:

(1) a $17 million loan to Carroll Kelly, secured by his Continental Savings stock. This loan had been transferred from Allied Bank, where it had been guaranteed by Beebe.

(2) a $17 million loan to William King, secured by stock in Title USA Insurance Company. This loan to the Houston attorney who controlled several savings and loans was arranged by Beebe, who got a commission of about $350,000, according to Dale Anderson.

Art Leiser, the retired Texas Savings and Loan Department chief examiner, said that after all the Beebe deals at San Jacinto, he was told by a top San Jacinto official that Beebe and his Louisiana group were basically running the S&L. Leiser said that when he first noticed Grosz's activities at San Jacinto, he asked people there about Grosz. "Nobody seemed to know anything about him, but none of them liked him," Leiser said.

(3) a $32 million loan to a group headed by Thomas Gaubert, who controlled Independent American Savings. The loan was a second mortgage on the Trophy Club outside Dallas. This loan was made in 1985, the same year that Gaubert placed Grosz on the board of directors of his company, Telecom, which Gaubert bought with a loan from Sunbelt Savings.

(4) a $76 million loan to a partnership led by Sunbelt Savings chairman Ed McBirney. The 1985 federal examination report stated that $21.5 million of this loan was "substandard," meaning that the collateral was not worth the amount of money that San Jacinto had lent. A 1988 lawsuit filed against McBirney and other Sunbelt insiders states

that "Grosz handled these loans for San Jacinto"—referring to the $76 million. On the flip side, Grosz received seven loans from Sunbelt totaling $23.1 million.

San Jacinto also made loans to other S&Ls through Grosz and Southmark Funding, according to the federal examination report. These savings and loans included Sunbelt, Independent American, Lincoln, Western and Vernon. Furthermore, Grosz's Southmark Funding purchased and sold loan participations to and from a number of S&Ls, including Sunbelt, Lincoln, Western, Vernon and Peoples Heritage Federal Savings.

Peoples Heritage is the Kansas S&L that lent big bucks to the John Riddle/John Ballis deal in Houston. In January 1991, Grosz was indicted by a federal grand jury in Kansas regarding a loan participation he was involved with at Peoples Heritage. A Kansas jury later acquitted him. According to officials, when the verdict was announced Grosz wept, and three members of the jury wept with him. But Grosz's troubles were far from over. In late 1991, a federal grand jury in Dallas indicted him for fraud regarding some San Jacinto deals.

One loan that San Jacinto *didn't* make was the big one on the $200 million St. Joe Paper Co. deal in the Florida panhandle. Southmark was all lined up for a joint venture with Mike Adkinson with the financing to come from San Jacinto. This was spelled out in the sales contract with Lawrence Freeman's company. (Another link between the Kanter group and the Gouletas group.) But the feds finally put a stop to San Jacinto funding Southmark's commercial real estate ventures. Of course, it was about a $1 billion too late for the American taxpayers.

San Jacinto was also involved in multi-million-dollar deals with Lincoln Savings and its master, Charles Keating. In 1985, the two institutions swapped more than $123 million in loans, each S&L booking about $8 million in profits. The following year, the federal regulators made them reverse the transaction because of irregularities. In fact, Lincoln's chairman, Andre Niebling, wrote a letter to Grosz on April 25, 1986, pointing out that "We call you on Tuesday to describe our initial problems with the San Jacinto loan files. Specifically, a very significant number of the San Jacinto files were not included, payment histories were not available, and it was apparent from the limited information available to us that a substantial portion of the loans did not meet Lincoln's internal underwriting criteria. . . ."

Two points about the letter: one, for Lincoln of all places to consider these loans bad, they must have been very, very bad indeed; two, why didn't Lincoln inspect the loans prior to making the swap, which occurred on November 27, 1985? As for the Lincoln loans transferred to San Jacinto, the federal examination report stated that San Jacinto "does not have any loan files or documents in its possession as of April 20, 1986, to support this recorded transaction."

In other transactions between Lincoln and Southmark, a Lincoln subsidiary lent Southmark about $64 million to provide working capital to the company and for the purchase of a hotel company. In turn, San Jacinto lent $36 million to a Charles Keating and Lincoln partnership on the Hotel Pontchartrain in Detroit. San Jacinto later foreclosed on the hotel after the Keating partnership defaulted on the loan. Not surprisingly, Charles Keating's diaries contain a number of telephone calls between Keating and Joseph Grosz.

Finally, there were a number of loans and sales between San Jacinto and Larry Mizel's M.D.C. Holdings. San Jacinto made at least four loans to M.D.C. affiliates totaling $14.3 million. And, in 1986, Southmark was going to sell J. M. Peters Company, a California homebuilding firm, to M.D.C., but the deal fell through. Then, in 1987, M.D.C. sold all the assets of its oil and gas subsidiary to Southmark and in turn acquired residential property in Virginia and an option to buy residential property in California.

In September 1988, a Dallas savings and loan regulator wrote Darrel Dochow, a top bank board regulator in Washington, about his concern with the "significant number and volume" of loans between M.D.C. and San Jacinto Savings, Lincoln Savings and Silverado Savings, "as well as the apparent shifting of loans among those institutions."

M.D.C. first told me that it had never borrowed any money from Silverado and had never engaged in any business deals with Neil Bush, the President's son, who sat on Silverado's board of directors. It was wrong on both counts.

18

SILVERADO

E llison Trine Starnes, Jr., may well be the biggest con man Texas has ever produced. In terms of dollar amounts he easily outdistanced Billie Sol Estes, the friend of LBJ and Morris Jaffe, and on a national scale is right up there with the fugitive financier from Detroit, Robert Vesco. However, there was more to Starnes than merely the following facts to elevate him in the annals of flimflamery:

Starnes grew up in that barren godforsaken Southern Baptist-dominated town of Waco, where his father, Trine Starnes, Sr., was a noted traveling evangelist with the Church of Christ, preaching the gospel of how religion makes "bad men good and good men better."[1] Starnes Sr. later moved to Houston, where he became the preacher at the Lawndale Church of Christ, while Abilene Christian University named part of its Bible studies college the "Trine Starnes Center for Evangelism."

"You can tell he [Starnes Jr.] is a preacher's son. He's solicitous of you. He has a way like a preacher. You ask him a question and he wants to give you a sermon," Tom Dyer, an attorney for a Memphis, Tennessee, bank suing Starnes, told the Associated Press.

The first time Starnes Jr. apparently strayed from the straight and narrow was in 1973, when he was twenty-eight. He put a Dallas company called CIC Cosmetics International Corp. into bankruptcy and was sued by an investor, who won a $247,296 judgment.[2] He also got

---

[1] Associated Press, by Scott McCartney and Marcy Gordon, September 22, 1990.
[2] Ibid.

into trouble for his involvement with a company called International Psyco-Cybernetics Corporation. The next year he lost two fraud judgments in Houston and then in 1976, at the tender age of thirty-one, he filed for personal bankruptcy, listing debts of $2.4 million and assets of a mere $6,600.

In January 1977, Starnes was discharged from bankruptcy and embarked on a career in real estate. His first job was with San Francisco-based Regency Development. He was also working part-time for a Las Vegas company, Scribe Property Group. At his zenith in 1984, Starnes controlled 175 companies and real estate partnerships, 50 properties, 500 employees and had an alleged net worth of $222 million.

He owned a $1 million house in Houston, a $2 million house in Dallas, a $1 million condominium in Vail, Colorado, and a luxury skybox at Texas Stadium to watch the Dallas Cowboys. He and his wife, Kathryn, ran up bills of more than $400,000 at super-exclusive Neiman-Marcus and once bought a single piece of jewelry for $295,000.[3]

Then, in October 1988, Starnes did something almost unheard of. He filed for personal bankruptcy for the second time, less than 12 years after being discharged from his first bankruptcy.[4] "He was able to do it twice. It's unique that a guy can file bankruptcy once, then go out and incur this much debt and put so much together," Gary Knostman, the court-appointed trustee in Starnes's bankruptcy liquidation, told the Associated Press.

Starnes's second bankruptcy was indeed a thing of great beauty and a joy forever, sure to warm the cockles of the coldest cynic's heart. The list of creditors takes up 70 pages, with a total of more than 800. There were at least 21 banks and savings and loans, all the way from New Jersey to Florida to Minnesota to Texas to New Mexico. Starnes and his wife had 34 checking accounts at 22 financial institutions, and Starnes listed 48 pending lawsuits against him. The Federal Deposit Insurance Corporation has sued Starnes in his bankruptcy filing, claiming he defrauded seven failed banks.

Although Starnes cited debts of approximately $103 million, that figure is very misleading. He didn't list the debt figure for most of his creditors, and omitted the figure for his largest single debt: $77.5 million

---

[3] Ibid.
[4] In re Ellison T. Starnes, Jr., and Kathryn E. Starnes, United States Bankruptcy Court for the Southern District of Texas, No. 88-0800-H2-7.

to Silverado Savings in Denver. The Associated Press estimated his total debt to banks and savings and loans to be "as much as $500 million."

If that is true, then Starnes even overshadows debtors and bankrupts like John Riddle, who borrowed more than $300 million, and Richard Rossmiller, who borrowed about $200 million from Hill Financial Savings and allegedly had the largest personal bankruptcy in Colorado at around $57 million.

Starnes's lifestyle and possessions were chimeras balanced precariously on a mountain of debt. But the question is: How was it possible for him to borrow that kind of money, particularly given his previous bankruptcy and fraud suits. In their profile of Starnes in September 1990, the AP writers imply that it was his charisma and charm that persuaded bankers to open their vaults to him.

But the real answer to the riddle of Ellison Trine Starnes, Jr., lies in the ultimate destination of all that money he borrowed. Did *he* get it, or was he just a front man or mustache for others? Since tracking the money is not possible for anyone without subpoena power—and may not even be possible for those with it, because Starnes had accounts and business in the Bahamas and on the Isle of Jersey—the next best clues are the people he did business with, his partners and associates and the banks and S&Ls he borrowed the money from.

According to his 1988 bankruptcy filing, the first bank loan Starnes got after his 1977 bankruptcy discharge, and still owes money on, was a 1978 real estate partnership loan from Allied Bank of Texas, Walter Mischer's flagship bank in Houston. Ten years after the loan, Starnes listed a debt of $85,000 still owing to Allied Bank, today First Interstate Bank.

Starnes listed two other Allied banks as creditors in his bankruptcy. He showed a $70,000 debt from a 1985 "corporate real estate acquisition" owed to Allied Addicks Bank in Katy, Texas, and an unspecified amount owed to Allied Bank North Central in Dallas. In his bankruptcy filing, Starnes stated that he had three checking accounts at Allied banks and that he received a dividend from Allied Bancshares of $3,421 in the period from October 1986 to October 1987, indicating he owned some Allied stock during that period.

The largest debt to a bank or savings and loan that Starnes listed on his bankruptcy filing was $15.6 million to Continental Savings, the same one owned by Carroll Kelly, controlled by Herman K. Beebe and financed by Allied Bank and then San Jacinto Savings. In fact, Starnes borrowed more than $25 million from Continental, including $12.7 million to buy the ten-story Marina City office building in Chicago on the north bank of the Chicago River.

Art Leiser, the former Texas S&L Department's chief examiner, said he remembered the Marina City loan because there was no appraisal in Continental's file, and the purchase price was less than $12 million. The loan also had a $1 million interest reserve in it. "We questioned it," Leiser said.

The $25 million-plus that Starnes got from Continental made him one of that S&L's biggest borrowers. There is no way he could have done that without the okay, and probably the participation, either direct or indirect, of Herman K. Beebe. "I remember him," said Dale Anderson, Beebe's former partner. "I have met with him. I don't know if we met him through Carroll, or it may have been Larry Parker" (referring to the former head of Surety Savings).

Leiser said that Starnes was "involved in flashy deals. He was in the Riddle/Corson/Aubin/Woods group." One person close to Riddle and Corson said that "Starnes was a John Riddle partner from the get-go. They called him E.T." Starnes had bank accounts and borrowed money from Riddle's Texas National Bank, and at least one of Starnes's Continental loans was run through Investors Title Co., owned by Riddle and his law partners, Wade Kilpatrick and Victor J. Rogers II.

In September 1985, Starnes bought a piece of property in Harris County from Westside National Bank, where Robert Corson and his mother were the largest stockholders. He also showed a debt of $60,000 to Westside in his bankruptcy and had one checking account there.

Further, Starnes apparently had some relationship to Riddle and Corson's buddy Mike Adkinson. In Adkinson's Development Group, Inc., files, there is a reference to "E. Trine Starnes Jr. financial statement" and to "Trine Starnes file." These references are on the same page of a 112-page listing of all of Adkinson's files together with a reference to the Compendium Trust Company in the Isle of Jersey, a reference to John Riddle and Riddle's Investors Title Company and a reference to an $8.5 million promissory note involving Corson.

Starnes also had a close relationship to West Belt National Bank, where Adkinson was a stockholder and where Sandsend Financial Consultants of the Isle of Jersey, an offshore company involved in secreting ill-gotten S&L and drug proceeds, had its Houston bank account. Starnes was one of the original stockholders in this bank, whose charter was handled by Robert L. Clarke, the future U.S. Comptroller of the Currency. In his bankruptcy Starnes listed four checking accounts and a money market account at West Belt.

Starnes's West Belt stock was financed by a loan from River Oaks Bank & Trust in Houston. This loan totaled about $280,000, indicating that Starnes owned a little less than 10 percent of the bank's stock, more than twice the percentage that Adkinson owned. Adkinson also financed his West Belt stock at River Oaks Bank & Trust. This venerable bank in the wealthiest section of Houston was controlled by Jimmy Lyon, the previously mentioned right-wing Republican, friend of George Bush and Walter Mischer, and a staunch supporter and fundraiser for the Contras. In fact, Lyon is mentioned several times by name in Oliver North's White House diaries. North wrote Lyon's name in his diaries at least four times, including one entry regarding a telephone call from Richard Miller, a major Contra fundraiser, on February 1, 1985; Lyon's name came right after the name of Clement Stone.

(Stone is a Chicago insurance magnate. His son-in-law is president of a Texas corporation, Avro Aviation, that has offices in Houston. Investigators traced an airplane once used by Corson and his associates for money-laundering trips to Latin America to a company affiliated with Avro Aviation. Stone's son-in-law is also a director of Republic Health Corporation, which is represented in Denver by Norman Brownstein's law firm. Dr. Michael DeBakey is another principal in Republic Health.)

Perhaps Starnes's relationships to Riddle, Corson, Adkinson and the banks of Mischer and Lyon go a little way toward explaining why a bustout and con artist like him was one of the biggest *private* donors to the Contras.

On January 27, 1986, Spitz Channell, the late convicted Contra fundraiser, associate of Oliver North and president of the National Endowment for the Preservation of Liberty, wrote a letter to Starnes. That letter, found in the files of the National Security Archive, states:

"Dear Mr. Starnes:

"You are cordially invited to a briefing in the Roosevelt Room of the White House. The briefing will be on President Reagan's legislative initiative in support of the Nicaraguan Freedom Fighters.

"The President is attending. Donald R. Regan, White House Chief of Staff, Elliott Abrams, Undersecretary of State for Latin American Affairs, and Admiral John Poindexter, National Security Advisor, will be conducting the briefing along with me.

"The success of the President's initiative is absolutely critical to the establishment of true peace, freedom and democracy in Nicaragua and the rest of Central America. The defeat of communism in Nicaragua is an urgent issue for the future of American national security.

"Your attendance and participation is vital to President Reagan's success. I look forward to being with you at 2:30 p.m. on January 30, 1986."

In *The Chronology*, a day-by-day account of the Iran-Contra affair assembled by the National Security Archive, the following description is given of the January 30 meeting:

"President Reagan meets with Spitz Channell and a small group of donors to Channell's groups, the National Endowment for the Preservation of Liberty and the American Conservative Trust, in the Roosevelt Room of the White House. The meeting begins at 2:30 p.m. with a welcome from Linas Kojelis (Special Assistant to the President for Public Liaison), remarks from Linda Chavez (Deputy Assistant to the President for Public Liaison), and a 'Central American Overview' by Elliott Abrams (Assistant Secretary of State for Inter-American Affairs). At 3:15 p.m. President Reagan addresses the group, followed by a 'Report on Nicaragua' by Oliver North. A Channell fundraiser, Jane McLaughlin, later tells reporters that the price for inclusion in this session with the President was a $30,000 or more contribution to Channell's groups."

A National Endowment for the Preservation of Liberty (NEPL) note on the meeting reported the following: "RR mtg. 1st contributors—Starnes $30,000 . . ." That $30,000 from Starnes placed him seventeenth on NEPL's list of its top 25 contributors.

Starnes's contribution was designated for Channell's Central American Freedom Program, a propaganda campaign to get Congress to pass the Reagan Administration's weapons-assistance proposal for the Contras. "Policymakers can be best reached through an effort that is visible in Washington and the national media," said an NEPL pamphlet entitled "Central American Freedom Program."

Specifically, this propaganda program produced film footage of the fighting in Nicaragua, purportedly showing evidence of Sandinista atrocities, as well as newspaper opinion articles portraying Nicaragua as a center of terrorism and narcotics trafficking.

The largest donor to Channell's NEPL was Ellen Clayton Garwood, the Austin widow of a former Texas Supreme Court justice and daughter of one of the founders of the giant Houston conglomerate, Anderson Clayton. One of the other founders, M. D. Anderson, left some of his fortune to a Houston foundation that is run and controlled by the law firm of Fulbright & Jaworski. The CIA used the M. D. Anderson Foundation as a conduit to launder and funnel money for its purposes, according to author and journalist Thomas B. Ross.[5] This was confirmed to me by L. Fletcher Prouty, a retired Air Force colonel who served as the Pentagon liaison with the CIA in the 1950s and 1960s and was author of *The Secret Team*.

(Also during Starnes's borrowing rampage at savings and loans and his contributions to the Contras, he managed to donate $57,500 to the Republican campaign coffers. These contributions began in February 1984 and continued through July 1987. Almost half of them were to the National Republican Senatorial Committee.)

On September 30, 1986, exactly eight months after Starnes made his contribution to the Contra cause, he and his associates received three loans from Silverado Savings totaling $77.5 million. That made Starnes the second largest borrower at the Denver S&L. "The loans were made," according to a $200 million lawsuit filed by the FDIC against the Silverado officers and directors, including Neil Bush, "despite the fact that Silverado had no previous experience with Starnes, and that Starnes had a previous history of financial instability."[6]

"However," the suit continued, "the D&O [directors and officers] defendants were willing to make large sums available to Starnes even for speculative and poorly underwritten projects in exchange for assistance in temporarily removing bad loans from Silverado's books and concealing the association's deteriorating financial condition. The Silverado loans to Starnes violated federal loans-to-one-borrower regulations, prudent lending considerations and Silverado's own internal lending limits."

The biggest of the three loans was $30.95 million for what the feds called the "orange juice loan." This was a loan on an orange-juice-processing plant in Fort Pierce, Florida, that was sold from one Starnes partnership to another. The plant was leased to TreeSweet Products,

---

[5] "Surreptitious Entry: The CIA's Operations in the United States," by Thomas B. Ross, in *The CIA File*, edited by Robert L. Borosage and John Marks (New York: Viking, 1976).

[6] The Federal Deposit Insurance Corporation, as receiver for Silverado Banking, Savings and Loan Association vs. Michael Wise et al., United States District Court for the District of Colorado, No. 90-1688.

which had been purchased at the end of 1984 by Starnes and his partner, Clinton E. Owens. To top it off, Starnes was on all sides of this transaction, as one of his companies got a $1.9 million commission on the sale, payable out of the Silverado proceeds.

Owens had worked 20 years in the food and beverage business, including six years with Coca-Cola Foods, before teaming up with Starnes. Owens had been a top marketing executive with the Houston-based Coca-Cola Foods, which makes Minute Maid orange juice, under president Gene Amoroso. This is the same company that joined with Walter Mischer to buy 700,000 acres in the interior of Belize.

The federal lawsuit ripped into Silverado's officers and directors for making the orange juice loan:

"The value of the physical plant and land securing this loan was worth much less than the loan amount. The value of the lease was equally suspect. TreeSweet, the lessee, had suffered operating losses during the prior 18 months and was likely to have serious difficulties making the lease payments.

"Silverado had no experience in making this type of loan; even its lending officer for this loan conceded that he did not understand the operation at the TreeSweet plant. This inexperience resulted in Silverado's failure to obtain a security interest on the plant's equipment and spray fields.

"Silverado closed the loan without receiving a written appraisal on the property.

"Predictably, TreeSweet continued to lose money. Less than one year after the loan was made, TreeSweet ceased operations at the plant and declared bankruptcy in January 1988. Losses to Silverado are substantial."

A federal examination report on Silverado stated that although the written appraisal on the property later came in at $31.5 million, this was $14 million higher than the price Starnes's group paid to acquire the plant in May 1985. There was no way it could have increased in value like that over such a short time.

The orange juice loan was tied into the second biggest loan that Silverado made to Starnes. This was a $30.5 million loan for a Starnes-controlled limited partnership to buy the Breckenridge Hilton Hotel in Breckenridge, Colorado, some 50 miles west of Denver in ski country.

The $10 million downpayment on the Breckenridge Hilton came from the orange juice loan, according to the federal lawsuit and the examination report. The $30.5 million Silverado loan was a renewal of a $27.2 million loan Silverado made to the previous owner, American Shelter Company-Breckenridge, Ltd. The first loan, according to the lawsuit, was "deeply troubled," and Silverado, "in its haste to remove the poorly performing American Shelter loan from its books, relied on an out-dated and inflated appraisal, [and] overstated the cash flow projections from which the loan would be repaid."

Finally, the lawsuit concluded, "the loan [to the Starnes group] quickly went into default. Losses to Silverado are substantial."

The federal examination report placed the total losses on the orange juice loan and the Breckenridge Hilton loan at $28.2 million, and noted that "reappraisal of the orange juice plant will likely give rise to significant additional loss recognition." In a separate fraud suit in Houston, the FDIC claims that Starnes falsified financial statements in the loan application to Silverado for the Breckenridge Hilton and states that the hotel loan was "calculated to cause willful and malicious injury."

The third loan to Starnes from Silverado was $16.5 million, secured by a mortgage on two office buildings in Colorado Springs and a second mortgage on an office building in Denver. According to the federal lawsuit, the loan was used to refinance existing debt on the Colorado Springs buildings and to purchase a bad loan Silverado held on the Denver building.

The suit stated that the security for the Colorado Springs loan was "substandard' and that the appraisal used was a year out of date. Furthermore, the loan provided that if a new appraisal reduced the value of the property, then the loan would be reduced. "A new appraisal did, in fact, indicate a reduced value of the property, but no reduction in the loan was made."

Starnes's group defaulted on the Colorado Springs loan, and the lawsuit concluded that "Silverado's collateral is worth significantly less than the amount of the loan, and losses to Silverado are substantial."

Although Starnes listed Silverado as a creditor in his bankruptcy filing, he stated that the amount of the debt was "unknown." Also unknown is exactly how Starnes got tied in with Silverado. But given both of their connections to the Corson/Bush/Mischer/Beebe circle, it is not too difficult to imagine. It is also known, for example, that some borrowers at Beebe-financed Vernon Savings were sent to Silverado to try to obtain refinancing.

Another Beebe associate who got a big loan from Silverado was Californian Wayne Reeder. The Denver S&L lent Reeder's company some $14 million for a real estate development in Caramillo, California, about 40 miles north of Los Angeles. The loan later went bad.

Reeder and Beebe probably met at the La Costa resort, said Dale Anderson, Beebe's former partner. The two never did much business together, although there were discussions, Anderson said. Anderson added that he believes Reeder got into the insurance business through Beebe. By 1990, Reeder's insurance operations were under federal investigation in Rhode Island, Tennessee and Arizona.

Reeder was also involved in bingo games run on Indian reservations with Dr. John Nichols, a self-described CIA operative who participated in assassination attempts on Fidel Castro. Nichols was in the middle of a bizarre, abortive scheme to manufacture night-vision goggles and machine guns for the Contras on the Cabezon Indian Reservation near Palm Springs.[7]

As for the $200 million federal lawsuit against the Silverado officers and directors, it was settled in 1991 for $50 million, which was paid by their liability bond and other insurance. News reports stated that the only bill Neil Bush was stuck with was his $250,000 legal fee. Reportedly, Neil's friends were passing the hat to take care of that, too.

The company that did the most business with Silverado was Larry Mizel's M.D.C. Holdings, whose loans, sales and purchases from and to the Denver S&L totaled about $340 million. Although M.D.C.'s spokesman, Bill Kostka, first told me that M.D.C. never borrowed any money from Silverado, in a statement submitted to the House Banking, Housing and Urban Affairs Committee, M.D.C. admitted borrowing some $20 million from Silverado, secured by mortgages receivable. It also stated that it signed a $33 million note to Silverado to purchase participation certificates.

In its congressional statement the company claimed it was not a "major borrower" from the S&L, and "never obtained commercial real estate financing from Silverado Banking. Silverado Banking never loaned money to MDC to purchase property from any third party." Then, two sentences later in its statement, it contradicted what it had

---

[7] *Inside Job: The Looting of America's Savings and Loans,* by Stephen Pizzo, Mary Fricker and Paul Muolo (New York: McGraw-Hill, 1989).

just affirmed: "Silverado Banking extended credit to M.D.C. in connection with M.D.C.'s purchase of one property from Silverado-Elektra in 1987."

So it appears from M.D.C.'s own statements that it borrowed more than $53 million from Silverado, which would definitely put it among the S&L's ten largest borrowers. M.D.C. might not think that makes it a "major" borrower, but there is little doubt that what was major was the sale by M.D.C. of some $208 million in mortgage loans to Silverado. These mortgage loans were, the company itself admitted in an SEC filing, "non-conforming mortgage loans," which the company defined as "mortgage loans that do not meet GNMA, FNMA and the Federal Home Loan Mortgage Corporation securitization guidelines, as a result of, among other things, 'low' or no down payment, less restrictive qualifying ratios, etc."

M.D.C. also sold some $60 million in raw land to Silverado and Silverado-Elektra. On the other side of the ledger, M.D.C. bought $6 million in Silverado preferred stock in 1984, and $14 million in subordinated notes in 1986. In its statement to the House banking committee, M.D.C. whined about losing its $20 million investment in Silverado when the S&L failed, but attempted to downplay the fact that these investments were part of deals in which Silverado was also buying things from M.D.C., and paying a lot more than $20 million.

In a March 1, 1990, statement to me at the *Houston Post*, Kostka said that M.D.C. "has never had a business relationship with" Neil Bush. Then, in a March 5 statement, Kostka wrote me, saying, "While the company has never had a 'business relationship' with Neil Bush, so that there will be no confusion, the company states that it sold Mr. Bush a home in Denver, Colorado, in the ordinary course of its business." This house is in an exclusive Denver neighborhood and cost more than $500,000; it was purchased in the name of Sharon Bush, Neil's wife.

Mizel is also one of the biggest, if not the biggest, Republican fundraisers in Colorado. In 1986 he was the chairman of a luncheon that raised $1 million in honor of President Reagan. And in 1989 he organized a luncheon for Colorado Republican senatorial candidate Hank Brown that raised $850,000 and drew President Bush's attendance.

The single largest borrower at Silverado was Denver developer Bill L. Walters and his affiliated companies, which borrowed more than $130 million from the S&L. In addition, Silverado purchased over $95 million in assets from Walters or Walters-controlled entities, according to the federal lawsuit against the Silverado officers and directors. In turn, Walters bought more than $48 million in Silverado stock and $6.5 million in Silverado's pool of bad loans, all with money from the loans to and purchases by Silverado to Walters.

In its deals with Walters, to cite the federal lawsuit, "Silverado compromised its underwriting and appraisal standards, made loan concessions that were unavailable to other borrowers, consistently violated its own internal lending and underwriting practices, and violated federal regulations."

In turn, Walters's purchases of Silverado securities "enabled Silverado to inflate artificially its reported capital, fuel continued imprudent growth and divert improperly Silverado funds for the personal financial needs of Michael Wise [Silverado's chief executive officer], James Mertz [Silverado's majority owner] and [Silverado's] preferred shareholders," according to the federal lawsuit.

This is the same Bill Walters who was discussed in Chapter 6 on the 1970s Texas rent-a-bank scandal. He and his partners, Richard Rossmiller and William Wall, bought control of an East Texas bank that was part of the Herman K. Beebe/Ben Barnes rent-a-bank circle. Barnes and Beebe then brokered a loan from Mile High Savings (which became Silverado) for Walters's group.

Walters grew up in Fort Collins, Colorado, north of Denver, and played football at the University of Kansas. He became an architect in Denver and hit the big time with Rossmiller and Wall. The partnership split up in the late 1970s when Wall went to jail on fraud charges. There were whispers that Wall took the rap for some other people. It seems that while Wall was in jail, his wife moved into a new house in the posh Cherry Hills suburb of Denver and was well taken care of. And despite the public split, Walters and Rossmiller stayed in close touch with each other.

In 1983, Walters Petroleum I, Ltd., owned by Bill Walters, invested $150,000 into a new oil company called JNB Exploration. In exchange for approximately 50 percent of the start-up capital, Walters got 6.25 percent of the profits. One of Walters's banks, Cherry Creek National Bank, extended JNB Exploration a $1.75 million line of credit. The beneficiary of Walters's benevolence was Neil Bush, one of the principals of JNB.

Walters had been active in the Republican party in Colorado since

the 1970s, and was an ardent Reagan-Bush man in 1980. When George
Bush came to Denver during the presidential campaign in the fall of
1984, Walters had his browning front-yard grass ripped up and replaced
by new green grass. He did this because the Vice President was coming
to his house to visit his son's silent partner and benefactor.

Neil Bush's other big backer was real estate developer Kenneth M.
Good, who contributed $10,000 in new capital to JNB Exploration, and
obtained and maintained the company's lines of credit at Cherry Creek
National Bank, in exchange for 25 percent of the profits. It was Good
who lent Neil the $100,000 in 1984 to invest in commodities, which Neil
didn't have to pay back if the investment lost money. It did, and he
didn't. As Neil told the House banking committee, the loan "sounded
fishy." Neil also didn't report it as income on his tax return until five
years afterwards.

By the end of 1986, Good had just about completely taken over from
Walters as Neil's sugar daddy. (Walters's company still retained a
$100,000 promissory note from JNB Exploration, which never got paid
back.) One of the reasons for this was that Good and Walters had a
falling-out. It seems that Good had begun an affair with Walters's
estranged wife, and had even assisted her in evaluating Walters's real
estate for the purpose of dividing the property in the divorce.

Over the next three years, Good provided more than $1 million to
sustain JNB, including a $120,000-a-year salary for Neil. In addition,
Good placed young Bush on the board of directors of one of Good's
Florida companies, Gulfstream Holding Corporation, and paid him a
staggering $100,000 a year in director's fees.

And what did Good get in return for all his largess? Well, in the 1988
presidential election, he was invited to Houston for the Bush victory
celebration party. In addition, Good and his affiliated companies did
about $77 million worth of business with Silverado, although a good
deal of this was before Neil joined the Silverado board in August 1985.
The $77 million included about $53 million in loans, $10.4 million in a
land sale from Good to Silverado-Elektra and Good's purchase of $14
million in Silverado preferred stock.

Who is Kenneth M. Good? The son of a Methodist minister, he grew
up Kansas and then earned an M.B.A. at Southern Methodist University
in Dallas, where he got his first crack at real estate speculation. In 1969
he formed Good Financial Corporation in Dallas and began buying
properties with bank loans. His first big project was a hotel and office

development by the Dallas-Fort Worth International Airport. It flopped before any concrete was poured.

After he bombed in Dallas, Good moved to Denver in 1979, where he began wheeling and dealing, buying land and companies with borrowed money. He cultivated his flamboyant image as much as he cultivated his bankers. And he built the largest, most expensive house in Denver—34,000 square feet for $10 million in Cherry Hills. But by 1986 the wheels were starting to come off the Denver real estate market.

So, in January 1986, Good bought Gulfstream Land & Development Corporation in Plantation, Florida, a major real estate development company. To do so, he borrowed approximately $250 million. This included $70 million of the usual junk bonds and $90 million from major East Coast banks and the rest from a group of mostly Florida savings and loans. Before that borrowing occurred, though, Good got two loans totaling $86.3 million from an old familiar face: Jarrett Woods's Western Savings in Dallas. These two loans wrapped around, or included, about $58.9 million in existing debt and provided Good with $27.4 million in additional cash.

In the savings and loan industry in Texas, there was a game played called the "last greatest fool." This was the S&L equivalent to musical chairs. The last S&L to make an inflated loan on a piece of property, after all the swaps and flips, would get caught holding the bag, and would be the last greatest fool. It is interesting that this expression has been credited to Jarrett Woods (although some say it started with Tyrell Barker), because Western Savings was the biggest "last greatest fool" in Texas. It was Western that took out Vernon Savings, Continental Savings and MBank on several Robert Corson and John Riddle deals.

The procedure that Western liked to employ to win that honor is called the wraparound loan. It includes all the previous debt on a piece of property and then adds some of its own. This is what Ken Good did with his Western loan. (Another S&L that liked to use wraparound loans was Mainland Savings.)

The owners of the company that Good bought, partly with S&L money—in other words, the ultimate recipients of the S&L money—were dominated by a Canadian group led by Edgar M. Bronfman, of the Bronfman family that controls Seagrams. A managing director of Drexel Burnham Lambert was also on the Gulfstream board of directors, as was an New York attorney named Arthur D. Emil.

Emil was a partner in the law firm of Surrey & Morse, whose name partner, Walter Surrey, was an old OSS hand and one of the founding directors and stockholders of Guillermo Hernandez-Cartaya's World Finance Corporation.

Emil was also a major fundraiser for New York Governor Hugh Carey, and was named in an October 31, 1979, *New York Times* story about the racketeering trial of Mafia *capo* and Teamsters official Anthony Scotto. Scotto testified that he had given $75,000 in cash to the campaigns of Carey and then-Lieutenant Governor Mario Cuomo. Emil denied receiving any cash in his position as treasurer of the Friends of Governor Carey, the governor's main fundraising committee. Carey testified in Scotto's trial as a character witness for the notorious Mafioso. Interestingly, in 1976, Emil was elected co-chairman of the Brooklyn Academy of Music, while Scotto was elected vice chairman.

In 1977, the *New York Times* reported that Emil had given his first $50,000 to Carey to help retire the governor's mammoth 1974 campaign debt. Around this time, Edgar Bronfman allegedly made a $350,000 loan to Carey to help pay off the campaign debt.

In a July 5, 1981, story in the *Times*, it was announced that Emil would not be running the fundraising operations of Carey's re-election bid if he decided to run again. Two paragraphs later, in the same story, it was reported that Evangeline Gouletas-Carey had registered to vote as a Democrat in Albany after giving up her independent status in Chicago and marrying Hugh Carey.

One of the key figures in the middle of the big Silverado borrowers from Denver was attorney Norman Brownstein. Not only was Brownstein heavily involved with Mizel and M.D.C. Holdings, his law firm represented Bill Walters's companies and Ken Good's companies. Brownstein helped Good set up more than 100 trusts (á la Larry Mizel) and also helped him negotiate the purchase of Gulfstream Land & Development. Good then placed Brownstein on the Gulfstream board of directors along with Neil Bush. Brownstein calls all of these connections and relationships "coincidences."

Brownstein is a local boy, who grew up on the poor side of the tracks in Denver. He graduated from the University of Colorado at Boulder with a bachelor's degree and then earned a law degree there. By the late 1970s and early 1980s, his law firm was representing companies controlled by Larry Mizel, Ken Good, Bill Walters, Charles Keating, the Gouletases, Ohio shopping center magnate Edward DeBartolo (who has been plagued with allegations of organized crime connections) and last, but not least, Marvin Davis.

Lurking behind Brownstein and looming over all the Denver crowd is the massive figure of billionaire oil tycoon Marvin Davis. Davis grew up in New York City, where he worked in his father's garment business. The family moved to Denver in 1953 and started Davis Oil Co., which became one of the largest wildcat well drillers in the country.

In 1981, Davis bought 20th Century-Fox and, after he failed in his efforts to bring a major league baseball team to Denver and failed in his bid for the *Denver Post*, began moving his operations from Denver to Los Angeles. Later, he sold 20th Century-Fox to Rupert Murdoch and in 1986 bought the famous Beverly Hills Hotel from the family of convicted stock trader Ivan Boesky. About a year afterwards, Davis sold the Beverly Hills Hotel to the Sultan of Brunei, who had just been revealed as a $10 million donor to Oliver North's "Enterprise." (That money was eventually returned to the Sultan after the boys put it in the wrong Swiss bank account.)

Brownstein and Davis apparently first made contact within the Jewish community in Denver, and Brownstein set out to get close to and ingratiate himself with the richest man in Denver. Brownstein moved into a house in Cherry Hills close to Davis, across University Boulevard from the Cherry Hills Country Club. When Davis began to complain about having to drive all the way around University to get to his house, Davis was graciously allowed by Brownstein to put an extended driveway through the latter's property.

By 1979, Brownstein's law firm was representing Davis's Denver bank, Metro National Bank. And Brownstein, Walters, Mizel and others were allegedly flying all over in Davis's private jet. One place they liked to go was the Vintage Club near Palm Springs, California, where Davis would reportedly hold court in the locker room. Maybe they ran into Robert Corson there, because he and his partner, Paul Lewis, owned a vacant lot at the club.

Los Angeles publicist Lee Solters, a spokesman for Davis, said Davis had "no relationships" with Brownstein. Solters said Davis did business with Brownstein's law firm, but not Brownstein. Solters has also said Davis has no relationships to Walters, and knows Mizel but has never done any business with him. Solters also said that Davis is not a member of the Vintage Club.

In the early 1980s, just a couple of years after Neil Bush and his wife, Sharon, moved to Denver, she started a small cookie business called Cookie Express. Her partner was Mary Davis Zarif, the daughter of Marvin Davis.

Neil liked to tell reporters, investigators, examiners and judges that he applied the "Smith smell test" to determine whether or not someone wanted to do business with him because of who his father is. He said he would ask himself if his last name were Smith, would he still be getting the offer? Perhaps it is just a coincidence that Sharon Bush's maiden name is Smith. Maybe that's why she forgot to apply the "Smith smell test" as to why Marvin Davis's daughter went into business with her.

Neil eventually got his hand slapped by the Office of Thrift Supervision for not revealing the details of his relationships to Bill Walters and Ken Good and to the other Silverado directors. His punishment was that he had to agree to avoid conflicts of interest in any future dealings with savings and loans.

During the administrative proceedings in 1990 on the question of whether Neil Bush should be sanctioned, two expert witnesses on his behalf testified that he didn't do anything wrong in his actions regarding Walters and Good. The first expert was Geoffrey C. Hazard, Jr., Sterling Professor of Law at Yale's law school. The second was Charles M. Pickett.

Pickett, as noted in the earlier chapter on Walter Mischer (Chapter 1), was the former general counsel to Mischer's Allied Bancshares. Before joining Allied Bank in 1983, he had been counsel to MCorp in Dallas, the parent company of banks that Herman K. Beebe used. Pickett testified that he didn't see any conflicts of interest in what Neil Bush did as a director, because, he stated, bank directors vote on loans to their business partners all the time.

And when asked by government attorneys what information directors should disclose to other directors about their possible conflicts of interest, Pickett replied, "Well, even if a prospective borrower was screwing around with a board member's wife, I don't think that board member has any responsibility to disclose that to his fellow board members. He's there to make business judgments, not personal ones." He added further, "If one director thinks he knows about a conflict of interest of another board member, he is not obligated to disclose this."

The question of making loans to partners, friends and associates is obviously a touchy one for bankers and S&L executives, because the truth is, they lend out very little money that doesn't fall into that category. They may make lots of small loans, such as home loans and consumer loans, to people they don't know, but the big commercial loans are almost always made to their friends and associates.

In one of my interviews with Walter Mischer, Sr., this was a point Mischer was adamant about. He claimed that 80 percent of Allied Bank's loans were made to people they didn't know. When I asked him if that were true of 80 percent of the total dollar amount lent by Allied, he didn't respond directly but didn't dispute it. Of course, this is absolute nonsense, but it was one of the major points Mischer was trying to push.

Henry Ford once remarked that if the American public really understood the banking system there would be rioting in the streets. Perhaps he was referring to these facts: (1) it is nearly impossible to succeed in any business without bank credit; (2) banks take in federally insured deposits from everyone and then lend out the money to their selected friends and associates; and (3) bank charters are awarded to the favored few by the government.

There were two relationships at Silverado, one business and the other personal, that led to one of the most fascinating characters in the S&L debacle.

The first relationship: A Silverado director, Dianne Ingels, a Denver real estate broker who was also on the board of the Federal National Mortgage Corporation, was living with a Denver businessman named Ray Near. The second relationship: Silverado lent $7.65 million to William Pauls to buy the Boston & Champa buildings in Denver from Bill Walters.

What Ray Near and William Pauls have in common is that they both worked for John W. Dick, whose background and story seem close to fictional:

Dick was born and raised in a Mennonite community near Kitchener, Canada, southwest of Toronto. His father's family, originally from Holland, emigrated to Russia. Just before the Bolshevik Revolution, his father, Peter Dick, traveled to Canada on business and then decided to stay there because of the turmoil in Russia.

John Dick's father eventually married a Mennonite woman and went to work in a meat-packing plant. His wife was the maid to a doctor. Dick was born in 1938 and spoke German for the first three years of his life. The family was poor. The Mennonites, an evangelical Christian group like the Amish, emphasize plain, simple living.

Dick quickly shed his Mennonite upbringing when he went to college and became a lawyer. When he was twenty-six he moved to Denver and started working for Denver attorney Clarence Arch Decker, a Colorado state senator who would later represent Dick's wife in a fierce divorce battle. Dick clerked for Decker for three years, after which Decker sponsored Dick for admission to the Colorado Bar.

But Dick wanted to get rich in a hurry and quickly left the practice of law for the real estate business. He was joined by his fellow Canadian and Mennonite William Pauls. Sometime during the mid-1970s, Dick become involved with people and businesses on the Isle of Jersey. This, reportedly, came about when he was searching around for financing to get involved in the new Denver Tech Center on the southeast side of the city. Dick first approached Barclays Bank in England, which allegedly sent him to the Isle of Jersey.

In a May 12, 1988, affidavit in his divorce action on Jersey, Dick stated that he had been considering moving to Jersey since 1975 and had resided there since 1980. Sometime in that period, Dick became acquainted with the principals of the Compendium Trust and Sandsend Financial Consultants, including Raymond Harvey—the same people whom Lawrence Freeman dealt with in laundering Jack DeVoe's drug money and whom Mike Adkinson dealt with in moving Texas S&L money to the Isle of Jersey (discussed in detail in Chapter 21).

In fact, some people close to Dick believe he was instrumental in having the Jersey trusts established. Compendium and Sandsend were set up in 1977 and 1978, after Ray Harvey and his associates moved to Jersey from the Bank of Nova Scotia in the Bahamas. Also in 1978, Harvey and his Jersey partner, John Wadman, were involved in a Denver land transaction with Dick, Pauls and Dick's brother-in-law, Werner Heinrichs. There were several lawsuits accusing Dick and his partners with fraud in this deal. Then, in 1979, Harvey and Wadman participated in a land deal, along with Dick and Pauls, involving a major part of the Denver Tech Center.

Also, at least one of Dick's family trusts was under the Compendium umbrella, and Dick entered into a real estate transaction with Sandsend that was reminiscent of those with Adkinson in the Meyerland and St. Joe Paper deals (discussed in Chapter 21).

This particular arrangement occurred in August 1986, just two months after Adkinson closed on the Florida land deal with St. Joe Paper Co. and Corson's S&L transferred $7 million to Sandsend. In this instance, Sandsend "lent" Dick $5 million, secured by $17.5 million in promissory notes on Colorado land, which had been transferred to Dick by Pauls several years earlier. These notes required no interest of principal to be paid until 1996. The California judge hearing Elisabeth Dick's divorce petition called the creation of the $17.5 million in promissory notes a "sham transaction."[8]

Another interesting tidbit leaked out during the divorce hearings. Decker, Elisabeth Dick's attorney, stated in court that Dick had helped his friend Bill Walters move $20 million in 1986 to the Isle of Jersey. Dick denied this under questioning by Decker.

Several sources close to Dick said that Walters definitely traveled to Jersey in 1986, where he stayed at Dick's mansion. In 1984, Dick purchased the seigneurie, or lordship, of St. John, one of the 12 seigneuries on the Isle of Jersey. It consists of a huge multi-million-dollar sixteenth-century manor house and 125 surrounding acres. When friends, including Dianne Ingels and Ray Near, would come to visit Dick on Jersey, any of the overflow crowd would be put up in the Little Grove Inn, which had been owned by St. Joe Paper Co.'s Ed Ball and Charter Oil's Raymond Mason.

There was at least one direct transaction between Dick and Walters: In August 1985, Walters sold a lot and house at the Vintage Club outside Palm Springs to Dick's company, Noramco Management Group. To buy the property, Noramco borrowed $1.7 million from Hill Financial Savings, Red Hill, Pennsylvania. Dick signed the mortgage as president of Noramco and also gave a personal guarantee.

Dick was introduced to Hill Financial by Richard Rossmiller, Walter's old partner and a $180 million-plus borrower at Hill Financial. Rossmiller, as noted, had done business with Herman K. Beebe back in the mid-1970s, and perhaps still was. There was evidently contact between Beebe and Dick, as Beebe's name and phone numbers, including the number for his house at La Costa, were in Dick's private rolodex.

Rossmiller, in an April 4, 1986, letter to Al Lutz, president of Hill Financial, stated that "John Dick visited me last night concerning a loan request." Dick had purchased four condominiums across the street from

---

[8] *Denver Post*, December 30, 1990.

his own house for his parents and their servants and wanted to purchase the remaining 19 condos.

In his letter to Lutz, Rossmiller continued, "John would like to borrow $4,000,000 for a period of three years. $3,000,000 used for acquisition and $1 million for an interest reserve." Rossmiller then closed his letter: "John, I think, just felt more comfortable asking me to write you because it was I who made the introduction. John spoke about using another local lender for the loan. I told him heck no, this is a Hill-type deal. It is a good deal with solid sponsorship. Please give John a call with your feelings."

Dick and Lutz eventually worked out a deal in which one of Dick's companies, Wellington Management Services, would get two loans totaling $3.5 million from Nationwide Lending Group of Colorado, Hill Financial's Colorado affiliate, with a guarantee from Dick. Dick, of course, defaulted on the "good deal," and the Resolution Trust Corporation, as receiver for the failed Hill Financial Savings, sued Dick in 1990 for the $3.5 million.

As noted in Chapter 6, on Surety Savings, Rossmiller told a number of people in Denver that he [Rossmiller] had worked for the CIA. Rossmiller also told several people that John Dick sold weapons to Saudi Arabia in the early 1980s. This was around the same time that Mike Adkinson was allegedly selling weapons to Iraq by means of Saudis and Kuwaitis. In addition, both Adkinson and Dick were dealing with the same Isle of Jersey trusts that were connected to wealthy Saudis. A person close to Dick confirmed that Dick traveled to Saudi Arabia in 1981 and entertained Saudis in his Denver home on occasion.

Rossmiller, who was a captain in the U.S. Air Force, apparently had a special relationship to the CIA. Joe Kelso, who shows up twice in Oliver North's White House notebooks and claims to have worked on a contract basis for the CIA, told Washington journalist Paul Muolo that Rossmiller laundered money for the CIA. Kelso, who went to jail for trying to sell missiles to Iraq, worked for Rossmiller once on a project trying to extract gold from water.

A Denver attorney close to Rossmiller, and one of Rossmiller's associates and neighbors, said that Rossmiller used to brag about working for the CIA. This bragging by Rossmiller was confirmed by a Denver friend of his.

Rossmiller lived several houses down from Dick on Sunset Drive in Englewood, and the two would get together and discuss business often. Another neighbor at the end of the street was William Pauls, who purchased his house from Bill Walters. Walters had purchased the property, torn down the house on it and built another house.

The person Walters bought the property from was the godfather of white-collar crime and con artistry in Colorado, John McCandish King. King moved to Denver in 1963 from Chicago after serving three terms in the Illinois State Legislature. He got into the oil business, made some money, went broke and then started selling oil tax shelters and mutual funds.

In the manner of international con men, King eventually met up with mutual-fund swindler Bernie Cornfeld and attempted to buy Cornfeld's IOS company. He lost out and IOS was eventually swallowed by Robert Vesco. In the mid-1970s, King did a year in jail for income-tax fraud and quietly retired to his Colorado ranch.

Before that happened, King had gotten close to Richard Nixon, and claimed to have been an adviser to Presidents Johnson, Kennedy and Herbert Hoover, when he ran the Hoover Commission under Truman.[9] King also had an account at Castle Bank & Trust in the Caymans, and some of his advisers included former astronauts Wally Schirra and Frank Borman, as well as Richard V. Allen.[10] (Allen later served as Ronald Reagan's first National Security Adviser and resigned under a cloud of scandal, fueled by stories in the *Wall Street Journal* by Jonathan Kwitny.)

King is also mentioned in an Iran-Contra document that is an exhibit to the testimony of Richard Secord. It is a 1986 letter to Albert Hakim, Secord's Contra resupply partner, from Willard Zucker, their attorney who helped set up the corporations and Swiss bank accounts to handle Contra and Iranian money. Zucker stated that he knows King and had told a mutual acquaintance that he would not be investing in one of King's new oil ventures.

Another person close to Dick said that King had taught Dick all he knew about the use of trust accounts to hide money.

Dick also cultivated Atlantic Richfield's Robert O. Anderson, Mischer's land partner. They had several things in common. They both

---

[9] *Vesco,* by Arthur Herzog (New York: Doubleday, 1987).
[10] *Spooks,* by Jim Hougan (New York: William Morrow, 1978).

knew and did business with Richard Rossmiller and they both borrowed money from Hill Financial. Dick had Anderson over to his house for dinner, while Anderson invited Dick to his annual Christmas dinner for the "world's most powerful men" at the Claridge Hotel in London. The only woman in attendance, according to a source close to Dick, was then-British Prime Minister Margaret Thatcher.

There are other indications that Dick moves in large international circles. He owns a farm in Manitoba, from which he sells wheat to the Soviet Union. He holds citizenship in the Dominican Republic. Private detectives have tracked his travel all over the world, from Europe to the Middle East and to the Far East. And he allegedly uses evangelist Billy Graham's Youth for Christ International to travel widely.

Dick was reportedly instrumental in establishing Youth for Christ International's headquarters in Singapore, where he travels frequently. In 1990 Dick attended a Youth for Christ meeting in Chicago where he was praised by Graham for heading a $10 million Youth for Christ trust fund. This fund, according to a source close to Dick, is operated out of one of his Isle of Jersey companies.

Dick also has a number of businesses in London. In 1987, Dick and his partner, Pauls, were attempting to buy an office building in London, across the Thames from Parliament, for 5,250,000 pounds, with a 20-year lease to a British government agency. Hill Financial was going to make the loan, and there was correspondence between property consultants in London and Al Lutz. Federal examiners said the deal apparently fell through. Also in London, Dick and Pauls owned a business called Hoopers Royal Carriage, which refurbished Rolls-Royces. They refurbished a Rolls for the Sultan of Brunei and also for Marvin Davis.

One of the biggest social events of the year in Denver was Marvin Davis's Carousel Ball, which has now moved to Los Angeles. The event was to raise money for the treatment and research into juvenile diabetes, which afflicts one of Davis's daughters. One year, Dick and Pauls took Hill Financial's Al Lutz to the Carousel Ball.

A source close to Dick said that Dick actively pursued Davis. This included his purchase of a house at Davis's reportedly favorite country club, the Vintage near Palm Springs, and the Rolls refurbishing. Then, in 1986, Davis's Denver real estate firm, Miller-Klutznick-Davis-Gray Company, entered into three joint ventures in the Denver area with a British company called European Ferries.

European Ferries owned the largest private drive-on car ferry company in Europe, and in 1979 had formed a joint venture with Noramco Holdings, a John Dick company in the Isle of Jersey, to buy into the Denver Tech Center. In January 1986, the giant London-based conglomerate Peninsular and Oriental Steam Navigation Company, known as P&O, purchased the holdings of Dick and Paul in European Ferries for $50.7 million. Dick and Pauls stayed on the board of European Ferries, and four months later Marvin Davis's company bought half of European Ferries' interests in three major Denver developments.

In the early 1980s, Dick persuaded his European Ferries' partners to begin buying real estate in other parts of the United States. For one reason or another, they decided to concentrate on Atlanta and Houston. Dick sent Ray Near to Houston in 1981 to look for properties. By March 1981 they were already buying land in Houston with their new partner, Houston developer Ned Holmes. In 1984, Holmes merged his real estate development company with European Ferries to form Parkway Investments, which bought eight pieces of property, totaling more than 1,000 acres, in the Houston area.

Holmes is a noted Houston developer with a good, clean reputation. He grew up in the city, the son of a wealthy businessman who served on Houston City Council. He earned a bachelor's degree and a law degree from the University of Texas. After two years at Morgan Guaranty Trust in New York, he returned to Houston in 1971 and started his investment and real estate development business.

In 1987, Parkway Investments was taken over by P&O in its purchase of European Ferries. Holmes stayed on as president of the company, and said in an interview in 1990 that he deals with P&O's people in London. Also in 1987, Holmes was appointed to the Port of Houston Authority Commission, which governs the Port of Houston, the third largest in the country, and, coincidentally or not, where P&O does quite a bit of business. Holmes has said there is no conflict of interest in this because he has no involvement with P&O's maritime business.

Then, in 1988, Holmes was named chairman of the Port Authority Commission. This appointment is a joint decision of the Houston City Council and Harris County Commissioners Court. Holmes is politically connected to both entities, being a big fundraiser for former Mayor Kathy Whitmire and County Judge Jon Lindsay. In fact, Holmes was the head of the 1986 appreciation dinner for Lindsay in which Robert Corson contributed $10,000.

Holmes replaced Archie Bennett as chairman of the Port Authority commission. Bennett, as noted in an earlier chapter, was a good friend of Walter Mischer. Bennett sold his hotel company to Southmark and moved to Dallas, where he filed for bankruptcy.

In 1991, the Port of Houston got into a legal battle with a couple of Houston developers over the sale of a large tract of land on the Houston Ship Channel. The lawsuits were settled when the Port got back a $250,000 down payment. But the Port ended up paying its attorneys $450,000 to handle the case. One of the outside attorneys hired by the Port was Tom Alexander, Walter Mischer's personal attorney and friend. The land the Port backed out of buying was later purchased by a group led by Mischer's close friend Kenneth Schnitzer.

In 1990, Holmes was a member of a group of local investors who were vying to win a $1 billion contract to build a rail-transit system for Houston. His partners included Leo Linbeck, a construction contractor and UT Kappa Sigma brother with Carroll Kelly, Kenneth Schnitzer and Walter Mischer, Jr.

In the summer of 1992 a controversy arose over the Port of Houston's dealing with Schnitzer. It appeared as if a closed-door agreement had been cut between Schnitzer and the Port Authority, led by Schnitzer's former mass transit partner, Ned Holmes. The Port Authority agreed to buy 500 acres from Schnitzer for $12 million and lease him a terminal on the Port. In apparent exchange, Schnitzer agreed to drop his bidding war with the Port over another terminal.

One Port commissioner, the president of the International Longshoremen's Association Local 24, questioned the deal and got the Texas Attorney General to investigate. Schnitzer denied any deal had been cut and said the ILA was mad because of his decision to use non-union stevedores at his leased terminal.[11]

An article about John Dick was the last one on the S&L crisis that I wrote for the *Houston Post*. It appeared on December 23, 1990, and was to be followed eight days later by a series of articles on Walter Mischer. Those articles were never published. Why they weren't is explained in Chapter 23. I then began a leave of absence to write this book.

Immediately after I took the leave of absence, in January 1991, I did something I should have done two years earlier. I went to Miami to pull all the public documents on the players there who were connected to the story. Not doing so earlier was a major, inexcusable mistake.

---

[11] *Houston Post*, July 30, 1992.

19

CRIME AND SAVINGS AND LOANS, FLORIDA-STYLE

At the same time Farhad Azima bought Buffalo Airways, he was engaged in a big controversy over two DC-8s in Spain with individuals who lead to a vast, interconnected labyrinth of airplanes, boats, drug smuggling, gun running, money laundering, banks, savings and loans, Colombians, anti-Castro Cubans, the CIA and the Mafia in—where else?—Miami, Florida.

Almost all of the mazes and threads, if followed far enough, eventually lead back to Texas, and many go straight to Robert Corson, Walter Mischer and their associates.

Fernando Birbragher is a Russian Jew from Colombia, whose father, Abraham, emigrated to Barranquilla, Colombia, from Russia in 1928. Birbragher is also an officer or director in a number of Miami companies that are involved in real estate development, restaurants and automobiles. In addition, he owns an aircraft-refurbishing company in Miami, in a joint venture with a major U.S. aircraft maintenance company.

On September 19, 1984, Birbragher incorporated his aircraft company, Quiet Nacelle, to manufacture and install noise-suppression equipment—called "hush kits"—on DC-8s in order to meet the new FAA noise requirements. After incorporating Quiet Nacelle, Birbragher needed almost three years to gear up to design and manufacture the hush kits and then get FAA approval to install them.

Quiet Nacelle works with Orlando-based Page Avjet, which markets the hush kits—selling for $2.5 million for a four-engine jet like the

DC-8.[1] Page Avjet performs maintenance for business aircraft and airlines and runs fixed-based operations at airports in a number of cities.

By the summer of 1987, Birbragher was looking around for DC-8s to put his hush kits in. Another person looking for DC-8s was Farhad Azima. In May 1987, Azima's Aviation Leasing Group signed a contract to buy two DC-8s from a Swiss Company, Industrie-Leasing, A.G., a subsidiary of Swiss Bank Corporation. Azima agreed to pay $500,000 each for the planes, which had originally been owned by United Airlines. However, there was a slight problem. The planes were leased to Air Cargo Spain, which was in the middle of bankruptcy proceedings in Madrid.

To further complicate matters, Azima and his right-hand man, Mansour Rasnavad, found out that they had some competition for the planes, according to a lawsuit they later filed.[2] Birbragher was also trying to buy the planes, and had succeeded in getting the bankruptcy liquidating committee to approve the sale of the planes to his company for $930,000.

But was it really a fight between Azima and Birbragher? Quiet Nacelle's biggest competition in the hush kit business is a San Antonio company headed by Doug Jaffe, the son of San Antonio businessman Morris Jaffe. In 1989, one of Jaffe's closest friends and associates, John White—lawyer, lobbyist and former Democratic National Committee Chairman—was telling reporters that Azima had gone into the hush kit business with Birbragher. (Both Azima and Buffalo Airways had previously purchased hush kits from Doug Jaffe.) Interestingly, Azima's Global International Airways listed a $71,000 letter of credit due to Page Avjet, Birbragher's future partner, as one of its liabilities owed to Indian Springs State Bank.

On the surface, it appears that the lawsuit between Azima and Birbragher was pretty hard-fought, with strong accusations and recriminations on both sides. But the suit was eventually settled in 1989, Birbragher's company buying the interest of Azima's group in the two airplanes for $2,125,000. Azima had more than doubled his money in less than three years.

---

[1] *Aviation Week & Space Technology*, June 1, 1987.
[2] ALG, Inc., d/b/a Aviation Leasing Group, a Missouri corporation, and Berwyn Trading, Ltd., a Gibraltar corporation, vs. ABG Corporation, Mike Acosta, Fernando Birbragher, Hernando Gutierrez, Quiet Nacelle Corp., Jose Mena Fos, and Juan Lorca Cano, United States District Court, Southern District of Florida, 89-2319.

That same year, 1989, Birbragher, his wife and his father purchased an expensive Torah for their small Orthodox Jewish synagogue in Miami in memory of Birbragher's mother, who had recently died. "After my mother died, I became very dedicated to the synagogue," Birbragher told the *Miami Herald*. "Our hopes are not only to dedicate this Torah, but also to help build a synagogue that will be used for the glory of God."[3]

Before Birbragher dedicated himself to the synagogue, he had been dedicated to something quite different. Three months before he incorporated Quiet Nacelle, Birbragher pleaded guilty to laundering drug money for the feared and powerful Colombian drug cartel. After Birbragher was indicted in 1982, he either fled this country for his native Colombia or was already in Colombia. A *Miami Herald* story about the indictments, in December 1982, described Birbragher as a "fugitive."

Birbragher's attorney claimed in his sentencing hearing that "we knew about the case, we knew about the pending indictment months and months before it occurred. Fernando went to the DEA here in Miami and tried to work something out with them, unbeknownst to me. What they started with him was, okay, let's go out and buy three hundred kilos, three thousand kilos or whatever. It was that kind of thing, like the normal type of activity that the Drug Enforcement Agency is interested in. He couldn't do that, he left. He did not leave the United States, your honor. He never left, he never ran. The fact remains that he came back voluntarily." (This attorney, Melvyn Kesler, was later convicted of investing drug money in the Bicycle Club, a South Florida card casino.)

After he was indicted, Birbragher decided to cooperate with U.S. authorities. He ultimately returned to Miami, pleaded guilty and turned state's evidence. When he was sentenced, he got off with a slap on the wrist: three years probation and a $10,000 fine. Prosecutors said he got off easy because of the evidence he gave them, including some that led to the highest echelons of the Medellín cartel. However, there were other relationships in Birbragher's criminal activities that indicated a connection to a higher authority: the CIA.

These relationships, while not proof of CIA connections, are suggestive, especially when combined with Birbragher's business with Azima and the identity of one of his Quiet Nacelle partners. Consider first the bank where Birbragher was caught: Great American Bank in Miami.

---

[3] *Miami Herald*, March 30, 1989.

At the time (1980 and 1981) Birbragher was laundering the cartel's drug money through Great American Bank, it was owned by Marvin Warner, an Alabama native whose businesses were based out of Cincinnati. Like Charles Keating, his fellow Cincinnatian, who also got caught in the savings-and-loan debacle, Warner is full of arrogance, bluster and hubris, a man who thought his political connections and influence mongering would save him, and when it didn't, carped bitterly about government interference.

Warner got his start building houses after World War II. In the late 1950s, he bought Home State Savings in Ohio and prospered, investing in race horses and professional sports teams. In 1977, his support of Democrats paid off when President Jimmy Carter appointed him U.S. Ambassador to Switzerland. During his absence overseas, Warner hired Donald E. Beazley, a Miami banker and former federal bank examiner, to run Great American.

Before Beazley joined Warner he had worked for a while for Guillermo Hernandez-Cartaya, according to author James Ring Adams in *The Big Fix*. CIA asset Hernandez-Cartaya had gotten involved with Warner's close associates at the fraud-infested E.S.M. Securities. In fact, E.S.M. files contained a note from Hernandez-Cartaya thanking an E.S.M. principal for his offer to help in the sale or purchase of Jefferson Savings and Loan in McAllen, Texas, from Lloyd Bentsen's family.

When Warner returned from Switzerland in 1979, he took Beazley's place at Great American Bank. Beazley then jumped to the presidency of the Nugan Hand Bank in Australia. That bank, the subject of a book by Jonathan Kwitny, *The Crimes of Patriots*, was crawling with ex-CIA (if there is such a thing as ex-CIA) and former high-ranking military officials, and was used in drug-money laundering, weapons transactions and the cheating of American investors, among other things. (Beazley was never charged with any wrongdoing at Nugan Hand.)

When Beazley was working for Great American Bank, he was approached by an individual on behalf of Nugan Hand, who wanted to buy a Great American subsidiary bank, the Second National Bank of Homestead, Florida, Kwitny reported. The deal eventually fell through, but there were allegations that Second National Bank had been connected to the late Paul Helliwell, the China OSS veteran and CIA master-operative who practiced law in Miami and was one of the powers behind Castle Bank & Trust, the offshore tax haven bank used by the CIA and the mob to launder money.

While Beazley was chief executive officer of Nugan Hand, he took part in the attempted acquisition of a London bank.[4] One of his partners in the deal was Ricardo Chavez, a Cuban exile and CIA contract agent who was a member of the Edwin Wilson, Ted Shackley and Tom Clines group. In fact, Chavez was an officer in Wilson's Houston-based A.P.I. Distributors.

Despite all these relationships to CIA operatives, Beazley has denied any connections to American intelligence.[5]

After Beazley left Nugan Hand (when it disintegrated following the alleged suicide of one of its principals), he returned to Florida banking—first as president of Gulfstream Banks, and then as president of City National Bank of Miami. City National was owned by Alberto Duque, a Colombian whose father was a wealthy coffee magnate. The attorney for the bank was Stephen Arky, Marvin Warner's son-in-law.

Arky's firm also represented Beazley in a threatened lawsuit against Kwitny for stories he wrote in the *Wall Street Journal*. No lawsuit was ever filed.

Arky committed suicide in July 1985 after the E.S.M. Government Securities fraud scandal broke. The collapse of E.S.M. wrecked the Home State Savings of Arky's father-in-law, Warner, and led to Warner's conviction for fraud. After Arky's suicide, he was praised by his former boss at the Securities and Exchange Commission, where Arky worked after getting out of law school. "He was one of my real success stories," Stanley Sporkin, then general counsel to the CIA, told the *Miami Herald*. "He was one of my finest young men."[6]

Meanwhile, Beazley found himself enmeshed in yet another financial institution in the tangled webs of scandal. His boss, Alberto Duque, got caught using phony bills of lading of coffee as collateral to get more than $100 million in bank loans. He was convicted in 1986 and sentenced to 15 years in jail.

Besides Beazley, another Miami businessman embarrassed by Duque's fall from grace was Jeb Bush, son of George. In 1983, just days before Duque's empire started collapsing, Jeb accompanied Duque on one of his private planes to the inauguration of the President of Costa Rica. At the time, Jeb and his partner, Armando Codina, were building

---

[4] *The Crimes of Patriots*, by Jonathan Kwitny (New York: Norton, 1987).
[5] Ibid.
[6] *Miami Herald*, July 24, 1985.

a 30-story office building in downtown Miami that was to be the new headquarters of Duque's General Coffee Corporation.

Before that, Beazley had managed to escape the drug-money-laundering scandal at Great American Bank, just by months. Warner, too, dodged indictment, although the bank itself, as well as three employees, were charged. Just before the indictments were handed down, in December 1982, Warner sold Great American bank to Barnett Banks. It was Barnett Banks, not Warner, that had to pay the $375,000 fine levied on Great American Bank for its guilty plea to drug-money laundering. Warner, however, reaped a profit of $18 million from the sale to Barnett.

Also about this time, Warner was trying to sell a bank holding company he owned in Florida to the problem-plagued Freedom Savings and Loan in Tampa, in which Warner owned a little less than 5 percent of the stock. Freedom refused to go for the deal, so Warner had his Home State Savings in Ohio buy 7.5 percent of Freedom's stock to try to get enough votes to swing the deal.

Another stockholder, and big borrower, at Freedom was Oklahoma con man and mob associate Charles Bazarian. And, in 1986, when Freedom was in its death throes after Warner, Bazarian and a mob associate from New York had looted it, Chicago businessman Sam Zell—the old business partner of Douglas Crocker and Burton Kanter—bought control of Freedom. But before Zell bought Freedom Savings, Warner was trying to get American Savings and Loan in Miami to buy Freedom, or at least purchase his Home State Savings stock in it. American Savings and Loan is a multi-billion-dollar S&L in Miami that was controlled by Shepard Broad, an attorney and Russian immigrant, and his son, Morris Broad.

In December 1982, Warner and the Broads signed a voting trust agreement on control of American Savings. The Federal Home Loan Bank approved this agreement in November 1983, and Warner purchased approximately $13 million in American stock. In January 1984, Warner took over as chairman of the board and CEO of American Savings. He then placed his good friend and "the best business partner I ever had," Ronnie Ewton of E.S.M. Government Securities, on American's board of directors. (Arky introduced Ewton to his father-in-law.)

Warner then had American Savings enter into a $1 billion deal with E.S.M. that involved the purchase and repurchase of U.S. government securities, with American giving E.S.M. $110 million in U.S. Treasury notes. Shepard Broad finally called a halt to the E.S.M. deals and had them reversed. That caused American Savings to lose at least $55 million and brought down E.S.M. Warner's Home State Savings lost $150 million because of E.S.M., and failed, precipitating an S&L crisis in Ohio. And, among others, the city of Beaumont, Texas, lost at least $20 million on its E.S.M. investments.

Warner eventually lost his liberty too. In 1987, he was convicted in Ohio for fraud involving Home State Savings and E.S.M. Two years later, his conviction was reversed by an Ohio appeals court and then reinstated by the Ohio Supreme Court. Finally, in 1991, the U.S. Supreme Court let his conviction stand. Also, a federal court jury in Miami ordered Warner to pay $22.7 million in restitution to E.S.M.'s bankruptcy estate for his fraudulent activities. Warner then filed for bankruptcy.

There's more.

While Warner was involved with American Savings, the S&L owned about 43 percent of General Homes Corporation in Houston, a home building company. In fact, American Savings bought its interest in General Homes in January 1983, one month after Warner signed the voting trust agreement for dual control of American with Shepard Broad. The CEO of General Homes, Jeffrey Payson, was placed on American's board of directors, while Morris Broad joined General Homes's board.

American also participated in General Homes's bank lines of credit, totaling hundreds of millions of dollars. And the savings and loan purchased $125 million in mortgages from the home builder.

Guess who bought more raw land from General Homes than anyone, who purchased some $100 million in surplus vacant property in the Houston area from General Homes? That's right. Robert Corson.

In a class-action lawsuit filed against General Homes and American Savings and Loan in Dallas federal court in 1988 by some of General Homes's junk-bond holders, the plaintiffs alleged that:

"General Homes would sell portions of tracts of land to 'friendly' purchasers at inflated price(s) and, upon information and belief, in some instances with provisions that General Homes would buy-back the property under certain circumstances. These friendly purchasers could then sell or 'flip' the property to other purchasers, taking out profits and fees. The purpose and effect of this scheme and course of conduct was to provide artificially high 'sales' prices which defendants could use as the basis for artificially inflated appraisals of the property retained by General Homes.

"These fraudulent sales of real estate were made to various parties occurred (sic) in connection with various General Homes projects in Houston, Texas, including Silvermill project, the Park 45 project and Hickory Creek/Mission Green North subdivision. Many of the sales from General Homes were to Robert L. Corson and/or persons and entities affiliated with him." (In the Hickory Creek sale, Corson sold his interest to John Riddle.)

In some of these transactions, General Homes would actually finance the sale and take a first mortgage with a promissory note. The buyer then would obtain second mortgages from savings and loans such as Vernon, Continental and Western, and later default on them all. Thus, the borrowers would walk away with the S&Ls' money and General Homes would take the land back.

General Homes is also the target of another class-action suit in Houston by homeowners who bought defective houses built by the company. The homeowners, whose houses have developed large cracks in the walls, among other problems, alleged that General Homes failed to put rebar in their concrete slab foundations and knowingly sold them their houses in that defective condition.

By the time General Homes was placed into bankruptcy in 1990, American Savings had written off its investment of more than $50 million, and moved most of General Home's loans to other lenders. Warner, however, made out like a bandit. The Broads bought out his shares in American in early 1985 (just before it announced a $55 million loss on its E.S.M. dealings) for $26 million, a gain to Warner in less than two years of approximately $13 million. The money, moreover, didn't come from the Broads, it came from American Savings.[7]

Later, in July 1987, the Broads sold American Savings to Kinder-Care, an Alabama-based child day-care chain, for $138 million. Warner had founded Kinder-Care in 1969 and then allegedly sold out in 1976.[8] A principal in Kinder-Care was Aaron Aranov from Montgomery, Alabama, a longtime friend of Marvin Warner. Another principal in the company was Richard Grassgreen, one of Michael Milken's minions.

Kinder-Care raised $350 million through Drexel Burnham junk bonds, while American Savings was buying other Drexel junk. In 1990,

[7] American Savings and Loan Association of Florida, 10-K report, September 30, 1985.
[8] Bankers, Builders, Knaves, and Thieves, by Donald L. Maggin (Contemporary Books, 1989).

Grassgreen pleaded guilty to illegal stock activity involving himself, Kinder-Care and Drexel Burnham.

In 1977 and 1978, Robert Corson and his mother were building day-care homes in Houston and leasing them to Kinder-Care. In June 1977, their partner, Paul Lewis, acting as a trustee, assigned the Kinder-Care leases on a Houston day-care center they had built to Mischer's Allied Bank as security for an Allied loan. Although Warner allegedly sold out of Kinder-Care in 1976, one researcher into Kinder-Care said Warner still had some involvement in the company when it was leasing day-care centers from Corson.

There is another familiar name involved with American Savings brought in by the Milken crowd. In 1988, Steven Mizel was named chief executive officer of Kaufman Alsberg, a securities subsidiary of American Savings. The next year Mizel was named to the board of General Homes.

Steven Mizel is the brother of Larry Mizel, chairman of M.D.C. Holdings in Denver, and he served on the board of directors of M.D.C. from 1985 to 1988. M.D.C. participated in multi-million-dollar deals with San Jacinto Savings in Houston and Silverado Savings in Denver, including a peculiar land flip in Houston involving an Albuquerque company that was in a joint venture with Corson, as previously discussed.

Finally, a search of American Savings transactions in the Miami property records reveals several other familiar names. For instance, in July 1981 American Savings lent $44,000 for the purchase of a condo in Miami to Fariborz Azima, another brother of Farhad's. Fariborz ran Global International Airway's operations in Hong Kong and later worked for Race Aviation, which shipped weapons to Iran.

And, in December 1981, American Savings made a $75,000 loan on a Miami condo to Leon Birbragher, who served as a fellow officer and director of two Florida corporations with Fernando. In January 1985, American Savings filed a $75,000 mortgage from Leon on the same condo, and the next day the S&L filed a satisfaction of the 1981 mortgage. Then, in January 1982, a Fima Birbragher got a $51,900 loan from American Savings for a North Miami Beach condo.

Barbara Studley, the former conservative radio talk-show-host-turned-arms-dealer to the Contras, got a $70,000, 30-year loan from American Savings on a Miami Beach condo in August 1982. Two years later, American filed a claim against the property of pending legal action, apparently because Studley defaulted on the note.

There is one more connection to Fernando Birbragher and his drug-money laundering at Warner's Great American Bank that needs to be unraveled.

In an affidavit dated May 15, 1984, Birbragher explained how he got together with a fellow Colombian named Manuel Garces and set up a company called International Finance Company, which Great American Bank erroneously contracted to Interfil:

"Interfil did no legitimate business, it existed only as a Great American Bank account, and was used only as a false front for Mr. Garces' narcotics (both cocaine and marijuana) sales and narcotics money-laundering service. I personally sold narcotics for Mr. Garces and received proceeds from his and other people's narcotics transactions in Miami on behalf of the Garces organization. The cash proceeds were brought to us in boxes and suitcases and taken directly to Great American Bank by me, Mr. Garces or by my employee, David Goldberger, almost on a daily basis."

One of the principal pilots for Birbragher and Garces was Jack DeVoe. DeVoe is important because, among other things, he used Miami attorney Lawrence Freeman to launder some of his drug money. Freeman had CIA operatives and mob figures as associates and was connected to a savings-and-loan land deal involving Robert Corson. Freeman laundered DeVoe's drug money through companies in the Isle of Jersey in the English Channel. These same companies received S&L money from Corson and his associates, and were involved in transactions with John Dick (more about this in Chapter 21).

Back to Birbragher and DeVoe. In a reported dated March 3, 1982, U.S. Customs Senior Special Agent Peter M. Balonon stated: "Twin-engine aircraft, primarily the Beech Baron and the Navaho Aircraft, were used to smuggle approximately 200 kilos [of] cocaine per month into the U.S. The cocaine was primarily distributed through contacts of Manuel Garces known to me as Willie (LNU [or last name unknown]) and Salvatore (LNU). These are both young Latin males between the ages of 25 and 30. The pilots of these aircraft included William Sundback, Jack DeVoe and Warren Bullock.

"I've been told by numerous members of this group that Jack DeVoe was successful on more than a dozen trips during this period. To my knowledge cocaine was never stored at any of the offices at Latina Import Export [Birbragher's company], but rather at the home of the individual known to me as Willy. During November 1980, this group was so successful that Fernando Birbragher offered me 200 kilos of cocaine a month with free credit for 21 days, in other words he would front the merchandise for 21 days.

"Fernando Birbragher told me on one occasion that Jack DeVoe had flown 13 successful cocaine flights of between 150-200 kilos per trip."

The Willie discussed by Balonon is identified in Florida Department of Law Enforcement (FDLE) reports as Augusto Guillermo "Willie" Falcón, a Cuban cocaine smuggler and DeVoe's partner.

In addition to flying the cocaine from Colombia for Birbragher, DeVoe used Birbragher's Interfil account at Great American Bank to wire $100,000 to an aircraft company in Spokane, Washington. DeVoe was investing in this company as a way to launder his drug money. The money was wired in the name of Dr. Robert K. Oka. This is the first time the mysterious Dr. Oka, the man who never was, appears.

One of DeVoe's pilots, Profullo "Prof" Mondol, invented Dr. Oka, supposedly a rich physician from Bombay, India, to serve as a front for DeVoe. Oka was made to be from India because it is easy to get a death certificate there. In at least one of the Jersey Island trusts set up by Lawrence Freeman for DeVoe's drug proceeds, Dr. Oka was the trustee, with DeVoe the ultimate beneficiary. So if the trust ever needed to be abolished so that DeVoe could get the money, they would just kill off poor Dr. Oka.

This was also one of the late-lamented spook Paul Helliwell's favorite tricks. In fact, Helliwell used two imaginary Greeks to hold part-ownership in Castle Bank & Trust. Many years later, in a tax matter involving Burton Kanter and Castle Bank, Freeman swore that Helliwell had actually introduced him to these men. Castle Bank records show that Freeman should know; he took one of their places as an officer at Castle Bank.

In the event that DeVoe ever had to actually produce a Dr. Oka for visual inspection, Prof Mondol would do the honors. Mondol, a native of India, operated airlines in Afghanistan and Nepal before emigrating to the United States in 1967. He is author of a book of fiction, *Operation Tibet*. But one of his book's fictional pilots is a Jim Serbin, the name of a real pilot procured by Mondol for DeVoe's smuggling operations.

As the son of the first Methodist Bishop of Indian descent, Prof

Mondol, who died in March 1992, had grown up around British MI6 and United States CIA personnel. His full name, Profulla Kumar, meant "Prince of Sunshine," and the closer Mondol could get to the sun, the happier he was.

Mondol traveled the spook circuit. When DeVoe Airlines was formed, Mondol envisioned a commuter-type operation that fed off a large carrier. The commuter operation would be used as cover to work for the CIA. In order to set up the operation, Mondol brought in a couple of his longtime associates, Jim Serbin and Robert "Denver Bob" Colquitt.

Colquitt, whom Mondol had known since the early 1970s, had a mutual friend with Mondol, Heinrich "Harry" Rupp, the earlier-described CIA contract pilot who went to jail in a mob bank scam. "Harry, Bob and I tried to get a couple of deals going. One involved the transporting of around 500 Ford Escort tractors from India to the Afghan rebels. It really involved obtaining certificates from three governments, India, Pakistan and Afghanistan, because we had to fly through their air space. I got the certificates. We were going to use Sharjah Airlines. I got permission from the ruler of Sharjah to form the airline," Mondol said. In the end, Pan Am got the contract.

In 1981, DeVoe invested in Tiger Tops Mountain Travel International, a worldwide organization with parks located in central India, Nepal, Mysore, Gilgit, Pakistan and Wyoming, where Serpas from Nepal helped Americans learn to climb mountains. Mondol, Colquitt, DeVoe and others trekked off to the Nepal resort in the early 1980s during a lull in their cocaine-importing operations.

Colquitt not only appears in the FDLE reports on DeVoe and Freeman, his name is mentioned in a statement submitted by the former president of Aurora Bank, Aurora, Colorado, during his sentencing for bank fraud involving Rupp and several East Coast mobsters. The former president, William J. Vanden Eynden, said he was introduced to Rupp in 1976 by his fiancée, who, it turns out, is related to one of Adnan Khashoggi's employees. Vanden Eynden stated that in May 1981 he traveled to Las Vegas with Rupp and several other people, including Robert Colquitt, a "partner" of Rupp's.[9]

At Warner's Great American Bank, DeVoe also used Birbragher's Interfil account to buy a condo in 1980 at the exclusive Ocean Reef Club

---

[9] Affidavit in Federal Deposit Insurance Corp. vs. John Antonio et al., United States District Court for Colorado, 85C1298.

on the north end of Key Largo. DeVoe used the Ocean Reef landing strip to fly in much of his cocaine from Colombia. His other landing field was at the Opa-Locka Airport in Miami. (This airfield was used as an operations center in the CIA's 1954 coup in Guatemala.)

The Ocean Reef Club is owned by Cincinnati billionaire Carl Lindner, the secretive, security-obsessed, semi-reclusive, Baptist corporate raider and major Republican donor. Lindner, who had been Michael Milken's biggest and most respected client,[10] started out in the milk business and gradually expanded into other areas. His business empire includes the insurance and financial services company American Financial Corporation, Chiquita Brands International (formerly United Brands and before that United Fruit) and Penn Central, which bought Marathon Manufacturing from Walter Mischer and Mischer's close partner Howard Terry in 1979. Terry joined the Penn Central board of directors under its chairman, Carl Lindner.

A spokeswoman for Lindner said he knows Howard Terry but not Walter Mischer.

Lindner also controls Hunter Savings and Loan in Ohio, a big buyer of Drexel Burnham junk bonds. It was Hunter which bought Marvin Warner's Home State Savings out of insolvency. And Lindner had the distinction of being the biggest individual S&L-connected contributor to congressional campaigns during the 1980s, according to a study by *Common Cause*, which found that his family contributed $828,920 to congressional candidates.

Perhaps Lindner's biggest contribution to the S&L debacle was Charles Keating. During the 1960s, Keating and his Cincinnati law firm represented Lindner and his interests. Apparently the two were so taken with one another that in 1972, Keating quit his law firm and went to work for Lindner directly as executive vice president of American Financial. Four years later, in 1976, Keating moved to Phoenix to take over Lindner's home building company, American Continental Homes. Two years later, Lindner sold the company to Keating, who changed its name to American Continental Corporation.

However, the next year, 1979, Lindner, Keating and an attorney associate were charged by the Securities and Exchange Commission with making improper loans to friends and associates from Lindner's Provident Bank in Cincinnati. Lindner and Keating signed a consent

---

[10] *The Predators' Ball*, by Connie Bruck (The American Lawyer/Simon and Schuster, 1988).

decree, agreeing not to violate the law again, and Lindner paid $1.4 million out of his own pocket to his company, American Financial. More than one observer has noted that the charges against the two were remarkably similar to the ones that would be leveled against Keating in his operation of Lincoln Savings, which American Continental bought in 1984 with $51 million from Drexel Burnham.

There are other interconnections between Marvin Warner, Lindner and Keating. Warner's Home State Savings used Keating's law firm for legal work. Also, one of Warner's best and oldest friends and biggest partners, Hugh Culverhouse, Sr., served for a time on the board of Lindner's American Financial.

Regarding Charles Keating, Lindner's spokeswoman said, "Mr. Lindner hasn't even seen him in 12 years. He hasn't had anything to do with him since then."

Allegations of CIA connections to Lindner waft around him, but nothing has ever been proved. One interesting link was Lindner's purchase of United Brands, which, as United Fruit, worked hand in hand with the CIA in the overthrow of the Jacob Arbenz government in Guatemala in 1954.

In February 1984, Lindner's American Financial Corp. increased its ownership in United Brands to 45.4 percent from 29.3 percent. The very next month there are two relevant note's in Oliver North's White House diary. The first, on March 10, talks about a meeting at the Ocean Reef Club among four U.S. representatives: Thomas Foley, Democrat-Washington; Dante Fascell, Democrat-Florida; Edward Boland, Democrat-Massachusetts; and Jim Wright, Democrat-Texas and the Speaker of the House.

Three of these—Foley, Fascell and Boland—would later serve on the House Select Committee to investigate covert arms transactions with Iran. Boland was the chief sponsor of the Boland Amendments, which prohibited the CIA and other U.S. government agencies from providing military support to the Contras. And Wright would later resign from Congress under the cloud of improprieties related to savings and loans, among other things.

The entry in North's notebook just before the Ocean Reef Club states, "VP [Vice President Bush] to talk to Boland." In addition, the Ocean Reef entry begins with the initials "HAK" and then a dash and then the names of the congressmen. The only person listed in the index of the *Iran-Contra Chronology* prepared by the National Security Archive with the initials HAK is Henry Kissinger. In July 1983, Ronald Reagan appointed Kissinger to head a bipartisan Presidential Commission on Central America. Reagan said then: "We must not allow totalitarian Communism to win by default."[11]

The second entry in North's notebooks just one month after Lindner increased his company's ownership of United Brands by 55 percent was a telephone call from Andy Messing on March 27. Messing, a former Green Beret in Vietnam, was head of the National Defense Council and worked with North and some congressmen to get the U.S. military to airlift relief supplies to the Contras.

Messing was close to retired Major General John Singlaub, who said of Messing: "He serves as my adviser on all matters relating to Congress and the general conservative community." Messing was an advocate of low-intensity conflict in Central America and would show conservative congressmen around some of the low-intensity battlefields in Central America. After Messing's name, North wrote in his notebook: "United Brands grant to Messing for study of Mexican political center."

Lindner's spokeswoman said that Lindner has never had any relationship with the CIA.

But Lindner does have a relationship with former CIA Director George Bush. The corporate recluse is one of Bush's biggest campaign donors. Bush likes to go fishing at Ocean Reef, and has held several important meetings there, including a 1990 summit with French President François Mitterand. During this summit, Bush held a press conference in the backyard of Lindner's Ocean Reef house.

In November 1985, Florida Department of Law Enforcement investigators interviewed Jack DeVoe in federal prison in Memphis, Tennessee, regarding his cocaine smuggling into the Ocean Reef Club. "DeVoe stated that the majority of the hangars at Ocean Reef were used for drug smuggling for many years and a lot of people knew about it," said an FDLE report. DeVoe also stated that Harper Sibley, the chairman of the board of Ocean Reef Club for Lindner, "just seemed to tolerate anything that went on at Ocean Reef, legal or illegal."

In 1982, DeVoe was having income tax problems with the IRS. One of his attorneys told FDLE investigators that Harper Sibley "was con-

---

[11] *New York Times,* July 19, 1983.

cerned about the IRS investigation of DeVoe. Martin [a partner of DeVoe's attorney] talked with Sibley, who stated although he liked DeVoe personally, he could not afford to have his club dragged down with DeVoe should the IRS pursue charges. Sibley was particularly concerned about Carl Lindner's reaction should charges be filed against DeVoe."

Lindner's spokeswoman said that Lindner has never even heard of Jack DeVoe.

However, in the summer of 1988 the Ocean Reef Club agreed to transfer title for 31 acres of mangrove to the state. This friendly takeover by the state of Florida was allegedly done in lieu of a formal RICO [Racketeering Influenced and Corrupt Organizations] forfeiture complaint that could have been filed against Ocean Reef for allowing an ongoing criminal enterprise (DeVoe's drug smuggling) to operate on its property. Ocean Reef also agreed to pay $150,000 toward the cost of investigation by the FDLE.[12]

Lindner did not respond through his spokeswoman to questions about the Ocean Reef RICO investigation and the land transfer.

A name just a big as Lindner's and even more familiar appeared in one of DeVoe's statements to FDLE investigators regarding smuggling at Ocean Reef: "DeVoe indicated that the hangars at Ocean Reef Club were almost all utilized for smuggling purposes." Of the seven hangars DeVoe listed at Ocean Reef, he himself used three. But one next to his, Hangar #6, was owned by Bebe Rebozo, Richard Nixon's closest associate and Watergate figure. (Rebozo was also good friends with Paul Helliwell.[13])

When DeVoe needed two sponsors to join the Ocean Reef Club, he and his associate, "Happy" Miles, used Bebe Rebozo's name as the second sponsor. "Happy suggested B.B. Rebozo's name. DeVoe said he only knew of Rebozo but had never met him. Carrier [an Ocean Reef Club official] said don't worry, no one will ever question it. Russell Post [another Ocean Reef official] was the first to question DeVoe's sponsor. The lady in membership [name unknown] told DeVoe that Post later retyped DeVoe's membership card in order to remove Rebozo's name," an FDLE report acknowledged.

However, a close associate of DeVoe said Rebozo was in fact DeVoe's sponsor.

12 *Miami Herald*, July 8, 1988.
13 *Masters of Paradise*, by Alan Block (Transaction Publishers, 1991).

DeVoe had troubles with the IRS long before he was caught smuggling drugs. It seems he neglected to file tax returns for several years during the mid- and late 1970s. Therefore, on March 25, 1980, he went to see an attorney on the recommendation of Jack Brock, one of his drug-smuggling partners. Brock steered DeVoe to Theodore Klein, a criminal defense attorney in Miami.

(Seven years later, during Iran-Contra, Klein would come to the nation's attention as the attorney for Ron Martin, the CIA-connected arms dealer who was supplying weapons to the Contras and allegedly owned a casino with Robert Corson.)

DeVoe swore in a deposition that he told Klein he was in the drug-smuggling business. "Mr. Klein knew I was in the drug-smuggling business."

"Did you tell him that or did he just know," an FDLE attorney asked DeVoe.

"I asked him. We discussed it. I asked him one time—I said, 'Things are getting pretty heavy. Do you have any tips?' He said, 'Yes. Always keep a third person to make it as far—make it three or more people away from you when you're'—is it buying or selling and dealing? I don't recall the conversation exactly. I have some notes someplace."

However, according to an FDLE investigative report on an interview with Klein: "Klein stated he suspected DeVoe was a drug smuggler when his representation started, mainly because of his association with Jack Brock. Klein had represented Brock on drug-related charges. DeVoe later told Klein that a long time ago he was involved in smuggling cocaine, but that was over and he was trying to run a legitimate airline."

The FDLE report then goes on to state: "Klein did not realize DeVoe was not happy with his representation until DeVoe hired Harvey Silets to assist on the case. . . . Klein received a letter from DeVoe dated September 9, 1981, that ended his representation."

An FDLE attorney asked DeVoe during a deposition, "After Ted Klein, you hired Harvey Silets to represent you on the tax problem?"

DeVoe answered, "Yes."

Then the FDLE attorney asked, "Mr. Silets is a nationally recognized tax specialist, isn't he?"

To which DeVoe replied, "Yes, he is."

Silets, from Chicago, also represented Burton Kanter in his Castle Bank-related indictment. Silets told an FDLE investigator that "he had been friends with Kanter for a long time and had represented him in the early 1970s when Kanter was indicted by the federal government on conspiracy charges."

The FDLE reports do not indicate how and why DeVoe got Silets to represent him. They do show at least one meeting at which both Klein and Silets were present, although Klein didn't admit introducing DeVoe to Silets. Silets then sent DeVoe to Lawrence Freeman for help in setting up foreign bank accounts and companies. "Freeman was hired to assist in laundering the smuggling proceeds," an FDLE report on DeVoe states flatly.

Lawrence A. Freeman was born in Washington, D.C., on January 5, 1939. He attended the University of Miami, getting a bachelor's degree in 1960 and a law degree in 1964. He joined the Air Force as a judge advocate, where he worked until 1969, and then he began work as an associate with the old CIA spook Paul Helliwell's law firm, Helliwell, Melrose and DeWolfe, in Miami.

In October 1988, Freeman was a witness in a federal court hearing in Denver, Colorado, in one of the longest-running IRS cases in history: the fight over more than $30 million in undeclared profits from the movie *One Flew Over the Cuckoo's Nest*. No taxes were ever paid on the profits that were funneled through a maze of offshore trust accounts at Castle Bank, with the assistance of Burton Kanter and Paul Helliwell.

Freeman was called to testify about the existence of the two imaginary Greeks whom Helliwell conjured up. During his sworn testimony, Freeman discussed some of his background.[14]

Freeman said he first met Helliwell when he traveled to the United States for a funeral in April 1969. "I advised my dad that I intended to separate from the service and continue to live in Europe, and my father, being a consul for the country of El Salvador, recommended that I speak with Paul Helliwell, who by coincidence my father knew because Paul Helliwell was the consul of Thailand.

"I met with Mr. Helliwell, and Mr. Helliwell suggested that I contact his business associate in Zurich, who was Phil Barry." Barry was in the OSS with Helliwell, Freeman said.

Later that year, Freeman was in Zurich to see Barry about arranging financing for an Arab airline in Egypt. Helliwell was also there, he stated, as was a man named George Bebas, to whom Helliwell intro-

---

[14] *Saul Zaentz vs. Commissioner of the Internal Revenue Service*, U.S. Tax Court, docket numbers 3273-86, 4372-86, 5836-86, 6584-86, and 38046-86.

duced him. (Bebas was one of the two imaginary Greeks.)

"The only other thing that I can recall that happened that day is, I had dinner that evening with Mr. Helliwell and Bill Casey—William Casey, who was also of the OSS, who I believe was then in private practice. The gentleman later became the head of the Securities and Exchange Commission and I believe sometime in early 1981 became the head of the CIA."

Freeman testified that he joined Helliwell's law firm in January 1970 and then six months later went to work as the in-house counsel for Castle Bank & Trust in Nassau, Bahamas. Castle Bank records show that Freeman was listed as a vice president in September 1970 and as a vice president and secretary in September of the following year. The previously listed secretary had been A. Alipranti (the other imaginary Greek).

Freeman said he returned to Helliwell's law firm in October or November of 1971, and then left to form his own firm in May 1972.

(Freeman's testimony in this case was abruptly halted by the judge after the IRS attorney, Gene Ciranni, asked Freeman about Jack DeVoe and Dr. Robert Oka. Freeman invoked attorney-client privilege and requested a private meeting with the judge, who afterwards would not allow Ciranni to question Freeman further.)

In a brief telephone conversation I had with him in 1989, just after he had gotten out of jail and could not practice law, Freeman refused to answer any questions. Asked if he had ever worked for the CIA, he replied, "I don't know." Then he caught himself and quickly said, "No comment."

When asked if he knew Burton Kanter, Freeman replied, "I know a lot of people."

In his sworn testimony in the *One Flew Over the Cuckoo's Nest* case, Freeman was asked about Kanter's relationship to Castle Bank. "To the best of my recollection, Mr. Kanter was the United States tax counsel to the bank," he replied. Later, he stated that he first met Kanter in Miami in the spring of 1970, when he was still with Helliwell's firm.

When he was in-house counsel for Castle Bank, Freeman testified at the IRS hearing, "I probably consulted with Mr. Kanter with regard to various tax matters. I may have traded professional opinions with him. I may have consulted him with why or why something was not done. I don't know."

Even though Freeman left Castle Bank and then Helliwell's firm, he kept in close touch with Kanter. They and their associates were involved in at least 21 companies incorporated in Florida. Almost all of them were registered in the late 1970s or early 1980s, and some are still active. Kanter also had a law office next to Freeman's in Miami for about a year, and when Florida state prosecutors and investigators raided Freeman's office in November 1985, they found Kanter's name on several documents.

One was a disbursement of $27,500 to Kanter from a $50,000 receipt from the Bank of New England. Freeman got $10,000 of this, while his law firm received $6,000. In a letter to me at the *Houston Post*, Kanter said the $27,500 was a "reportable fee and was, in fact, reported on my personal income tax return."

In his letter, Kanter also makes the unbelievable statement that "Mr. Freeman has acted as counsel, both for me personally and for various activities in which I may have had an involvement from time to time, but neither of us have ever been associated in business." Kanter doesn't address the more than 20 companies in Florida that list Freeman as an officer or director, along with the names of women with the same Chicago street address and suite number as Kanter's.

One of the attorneys in the *One Flew Over the Cuckoo's Nest* case made the statement that Kanter was introduced to Helliwell by General William J. "Wild Bill" Donovan, the famous leader of the OSS during World War II, and Helliwell's OSS boss.

Kanter denied that. "I personally never met Bill Donovan. I believe I may have spoken to him once by phone at Paul Helliwell's request . . ."

In his 1991 book *Masters of Paradise*, Alan Block states that Kanter "had direct ties to organized crime," pointing to his connections with the La Costa resort, to mob associate and Teamsters Union pension fund guru Allen Dorfman, as well as to Cleveland mobster Morris Kleinman, who was probably one of the founding owners of Castle Bank.

Helliwell once reportedly told a Castle Bank colleague that they had to transfer some Kleinman accounts from a sister Caribbean bank to Castle Bank to protect them. "If you don't do it, Kanter will end up face down in the Chicago River," Helliwell said.

Block's book comes down stronger on the side of mob control and presence at Castle Bank than that of the CIA, but he does recognize the ground-breaking story in the *Wall Street Journal* by Jim Drinkhall in

April 1980, which stated that the CIA was responsible for stopping a Justice Department investigation of Castle Bank. The CIA, it seemed, was using some Castle Bank accounts to fund covert activities.

Helliwell was identified by journalist Jim Drinkhall as being the reputed paymaster for the abortive Bay of Pigs invasion. Drinkhall also reported that Helliwell and the CIA used Castle Bank accounts to fund later anti-Castro activities.

According to author and journalist Jonathan Kwitny, "Amidst all the speculation that has swirled around CIA agents who were also involved in narcotics smuggling over the years, the one CIA career officer definitely known to have planned narcotics smuggling as an instrument of American foreign policy was Paul Helliwell."

Helliwell established one of the CIA's first proprietary front companies, called Sea Supply Corp., to funnel weapons to the anti-communist Chinese in Thailand in the 1950s. The Chinese manufactured heroin to help pay for their military needs, and the heroin was transported out of the isolated mountains on the pack mules of Helliwell's Sea Supply Corp.

Like Kanter and Helliwell, and like Walter Mischer and Robert Corson, Lawrence Freeman lived in a world where the distinctions between the CIA and organized crime become blurred. Not only did Freeman have direct business associations with Kanter and Helliwell, and indirect ties to Corson, he had other links to organized crime figures.

One Florida Department of Law Enforcement report contains an interview with Jack DeVoe's main partner, James Malone, a former newspaper and television reporter. Malone explained how Freeman would launder some of their drug money by turning the cash over to one of his other clients and then moving money from that client's offshore bank accounts to DeVoe's offshore accounts.

"Malone and DeVoe nicknamed this other client the 'Cobra,' " the FDLE report recorded. "Based on numerous conversations with Freeman, Malone got the impression that the 'Cobra' was a prominent organized crime figure possibly from the Tampa area."

The head of the Florida Mafia, who lived in Tampa, was Santo Trafficante. Another FDLE report, based on an interview with DeVoe, states that "Malone told DeVoe that Freeman at one time told him that he [Freeman] handles Santo Trafficante's money."

Such an association is not far-fetched. Freeman's former boss, Paul

Helliwell, and Trafficante both worked hard on the same thing: the ouster or untimely demise of Fidel Castro. Trafficante wanted his Havana casinos (where Frank Sturgis worked) back, and was one of the two top-ranking Mafia bosses who were in on the CIA's use of the Mafia to try to take out Castro.

(The other one was Chicago don Sam Giancana. However, Trafficante's close associate, Carlos Marcello, once told an FBI informant that he was in on it too.[15] Author John H. Davis also reported that Marcello's close friend in Washington, lobbyist Irving Davidson—who was indicted with Marcello on Brilab and then acquitted—often "functioned as an unofficial lobbyist for the CIA on Capitol Hill. With a mere phone call, Davidson could have put Carlos Marcello in touch with most anyone in the CIA, including the director himself."[16])

When FDLE investigators subpoenaed the telephone company for the names behind the telephone numbers called by Freeman, they found Louis Chesler. They apparently didn't know who the mobster was, because there is no more mention of him in the FDLE reports on Freeman. Chesler, Meyer Lansky's partner, was also a casino partner with Wallace Groves, who headed a company called Intercontinental Diversified Corporation that washed money for the CIA through Castle Bank.[17] Another top official at Intercontinental Diversified was Mary Jane Melrose, a senior partner in Paul Helliwell's law firm.

It doesn't take too much cogitating about this to see why Lawrence Freeman might be calling up Louis Chesler on the phone, but would not have listed his name and phone number in any of his office records.

In 1982, DeVoe, on the recommendation of James Malone and Lawrence Freeman, hired Albert Krieger as his criminal defense attorney. DeVoe paid Krieger about $140,000 before his trial. After DeVoe was finally arrested on drug charges in July 1983, he wanted to plea-bargain with the government, but "Krieger would never consider a plea bargain," said an FDLE report.

The report went on to describe a meeting Krieger had with DeVoe at the Miami Correctional Center. "DeVoe mentioned plea bargaining again, but Krieger was not at all interested, especially since one of the

---

[15] *Mafia Kingfish*, by John H. Davis (New York: New American Library, 1991).
[16] Ibid.
[17] *Wall Street Journal*, "IRS vs. CIA," by Jim Drinkhall, April 18, 1980.

individuals Jack would have to inform on was Larry Freeman, Krieger's close friend," the FDLE report stated.

DeVoe eventually fired Krieger, pleaded guilty, turned state's evidence against a number of drug smugglers and received eight years in prison in 1986. He is now out of jail and in the federal witness protection program.

When Freeman was arrested and his office was raided in November 1985, the first person he telephoned was Krieger, his attorney. Freeman also told FDLE investigators that several of his files, including some on Dr. Robert Oka, had been turned over to Krieger.

One FDLE report discusses a telephone conference on April 23, 1983, among Freeman, Krieger, Harvey Silets, James Malone and Dr. Oka (probably Prof Mondol), regarding Oka's "position," presumably on tax or criminal matters.

After Freeman was arrested, Krieger described Freeman to reporters as a "taxation specialist of international reputation."

This is the same Albert Krieger who was the registered agent and secretary of C.I.C. Enterprises, whose president was Clemard Joseph Charles, the CIA's man in Haiti and money launderer for Mario Renda. In 1992, when John "The Dapper Don" Gotti, head of the Gambino Mafia family, was being tried for the murder of the former Gambino boss, Paul Castellano, guess who was brought in from Miami as his defense attorney? Albert Krieger.

Freeman ended up pleading guilty in February 1989 to two counts of racketeering in laundering drug money for DeVoe. He forfeited his law license for a limited period and was sentenced to three years in jail—but was already out when I talked to him in the fall of 1989.

Prof Mondol, the late Indian and one of DeVoe's main pilots, asserted that half of the runs involving the DeVoe organization were guns down and drugs up. Mondol said the drug-running profits were to be used to get DeVoe Aviation's commuter operations off and running.

Also, DeVoe's favorite transshipment and stopping point between Colombia and the United States was Belize. At least two Belize residents were indicted with DeVoe in Florida, but since the United States has no extradition treaty with Belize, they have escaped United States justice. Several of DeVoe's pilots testified that they received assistance from Jules Weatherbourne, who runs the airport in Belize City, and from a

Rudy Flowers, who provided them gas. Both Weatherbourne and Flowers were indicted in Florida.

One pilot, Andrew James, testified that Vallan Gillett, the head of the narcotics police in Belize, was also on the take.

Another pilot, Olmond Lawrence Hall, testified that one time he and Andy James crashed after attempting a takeoff from a landing strip in central Belize near the Guatemalan and Mexican borders. This is the same general area where, some two years later, Walter Mischer and his partners bought 700,000 acres.

This doesn't mean, of course, that Mischer had anything to do with this drug smuggling, only that the land he bought was in a very convenient transshipment point between Central and South America and the United States.

There is one final connection to be made from Fernando Birbragher to another character in the book. It is a connection that was alluded to earlier.

At the same time that Birbragher and DeVoe were smuggling narcotics and laundering drug money for Manuel Garces and Willie Falcón at Marvin Warner's Great American Bank, DeVoe's criminal defense attorney on taxes was Ted Klein, who later gained fame as the lawyer for CIA and Contra gun dealer Ron Martin.

Also around this time, Ron Martin's weapons firm, R M Equipment, lent $72,500 to Miguel C. Acosta. Five years later, Acosta showed up as Birbragher's right-hand man, and fellow officer and director, at Quiet Nacelle.

The loan from R M Equipment to Acosta was a one-year loan, secured by a Miami house that Acosta's company, MCA Leasing, had just deeded to Acosta and his wife. Acosta didn't pay off the note when it became due, and R M Equipment filed a lawsuit against him. The matter was settled, for an unknown amount, on January 20, 1981. Acosta's attorney then was Harry Bender, who became Quiet Nacelle's attorney after it started business. It was Bender who represented Birbragher, Acosta and Quiet Nacelle in their legal "fight" with Farhad Azima over the two DC-8s in Spain.

There were intimations that Ron Martin's weapons deals with the Contras were also mixed up with narcotics. Martin and his partner, James McCoy, the former defense attaché to the U.S. Embassy in Managua, Nicaragua, when Somoza was in power, had set up a so-called "supermarket" for arms in a warehouse in Honduras. In Oliver North's White House notebooks, there is an entry dated July 12, 1985, regarding a phone call from Dick Secord, which states: "discussion re: supermarket; Ho[nduran] army plans to seize all [the next word(s) is (are) illegible] when supermarket comes to a bad end. [Illegible] finance comes from drugs; [deleted by CIA] expects (HOAF) [Honduran Armed Forces] to seize the supermarket's assets when the supermarket folds."

A 1989 report by the Senate Subcommittee on Terrorism, Narcotics and International Operations found that a company called Hondu Carib was shipping some of Martin's weapons to the Contras. Hondu Carib was formed by a pilot named Frank Moss, who had come under investigation for alleged narcotics trafficking. Moss was also a pilot for SETCO, a Honduran company selected by the U.S. Department of State to supply humanitarian relief goods to the Contras. SETCO, which was established by a Honduran cocaine smuggler, had already been ferrying supplies to Contras in Honduras.

The U.S. Customs Service had been following a DC-4 aircraft used by Moss to carry equipment to the Contras. A May 18, 1983, Customs report regarding the DC-4 and one of its pilots, Guy Owen, stated that "arrangements had been made to airdrop large quantities of marijuana and cocaine at an isolated farm near Baton Rouge, Louisiana. The farm's address Rt. 6, Box 282E in East Baton Rouge, Louisiana, belonging to Adler B. [Barry] Seal and Wendell K. Seal, both allegedly major narcotic smugglers and distributors throughout the eastern and southern United States.

"The investigating officer was able to obtain copies of Guy Penilton Owen telephone tolls for the year of 1981 through the Mississippi Bureau of Narcotics Agent Norton. The tolls were submitted through TELAM [telephone analysis] and revealed that Guy Owen had called 912-638-3191, which is listed to Bill Walker and Associates, address of 2606 Frederica Rd., St. Simons, GA. William Oualy Walker is a well-documented narcotics smuggler."[18]

Bill Walker showed up in Houston in the summer of 1987 to buy a twin-engine Cessna out of repossession by NBC Bank Houston. The previous owner had been a company owned by Robert Corson's associate Mike Adkinson, for whom Lawrence Freeman was fronting in the

---

[18] U.S. Customs Service investigation report, New Orleans, Louisiana. Guy Penilton Owen et al., May 18, 1983.

21,000-acre land deal in the Florida panhandle.

This transaction will be dealt with in detail later. First, the rest of the Florida deals that lead back to Texas must be explored. They also lead to the Mafia, Paul Helliwell, Bebe Rebozo, the Contras, drugs, the CIA and George Bush.

20

SUNRISE, SUNSHINE, SUNSET: FLORIDA AND THE TEXAS CONNECTION

Eulalio Francisco "Frank" Castro is one bad hombre. Although he is a well-known terrorist and drug smuggler, his rap sheet shows only one conviction—for carrying a weapon in Miami in 1981. That same year, he was charged with four counts of importing, delivering and selling marijuana. The case was later dismissed.

Then, in 1983, he was indicted for conspiracy and smuggling 425,000 pounds of marijuana into Beaumont, Texas, as a spinoff of the Drug Enforcement Administration's "Operation Grouper." (Some of the Grouper targets' drug money was laundered through Marvin Warner's ComBanks in Florida.) These charges against Frank Castro were also dropped, in June 1984.

From July 1983 to January 1984—the same time period in which he was under indictment for drug smuggling—Castro was providing food, equipment and weapons for a secret military training camp for Nicaraguan Contras in the Everglades near Naples, Florida. Castro told FBI agents that he provided food, ammunition and an M-14 rifle to the camp. He would go to the camp almost weekly to take supplies, Castro told the FBI.

Castro also traveled to Costa Rica and met with John Hull and a Contra leader. "Castro went to Costa Rica in order to assist [René] Corvo and the Cubans fighting there," said an FBI report. Castro tried to tell the FBI agents that John Hull "does not work for the Central Intelligence Agency but funnels information to them."

That statement is laughable. John Hull not only worked directly for the CIA, he worked for Rob Owen, who was a gofer for Oliver North, who was a cutout for the CIA. More important, according to the CIA's official pronouncements, its primary work is the funneling of information. Perhaps Castro didn't realize that stated purpose when he has worked for the CIA. Perhaps he perceived its work to be the elimination of foreign politicians it doesn't like.

A Cuban exile, Frank Castro was a member of the famous Brigade 2506 that participated in the CIA-supported Bay of Pigs invasion to oust Fidel Castro. The head of the National Front for the Liberation of Cuba, Frank Castro was also a top dog in CORU, an alliance of anti-Fidel Castro Cuban terrorist organizations that was connected to and partly financed by Guillermo Hernandez-Cartaya. Castro, who owned the Golden Falcon Skydiving Club in the Florida Everglades, shuttles between Miami and the Dominican Republic, where he is lives with his wife, the daughter of an admiral close to the president of the republic.[1]

"Frank Castro is a very dangerous individual. He's CIA trained," according to Assistant U.S. Attorney Daniel Cassidy, who prosecuted some of Castro's associates involved in drug smuggling and control of a bank.

In the mid 1970s when Castro's *compadres* Orlando Bosch and Rolando Otero were going around blowing up all sorts of things, like post offices and passenger airliners, Castro told the *Miami Herald*, "I believe that the United States has betrayed freedom fighters around the world. They trained us to fight, brainwashed us how to fight and now they put Cuban exiles in jail for what they had been taught to do in the early years."

In June 1988, Frank Castro and five others were indicted for violating the U.S. Neutrality Act for taking part in a "military expedition and enterprise to be carried on from thence against the territory of Nicaragua, a foreign state with whom the United States, at all times mentioned herein, has been and is now at peace."[2]

In announcing the indictment, Assistant U.S. Attorney Mark Schnapp said that Castro financed the 60-man training camp near Naples. In defiance, Castro's attorney, Kirk Munroe, said that Castro

---

[1] *Labyrinth*, by Eugene M. Propper and Taylor Branch (Viking, 1982).

[2] United States of America vs. Rene Corvo et al., United States District Court, Southern District of Florida, 88-6098 CR.

would provide aid to the Contras again if he were asked. The defendants took the position that they had set up the camp and trained the Contras with the approval of the White House, but the prosecutors claimed the operation was not "sanctioned" by the Reagan Administration.

The argument was rendered moot and never adjudicated when the judge threw out the charges, ruling that the United States was not technically at peace with Nicaragua at that time. But the question remained whether Castro used drug money to finance the Contra operations.

A May 21, 1986, letter from the chief counsel of the Senate Foreign Relations Committee to the Justice Department detailed allegations that Frank Castro and his associate, Francisco Chanes, "are said to be partners in seafood business and use business to smuggle cocaine into the U.S. from Costa Rica. Funds from cocaine sales said to be used to purchase weapons for Contras." This information was based on a investigation by the staff of Senator John Kerry (Democrat-Massachusetts), who headed the Senate Subcommittee on Terrorism, Narcotics and International Operations. This was apparently the only investigation into the allegations.

In Frank Castro's most famous drug-smuggling exploit, he was not even charged—he was named as an unindicted co-conspirator in the marijuana-smuggling syndicate headed by fellow Cuban exile and CIA contract agent Tony Fernández. From 1977 to 1981, Fernández and his associates smuggled more than 1.5 million pounds of marijuana into the United States from Colombia. In early 1981, Fernández, known on the streets as La Mentirita—"the little lie"—was arrested and jailed in New Orleans for his smuggling activities.

Fernández made bail with the help of a banker friend. Upon release, he was promptly kidnapped by Frank Castro and taken to Colombia, according to Assistant U.S. Attorney Daniel Cassidy. His Colombian suppliers had some questions to ask about payment for a marijuana shipment that had been confiscated by the DEA. Fernández managed to scrape up the money to satisfy the Colombians, then bounced around to Spain, Costa Rica and finally Brazil, where the DEA caught up with him. In 1984, he was extradited to the United States, where he turned state's evidence against his banker associates and received a 30-year prison sentence. By 1990, La Mentirita was back out on the streets.

But all that is just the prologue to this story. In 1977, Fernández wanted to use some of his drug-smuggling proceeds to buy a bank in Miami. His Panamanian money launderer, Steven Sandor Samos, advised against it because of the inevitable scrutiny from bank regulators.[3] This is the same Steve Samos who helped New York Mafioso Lawrence Iorizzo launder money through offshore companies and who was linked to Amalgamated Commercial Enterprises, which was funneling money and equipment to the Contras.

According to an attorney close to the case, Samos's grand jury testimony made reference to a Nestor Sanchez, who originally told Fernández about Samos and his services. Samos testified that this Nestor Sanchez was in the film distribution business in Panama, according to the attorney.

It is not known if this is the Nestor Sanchez who was Oliver North's associate and the former Deputy Assistant Secretary of Defense for Inter-American Affairs during Iran-Contra, and before that, a CIA official for more than 30 years. Sanchez was also in Panama during the mid-1970s, according to his testimony before the Senate Subcommittee on Terrorism, Narcotics and International Operations. So he could very well have had contact with Fernández, who was a CIA contract agent at this time, and with Samos, who was setting up off-the-shelf offshore companies in Panama then. In his 1988 congressional testimony, Sanchez denied that he had any business relationships in Panama, but he phrased his answer in the present tense.

Sometime in 1976, Fernández was introduced to a fellow Cuban, José Alvero-Cruz, then the biggest drug smuggler in Miami. Fernández went to work for Cruz, who then introduced him to Miami banker Ray Corona.[4] Corona, like Fernández, hungered after a bank of his own. He was a vice president at Totalbank in Miami, where his father, Rafael, was chief executive officer and where his three brothers worked. In the early 1960s the family had moved to Miami from Cuba, where the father had been a banker.

So Corona, Fernández and Samos cooked up a scheme to buy a bank. The money would come from Fernández's drug smuggling and would be funneled to Corona through Samos's wife, Alma Robles Chiari. The first bank they picked was the National Bank of South Florida, which was owned by none other than Guillermo Hernandez-Cartaya.

---

[3] *The Big Fix,* by James Ring Adams (John Wiley & Sons, 1990).
[4] Ibid.

Hernandez-Cartaya had managed to defraud the bank into the ground in less than a year, but the Comptroller of the Currency's office rejected Corona's bid, based on questions about his banking experience. Finally, in May 1978, Corona won permission to buy Sunshine State Bank in Miami. As a downpayment, Samos wired him $1.15 million from Fernández's bank account at Banco de Iberoamérica in Panama. Later, Fernández turned more than $1 million in cash over to Corona to consummate the deal.

After Fernández was indicted and then kidnapped to Colombia, he sold his shares in Sunshine to Corona—putting the Coronas in full control of the bank by the middle of 1982. Before the end of that year, federal examiners were expressing concern about lending practices there, citing insider abuse and insufficient collateral for loans.

Like many of the crooked savings and loan owners, Corona cultivated politicians. One of Sunshine's directors was Howard Gary, the Miami City Manager, who borrowed $95,000 from the bank to buy two apartment buildings for $85,000. Another stockholder was South Miami Chief of Police Sal Vizzini. And a big borrower was Lazaro Albo, the right-hand man of former Miami mayor Maurice Ferre.

But the politician who most helped the Coronas was Florida Comptroller Gerald Lewis, whose office continually frustrated the efforts of the Federal Deposit Insurance Corporation to remove the Coronas or shut down the bank. Two of Lewis's biggest campaign contributors were large borrowers at Sunshine.[5] Lewis also presided over the failure of E.S.M. Government Securities, which was located in Fort Lauderdale. It was E.S.M. that caused the failure of Marvin Warner's Home State Savings in Ohio and led to a $55 million loss at American Savings in Miami while it was headed by Warner. Gerald Lewis is Warner's second cousin.

Meanwhile, Ray Corona was living it up. The former Golden Glove boxer bought a white Rolls-Royce Corniche, a cigarette boat and a calf-length mink coat. He had a gold Rolex pocket watch and favored three-piece silk suits. He also became addicted to cocaine. From October 1981 to October 1984, Corona bought nine guns while hooked on the drug and then lied about this on gun dealers' forms. In 1986 he was convicted of illegally purchasing the guns while addicted to cocaine.

Corona may have gotten his cocaine from Willie Falcón, the drug smuggler and partner of Jack DeVoe and Fernando Birbragher. Sun-

---

[5] *Forbes*, May 5, 1986.

shine State Bank made Falcón and his wife a mortgage loan in 1979 and then renewed it in 1984. And, although Fernández apparently never used Sunshine to launder his drug profits, Falcón did, according to an assistant U.S. prosecutor and an attorney who represented one of the Sunshine State Bank figures.

Another Miami attorney who keeps turning up is Theodore Klein, the attorney for CIA-connected gun dealer Ron Martin, and also, for a while, for Jack DeVoe. Klein represented Rafael Corona, Ray's father, in their racketeering and money-laundering trial.

Something else was going on at Sunshine besides the high rolling, fast living, drug smuggling, money laundering, questionable lending, political logrolling, and connections to CIA-trained Cuban exiles. In addition to all that, the $100 million bank was doing business with the Mafia—quite a bit of business, it turns out.

This part of the story begins in 1971, when twenty-three-year-old Ray Corona returned to Miami to start his banking career at Miami National Bank. At that time, this bank was controlled by Sam Cohen, an associate of the legendary mob financier Meyer Lansky. Cohen was indicted in 1971 along with Lanksy and a Caesar's Palace official, Jerry Gordon, for illegally skimming money from the Flamingo Hotel in Las Vegas. Cohen copped a plea and did four months in Club Fed.

One of Corona's customers at Miami National was Joseph Klein, the chief executive of a company called Cavanagh Communities Corporation. Cavanagh, according to the *Miami Herald*, was a "controversial outfit that sold Florida swampland in the 1970s and tried unsuccessfully to get into the casino gambling business."[6] Klein was also connected to organized crime figures in the Philadelphia area, according to articles in the Philadelphia *Daily News*. In one of his business deals, Klein bought some property at the Cricket Club in Miami, which had been owned by Sam Cohen and Alvin Malnik, one of Meyer Lansky's protegés.

After Corona took over Sunshine State Bank, he put Joseph Klein's wife on its board of directors and began to do business with Royale Group, Ltd., the successor company to Klein's Cavanagh Communities Corp., and its new chief executive, Leonard Pelullo, a Mafia associate from Philadelphia who had taken over from Klein.

Pelullo's ties to organized crime first came to the public's attention in December 1985, when the New Jersey State Commission of Investiga-

---

[6] *Miami Herald*, July 6, 1986.

tion released a report on organized crime in boxing. The report stated: "The previous episode described boxing manager Barry Shapiro as being a part of a mob-tainted supporting cast for his brother Kenneth Shapiro's financial machinations. A similar relationship exists between boxing manager Arthur R. Pelullo, thirty, of Vorhees and his brother, Leonard, a key organized crime associate from Philadelphia, currently based in Florida."

Pelullo vehemently denied any connections to organized crime, and in 1990 filed a libel suit in federal court in Miami against the New Jersey commission. The New Jersey commission responded to the suit by denying Pelullo's claim that he has no connections to organized crime. Pelullo's suit was apparently aimed at stopping journalists from printing the statements because, as the New Jersey commission pointed out, the statute of limitations for a libel suit had already run out and, regardless, the commission could not be sued for such statements, as Pelullo himself admitted to a reporter before he filed the suit.

In 1991, the roof fell in on poor Lenny. First, he got thrown in jail in New Jersey on contempt charges relating to a lawsuit accusing him of "pillaging" $1.75 million from the pension fund of a printing company he controlled. Then he was indicted by a federal grand jury in Philadelphia for cheating American Savings and Loan in Stockton, California, of $1.6 million out of some $16 million he borrowed to renovate six hotels in Miami Beach.

The 55-count indictment also charged that Pelullo took $114,000 from Royale Group, Ltd., to pay back a personal loan from a Philadelphia man named Anthony DiSalvo, at the request of Nicodemo Scarfo and Phillip Leonetti. Scarfo, the boss of the Philadelphia Mafia, is currently serving a 60-year prison sentence for racketeering. Leonetti, Scarfo's underboss, was also convicted of racketeering and is now cooperating with law enforcement officials in turning state's evidence against Mafia figures.

Fred Martens, executive director of the Pennsylvania Crime Commission, told *Wall Street Journal* that DiSalvo "is a longtime Scarfo associate," and that Pelullo "is a very close associate of Nicodemo Scarfo."[7]

In July 1991, Pelullo was convicted of 50 of the 55 counts against him in Philadelphia, including the theft of $114,000 to repay a loan shark at

---

[7] *Wall Street Journal*, February 21, 1981.

the command of Philadelphia Mafia boss Scarfo. (All of these convictions except the $114,000 theft were later overturned by an appeals court on technicalities.)

Before he was jailed on contempt charges, Pelullo had already dodged a couple of bullets regarding bank and savings and loan fraud. He was the vice chairman of Dominion Bank in Denver when it failed. Although he was never formally charged with any criminal wrongdoing, regulators questioned whether some of his property pledged for Dominion loans had also been pledged for Sunshine State Bank loans.

Then in 1989, he was indicted for fraud at Savings One, an S&L in Ohio. Pelullo and Savings One owner David A. Friedmann, a Houston businessman, were charged with five counts of fraud, regarding a $145,-000 payment to Friedmann out of a $1 million loan to a Pelullo company. Pelullo, claiming the payment was prepaid interest that was not supposed to go to Friedmann, was acquitted by a jury, but Friedmann was convicted.

Friedmann had bought Savings One in 1983, around the same time that Mario Renda and Martin Schwimmer were also attempting to buy the S&L. Little is known about Friedmann in Houston, where his companies are headquartered. Art Leiser, former chief examiner for the Texas Savings and Loan Department, said Friedmann was originally from Ohio and was connected to Tyrell Barker, the Herman K. Beebe associate who owned State Savings in Lubbock. Friedmann was "trying to arrange for the purchase [by Barker] of several other savings and loans around the country," Leiser said. (In 1980, Friedmann was involved in a scam to sell grain to Iran in violation of the embargo imposed because of the American hostages. Friedmann lost a federal lawsuit over this in New York.)

Meanwhile, before any of the S&L fraud hit the fan, Pelullo and his companies and relatives were borrowing from Sunshine State Bank to the tune of more than $15 million, making them the single largest borrower at the bank. Pelullo was also a director of King Crown Corporation, which owned about 6 percent of the stock of Sunshine. All the other officers and directors of King Crown were members of the Corona family. Also, long after Sunshine State Bank was closed down and Ray Corona went to jail, one of the Coronas was working for Pelullo.

Needless to say, all of Pelullo's loans from Sunshine became delinquent. So he sold Don Pedro Island on the west coast of Florida to the bank for forgiveness of $2.5 million in debt; plus Sunshine paid to settle some lawsuits against Royale Group, Ltd. In November 1984, when the bank was struggling to stay alive, the Florida state cabinet voted to buy the island for $6 million as part of the state's Save Our Coast program, and provided Sunshine with badly needed capital.[8] (One of the members of the Florida cabinet was Gerald Lewis.)

Even after that deal, Pelullo again defaulted on his loans. This time, in late 1985, the bank was on its last legs. So what did it do—it hired two of Royale Group's senior executives. Then Pelullo and the bank agreed that the bank would take back the collateral for the loans and forgive the debt, and, in addition, issue $15 million in bank stock to Royale.

The banking regulators halted this transaction, pointing out that the upshot would be to wipe out Pelullo's personal guarantees. Furthermore, the bank would have to fork over another $3.5 million in cash to Pelullo. The collateral in question was some land in Vermont and a two-acre tract in Atlantic City that Pelullo wanted to develop for a casino. To that purpose, Pelullo had made an agreement with Resorts International, a casino company with past ties to Meyer Lansky and the mob.

Like any good mobster, what Pelullo coveted the most was a casino of his very own. He finally got his wish in 1988, when he bought the unfinished Dunes in Atlantic City, a project with a checkered history. The late mob lawyer Morris Shenker had started it and then defaulted on his union pension fund loan. Shenker sold the project to San Diego developer Jack Bona, one of that select group that borrowed more than $200 million from savings and loans that later failed. Bona defaulted on his loans and put the project into bankruptcy, from whence Pelullo purchased it in 1988.

By that time, Sunshine State Bank had been closed for two years, and Ray Corona was in jail serving a 20-year term, after Tony Fernández and Steve Samos testified against him. (Samos got immunity from prosecution, and Rafael Corona's three-year sentence was overturned by an appeals court.)

However, before Sunshine State was closed in the summer of 1986, the Coronas and Pelullo had fought a hard protracted battle with the feds to keep it open. The first real trouble occurred in late 1983, after federal bank examiners found that Sunshine had a "high probability of

[8] *Forbes*, May 5, 1985.

failure" and decided to take the Coronas out of Sunshine. Nevertheless, in January 1984, the State Comptroller's Office under Lewis intervened and issued a less severe memorandum of understanding that the bank would improve its situation.

To bolster the bank's capital and keep it alive, Ray Corona bought the land that the bank's headquarters was on and some surrounding property, including tracts that Pelullo had sold to the bank for a profit of $160,000. And where did the money to do this come from? Why, where else? Peoples Savings and Loan in Llano, Texas, population 4,147.

On February 16, 1984, Peoples Savings and Loan wired $2,967,000 to Sunshine State Bank. At that time, there was little documentation for the loan at Peoples. There was no loan-closing statement. There was no recorded mortgage. There was not even a loan application. All of these omissions were violations of federal statutes. The loan was a six-month loan, which was highly irregular for a small savings and loan (assets of $129 million) to be making, especially to recapitalize a bad bank in another state. However, the loan was paid back, 20 days after it was due, and four months before Ray Corona was indicted for racketeering and money laundering. Corona paid back the loan after he sold the property to South Miami Hospital for a profit of more than $1 million.

Joel Daniel, the managing officer at Peoples then, said he didn't want to make the loan, but was told to do so by the new Peoples owners, who had taken over in November 1983, just three months before the money was wired to Corona. The new owners were Marvin Haass, from San Antonio, and Jerry Holley, from Waco. They were construction contractors who also owned some nightclubs and bars in San Antonio, Austin, Waco and El Paso, with charming names like Abracadabra, Doc Holiday's, Rocky Racoon and Texas Down Under.

Needless to say, they knew nothing about savings and loans, according to Daniel. They borrowed the money to buy Peoples from another dirty S&L, First South Savings in Houston. First South was controlled by two attorneys, one of whom bought a title insurance company with a $20 million loan from San Jacinto Savings that was brokered by Herman K. Beebe. The former Texas Savings and Loan commissioner, Alvis Vandygriff, became counsel to these attorneys' law firm after he retired, and had the distinction of shepherding through the regulatory process Robert Corson's application to take control of Kleberg County Savings and Loan.

Anyway, Haass and Holley are two fairly undistinguished gentle-men, whose takeover of Peoples gives them the appearance of either being front men for someone bigger or gofers who were tossed a small bone called Peoples Savings for past services. Holley ended up being convicted of perjury for statements made during the investigation of the failure of Peoples, while Haass apparently escaped any serious legal problems.

A search of the public records in San Antonio reveals that Haass is connected to two influential entities. One is the Longoria family from the Rio Grande Valley, a rich, powerful Mexican-American family; the other is Morris Jaffe. (After Jaffe and his first wife divorced, she married a Longoria, who was a good friend of Jaffe's.)

Asked to characterize his relationship with Jaffe, Haass replied, "I worked for him. He's been a friend of mine for 29 years, 27 years, 26 years, 20 years, I guess. I don't know."

Joel Daniel, the managing officer at Peoples, said Haass and Jaffe were "supposedly tight." Jaffe reportedly financed Haass's nightclub at the Central Park Mall in San Antonio, which Jaffe and his family own. (Jaffe got his original financing for this mall from Farm & Home Savings, the Missouri S&L with connections to Walter Mischer and his associates.) But Haass denied that Jaffe financed the bar. "He's a land-lord is all," Haass said.

In February 1984, the same month Peoples lent $3 million to Ray Corona, a Mischer Allied Bank affiliate in San Antonio lent $500,000 to Perseus, one of Haass's and Holey's nightclub companies. As collateral for the loan, Perseus assigned to the bank, Allied American Bank of San Antonio, its interest in a lease with Morris Jaffe.

Haass did not answer a question about whether Peoples Savings ever did any business with Jaffe. However, Daniel denied that the S&L did anything with Jaffe, but acknowledged that it purchased a fixed-base operation at the San Antonio airport right next to Jaffe's. Peoples lost about $2 million on that deal, Daniel said.

Morris Jaffe is a unique individual in Texas, as unique as Walter Mischer. In fact, Jaffe could be called the Walter Mischer of San An-tonio. Both men exercise a great deal of political influence, but they do it quietly and behind the scenes. Both were strong supporters of Lyndon Johnson, Jaffe perhaps more than Mischer. Both are feared and talked about in hushed tones. And both had contact with New Orleans Mafia boss Carlos Marcello regarding business deals.

Jaffe returned to his native San Antonio after serving as an aircraft engineer in World War II and went into the construction business. He made his first fortune after he allegedly discovered uranium in Karnes County (where Mischer grew up) by flying over it with a new-fangled detection device. He managed to sell his leases and options for a nice profit before the uranium boom busted.[9] Jaffe also got into the oil business with his buddies Oscar Wyatt, the cantankerous Texas oilman who went to Iraq with John Connally during the Gulf War to get some Americans home and to osculate upon Saddam Hussein's gluteus maximus, and John Mecom, Sr., the rich Houston oilman whose son, John Mecom, Jr., allegedly hobnobbed with mobsters.

Jaffe, like Mischer, has never been too proud to suck off the government teat. In a celebrated incident in 1957, Jaffe got into a dispute with an Air Force colonel at Lackland Air Force Base who wouldn't go along with Jaffe's efforts to get more airmen to frequent his skating rink. Jaffe went over the colonel's head and eventually got the base to bus the airmen to his rink.

In 1962, Jaffe bought the assets of West Texas con man Billie Sol Estes out of bankruptcy for an announced $7 million to be paid over a 10-year period. However, by 1971 he had only paid off $1.3 million. So the IRS auctioned off the remaining $5.7 million note. And who bought that note? Why, Morris Jaffe, of course, for $200,000.[10]

Then in the early 1970s, a number of mob connections to Jaffe came out. First, Jaffe claimed that he had been trying to buy Carlos Marcello's Churchill Farms, the 6,400-acre spread outside New Orleans. The deal allegedly fell apart when Marcello went to jail in 1970 for assaulting an FBI agent. "I'd have served his time for him if he had sold me that land," Jaffe told Texas Monthly.

Key points of the alleged explanation for this deal don't make sense. Churchill Farms was one of Marcello's greatest pride and joys. It's where he went to do a lot of his scheming. He had grandiose plans for it too. First, he had gotten the state of Louisiana to put dikes around the swampland, and then he had had the state install huge pumps to drain it. The next thing he wanted was a superhighway going through it. But that was too much even for Louisiana to swallow.

That was when Jaffe appeared on the scene wanting to buy the

---

[9] A Texan Looks at Lyndon, by J. Evetts Haley (Palo Duro Press, 1964).
[10] Dallas Morning News, March 21, 1975.

property. Perhaps Marcello figured he never would be able to get a highway through his property and would just sell to the highest bidder. But perhaps Jaffe was brought in, as one organized crime investigator believes, to front for Marcello so that the good state of Louisiana could then build the highway in good conscience. But then Marcello's assault conviction made him too hot for Jaffe.

Also, the events leading up to Marcello's assault on the FBI agent did much to blow Marcello's cover. Up until then, he had consistently denied being connected to the Mafia, and there were enough fools, or people who had been bought off, in law enforcement to give this declaration credence.

But, in September 1966, Marcello was caught by New York police having lunch at the La Stella restaurant in the Queens. Seated at Marcello's right at the dinner table was Carlo Gambino, boss of the biggest New York Mafia family; seated at Marcello's left was Santo Trafficante, boss of the Florida Mafia; seated directly across from Marcello was Thomas Eboli, acting boss of the powerful Genovese family; and seated at Eboli's left, across from Gambino, was Joseph Colombo, boss of the Colombo family. After being arrested, Marcello returned to New Orleans, where he took a swing at an FBI agent in the airport.

In an August 1990 *Texas Monthly* story about Jaffe's son, Doug's, traveling to Romania to try to drum up some capitalism, Jan Jarboe, a former San Antonio columnist who wrote occasional fluff about the Jaffes, stated that Marcello is "known as the Little Man and has wide-ranging Mafia connections. When I first met Morris [Jaffe] in 1975, I asked him straight out if he was in the Mafia, and he laughed so hard he practically fell out of his desk chair at his office in Central Park Mall. 'No,' he told me. 'As a matter of fact, hell no.' "

Well, when I read that description of Marcello ("wide-ranging Mafia connections"), one of richest, most powerful, most feared, and most convicted Mafia bosses in this country, *I* laughed so hard I practically fell out of my desk chair.

I laughed even harder when I read Jarboe's question to Jaffe. *Of course* Jaffe, whose father was Jewish and mother was Hispanic, isn't in the Mafia. Only Sicilians and Italians can be in the Mafia. The questions are what associations, enterprises, businesses and contacts Jaffe has had with members of the Mafia and their associates, and how, why and under what circumstances such associations, enterprises, businesses and contacts occurred.

One curious business deal Jaffe attempted in 1972 was the purchase of the King's Castle Hotel and Casino at Lake Tahoe, Nevada. The casino had been owned by Nathan Jacobson, who bought it after he sold his interest in Caesar's Palace, where he had been one of the original owners along with the Rogers brothers from Beaumont. Jacobson bought King's Castle with a loan from the mob-controlled Teamsters Union pension fund, but went broke in 1972. The pension fund had begun fishing around for new owners when Jaffe put his bid in. But he was beaten out by the Pritzkers from Chicago—whose attorney was Burton Kanter and who probably had more accounts at Castle Bank & Trust than anyone.

Another mob association to Jaffe was dug out by journalist Jonathan Kwitny, whose 1974 book, *The Mullendore Murder Case*, describes the events leading up to the 1970 murder of E. C. Mullendore III, an Oklahoma rancher. Mullendore's sister, Katsy, married John Mecom, Jr. (Katsy and Mainland Savings's Raymond Hill are good friends.) Through Jaffe, Mecom had met loan-scam artist and mob associate Leroy Kerwin.

Kerwin had earlier gone to jail in a car and bankruptcy scam run by Chicago Mafia *capo* Felix "Milwaukee Phil" Alderisio, a feared killer and scam artist. Jaffe apparently first encountered Kerwin through a restaurant franchise Jaffe started with former New York Yankee star Mickey Mantle. Kwitny reported that when Kerwin went to Chicago to appeal a tax-evasion sentence, Jaffe accompanied him to petition the judge on his behalf. "I would be willing to stick my neck out to guarantee Mr. Kerwin as I know him. If there was some way I could personally take responsibility, I would do it," Jaffe told the judge there.

Jaffe hired Kerwin as a "special consultant" to his insurance company at $1,000 a month, according to Kwitny, and then Kerwin used a Jaffe company as a front for loan swindles. Jaffe claimed later than this swindle cost him $250,000 and that he then turned Kerwin in to authorities. Kerwin fled the country and his body was found later in a shallow grave in Canada. He had been shot in the head at close range. No one was ever charged in the killing.

John Mecom, Jr.'s, involvement with mob figures didn't stop with Leroy Kerwin. In testimony before the House Select Committee on Crime in 1972, Aaron Kohn, the director of the New Orleans Metropolitan Crime Commission, stated that Mecom, who owned the New Orleans Saints professional football team, was seen frequently at a New Orleans restaurant connected to the Marcellos. The restaurant, La Louisiane, was owned by the Moran brothers, who received financing from the Marcellos.

"Mecom became closely affiliated with the Moran brothers, frequented the La Louisiane and hosted the Morans on trips," Kohn testified.

"Finally," Kohn stated, "I make reference to another astonishing involvement of the president and major owner of the New Orleans Saints. Last month, on April 12, 1972, John Mecom, Jr., was a principal in the organization of two corporations at Fort Walton Beach, Florida. Two other principals are a convicted gambler and a developer with ties to the Marcello syndicate." One of the principals was Sam Presley, Jr., a notorious gambler, sentenced to one year in prison for gambling in 1971. The other, Gerald E. Senner, "has a considerable record of forming business partnerships with individuals who are also partners of Carlos Marcello or other major member of the Marcello structure," including Roy and Frank Occhipinti, Kohn testified.

Mecom later sold the Saints to San Antonio and New Orleans car dealer Tom Benson, who, according to the 1985 Comptroller of the Currency report on Herman K. Beebe, "has purchased Pontchartrain State Bank, Metairie, Louisiana, from Beebe's interests and has other business relationships with Beebe's associates."

Mecom also owned the venerable Warwick Hotel in Houston. When Marcello would come to Houston to visit his properties and friends, one of his favorite places to stay was the Warwick, where he would be "comped"—given free rooms and service—by the management, reported former Houston police criminal intelligence officers. Another prominent Mafioso who stayed at the Warwick, after he had been operated on by Dr. Michael DeBakey at Methodist Hospital, was Chicago boss Sam Giancana.

According to author and journalist Thomas B. Ross, who was Washington bureau chief for the *Chicago Sun Times*, Mecom's father and Jaffe's close friend and partner, John W. Mecom, was one of the original incorporators of the San Jacinto Fund, which was used by the CIA to launder and funnel money.[11] As previously noted, Mecom Sr. was also close to CIA asset George DeMohrenschildt.

---

[11] "Surreptitious Entry: The CIA's Operations in the United States," by Thomas B. Ross, in *The CIA File*, edited by Robert L. Borosage and John Marks (Viking, 1976).

When I submitted a two-page list of questions to Mecom Jr. about his reported connections to mobsters and other people in this book, he replied in writing, "After reading all of these questions, I find this is just a rehash of supermarket tabloid trash from years ago, that does not even justify my taking the time to respond to them."

When Jaffe's son, Doug, wanted to get into making hush kits for Boeing 707s, one of his original investors and limited partners was John Mecom, Jr. Doug then formed a joint venture with Tracor, the Austin-based defense contractor with connections to the Mischer circle in Houston, to manufacture and install the hush kits.

By 1985, Doug Jaffe was supplying hush kits to Farhad Azima, Buffalo Airways and others. Jaffe's company bought five 707s from Pan Am that had belonged to Azima's Global International Airways and were repossessed after Global filed for bankruptcy. The financing for this purchase came from Tesoro Savings and Loan in Laredo, Texas (which had been implicated in a drug-money-laundering scheme), and Western Savings and Loan in Phoenix.

During this time, Doug Jaffe was also borrowing big bucks from two other fraud-ridden savings and loans. In January 1984, Doug, as a trustee, bought seven tracts of land totaling 92 acres in Llano County and signed a $7.1 million promissory note to Commerce Savings in Angleton, Texas. Jaffe defaulted on the loan in November 1986, still owing $5 million. (Commerce Savings also lent a Longoria partnership $20.7 million on land in Austin.)

The Jaffe property was foreclosed on and sold back to Commerce Savings for $3.8 million, leaving a deficiency of $1.2 million, for which Commerce sued Jaffe.

When this loan was made, Commerce Savings was owned by San Antonio developer John H. Roberts, Jr., the Khashoggi business partner who bought the S&L from Jarrett Woods and Woods's brother-in-law, Thomas Perry. They, in turn, were assisted in the sale by Ed McBirney. Woods then bought Western Savings in Dallas, while McBirney went on to greater glory at Sunbelt Savings. Roberts sold Commerce in late 1984 and bought Summit Savings in Dallas. In 1989, he pleaded guilty to fraud at Summit and Western Savings for using a straw borrower to get a $4.5 million loan to buy a private jet for his use. He was sentenced to five years in prison.

After Doug Jaffe borrowed $7.1 million from Commerce Savings in

1984, the next year he and a partner borrowed $13.1 million on an •
apartment project in Austin from McBirney's Sunbelt Savings. Jaffe and
his partner, Bob Goodson, defaulted on the loan and then sued Sunbelt's
federal receiver to keep the S&L from foreclosing on the apartments.
They later settled the suit by deeding the apartments over to Sunbelt and
paying an additional $1.5 million.

The Sunbelt loan takes on added significance when U.S. Congressman Henry B. Gonzalez (Democrat-San Antonio) is factored in. Gonzalez, as head of the House Banking Committee, did an admirable job
of putting the public spotlight on Charles Keating and his Lincoln
Savings and Neil Bush and Silverado Savings. But he did little in regard
to all the rotten Texas savings and loans, many of which were just as
bad as, if not worse than, Lincoln and Silverado. The only failed Texas
S&L that got much attention from Gonzalez's committee was Sunbelt,
but there was no mention of the Jaffe loan.

Perhaps that was because Gonzalez, considered to be a fierce and
eccentric independent, owed more political debts to Morris Jaffe than to
just about anyone. Jaffe was one of Gonzalez's first major backers when
he ran for Congress in a special election in 1961, and continues to
support him. "Frankly I have a great deal of admiration for Morris,"
Gonzalez told the San Antonio *Express News*.

Gonzalez has said that he knew Jaffe because their mothers were
good friends when they were growing up on the West Side in San
Antonio. "He was the one who opened up [San Antonio] home ownership for Mexican-American purchasers," Gonzalez told the *Express
News* in 1989.

And why was Gonzalez saying all those nice things about Jaffe then?
Because Jaffe and his son were under fire for being in the middle of a
sweetheart oil deal for House Speaker Jim Wright, another Democratic
congressman from Texas. Doug Jaffe arranged for the sale of a practically non-producing oil well in East Texas to a company partly owned
by Wright. This company then sold the well to a West German firm at
a price of more than $400,000 over what Wright's company paid. Some
$325,000 in the profits from this deal went into Wright's blind trust.

Wright resigned from Congress after being criticized for this deal
and others that involved conflicts of interest. He was also investigated,
but not officially criticized, by his House colleagues for his attempt to
get federal regulators to go easy on several dirty Texas savings and
loans, including Don Dixon's Vernon Savings, Tom Gaubert's Indepen-

dent American Savings and Scott Mann's CreditBanc Savings.

I bring up the relationship between Gonzalez and Jaffe not to try to discredit Gonzalez's integrity—which is beyond question—but to show the deep and wide-ranging influence people like Jaffe have in the halls of our elected representatives.

One question was left dangling about the Peoples Savings loan to Ray Corona to add capital to Miami's Sunshine State Bank: How did Haass and his co-owner, Jerry Holley, come into contact with Miami bad boy Corona?

Haass said he did not meet Corona until January 1984, about a month before the $3 million loan was made to him. "I think it was only a couple of times I saw him," Haass said to me. "It wasn't even a meeting. It was just a drink."

Perhaps Frank Castro made the introductions. Peoples's managing officer Joel Daniel said that Haass and Frank Castro were "big buddies," but that Peoples Savings never did any business with Castro. Haass danced around my questions about Castro. "Frank Castro? Can you tell me what town he's in?" Haass asked when queried about Castro. When asked whether he was "big buddies" with Castro, Haass replied, "I did not meet him, I did not even . . . that name at this point, unless you can jar my mind. I'm not saying that . . . Tell me what he does, then I might."

Later in the interview, Haass said he thought Castro was a lawyer. Then he began speculating on who told me about him and Castro. "But Frank Castro? Tell me more so I can maybe . . ." he said. When told about Castro's relationship to Tony Fernández, who used Corona as a front man, Haass replied, "Harold White was probably . . . Harold White would have been the one who would have alluded to the fact that somebody else knew these people."

Peoples's managing officer Joel Daniel agreed that the introduction to Corona came through a Florida developer named Harold White. When I asked how he met Harold White, Haass said, "Let me get back and I'll give you something on this thing." He never did.

Researching Harold D. White in the Florida public records reveals a number of interesting names and connections. White, the son of Armer E. White, was a principal along with his father in Context Industries, a Miami real estate firm. Beginning in June 1979, Context started borrowing money and doing business with Sunshine State Bank. This was a little more than a year after Corona took over the bank.

(Armer White was the chairman of the executive committee of the board of Context and third largest individual stockholder. His son, Harold, was a director and vice president of sales, at an annual salary of $203,000.)

Several people, including Art Leiser, the former chief examiner for the Texas Savings and Loan Department, said they had heard that Armer White was a friend of former President Ronald Reagan. This could not be corroborated. But he is a close associate of Victor Posner, the secretive, reclusive, security-obsessed corporate raider and convicted tax evader. Posner is an old friend of Carl Lindner, and as part of the Michael Milken inner circle was rewarded with more than $350 million in junk bonds as well as an SEC lawsuit charging illegal stock trading.

In 1974, there were five trustees for Posner's own irrevocable trust: Posner himself, his son, Steven, two other close associates, and Armer White, who was also on the board of directors of Posner's Sharon Steel Corp. (In a list submitted to the Senate Intelligence Committee during the confirmation hearings of William Casey as CIA Director, Sharon Steel was listed as a client of Bill Casey's when he was in private practice from 1976 to 1981.[12])

Another connection between Posner and the Whites is Mafioso Leonard Pelullo. In 1982 and 1983, the Whites' Context Industries paid Pelullo $80,000 in "consulting" fees for his work in arranging at least $800,000 in loans from Sunshine State Bank.[13]

The *Miami Herald* reported: "After months of fruitless pleading with the bank, Context Industries got a new $800,00 loan—imediately after Pelullo's company received its first payment, according to former Context executives. "Sunshine's sudden generosity surprised even the Context officials. 'It was a loan agreement beyond our wildest hopes and dreams,' said Context's ex-president Wallace Dill, who had met Pelullo through mutual acquaintances in the Atlantic City casino industry. 'We were so desperate then we couldn't pay our bills.'

"What did Pelullo do," the *Herald* went on, "to help Context merit the new loan? Neither Dill nor other company officials involved said they knew, although they considered the payment a cost of doing business."

But something doesn't compute with the Context explanation. For

---

[12] *Reagan's Ruling Class*, by Ronald Brownstein and Nina Easton (Pantheon Books, 1982).
[13] *Miami Herald*, October 9, 1986.

one, the company had been borrowing from Sunshine State Bank since 1979, and Harold White received a personal loan from the bank in 1981.

Pelullo claimed that he restructured the company's finances and "educated them about finance," according to the *Miami Herald*. However, the chairman of the board and largest stockholder of Context was Robert B. Evans, the former chairman of American Motors Corporation, the chairman of Evans Industries and the owner of Robert B. Evans Oil Company. What could a Mafia associate and bustout artist like Pelullo teach a man like this about finance?

Several years after "arranging" the Context loans from Sunshine, Pelullo offered to buy Posner's beleaguered Sharon Steel, where Armer White was a director. Posner turned down Pelullo, but then hired him as a "consultant." From late 1987 to the middle of 1988, Posner paid Pelullo $1.2 million for his services. Pelullo then tried to buy some of Posner's companies, including his flagship DWG Corp., and Posner again declined, leading to lawsuits between them.

"I like Victor," Pelullo told *Business Week.*. "He's a fighter, and I'm a fighter."

By the time Robert Evans bought the Whites out of Context Industries in 1985, Harold White was doing real estate deals with Peoples Savings and also with a Key Biscayne restaurant owner named Donald Berg. Berg is an associate of Richard Nixon's banker, Bebe Rebozo, and of Lou Chesler, the Meyer Lanksy front man whose phone number appeared in Lawrence Freeman's telephone tolls. (Berg told *Newsday* that he is "well acquainted" with Chesler.) Berg and Rebozo, along with former U.S. Senator George Smathers's brother, formed Cape Florida Development Company, in which Nixon invested.

In *The Fish Is Red*, by Warren Hinckle and William W. Turner, Berg is described as "a Key Biscayne boniface who fraternized with Lansky gaming manager Lou Chesler on the one hand and Dick Nixon on the other (the Secret Service later cringed every time Berg and Nixon got together). In 1967, Rebozo brought Nixon to Key Biscayne to pose for publicity pictures with him and Berg in order to promote the lagging development. In gratitude Nixon was allowed to buy two lots at greatly discounted prices."

Berg and Harold White are involved together as officers and directors in at least six Florida corporations, including one named Berg and White, Inc.

Their attorney, registered agent and, in several cases, fellow officer and director is Truman Skinner. In 1982, Skinner pleaded guilty to two misdemeanors in the so-called Outrigger scandal involving loans to organized crime associates from Miami National Bank, the bank formerly controlled by Lansky associates in which Ray Corona got his start in banking. In 1976, when the Outrigger loans were made, Skinner was Miami National's lawyer and chairman of its loan committee. He was indicted for mail fraud, making false statements to bank examiners, filing false bank records, loan fraud and racketeering. His criminal defense attorney would later represent Ray Corona in his criminal problems.

At that time, Skinner was a senior partner in the law firm of super CIA spook Paul Helliwell, who had also represented Miami National. When Helliwell died on Christmas Eve, 1976, Skinner took over as head of the law firm. He resigned from the firm after pleading guilty.

Skinner has apparently represented Berg for some time, according to Dade County court records. Berg is also a director of Creditbank in Miami, which was connected to Helliwell back in the Castle Bank & Trust days.

When Peoples Savings lent $3 million to Ray Corona in February 1984, it also made a $2.3 million loan to Harold White. The loan was a second mortgage on a White Miami office building project. The first mortgage was a $6.8 million loan from Sunrise Savings in Boynton Beach, Florida. Sunshine State Bank also made it into the deal when it lent $2 million and then bought a $500,000 mortgage on the property. And eventually, Haass and Holley got a piece of the construction action in the project for a company they formed in Florida.

Then Sunrise failed in July 1985 and claimed that White defaulted on his loan, owing $4.9 million. White sued Sunrise, claiming it had stopped funding his loan. Sunshine jumped in with its own lawsuit, and then Haass and Holley followed suit. It was a great big legal mess, but the ultimate outcome was that the project was never built, and Sunrise, Sunshine and Peoples—as well as ultimately the taxpayers—never got their money back.

Sunrise, which Victor Posner was trying to buy at one time, was one of the first big S&L failures in the country, at a cost to citizens of about $680 million. In 1989, the federal agency responsible for managing the assets of failed S&Ls stated that four-fifths of its holdings east of the

Mississippi were the result of Sunrise's failure.[14] Sunrise was founded and controlled by Philadelphia's second largest law firm, Blank, Rome, Comisky & McCauley, which agreed to pay $50 million in 1988 to settle a civil suit by the feds alleging misconduct in its oversight of Sunrise.

Among the borrowers at Sunrise were: Ray Corona, whose company, Litico, owed $5.4 million, which was guaranteed by Corona; Rafael Corona, who borrowed $150,000 to pay the interest on Litico's delinquent loans; Harold White, who in addition to the $6.8 million for the office building project, had also borrowed $400,000 on 12 condos in Miami and then was sued by Sunrise's federal receiver to foreclose the mortgage that he still owed $294,000 on and hadn't paid.

One of the biggest borrowers at Sunrise, with a total topping $30 million, was Kappa Sigma's own John Riddle, who borrowed the money on some seven Houston area strip shopping center projects. Sunrise's federal receiver sued Riddle in 1988 for $15.2 million he still owed on the loans. Riddle was reportedly introduced to Sunrise by Laddie Howard, who had worked for Mainland Savings and Lamar Savings in Austin before heading Sunrise's Houston office. Howard had borrowed $150,000 from McBirney's Sunbelt Savings in Dallas to buy stock in Sunrise Savings.

Unbelievably, the Florida prosecutors, who apparently had no idea who Riddle was or what he had done to savings and loans in Texas, gave Riddle immunity from prosecution for testifying against Sunrise officers.

During the 1989 criminal trial of several top Sunrise executives, there was incredible testimony about then-Vice President George Bush's interference into Sunrise's federal oversight. This testimony for the prosecution, by a convicted white-collar criminal, received little media attention in Miami, much less nationwide. But the *Miami Review*, a local legal newspaper, wrote an extensive story on the trial and spotlighted the testimony.

The story told by Ronald Berkovitz, a loan adviser, was confirmed by an official close to Sunrise. Berkovitz testified that in 1984 Sunrise CEO Robert Jacoby met with Bush in his vice presidential office, where Jacoby complained that federal examiners were being too tough on Sunrise.

"The embarrassing situation was created when Mr. Bush, Vice President Bush at that time, called a lady who was in a position underneath

---

[14] *Miami Review*, May 22, 1989.

Edwin Gray at that time, who was the head of the FSLIC [Federal Savings and Loan Insurance Corp.], and reprimanded her in front of him [Jacoby]," Berkovitz testified. Bush told the unidentified woman to back off from Sunrise, Berkovitz stated.

Jacoby's meeting with Bush was arranged by an unidentified "strong political friend," according to Berkovitz.

This is the first and only public evidence of George Bush's directly intervening in a savings and loan matter. It seems curious that it would be for a Florida S&L rather than one in Texas or Colorado. However, considering Sunrise's big Houston office run by a former Mainland Savings official, its loans to Corona and White and the big loans to John Riddle, who was Robert Corson's buddy and an alleged weapons transporter to the Middle East, perhaps it is not that surprising.

One officer at Sunrise who bailed out before the trouble hit was David Devaney, who had come to Sunrise from Hill Financial Savings Association in Red Hill, Pennsylvania, north of Philadelphia. Devaney became an S&L consultant after leaving Sunrise and helped bring together all the various participants in the $200 million 21,000-acre land sale in the Florida panhandle. These parties included the Du Pont-controlled St. Joe Paper Co., the largest private landowner in Florida; Robert Corson's and John Riddle's sidekick, Mike Adkinson; Lawrence Freeman; Hill Financial Savings; and Corson's Vision Banc Savings, which provided financing. Some $7 million of Vision Banc's money went to an Isle of Jersey company that was also handling Jack DeVoe's drug profits and John Dick's trust funds.

If this complex deal has confounded many an FBI agent, federal prosecutor, federal regulator and journalist, there's a reason, and that reason probably has Ed Ball lifting his glass, muttering his epitaph and smiling from beyond the grave.

21

"Confusion to the Enemy!"

Every evening after suppertime, Ed Ball would sit around with his close circle of friends and associates, talking and sipping Wild Turkey or Jack Daniels bourbon whiskey. Each session would end the same way, with Ball—arguably the most powerful man the state of Florida has ever seen—raising his glass for the final toast and benediction: "Confusion to the enemy!"

Originally from Virginia, Ball began his career as a traveling salesman in California. He ended up in Jacksonville, Florida, in the early 1920s, following after his brother-in-law, Alfred I. du Pont, the best black gunpowder man in the country. Alfred had feuded and split with his Wilmington, Delaware, kin, one of the richest, most powerful, most famous families in America, and moved with his third wife, Jessie Ball du Pont, to the warmer climes of Florida.

The first order of business in Florida was, of course, to buy a bank. Ed Ball was assigned that job, and like a good cutout he surreptitiously bought up controlling shares in Florida National Bank of Jacksonville. Next on the empire-building agenda was, of course, land, lots of it. Du Pont and Ball bought hundreds of thousands of acres in Florida, much of it in the backwater, neglected panhandle—for $2 and $3 an acre.

But Alfred died in 1935, before he could get much further in his Florida dealings. He left most of his $55 million (before taxes) estate in trust for his wife, Jessie, who along with her brother, Ed, took control of the fortune. For her part, Jessie established the Nemours Foundation and built a hospital in Delaware for the elderly and for crippled children, even though she, not the foundation, received the lion's share of the income of the estate.

For his part, Ed Ball, a right-wing skinflint, curmudgeon and union buster, devoted his energies to preserving, protecting and expanding the du Pont empire, rather than to helping the less fortunate. This was not unlike many of his Houston counterparts who came to control huge charitable foundations left by wealthy oilmen and businessmen.

(The most infamous of these Houston foundations is the Hermann Hospital Estate, which made headlines in 1985 with a scandal involving self-dealing, theft and extravagant perks. The hospital was established as a charity but was spending less than 10 percent of its income on poor patients. One of the Hermann trustees is Walt Mischer, Jr., who took his father's place on the board. The *Houston Post* published a story about how Walt Jr. engineered a deal in which the Hermann Estate bought a big tract of land north of Houston at the same time he and his father's company bought a large adjacent tract. They bought the land cheap because of a planned landfill nearby, and then stopped the landfill at the state permit level. Later, Vinson & Elkins created a non-profit pseudo-government corporation to perform flood-control work to drain the flood-prone area—exacerbating the flooding problems of downstream residents, the residents claimed. The Mischers then sold out for an unknown profit, when it became clear they were not going to be able to put a horse-racing track there. Hermann Estate continued to hold its land. As previously reported, when Mischer Sr. was on the Hermann board, it instituted its famous Life Flight helicopter service. The hospital hired Evergreen Air, the CIA-connected firm previously discussed, to run Life Flight.)

One of the first moves Ed Ball made after Alfred du Pont died was to build up the St. Joe Paper Co., which Alfred had just started. At the town of Port St. Joe on the northwest coast of Florida, Ball had a huge paper mill constructed; today it puts out half a million tons a year of pulp and paperboard. Ball then increased his timberland holdings to more than one million acres to feed the mill.

Ball expanded the Florida National Bank umbrella to 30 banks across the state, making it the largest in the state and the largest in the country south of Philadelphia. He then bought Florida's most important railroad, the Florida East Coast Railroad, running from Jacksonville to Miami. He also purchased more than 50,000 acres of sugar cane property in South Central Florida and constructed a processing plane for the cane.

Finally, no empire is complete without its politicians, and Ed Ball bought and controlled many. In the most infamous incident that became public, Ball took on U.S. Senator Claude Pepper—after supporting him for years—because he thought Pepper was getting too liberal. In 1950, Ball put up George Smathers to run against the senator and then orchestrated a dirty smear campaign. This included calling the incumbent senator "Red Pepper" and hiring an ex-FBI agent who put together a pamphlet entitled *The Red Record of Senator Claude Pepper*. Smathers won.

In a 1972 article in the magazine *Sundance* entitled "Nixon and the Mafia," *New York Times* reporter Jeff Gerth described how Smathers, Ball and Bebe Rebozo were good friends, and that Ball was involved in Key Biscayne real estate deals that touched these men as well as Donald Berg.

One of Ball's closest friends and business associates was Raymond Mason, who controlled the Charter Company, the primary affiliate of which was Charter Oil Co. In 1972, Ball and Mason swapped stock in their companies, Charter getting 8 percent of St. Joe and St. Joe getting 23 percent of Charter, making it the oil company's largest shareholder. (Charter Oil was in the middle of the so-called "Billygate" scandal, in which Billy Carter, the brother of President Jimmy Carter, was being paid as a middle man to secure oil from Libya for Charter.)

Ball also sold Mason the Alfred I. du Pont estate and mansion south of Jacksonville, where his sister, Jessie, had lived until close to her death in 1970. And Mason co-authored a sycophantic biography of Ball titled *Confusion to the Enemy*. Together the two traveled all over the world in Mason's jet, rubbing elbows with Middle Eastern sheikhs, the Shah of Iran, King Hussein of Jordan, and even Robert Vesco. When Vesco was trying to get Ball and Mason to buy one of his companies, Ball allegedly told Vesco, "I had a dream. You and I slept together on a cold night. In the morning, you had all the blankets."[1] (At one time Vesco served on the board of directors of a du Pont company, All American Engineering.)

Ball and Mason also owned together the Little Grove Inn on the Isle of Jersey. This inn was discussed in Chapter 18, on John Dick, who owns a mansion on Jersey.

---

[1] *Vesco*, by Arthur Herzog (New York: Doubleday, 1987).

Although Ball was a right-wing security nut—in one house he owned he allegedly cut portals into the wall in which he could place machine guns to shoot out—there is no direct evidence that he worked for or with the CIA. But he certainly ran in those circles with Raymond Mason, who describes in *Confusion to the Enemy* a trip they took in 1973:

"The next item on the itinerary was one of the most exciting and pleasurable experiences of the trip, a meeting with His Majesty the Shah of Iran.

"Teheran was the site of the longest layover on the trip, and we stayed for almost a week. While visiting with His Majesty, Mr. Ball confessed his regrets that he was not 'forty-five years younger' so that he would be around to watch the growth and development of the country, which had so impressed him on his many visits there. Among the people he met in Iran and the subjects that were discussed were the following: a meeting with the Ahwaz Sugar Corporation, with the idea of taking over some sugar land to grow sugar using the expertise of the Talisman Sugar Company [a subsidiary of St. Joe] and selling it to Iran—the Shah expressed interest in building sugar refineries on land in Australia if our trip there proved successful; a meeting with the housing and insurance officials with whom the Charter Company has negotiated the planning and financing of insuring mortgages on a $520 million New Town in the industrial south of Iran; Mr. Ball spoke with the American Ambassador to Iran, former CIA Director Richard Helms and several banking groups about a 35 percent interest in an Iranian bank (he has been greatly moved by the accomplishments of Iran, in the stability of their government and the methods they are employing to bring their country solidly into the twentieth century); and finally, a stop at an oil sheikhdom on the southern coast of the Persian Gulf, known as Doha Qatart (pronounced Guitar), for another discussion about an oil concession (one which covers an area of over three million acres all on dry land)."

Ball had purchased Talisman Sugar Co. from William Pawley, who had been U.S. Ambassador to Panama under Truman and was involved in the formation of the Flying Tigers airline company. In fact, it was Pawley who had helped transform that airline company into the CIA's airline, Civil Air Transport,[2] the umbrella company over Air America.

---

[2] *Bitter Fruit,* by Stephen Schlesinger and Stephen Kinzer (New York: Doubleday, 1982).

Pawley also was involved in the CIA coup in Guatemala in 1954, and helped the CIA recruit anti-Castro Cubans for its war against Castro.[3]

After Ball died in 1981, his successor J. C. "Jake" Belin reversed the stock swap with Charter in 1983. The next year, Charter filed for bankruptcy, and then, in 1987, 51 percent of its stock was purchased by Mason's friend and associate Carl Lindner. More than ten years earlier, Mason had met Lindner and bought several of his companies.

In 1966, Ball lost his fight in Congress to stop a law that required him to divest the A. I. du Pont Trust of its controlling share of the Florida National Banks (primarily because of his gruesome labor practices and union busting at his railroad, which were interfering with the operation of Cape Canaveral). But the Trust and he and his sister still owned 35 percent of the shares in the banks and maintained virtual control.

Ball also carried on a continuous fight with the attorneys general in Florida and Delaware over the amount of money remitted by the Trust to the Nemours Foundation, which operated several hospitals and clinics in Delaware and Florida for the elderly and crippled children.

The Alfred I. du Pont Testamentary Trust owns the assets of the empire, primarily in the form of stock in the various companies, including St. Joe Paper Co., the Florida East Coast Railroad, etc. The Trust's beneficiary is the Nemours Foundation, which owns and operates the hospitals and clinics. The money flows this way: The companies make profits and pay stock dividends to the Trust, which in turn, makes contributions to the Foundation.

If this were a normal charity, it would be required to pay an amount equaling at least 5 percent of the assets of the Trust to the Foundation each year. But the way it is set up, there can be several impediments in the flow of money. For instance, the companies might not make a profit and thus might not pay any dividends to the stockholder: the Trust. Or the companies might retain their profits rather than paying them as dividends.

Ball evaded the requirement that charitable foundations make annual expenditures on charity equal to at least 5 percent of their total assets by classifying his system as a hospital. Then, before he died, Ball was sued by the states of Delaware and Florida, which alleged he was not spending enough of the profits of his companies on charity. Ball preferred reinvesting his profits in the paper company and the railroad rather than spending them on medical care for the elderly and children.

---

[3] *The Great Heroin Coup,* by Henrik Kruger (South End Press, 1980).

The Trust, which had been paying about 1 percent of its assets to the Foundation each year, agreed to settle the Delaware and Florida lawsuits by upping the percentage to 3. Ball then hired an auditor to lower the appraised value of the assets of the Trust from $1.1 billion to $640 million (when its fair market valued was closer to $2 billion). In effect, this lowered the amount it would have to pay to charity rather than increasing it.

Thus, if the Trust were treated as a normal charity, it should be paying out about $100 million a year to the Foundation (5 percent of $2 billion). Instead, under the settlement and new value of the Trust's assets, it would have to pay out $19.2 million.

Fred Silverman, an assistant attorney general in Delaware, has lead the fight to try to get more money spent for charitable purposes. "We try to keep an eye on them as best we can—which is not good at all. They cook the books to make the 3 percent as small as possible," Silverman said.

Finally, Ball died in 1981 at the age of ninety-three. Even in death he confused his enemies by leaving his entire personal estate, valued at a little less than $100 million, to the Nemours Foundation, for "curable crippled children in Florida," whom he hadn't cared a whit about in life.

Author Gerard Colby, who wrote an eye-opening book about the du Ponts, *Du Pont Dynasty; Behind the Nylon Curtain*, believes that Ball was still up to no good in his bequeathal: "And what of crippled children?" wrote Colby. "Belin, as trustee of Ed Ball's personal estate, is dipping into the $100 million fortune the old curmudgeon left behind. This includes sizable chunks of real estate near Titusville. 'We've sold some to McDonnell-Douglas and some to Hughes Aircraft,' he explains. 'We've reinvested the proceeds in government securities to produce income. As we continue to liquidate assets of Mr. Ball's estate, the income flow will increase.'

"This leaves the Alfred I. Du Pont estate intact. Ed's personal fortune proved to be his greatest secret weapon, a ready source of cash that Belin could use to protect Ed's empire from the ravages of crippled children."[4]

Ball's successor, Jake Belin, has a personality that is entirely different from his old boss's. A Florida redneck and good old boy whose voice reeks of corn pone and molasses, Belin replaced Ball's picture of the

---

[4] *Du Pont Dynasty: Behind the Nylon Curtain*, by Gerard Colby (Lyle Stuart, 1984).

Shah of Iran in his office with those of his favorite Confederate generals, Robert E. Lee and Stonewall Jackson. (In 1988, St. Joe Paper Co. paid $2 million to settle a racial discrimination lawsuit that charged that the company had separate job categories for whites and blacks.) But in terms of being miserly with the du Pont's assets and with expanding the empire, Belin—who had started working for St. Joe Paper Co. in 1938— was every bit the equal of Ball.

Consider, for example, the 21,000 acres and six miles of beachfront property that St. Joe Paper Co. owned in Walton County near Destin, between Pensacola and Panama City. Its pristine beaches and inland freshwater lakes have been called the finest Gulf Coast property left available for development.

Ed Ball, fronting for Alfred I. du Pont, bought most of this land in 1925 for $11 an acre. In 1981, just after Ball died, Belin announced that in the next ten years he wanted to turn the property into "the playground of America," complete with condominiums, shopping centers and recreational facilities.[5] But Belin, like Ball before him, came under pressure from Delaware and Florida to increase the contributions of the Trust to the Nemours Foundation. So instead of developing the property, in 1984 he put it on the market for sale.

Many major Florida developers expressed interest in the property, but, according to Belin, they all wanted to do some kind of joint venture. "No one wanted to put up any money," he told *Florida Trend*. No one, that is, until Mike Adkinson, a small-time Houston home builder, showed up in early 1985, wanting it. "I like Mike. We're a couple of West Florida rednecks. He's from Crestview and I'm from De Funiak Springs, so I figured we'd get along fine," said Belin.[6]

On the surface, Adkinson appeared to be just another two-bit home builder who had kicked around a lot of places and never made much money. Born in 1948, he grew up in Florida and southern Mississippi. Drafted into the Army in 1968, he served for two years, including a stint in Germany. Afterwards, he went to work as a foreman for a Florida construction company. From there he formed his own company, which made construction materials, such as roof trusses. He went broke two years later, in 1974.

Adkinson then joined Taylor Construction Company, for which he

---

[5] *Florida Trend*, November 1981.
[6] *Florida Trend*, March 1987.

traveled across the country building houses on Air Force and Army bases. After three years of that, he settled in San Antonio, where he worked for Regal Homes, a home builder. Two years later, in 1979, he transferred to Houston, where he worked for another two years as vice president in charge of the Houston operations. In July 1981, Adkinson quit Regal Homes and formed the Development Group, Inc., with Frank M. Gammon, Jr., the treasurer at Regal Homes.

So far, so good. But two months after he and Gammon created the Development Group (referred to by everyone as DGI, also the acronym of Fidel Castro's "CIA"), Adkinson got involved in something that showed that he had moved into a different circle of acquaintances. He traveled to Kuwait and other Middle Eastern countries and began representing some wealthy Arabs.

Adkinson was taken to Kuwait and introduced around in September 1981 by Mary Faza, who came from a wealthy Kuwaiti family with connections to the royal family. Faza said she met Adkinson when she bought a house in Houston from his brother. "Michael didn't have a penny when I took him to the Middle East," she said.

Among the Arabs whom Faza introduced to Adkinson were Ahmad Al-Babtain, a wealthy Saudi Arabian who had a car dealership in Kuwait, and Nazih Al-Dajani, who owned a construction company in Saudi Arabia. Adkinson began arranging investments in Houston for his newfound clients, but ended up cheating Faza, Al-Babtain and many others, according to Faza.

By then, Adkinson had moved on to work with other people in Kuwait, Saudi Arabia and Iraq, Faza told me. "I believe he was into arms. I heard about gun deals, but I don't know anything about them. He had a lot of money quickly," she said. Joseph Hailey, who was his accountant, said Adkinson bragged about his gun deals: "He would make remarks about a far-reaching power that could get arms out of the country. He was aware that he was part of something big. Mike was too dumb to be in the CIA, but he could have been used as a pawn by them."

One official close to a federal investigation of Adkinson and the Florida land deal said that Adkinson was asked in a deposition whether he worked for the CIA, and he replied that he was not at liberty to disclose that information.

Hailey also volunteered that both he and Adkinson know Harry "Heinie" Aderholt, a retired Air Force general who lives in Fort Walton Beach, just down the road from the St. Joe Paper Co. land. Aderholt, a

longtime veteran of unconventional warfare, served under General Singlaub in Southeast Asia as chief of covert air operations, where he was
succeeded by Richard Secord. Aderholt, the unconventional warfare
editor of *Soldier of Fortune*, is president of the Air Commandos Association, which provides "relief" assistance to counter-revolutionary
groups in Central America, such as the Contras.

Hailey told me that Aderholt asked Adkinson about sponsoring
medical facilities in Third World countries. But, he said, "Heinie didn't
trust him."

By the end of 1982, Adkinson had come to the attention of several
heavyweights in Houston, perhaps through his Middle East activities
and connections, perhaps through his home building. In a financial
statement dated November 1982, Adkinson listed one of Walter
Mischer's companies as a credit reference. And it was reportedly
through Mischer that Adkinson got into the deal that really put the
Florida redneck on the map. It happened like this:

In 1983, Adkinson approached the owners of a Houston shopping
center with an offer to buy it. The property was the venerable old
Meyerland Shopping Center, built by George Meyer in the 1950s in the
midst of a large, wealthy Jewish community in southwest Houston.
Adkinson and his lawyer, Robert L. Collins, went to see the matriarch
of the Meyer family, Leota Meyer Hess, a 1933 graduate of the Rice
Institute (today Rice University), the daughter of George Meyer and one
of the grandes dames of Houston.

"I couldn't stand them," Leota Hess said to me of Adkinson and
Collins. She even ran the two out of her office at one point. Hess didn't
want to sell the shopping center, much less sell it to Adkinson. But, she
admitted, "I had some younger members of my family who wanted to
sell. I fought it."

Hess finally went along with her family, but they decided that they
wanted at least $35 million for the property. New York developer
Arthur Fisher, who operated another shopping center in Houston, was
the first who wanted to buy it, but he dropped out, saying the center was
worth only $25 million. "Eventually, Adkinson and Collins showed
up," said Hess. "They said they would pay it [the $35 million], but they
weren't interested in the shopping center. There's something wrong
with people who want to spend $35 million and not ask any questions
about it. He [Adkinson] never read our financial records. He never read
our leases. He didn't seem to care," Hess said. The property, she states
flatly, was not worth $35 million.

Several weeks before Adkinson showed up at her door, Hess was in downtown Houston visiting her attorneys, Fulbright & Jaworski, regarding a lawsuit involving the shopping center. "I ran into Walter [Mischer]. Walter and I were real good friends. He asked me, 'Why don't you sell that place—you're not doing anything with it.' He said, 'You just need to retire.'"

Several weeks later, Adkinson introduced himself to Hess. He told her that Walter Mischer had sent him.

Hailey, Adkinson's accountant who joined him after the Meyerland deal and before the Florida transaction, told me that "Mischer got him [Adkinson] into Meyerland." However, Mischer, when asked about Adkinson, replied, "I never did know him. Is he a Houston guy?"

Not only did Adkinson use Mischer as a reference, Mischer's Allied Bank lent Adkinson $5 million, secured by part of the shopping center, while Southmark's San Jacinto Savings lent at least $7 million and Carroll Kelly's Continental Savings made a $25 million loan. All these institutions were intertwined in another previously described deal: San Jacinto purchased Allied's loan to Kelly on his Continental Savings stock that was guaranteed by Herman K. Beebe.

Adkinson said that Beebe was "partly responsible for his [Adkinson's] original rise to stardom," Hailey related. "Adkinson knew Beebe well. There was correspondence between the two. Beebe was on the private rolodex."

Joe Cage, the U.S. attorney in the Western District of Louisiana who prosecuted Beebe, said that one day Adkinson showed up in his Shreveport office wanting to do a deal. Adkinson offered to turn state's evidence against Beebe in exchange for leniency from prosecution in Houston. For some reason, Cage shuttled him off to an assistant attorney and nothing apparently ever came of it.

(Both Beebe and Adkinson are now living in the Destin, Florida, area and both filed for bankruptcy in federal court in Pensacola. Adkinson's bankruptcy attorney is John Venn, who is the trustee in Beebe's bankruptcy.)

The sale of the Meyerland Shopping Center was consummated in the first week of January, 1984. Leota Hess and her family sold the stock in their company, the Meyerland Co., which owned some other property in addition to the shopping center, to an Isle of Jersey company, Vorvados, for around $35 million. The same day, Vorvados flipped the property to DGI for an apparent $70 million. Adkinson said later he was representing Vorvados and then decided to buy the shopping center himself.

The entire deal was financed by a $58 million loan from Lamar Savings in Austin. But the collateral for the Lamar loan was only the east half of the shopping center. This means that in one day Adkinson and his cohorts had taken property worth around $25 million and inflated its apparent value to more than $100 million. The purpose of that exercise was to borrow more money from banks and savings and loans; eventually the loans against the property would total around $150 million. That meant someone was going to lose at least $100 million on this deal. Guess who? That's right, the American taxpayers.

The money on the closing table at the sale from the Meyer family to DGI was $47.1 million, wired from Lamar Savings. This is an Austin S&L that had special interest rate deposit deals with Mario Renda; that lent $46 million to Adnan Khashoggi; that lent $30 million plus to George Aubin and J. B. Haralson on a Houston tract; that made several big loans to Joe Russo; that was heavily involved with Robert Strauss's son, Ricky; and that also engaged in deals with Monzer Hourani.

Lamar was owned by Stanley Adams, a huge man with a soft voice and eccentric ideas, such as applying for a branch of his S&L on the moon. During interviews with me, Adams implied and indicated that there were larger forces and figures than his in control of Lamar, but he was too afraid to reveal them. Plagued by alleged emotional and physical problems, Adams pleaded guilty to fraud at Lamar and was sentenced to a short prison term.

Most of the Lamar money on Meyerland, a little over $40 million, went to Vorvados. About $30.5 million of that came back to the Meyer family—this figure is approximately the sales price of $35 million less the $4.4 million first mortgage to Connecticut General Life Insurance, which was paid off out of the Lamar money. This means that Vorvados made a pure profit of some $10 million in one day, just for signing a few papers.

Vorvados is an Isle of Jersey company whose principals are the same as those of the Compendium Trust, the umbrella trust company tied to John Dick that Lawrence Freeman used to launder Jack DeVoe's drug profits. During this time period, the principals and directors of Compendium were Raymond Sidney Richard Harvey, John Wadman and Leslie Norman, all of whom worked together in the Compendium Trust office on Jersey. The registered principals of Vorvados were Harvey, the

Compendium Trust and a secretary at the Compendium Trust.

However, the way that trusts are set up within the Compendium Trust, the real, or beneficial, owners are usually different from the registered principals, who merely serve as front men. For example, the Jersey trusts that Freeman set up for Jack DeVoe, which had names like Katmandu and Himalaya, were registered under Freeman and the imaginary Dr. Robert Oka, but DeVoe was the beneficiary. In the case of Vorvados, the owners were allegedly the Arabs whom Adkinson was representing, such as Ahmad Al-Babtain. But there is nothing on the record that shows who the *beneficial* owners of Vorvados were.

Raymond Harvey was the primary official whom both Lawrence Freeman's and Adkinson's representatives dealt with on the Isle of Jersey. A Florida Department of Law Enforcement report states that Harvey, as well as most of the other Compendium Trust officials, had previously worked for the Bank of Nova Scotia in the Bahamas before coming to Jersey in the late 1970s.

The Nassau branch of the Bank of Nova Scotia, a Canadian bank, was hit with $1.25 million in contempt fines by U.S. courts for failing to produce documents in a criminal case. And, as reported by author Jonathan Kwitny, the infamous CIA-connected Nugan Hand Bank was incorporated in 1976 in the Cayman Islands by the Cayman lawyer for the Bank of Nova Scotia. There is speculation that the Nugan Hand Bank was a successor to Castle Bank & Trust after Paul Helliwell died. Some federal investigators who have followed the use of Isle of Jersey companies to launder and hide money believe that the Jersey operation also was a successor to Castle Bank.

There exists evidence in Florida Department of Law Enforcement documents that Freeman, the former in-house counsel for Castle Bank & Trust, was in on the ground floor of the Compendium Trust. A December 31, 1981, letter to Freeman from Raymond Harvey asks about "fees, procedures and documentation used by the Compendium Trust Company, Ltd., when setting up corporations for clients in the Channel Islands, Cayman Islands, United Kingdom and Liberia."

Another entry in the FDLE reports on Freeman and DeVoe states that "on January 21, 1983, Harvey initiated a discussion via teletype about a group of Europeans joining U.S. citizens in a real estate purchase and development in Texas. Harvey was asking for advice on what corporate vehicle should be used to shield all parties concerned. Freeman replied by sending some U.S. statutes relating to joint ventures and royalties." It is not known whether this development is the Meyerland shopping center. If it is, it puts a new twist on things by referring to European investors rather than Arab investors.

The next event in the Meyerland saga occurred in December 1984, when another Isle of Jersey company filed a $30 million mortgage against the western half of the shopping center. This company, Sandsend Financial Consultants Limited, had the same directors as Vorvados and the Compendium Trust. Sandsend's attorney, Keith Alan Cox, a London solicitor, indicated in a deposition he gave in Adkinson's bankruptcy that Al-Babtain was one of the owners of Sandsend. Cox also stated that by the time Sandsend got involved in the St. Joe Paper Co. deal in Florida, Al-Babtain was no longer a Sandsend owner.

The Sandsend $30 million mortgage was apparently bogus; that is, Sandsend did not pay any money to DGI. The mortgage was filed in December to secure a $30 million promissory note Adkinson had allegedly signed in January. But that meant that for almost 12 months Sandsend's mortgage was unprotected against other possible claims. For example, Adkinson could have borrowed more money against the property, and if a mortgage had been filed, it would have been superior to Sandsend's mortgage. Cox stated in his Adkinson bankruptcy deposition that he made a mistake in not filing the mortgage sooner. However, attorneys for Continental Savings said during their later litigation with Adkinson that their experts had determined the promissory notes Adkinson signed were made of paper that had been manufactured between 1986 and 1987, at least two years after he allegedly signed them.

The purpose of the Sandsend mortgage soon became apparent: to transfer more money from Texas banks and savings and loans to the Isle of Jersey. In early 1985, Mischer's Allied Bank and Southmark's San Jacinto Savings each filed $5 million mortgages against the western half of the shopping center. Sandsend subordinated its mortgage to them, indicating that some or all of the money the two institutions lent DGI was paid to Sandsend.

Next, in January 1986, Carroll Kelly's Continental Savings made a $25 million loan to DGI, secured by a mortgage on the western half of the property. This loan was a wraparound loan—a second mortgage—and included the $5 million Allied Bank first mortgage. No one seems to know what happened to the San Jacinto Savings mortgage; no release was ever filed, yet the Continental mortgage made no mention of it. This means that some lawyer involved in the deal was negligent—or worse, committed fraud.

In making the loan, Continental paid DGI $20 million (the $25 million face amount of the mortgage less the $5 million first mortgage). Approximately $10 million of this went to Sandsend as partial payment on its bogus $30 million note. The other $10 million was paid back to Continental to buy bad loans that were on Continental's books—cash for trash.

In this particular case, $1 million went to pay the interest on a Continental loan to Harry Terry, Carroll Kelly's Kappa Sigma brother, who was serving as a front man for Kelly and Beebe on some San Antonio property they wanted to make into a parimutuel horse racing track. Most of the remaining trash money went to DGI to buy bad loans Continental had made to John Riddle.

Also, in January 1986, the $5 million Allied loan to DGI was sold by Allied to West Belt National Bank in Houston. This is the Houston bank that had been chartered in 1983 by Robert L. Clarke, the agent and attorney for the original investors, who would go on to be named the U.S. Comptroller of the Currency in 1985. West Belt stockholders included Adkinson and E. Trine Starnes, Jr.

Although Adkinson's name does not appear on West Belt's charter papers, sometime in 1983 he became a minority stockholder of the bank, with about 4 percent of the stock, listed on his financial statement at $100,000. He was later named to the bank's board of directors. One of the original stockholders of this bank was Starnes, the previously introduced private donor to the Contras and a major borrower at Continental Savings and Silverado Savings in Denver.[7] (Sandsend also had its bank account at West Belt.)

Then, in March 1986, Robert Corson's Vision Banc Savings bought the $5 million Allied note from West Belt National Bank. This was one of the very first transactions Corson did after he got control of the S&L; in fact, he hadn't even changed its name from Kleberg County Savings and Loan to Vision Banc Savings yet. Continental Savings later bought this note from Corson's S&L, for $5 million plus $1.2 million in interest.

Finally, another $60 million in mortgages were filed against the other property in the Meyerland sale. This consisted of the strip shopping center across the street and other tracts in the area. These mortgages included $12.7 million from Sandsend. Loan-closing documents show that at least $4.7 million was wired to Sandsend from Delta Savings, a

---

[7] Application to organize a national bank, West Belt National Bank, and other documents on file with the Comptroller of the Currency.

fraud-riddled S&L in Alvin, Texas, a small town south of Houston (and the home of Nolan Ryan).

This means that between $30 million and $40 million went to Isle of Jersey companies in the Meyerland transaction. Where did it eventually go?

The private attorney hired by Continental Savings to go after Adkinson and the money was Tom Alexander, Walter Mischer's close personal friend and attorney. Alexander, of course, vowed publicly to pursue Adkinson and his money to the "ends of sand." (Get it? Sandsend.) However, as far as I know, the only money Alexander recovered was his fee from Continental.

The S&Ls sued for the money they lost, but Adkinson filed for bankruptcy and claims to be broke. Regardless, these lawsuits were just farces, smoke screens and red herrings, designed to conceal the fact that the S&Ls were in on it with Adkinson from the beginning. The proof of this is in the pudding: So far these lawsuits have not recovered one dime for the taxpayers—but enormous fees for the lawyers have been paid.

One farcical hearing in the case was before U.S. District Judge John Singleton, who, years earlier, had narrowly escaped getting tied into the Sharpstown scandal. During the middle of the court hearing, Tom Alexander reminded the judge that they had played golf together the day before. Not surprisingly, when Singleton retired in 1992, he became counsel to Alexander's law firm.

Alexander tried to portray the case as a money-laundering scheme in which the money was eventually funneled back to Adkinson and to Robert L. Collins, his attorney. Other than the 1 or 2 percent they got for fronting and papering the deal, there is little evidence for that. Besides, the money was not being laundered; its source was known: S&Ls, and thus ultimately the taxpayers. It was just being stolen and taken offshore.

And, so far, no one involved in the Meyerland deal has been indicted for that particular deal. Lamar and Continental Savings, and ultimately their federal receivers, eventually foreclosed on DGI's loans and took the property back. Lamar's successor auctioned off the eastern half of the shopping center for an estimated $18 million—which means the taxpayers took a $30 million loss on the deal.

Meanwhile, all the grandiose plans Adkinson had announced for the Meyerland Shopping Center came to nothing. In fact, he let the strategically located center go to pot. His company cut down all the trees there and even closed the public restrooms, before being forced by the city of Houston to keep them open. He and his minions tried to run renters off and threatened to cancel the leases of some of the best stores there, including Walter Pye's. "They really hurt a lot of people here," said Walter Pye, Jr.

This was simply more evidence that the whole scheme was a just a scam to take money from Texas banks and savings and loans —which had connections to mob associates and CIA operatives—to Isle of Jersey companies reportedly fronting for wealthy Arabs.

After Adkinson closed on the Meyerland deal, his stock and his lifestyle soared. His companies bought three airplanes, including two jets. One was a Lockheed Jetstar that DGI acquired from Hughes Tool Company in March 1984. (In 1987 this plane was sold to Aero Center, Inc., in Laredo, for export to Mexico.) Another plane was a Dassault Falcon 10, purchased in 1985 with a $1 million loan from West Belt National Bank.

Adkinson's airplanes were constantly flying south of the border, according to Hailey, his accountant. One destination was Belize. Hailey said that they looked at some land in Belize to purchase: 16,000 acres of rosewood trees. Another frequent destination was Panama, where Adkinson had a company called Panamanian International Oil Co. No one seems to know what this company did, but it had a $10 million letter of credit from San Jacinto Savings.

Adkinson also formed an airplane company called Skyways Aviation and hired a couple of pilots. According to Hailey, Beebe was one of the powers behind this company and Adkinson was brought in as the patsy, in case Skyways was ever caught with the "packages going back and forth," Hailey said. Perhaps this is why Joe Cage shuttled Adkinson off to a drug task force attorney when he showed up in Shreveport to talk about Beebe.

In 1984, Adkinson bought a yacht and named it after himself and his girlfriend, Cathy Fawcett. The Mica (Michael/Cathy) was later repossessed by San Jacinto Savings.

Adkinson began taking hunting trips to Mexico, where he would be accompanied by bankers from West Belt National Bank and from San Jacinto Savings. Hailey said Adkinson loved to indulge in high-stakes poker games on his trips to Mexico. In one such game, according to Hailey, there was $300,000 on the table.

In the summer of 1986, Adkinson went with Riddle and Corson on vacation to the Moonlight Beach Club in Encinitas, California, which had been created by Vernon Savings's Don Dixon. Dixon got some financing from Sandia Savings in Albuquerque for the club, and would suggest to Vernon borrowers that they buy memberships in the club.[8] Riddle, of course, was a big borrower at Vernon.

Sometime in 1981 or 1982, Adkinson met up with Mel Powers, one of the most notorious and disreputable characters in Houston. In 1966, Powers was tried and acquitted, along with his aunt, Candace Mossler, for the strangling and stabbing death of his uncle and her husband, Jacques Mossler, a mob-connected financier. The allegations were that Powers, then twenty-four, and Candace were carrying on an affair and killed Mossler in his Key Biscayne apartment for his money.

Mossler later filed an aggravated assault charge against Powers, but she never appeared in court to press it. She and Powers then announced they were in love. But several years afterwards Mossler married an electrical contractor, divorced him four years later and then died of a drug overdose in Miami in 1976. She was buried beside Jacques in Arlington National Cemetery.

Powers started out in the mobile home business in Houston. According to an investigator who has worked on organized crime probes with the FBI, Powers received his initial financing from a New York company associated with the mob. A lawsuit filed in federal court in Houston in 1984 by one of Powers's creditors states that he was under investigation by the Houston-based Organized Crime Drug Enforcement Task Force. But Powers was never charged in the inquiry.

Instead, he turned into a wealthy developer in Houston and lived the good life for a while. He purchased a multi-million-dollar mansion on Clear Lake, complete with helicopter pad, as well as a 166-foot yacht, the largest privately owned yacht in the Western Hemisphere. But in 1984 Powers filed for bankruptcy and began losing his empire. At one point in his bankruptcy proceedings, he was jailed for refusing to account for $2 million in revenue generated by an office building he lost to foreclosure. Powers's most notable development was the Arena Tower office and entertainment complex in southwest Houston. He lived in a penthouse at the top of one of the two office towers there and during his bankruptcy tried to exempt the entire building from foreclosure by claiming it as his homestead.

---

[8] *The Daisy Chain,* by James O'Shea (New York: Pocket Books, 1991).

When Powers first began getting into financial problems in the early 1980s, his buddy, Mike Adkinson, moved his companies to the Arena Tower, to pay rent and thus help with the cash flow. Powers's largest tenant in the office building was General Homes, thè former bankrupt home builder that was partly owned by American Savings and Loan in Miami and that did around $100 million worth of land deals with Robert Corson.

According to several people close to Corson and Powers and a number of law enforcement officials, Walter Mischer flew with B. J. Garman (Corson's mother) and Powers in a Powers airplane from Lajitas to Belize in early 1987.

Mischer said Powers would fly into Lajitas occasionally to raft down the Rio Grande, but he denied going on any plane trip to Belize with Garman and Powers. "I've never been on a plane with her or Mel either. The only way they could have got me on that plane was shanghaied me." Still, several independent sources, including law enforcement officials who had access to federal records regarding the trip and one of Garman's closest friends, said that Mischer and Garman made at least one trip to Belize around Christmas in 1986. "They were looking at some property there," Garman's friend said.

The U.S. Customs Service denied Freedom of Information Act requests by me for entry and exit records on Garman, Corson, Mischer and Powers.

After Powers declared bankruptcy, leaving numerous creditors holding the bag for millions of dollars in unpaid obligations, he showed up in 1990 in the S&L mess. Along with his partners, Gayle Schroder and Schroder's son, Powers purchased $125 million in mobile home loans from a group of Texas savings and loans that went broke and were taken over by the feds. According to a person familiar with the deal, Powers and the Schroders may clear $10 million on this transaction without having to put up any front money.

Schroder is a Baytown, Texas, banker who borrowed heavily from Continental Savings. On November 21, 1989, Continental's federal receiver won a $1.5 million judgment against Schroder for an unpaid 1985 loan. Century Savings and Loan also received a judgment against Schroder on May 11, 1989, for $2.6 million. Yet despite all their financial troubles, Powers and Schroder were able to garner a very lucrative contract with an S&L that had been taken over in the feds' Southwest Plan.

When Powers moved out of his Clear Lake mansion and into his Arena Tower penthouse in 1982, he put his mansion on the market. Adkinson shopped it with his Arab investors and partners, eventually selling it to Al-Babtain. The newspapers said the sales price was $1.5 million, but Mary Faza, the Kuwaiti who introduced Adkinson to the Arabs, said Adkinson charged Al-Babtain $5 million for the house and some other property and services, cheating the Kuwaiti out of several million dollars. Then, Faza said, Al-Babtain was unable to enjoy his new mansion because he couldn't leave Kuwait for some reason. So Adkinson just helped himself to the house, she said.

In 1983, Adkinson found himself another house, located on 7.5 acres in the Pecan Grove Plantation subdivision outside Richmond, Texas, some 20 miles southwest of Houston. Adkinson had one of his companies buy the property from the CEO of San Jacinto Savings. Allied Bank had lent $300,000 on the property, while Texas Commerce had a $200,000 loan and San Jacinto Savings had kicked in $50,000. In 1987, San Jacinto extended its loan to include $279,167 that was due.

An inspection of the property in 1988 found large, locked, electronically controlled iron gates, with closed-circuit television cameras installed to view incoming visitors. In addition, according to one of Adkinson's former employees, pressure plates had been buried around the grounds to detect intruders.

Horses grazed in pens behind the house, and beside the house was a big, long, black trailer with the words "Watkins Racing Team" on the side. This turned out to be a stock-car racing group out of Jackson, Mississippi.

Adkinson's house is on one dead end of the top of a short T-shaped road. At the other end is the house of the subdivision's developer, J. Bruce Belin, Jr., a successful developer of residential and recreational communities who was president of the American Land Development Association, 1977-78. One of his more notable developments is at April Sound on Lake Conroe, north of Houston.

A Salt Lake City company that sold time-share vacation condos at April Sound in the early 1980s was sued by the Texas Attorney General for alleged deceptive trade practices by making false presentations to customers to get them to buy into its resort properties. The company, Sweetwater, agreed to make restitution of $48,000 to some of its customers. A director of Sweetwater was Chicago attorney Burton Kanter. In a letter to me, Kanter stated, "As for participants in any 'deceptive trade practices,' I certainly did not personally engage in any such practices at any time, and moreover, I doubt that I was personally accused of such."

Another interesting connection is that Bruce Belin's father was the first cousin of Jake Belin, the head of St. Joe Paper Co. (I believe that makes the two of them first cousins once removed.) When questioned about their relationship, Bruce said that he had never met Jake but had talked to him on the phone. He later admitted, "I believe I did meet him, 20 to 25 years ago." When asked about Bruce, Jake replied, "I haven't seen him recently. I was in Conroe [Texas] recently and saw his footprints."

When told about Adkinson living down the street from his cousin, Jake replied, "I was not aware that Bruce was Adkinson's neighbor." When asked about Adkinson, Bruce said, "I do not know Mr. Adkinson at all. I never met him. I knew he was living down there, but as far as I know, I never talked to him."

Perhaps it is merely a coincidence that Adkinson moved into a house (previously owned by a San Jacinto Savings executive with a San Jacinto mortgage on it) close to Bruce Belin (whose latest Houston-area development was financed by San Jacinto Savings) in 1983, and less than two years later was negotiating with San Jacinto's parent company, Southmark, to buy 21,000 acres from Jake Belin in Florida. Perhaps it is another coincidence that Lawrence Freeman was working with Adkinson to buy the land from Jake while Freeman's good friend and business associate, Burton Kanter, was a director of a company doing business with Bruce.

It certainly appears that Adkinson was introduced to Jake Belin either through Bruce Belin or San Jacinto Savings. But Jake said he didn't meet Mike Adkinson until 1985, when Adkinson was interested in buying the 21,000 acres from St. Joe Paper Co. The official story is that a couple of real estate brokers put Adkinson and Belin together and the two Florida panhandlers hit it off.

The first document regarding the sale, a land purchase contract, was signed on October 3, 1985, by W. L. Thornton, president of St. Joe Paper Co., as the seller, and by Michel Beauvais-Wagoner, president of Panhandle Coast Investments, as the buyer. At that time, Beauvais-Wagoner was Lawrence Freeman's office manager and legal assistant. Freeman is the registered agent for the company, whose incorporation papers were filed in Florida one day before the contract was signed.

Jake Belin said to me that Freeman was "supposed to be representing Adkinson in some manner," while Hailey, Adkinson's accountant, said the company (Panhandle Coast Investments) was just a front for the Isle of Jersey boys, Raymond Harvey and Keith Alan Cox, to create an artificial $20 million debt to them from Adkinson. Florida corporation records show that by 1988 the only officer and director listed was Martin Clitheroe, the London law partner of Cox.

The purchase contract provided that Panhandle Coast Investments would assign its rights to a joint venture of DGI and Southmark. This assignment was made less than a week later—and not a moment too soon. The following month, Freeman, who notarized Beauvais-Wagoner's signature on the assignment, was indicted for laundering Jack DeVoe's drug money.

Southmark had lined up its subsidiary, San Jacinto Savings, to provide the financing for the sale. However, by the next month, the federal regulatory authorities had stopped Southmark from getting any more financing for its deals from San Jacinto—about a billion dollars too late for the taxpayers. So now Adkinson et al. had to scramble to get new financing.

The first savings and loan to step up to the plate was Jarrett Woods's Western Savings. A February 1986 letter from a Western Savings official to one of Adkinson's attorneys discussed a loan of $86 million on the Florida tract. But Western dropped out for some reason.

The next S&L to appear was Hill Financial Savings in Red Hill, Pennsylvania, the S&L that lent almost $200 million to Denver developer and Herman K. Beebe associate Richard Rossmiller and his partners, including Robert O. Anderson. Hill Financial was reportedly brought into the deal by W. A. "Andy" Erskine, a loan broker who had worked at Delta Savings, one of the Meyerland lenders. Erskine is the son-in-law of the former mayor of Alvin, who is a business associate of Continental Savings's Carroll Kelly. The broker involved on Hill's side was David Devaney, formerly of Sunrise Savings of Boynton Beach, Florida.

Then two entities came forward announcing their intentions to provide a $30 million takeout commitment to Hill Financial. A takeout commitment (Beebe's standard way of guaranteeing a bank loan for an associate to buy an S&L) means that they would guarantee $30 million of the Hill loan and actually pay Hill off and take over the mortgage at a certain time in the future. In April 1986, Richard Dover wrote to Hill about a $30 million takeout. Dover was John Riddle's real estate partner and was later convicted for income tax fraud.

Then, in May, BancPlus Savings Association in Pasadena, Texas, wrote to Adkinson proposing a $30 million takeout commitment. In addition, BancPlus's owner, Kenneth Schnitzer, would buy a parcel of the Florida land for $15 million. This is the same prominent Houston developer who hung out with the Susalas at La Costa Country Club, who was found by Houston undercover police allegedly associating with family members of Carlos Marcello and who built the Allied Bank building in downtown Houston for Mischer. Former employees of Schnitzer included H. Stephen Grace, the Mainland borrower involved with Ian Paget-Brown.

Schnitzer had purchased Southmore Savings from another Mischer associate and business partner, Tommy Adkins, and then changed its name to BancPlus. When Schnitzer fell on hard financial times, he sold his Century Development company to BancPlus for approximately $60 million, and then when the company and the S&L went broke he tried to buy it back for $12 million. The company was eventually purchased by former associates of Schnitzer.

Regarding the $60 million in cash that BancPlus paid for Century Development, Schnitzer told the *Houston Post:* "Neither I nor anyone in my family received so much as a penny from the assets sold to BancPlus. All the proceeds of the cash sale were used to pay debts on the remaining assets owned by the Century Corp." In a letter to me, Schnitzer said the cash payments "were made to a number of banks and financial institutions." He stated that the other alternative would have been to sell some of these assets to third parties. In other words, Schnitzer would have lost control over these assets of his company.

According to federal investigators, Schnitzer flew out to Florida, looked at the land and met with Adkinson and the Governor of Florida. But the BancPlus deal fell through too.

Schnitzer said he didn't go through with the transaction because he did not feel "completely comfortable" with Adkinson. When asked how and why he got involved in the deal in the first place, he answered, "I do not remember how or why I became interested in this deal in the first place."

Adkinson and the boys still wanted to come up with another $20 million to $30 million in addition to Hill Financial's $70 million. By this time, Robert Corson had purchased his savings and loan in South Texas, so it was used to loan $20 million to the deal, even though the assets of the S&L were around $70 million. (To get around federal loan limits to one borrower, they cut up the $20 million into four different loans to four different straw borrowers.)

Everything was set. On June 5, 1986, Adkinson's company bought 2,850 acres of beachfront and 18,000 acres of inland property from St. Joe Paper Co. for $200,000,000—$70 million in cash from Hill Financial and Vision Banc Savings and a $130 million promissory note from Adkinson's company. It was the most expensive sale of raw land in Florida history, approximately 37 times what Disney paid for 27,000 acres near Orlando for Disney World. (This had been handled by ace spook Paul Helliwell, who surreptitiously bought up the land for the entertainment center in small tracts with different dummy owners to keep the prices from skyrocketing.)

All other developers who looked at the deal said they couldn't believe it, that there was no way in the world the property was worth that much money—which is about the same thing that developers had said about the Meyerland sale. "This deal is not even marginal," R. Thomas Powers, vice president of Goodkin Research, the Lauderdale-by-the-Sea-based real estate consulting firm, told *Florida Trend* at the time. "The only way it would work is if turpentine [yielded from trees on the property] became the hottest product in the futures market in the history of the country. It's an annuity for the year 3000." "There's no way you can pay that kind of price and make it work," a spokesman for Arvida/Disney told *Florida Trend*. "It's outrageous."[9]

Outrageous for whom, is the question. The grandiose plans for development again came to nothing. But every participant in the deal walked away from it with money or land, or both. The only losers were the American taxpayers, who probably lost at least half of the $100 million in cash paid out by the two savings and loans.

Du Pont's St. Joe Paper Co. came out the biggest winner. At the sale closing, the company got $62.1 million in cash from Hill Financial, plus $5.2 million in cash from Corson's Vision Banc Savings. Hill also put $7 million into an interest reserve account. Adkinson's company defaulted on the interest payments due, and Hill paid the $7 million to St. Joe and then lent Adkinson's firm another $12 million for interest payments, which was paid to St. Joe.

The next year, Adkinson's company defaulted on the first principal payment due, so St. Joe Paper Co. foreclosed on 1,850 acres of the prime

9 *Florida Trend*, March 1987.

beachfront property that it had the mortgage on in order to secure its $130 million promissory note.

To recapitulate: St. Joe Paper Co. ended up with about $86 million in cash, plus 1,850 acres of the most valuable land back. This acreage accounted for about 60 percent of the value of the original $200 million deal. Taxpayers might be able to stomach this if the money went to the Nemours Foundation and then to help crippled children in Florida and Delaware. In fact, almost none of it did.

In 1986, according to its annual report, St. Joe Paper Co. recorded a company-wide profit of $100.4 million, including $71 million from its sale of beachfront property. This means that about 70 percent of its profit came from the land sale. Then, out of its total profits, it paid dividends of $5.53 million to its stockholders, including $10 a share in cash and $53.50 a share in stock of a St. Joe-related limited partnership.

Since the Alfred I. du Pont Testamentary Trust owned about 80 percent of the St. Joe shares, in 1986 it received approximately $700,000 in cash and $3.7 million in the partnership stock. Taking 70 percent of that yields a final figure of about $3 million: $3 million—that's how much the Trust got from the land deal to pass on to the Nemours Foundation for crippled children—and less than half a million of that was actually in cash.

Where did most of the money go? According to St. Joe's annual reports, *it* kept it. In 1986, about half the company's profits went for additions to plant, property and equipment; the rest went for reduction of the company's long-term debt and the purchase of certificates of deposit and municipal bonds.

In its 1987 annual report, the company stated: "The company has approved a very aggressive capital expenditure budget over the next several years. The budget for this year and next year includes over $7 million for the timberland operations, approximately $100 million for the mill, and almost $15 million for the container company." And the money for this was raised from profits, not from borrowing.

Ed Ball would have been proud—Jake Belin was building up the assets of the company. But he was doing it at the expense of the American taxpayers and the beneficiaries of the Nemours Foundation, created to aid the elderly and crippled children of Delaware and Florida.

What about the rest of the $100 million in the deal, about $15 million that came from Corson's S&L? Who got it? Sandsend Financial Consultants, Ltd., of the Isle of Jersey got almost half of Vision Banc's money: $7 million. Sandsend also got 260 acres of some of the best beachfront property, which was valued in the sale at about $16.6 million. This money and land came from another one of those bogus debts deal, in which Sandsend claimed that Adkinson owed it some $20 million. There is no evidence for this debt. Sandsend apparently got $7 million in cash and 260 acres—for nothing.

The $7 million does not appear on the loan-closing documents. The only payment to Sandsend on these documents is $900,000. However, thanks to the efforts and determination of one single federal regulator, Ken Cureton, Associate Director of the Office of Thrift Supervision, who got the assignment to examine Vision Banc Savings, we know what happened to the other $6.1 million.

The $6.1 million started out as a single payment to Plantec Realty Corporation, a subsidiary of Florida's largest engineering firm, Reynolds, Smith and Hills, that was assisting DGI in its development plans. Reynolds, Smith and Hills had also done work for St. Joe Paper Co. (Plantec got an additional $3 million in two other payments out of the closing.)

Plantec then signed over the $6.1 million check to Ben Koshkin, one of Adkinson's associates and sometime partner. Mary Faza said Koshkin was with Adkinson back in 1981 when Adkinson was first getting started.

Koshkin deposited the check in his account at West Belt National Bank and then wrote a $6.1 million check the same day to Sandsend. One Houston attorney familiar with the case said that this check originally bounced because the bank had not yet credited Koshkin's account for the Plantec check. This attorney also said Koshkin received for his services about $30,000—which would be approximately one-half of 1 percent of the $6.1 million.

The Isle of Jersey company then started sending out the money in big chunks. It wired $1.5 million to its account at Bank Cantrade Switzerland (C.I.), Ltd., and put $1.8 million in a certificate of deposit at West Belt, which was pledged to an unspecified commercial loan.

Sandsend also transferred $1 million to DGI and $600,000 to Adkinson's attorney, Robert L. Collins.

The documents showing these transfers were placed into evidence at the Fifth U.S. Circuit Court of Appeals by the Federal Home Loan Bank Board after a federal judge in Houston, Lynn Hughes, refused to allow the feds further access to Sandsend's records at West Belt National

Bank. Hughes made his ruling without hearing arguments from the federal regulators, and his decision was overturned by the appeals court.

Corson himself got $3 million in cash out of the deal, plus a 23-acre tract on the beach, plus a Ferrari and some townhouses in Houston. On the date of the sale, the 23-acre tract was sold three times, the value jumping from less than $1.5 million to $20 million. The property was transferred from St. Joe Paper Co. to an Adkinson company to Corson, then to another Adkinson company and finally back to Corson.

In the last transaction, Corson got the $3 million in cash plus a $17 million promissory note. Adkinson's company defaulted on the note, of course, and Corson took the land back and then pledged it against a $7 million loan from MBank Houston that he had used to buy Vision Banc Savings.

Also making out on the deal was John Riddle, who used a $2.9 million promissory note that Corson received to pay off a loan from Vernon Savings. From Riddle, Corson got the townhouses and the Ferrari, which had belonged to Vernon Savings. This came about because of a related deal involving the swap of two pieces of property north of Houston for some of the Florida land that Adkinson got.

Vision Banc lost several million dollars on this swap deal because it had a second mortgage on some of the property north of Houston, and then the S&L lost it all when the first mortgage holder, General Homes, foreclosed.

But that loss was not nearly as much as Vision lost on the Florida land. The $20 million loan was secured by four mortgages on four pieces of property totaling 107 acres. The four companies buying the property were fronts for Adkinson and Corson. One of the straw borrowers for Corson was Robert Ferguson, the Kappa Sigma who said in a deposition in his divorce that he got $100,000 to front the deal for Corson.

All of the borrowers defaulted on their loans, and Vision Banc Savings foreclosed and repossessed the land—then estimated to be worth about $3 million—leaving Vision with a loss of $17 million, which basically bankrupted the small S&L.

What happened to the money that was taken offshore, including the $30 million to $40 million from the Meyerland deal?

One theory holds that the money taken offshore was used to buy war supplies for Iraq. The evidence for this is circumstantial and includes the following:

(1) Before this deal, Adkinson was allegedly running guns to Iraq

with some Kuwaitis and Saudis, who were reportedly behind the Isle of Jersey companies.

(2) One of the banks where some of the proceeds from the Texas S&Ls were deposited was a Jersey branch of an obscure Swiss Bank, Bank Cantrade Switzerland (C.I.), Ltd., a subsidiary of Union Bank of Switzerland.[10]

Bank Cantrade is one of the banks the CIA used to launder funds for arms purchases, according to Robert Maxwell, a former Maryland banker who worked on moving money around for a CIA front, Associated Traders. Maxwell, who was an officer at First National Bank of Maryland, has alleged that he was told by an official at Associated Traders in December 1984 to transfer approximately $5.4 million to Bank Cantrade. The money went from a CIA account in the Cayman Islands to Banco Sudameris in Panama to Union Bank of Switzerland and then on to Bank Cantrade.[11]

Maxwell filed a $4 million lawsuit against the First National Bank of Maryland, Associated Traders and the CIA, after he asked to stop working on the Associated Traders account and requested written authorization for his money-moving activities, fearing they might be illegal. Maxwell never got his written authorization and claimed he was intimidated, threatened and had his constitutional rights violated.

Bank Cantrade on the Isle of Jersey was also used by Lawrence Freeman for the deposit of some of Jack DeVoe's drug-trafficking profits. Some of DeVoe's legal fees paid to Harvey Silets, the Chicago tax attorney who also represented Burton Kanter, came from this account at Bank Cantrade, according to an FDLE report.

(3) A former Israeli intelligence officer, Ari Ben-Menashe, has alleged that John Riddle and one of his companies, First Western Aviation, were part of the arms-to-Iran operation that worked out of Arizona. According to Ben-Menashe, in late 1985 First Western began shipping arms to Iraq as well.

(4) The Reagan and Bush Administrations were seriously considering sending arms to Iraq during the Iran-Iran War, to try to balance out their arms-for-hostages deals.[12]

---

[10] Federal Home Loan Bank Board vs. Sandsend Financial Consultants, Ltd., United States Court of Appeals for the Fifth Circuit, No. 88-2991.

[11] Jack Anderson, December 1986.

[12] Associated Press, June 7, 1992.

(5) Mixed into the middle of the bogus notes payable to various Channel Islands companies were invoices for 100 Volvo trucks valued at $10.77 million. The bill of exchange relating to these trucks involves a substantial Kuwaiti company that would not have needed the assistance of Adkinson in procuring financing of its business operations.

Investigators looking into the BCCI scandal have found instances where weapons were purchased using fake invoices for trucks. For example, the respected congressional newsletter *Roll Call* reported that December 1985 documents showed BCCI providing a $9.3 million letter of credit for the sale of U.S.-made TOW missiles. The invoice by the seller, a British company, accurately described the weapons, but the BCCI letter of credit describes the merchandize as "lift trucks." On January 23, 1992, *Roll Call* reported that "the BCCI letter of credit indicates that bank officials may have known the 'trucks' were weapons and participated in disguising them because the letter indicates they were in possession of the invoice. The letter makes reference to the invoice but describes the missiles only as lift trucks."

Also, in the recent investigations into Banca Nazionale del Lavoro in Atlanta (which lent $4 billion to Iraq, some of which was backed by U.S. government credit and may have been used for weapons), it was learned that Volvo trucks were used as a code word for what may have been Scud missile launchers.

Although these weapons were supposed to be used by Iraq in its war against Iran, it would be a terrible irony if the American taxpayers' dollars that were siphoned out of some Texas savings and loans by mob associates and CIA operatives were used to buy weapons for Iraq that were in turn used against American soldiers in the Gulf War.

Another interesting relationship in the Florida land deal involves the attorneys for Corson's S&L, the Houston law firm of Lackshin & Nathan. This law firm also represented Continental Savings, and one of its name partners, Marvin Nathan, served on the board of directors of Continental.

This is a curious fact because Adkinson never made a payment on his Continental loan for Meyerland that he got in January 1986. Then, by June 1986, Continental's law firm was representing Vision, funneling money to Adkinson and his fronts. Didn't they know Adkinson was in default of his Continental loan, and, if so, why did they allow Vision to lend him more money?

Marvin Nathan said he did not work on the Vision loan and was not aware that the Continental loan was in default until after the Vision loans were made. Marc Gordon, the Lackshin & Nathan attorney who worked on the deal, said he doesn't "recall" if he knew that Adkinson's company was in default on the Continental loan when he worked on the Vision loans.

But Gordon appeared to have a possible conflict of interest in handling an Adkinson loan. Gordon was the registered agent for Houston International Securities Corp., which was incorporated in Texas in 1982 and forfeited its charter in December 1985. In his 1982 divorce, Adkinson showed that he owned this company. The president was his partner, Ben Koshkin. Gordon said he was asked by Koshkin, a client of his firm, to incorporate the company. "I don't remember if I knew about Adkinson's role" in the company, he told me.

There are other connections between this law firm and Robert Corson. In the early 1980s, Marvin Nathan was the trustee in a complicated land deal involving Corson and his partner, Sandy Aron. One of Aron's clients, an Emily Todd, sued Aron and Corson over the deal, claiming they used Nathan as a trustee to buy a piece of property at a low price and then sell to her at a much higher price. The suit was eventually settled.

Also, Nathan's partner, Herbert Lackshin, represented Corson's mother, B. J. Garman, in her 1985 divorce from William L. Garman.

Between the time that Nathan was representing Corson and Aron in the disputed land deal and the time that his partner was representing B.J. in her divorce, Nathan and his brother-in-law, Neil Strauss (who is related to Robert Strauss, the U.S. Ambassador to Moscow), participated in a noteworthy land purchase. They bought a 1,185-acre ranch northwest of Houston from the family of the late Nicaraguan dictator Anastasio Somoza Debayle.

Somoza's family, consisting of his nephews and cousins, purchased the ranch in September 1977 from William Stamps Farish III. Farish, the grandson of a founder of Exxon, is one of George Bush's closest friends and has handled Bush's blind trust investments. Every autumn, Bush visits Farish's ranch near Beeville in South Texas to hunt quail.

The purchase of the ranch by the Somozas occurred about the time that the Sandinistas were stepping up the pressure on Somoza, who complained bitterly that the United States, under Jimmy Carter was not doing enough to help him. Perhaps seeing the writing on the wall, wealthy Nicaraguans began moving their money offshore and to the United States.

Six years later, in July 1983, about the time that private assistance to the Contras was cranking up, the Somozas sold the ranch to Nathan and Strauss. Nathan said it is "absurd" to believe that any of the money he and Strauss paid the Somozas for the ranch went to the Contras.

Before St. Joe Paper Co. foreclosed on its mortgage to Adkinson's company, there had been a big legal fight between Adkinson and Hill Financial. Like the Meyerland litigation, it was another of those smoke screens to cover up the fact that all the parties were in collusion together. One of Adkinson's former employees told investigators that Adkinson and his people were drawing up the lawsuit papers at the same time they were drawing up the loan documents to close the sale.

After St. Joe Paper Co. foreclosed on its 1,850 acres of beachfront land, Keith Cox and Sandsend took over the project from Adkinson and proceeded to get into a big fight with Hill Financial over foreclosure of the 18,000 interior acres that Hill had a mortgage on.

Ostensibly, Cox kept trying to line up partners and investors, but it appeared as if he were simply going through a song and dance to convince federal authorities that the whole transaction had been a good-faith effort from the beginning to develop the land, rather than a scam to take S&L money to the Isle of Jersey. And, he wanted to sell the 260 acres too.

One potential partner Cox said he was courting was E-Systems, the Dallas-based electronics firm and defense contractor. E-Systems had originally been part of James Ling's LTV. In 1970, William F. Raborn, CIA Director in 1965 and 1966, was put on the E-Systems board of directors, and the company was spun off LTV in 1972, Raborn staying on the board.[13]

In 1975, E-Systems bought Air Asia, the CIA's repair and maintenance facility on Taiwan and the sister company to Air America. One year after that, the company was "awarded a $16.6 million contract to install and maintain the sensoring devices that monitor the Sinai buffer zone between Egyptian and Israeli forces. But president [John] Dixon insists, 'We have never done any business with the CIA.' "[14] However,

---

[13] *Air America,* by Christopher Robbins (New York: Avon Books, 1990).
[14] Ibid.

E-Systems is a major supplier of electronic spying equipment for the CIA and the National Security Agency.[15]

Another company that made noises about buying the 18,000 acres out of foreclosure was a Jacksonville insurance company, Old Dominion Insurance Co., owned by Gary Vose, a Denver developer and sometime partner and associate of Richard Rossmiller. Vose bought controlling interest in the Florida insurance firm from J. Edward Houston, a Fort Lauderdale attorney, judge and banker. (Houston had been involved in a Florida S&L/real estate deal with Jeb Bush, one of President Bush's sons. The deal went bad and the taxpayers had to pick up the pieces.[16])

Last but not least, Roy Dailey, Robert Corson's first cousin, approached Hill Financial about buying the Florida land. Dailey told Hill officials that he was working with a company called Government Securities and he had a letter of credit from the Bank of Credit and Commerce International (BCCI). Nothing came of it.

For its part, Hill Financial brought in one of its borrowers, Patrick Harrison, to try to run things and get some development going. Harrison had borrowed tens of millions of dollars from Hill Financial to buy repossessed real estate in Colorado and Texas, under the name Warehouse Associates, including some that had been controlled by John Riddle and Richard Rossmiller.

Harrison's father was Nat Harrison, a Florida construction contractor whose lawsuit against the IRS in 1964 is noted in a 1985 report by the Senate Permanent Subcommittee on Investigations on "Crime and Secrecy: The Use of Offshore Banks and Companies." The Senate report, which was worked on by Robert Corson's attorney-to-be, S. Cass Weiland, stated that Nat Harrison's company had entered into three contracts to construct missile facilities in the Caribbean, and then formed a Panamanian company to do the work in order to try to keep the profits offshore and untaxed.

One of Nat Harrison's partners in his construction company was his father-in-law (and Patrick Harrison's grandfather), Alto Adams, a former chief justice of the Florida Supreme Court. Adams was also one of the five trustees of Victor Posner's irrevocable trust along with Victor Posner and Armer White, the Miami businessman and father of Harold

---

[15] *Dallas Morning News*, May 20, 1990.
[16] *New York Times*, October 14, 1990.

White, who was involved with Sunshine State Bank and Peoples Savings. The Houston law firm that represents Harrison and his company, Warehouse Associates, is Stumpf & Falgout, the name partner of which is T. J. Falgout III. Falgout is a cousin of Tilman Fertitta; in fact, they share the same first names, Tilman Joseph. Fertitta, as previously mentioned, is a relative of the Maceos, the old Galveston Mafia family.

Falgout's father, T. J. Falgout, Jr., a boat company owner in Louisiana, appears in the bankruptcy papers of Commercial Helicopters, the Baton Rouge company that was financed by Herman K. Beebe and supplied helicopter parts to CIA agent Carl Jenkins. As Commercial Helicopters teetered on the edge of bankruptcy in 1983, Falgout and his partners came in to buy the company. Their proposed purchase, however, never materialized.

Finally, Cox and Sandsend are now trying to swap their 260 acres for more than 300 acres of nearby land owned by the state of Florida. This swap was proposed after adverse publicity about the St. Joe Paper Co. deal apparently stopped an attempt by Cox et al. to sell their land to the state of Florida as part of the state's Conservation and Recreation Lands program.

22

WHERE ARE THEY NOW?

In the early-morning hours of September 21, 1990, undercover agents with the Arizona Department of Public Safety and the Phoenix Police Department swooped down on the spacious ranch-style house. They had gotten an anonymous tip that a large, Las Vegas-style gambling operation was being conducted in the house there at the foot of Camelback Mountain in the ritzy Phoenix suburb of Paradise Valley (the neighborhood of luminaries such as Charles Keating). Arizona DPS officers said after the raid that the operation was the biggest full-scale private gambling setup in the Valley of the Sun. Approximately $50,000 a night was being wagered by the 15 or so players congregating there to play cards and dice.

The proprietor of the casino, who was leasing the $3 million house for $2,500 a month and was booked into the Maricopa County jail on suspicion of promoting gambling, was none other than Robert L. Corson. Also arrested were his wife/ex-wife (Corson told the police that they were divorced), Randi, and five others helping them run the games, including a six-foot-eight-inch, 300-pound bodyguard. B.J., Corson's mother, in whose name the house was leased, was nowhere to be found on the night of the raid.

Corson had come to Phoenix from Houston by way of La Costa, California. In 1988, the Federal Home Loan Bank had removed him from Vision Banc Savings and prohibited him from ever again participating in the activities of a federally insured financial institution. This so-called removal and prohibition order on Corson was never made public. However, a year later, the same order was issued against B. J.

Garman, the first such order made public under the Financial Institutions Reform, Recovery, and Enforcement Act of 1989.

The order prohibiting Garman from ever again participating in the activities of a federally insured financial institution made allegations against her and other unnamed Vision Banc insiders that were obviously criminal in nature. A press release on Garman's prohibition, issued by the Office of Thrift Supervision (OTS), stated:

"Examiners discovered a number of large, speculative loans that were tainted with conflicts of interest and other violations of law and regulation.

"Further investigations by OTS revealed that Vision Banc insiders had received financial benefit from loans made by Vision Banc that resulted in substantial loss to the thrift. Extraordinary loan commissions were paid to a firm associated with Vision Banc insiders, which in turn, paid a substantial amount of those commissions to the insiders. Insiders also arranged to have proceeds of significant dollar amount loans made by Vision Banc diverted through the borrowers and others back to themselves."

When federal prosecutors in Houston were questioned about these allegations, they acknowledged there were two active investigations of Corson, which involved federal agents in Pennsylvania and Florida. These were obviously the investigations of the Florida land deal with St. Joe Paper Co. and Hill Financial Savings. By the summer of 1991, there were supposedly sealed indictments issued in Pensacola, Florida, in the investigations.

Finally, Corson, his mother and partner Robert Ferguson were indicted in late 1991 in Houston for the Florida land deal. Adkinson, his attorney Robert Collins and several others were indicted in Florida, and then convicted. (Lawrence Freeman was given immunity from prosecution to testify against Adkinson and his partners, but during his testimony appeared to suffer from sporadic memory losses.) At the time this book went to press, Corson and his mother had not gone to trial.

Before the indictments, in March 1989 both Vision Banc Savings and Hill Financial had been taken over by the federal regulatory authorities. Hill Financial had suffered estimated losses of $2 billion. The feds could not find a buyer for Vision and eventually closed the institution in December 1990, paying off $87.6 million in insured deposits. The Resolution Trust Corporation estimated that the closing of Vision Banc cost taxpayers about $63.5 million.

After Corson had been banned from the industry in 1988, he, his wife and his mother moved to Southern California. They had at least two houses in La Costa and a third in the vicinity. Allegedly they also had set up a real estate business in La Jolla, although there is nothing on the public record in San Diego County indicating any activity by the three.

Then in the summer of 1990, they moved to Phoenix and leased the $3 million house in Paradise Valley from an absentee landlord living in El Salvador. When Phoenix law enforcement officers raided the house they found a great deal of opulence inside. "Corson probably had 30 pairs of custom-made cowboy boots with exotic skins—the stuff is illegal to buy—at $1,000 a pair," said Lieutenant Dave Gonzales of the Arizona DPS. Corson also had "20 to 30 beautiful custom-made suits," and other expensive possessions, such as Rolex watches, Gonzales added.

While he was running the gambling operation, Robert Corson was also dealing in art and jewelry, Phoenix officials said.

After Corson was arrested and booked, he was released on his own recognizance. The original charges against him were dropped, as a formality, officials said, so that the case could be taken before a grand jury for indictment. However, by the summer of 1991 Corson's case had still not come up before a grand jury.

A couple of weeks after the gambling raid, something far more serious happened to Corson. The IRS paid him a visit, searched his house and issued a subpoena to him to appear in Houston. Corson may laugh and scoff at the efforts of the FBI and local police to catch him, as Raymond Hill did, but the IRS is no laughing matter to people of his ilk.

After the IRS arrived, Corson pulled up his Phoenix stakes and moved. Lieutenant Gonzales said that Randi told the real estate agent handling the house that Robert had had a heart attack and had to return to Houston. They ended up stiffing the landlord for two months rent. Also true to form, the undercover DPS officers found that Corson had been using marked cards to cheat the gambling customers. One of the card decks seized in the raid had slight ridges on the cards' edges so that an experienced dealer could tell which cards were being dealt, officers said. Cherry busters forever!

Then, sometime in 1991, things were apparently getting too hot for Corson, so, according to Gonzales of the Arizona DPS, he skipped the country and fled to Tegucigalpa, Honduras. An FBI source said Corson then went to Belize, which doesn't have an extradition treaty with the United States. However, by the summer of 1991 he was back in Phoenix. And after he and his mother were indicted in late 1991 for the Florida land deal, the FBI found them in Sedona, Arizona, a small tourist trap south of Flagstaff, where B.J. was allegedly selling jewelry.

Meanwhile, the Justice Department had built up a big file on Vision Banc Savings, but it was not receiving wide dissemination. Marked on the front of the file were the words: "Classified. Do not discuss this case with anyone." A federal law enforcement source said the file had been classified at the request of the CIA.

By the middle of 1991, the old warhorse Walter Mischer was practically out to pasture. His company, the Mischer Corp., was losing money. It no longer owned any land in Cinco Ranch. Mischer and his son failed in their attempts to win the horse-racing franchise in Houston. And Mischer never could defeat Houston Mayor Kathy Whitmire. That lack of control may have cost Walt Jr., Ned Holmes, Kenneth Schnitzer and Leo Linbeck the $1 billion Metro rail contract. (In 1991, Houston developer and former S&L owner Bob Lanier defeated Whitmire, with the help of a $10,000 campaign contribution from his friend Mischer.)

In what was an incredible reversal, one of Mischer's major lending banks, First City, foreclosed on some Houston property his group owned. This was property just west of downtown that Mischer had amassed in typical Mischer fashion—quietly, using front men, so that no one would know what he was doing. He was also counting on the city of Houston to demolish a nearby low-income housing project, thus raising land values and making his secretly acquired land much more valuable.

Before that could happen, First City foreclosed. Mischer's old financing bank had changed hands. Judge Elkins was probably spinning in his grave, when he found out that his bank had foreclosed on Walter Mischer—the man who had gotten his first $1 million loan from Elkins.

But Mischer is not completely down and out. Although he sold Allied Bank to First Interstate of California, in 1990 he invested in a little Houston bank called Southwest Bank of Texas, whose growth has skyrocketed and whose chief executive officer, Walter Johnson, was the former president of Allied Bank. Mischer also joined with Jim Elkins, the son of Judge Elkins, to develop a residential area close to downtown, with homes priced from $700,000. Their director of sales is Martha Adger, sister of John and Stephen. This is the development that President Bush visited in March 1992, when he paid a call on Mischer's daughter.

Finally, one of the biggest questions in political and business circles in Houston and Texas today is who will be the next Walter Mischer. It won't likely be Walt Mischer, Jr. The son just doesn't have his father's ruthlessness and instinct for the jugular.

Herman K. Beebe, Sr., spent about ten months in federal prison for copping a plea to bank fraud. His federal tenure began in the country-club atmosphere of the penitentiary in Fort Worth, Texas, but he was later transferred to Texarkana, a medium-security prison, because he allegedly got into an altercation at Fort Worth. When Beebe was transferred to Texarkana, he may have bumped into his old boss, Carlos Marcello, who was also incarcerated there.

When Beebe got out of jail, he moved into a condo at Destin, Florida, owned by his dentist brother, Elton. He also filed for bankruptcy. But the FDIC has been after him, serving several legal actions on him, alleging fraud and asking that his debts not be discharged. There are even one or two federal regulators who are apparently trying to find out whether Beebe has any money offshore and, if so, where.

Occasionally Beebe will be spotted in a restaurant in Dallas, where some of his children live. People who have seen him say he looks great, surrounded by his typical entourage and talking up deals in his usual manner. One deal he apparently never did was cooperate in other federal investigations as he had promised.

Mike Adkinson also moved to the Destin, Florida, area—and filed for bankruptcy as well. At first, Sandsend Financial Consultants, the Isle of Jersey company, put Adkinson up in a luxurious penthouse. Later, he was reported living in a trailer house and restoring 1955, '56 and '57 Chevrolets for a living. Adkinson got indicted and convicted for the St. Joe Paper Co. deal. But that was his designated role: front man and fall guy. In turn, the Florida redneck got to live the good life while it lasted.

Mario Renda, the hot-money broker and Mafia associate who knew Khashoggi and several other CIA assets, went to jail for 30 months, but ended up making fools out of the federal authorities. His plea bargain, for which he testified against Martin Schwimmer, called for him to pay $9.9 million to the FDIC as restitution. He also agreed to pay the Justice Department $4.25 million in fines, but the FDIC agreed to pay that amount out of the restitution it got from Renda.

Unfortunately for the taxpayers, the Department of Justice let Renda out of jail before he made restitution, and now the FDIC is left holding the bag, including the $4.25 million Justice wants.

The feds did get Renda to turn over his 101-foot yacht, which he claimed was worth almost $900,000. However, after the FDIC auctioned the boat and paid off the liens against it, only $10,000 was netted. Take away the costs of the auction and other expenses and our federal agency actually *lost* $5,800 on the sale. It makes you wonder how they caught him in the first place. Maybe we would have been better off if they hadn't.

Neil Bush, the S&L poster child, decided he had had enough of Denver, and in the summer of 1991 put his house there up for sale and moved to the more friendly clime of Houston. He went to work for a cable TV company and appeared regularly in the gossip columns of the newspapers, as if nothing untoward had happened in the last five years.

After John Connally failed in his 1980 Republican presidential bid, in which Charles Keating was his West Coast finance chairman and briefly managed the campaign in its last, dying moments, he joined up with Ben Barnes in a business partnership called Barnes-Connally Interests. They went into the commercial real estate development business in Texas and borrowed money from Keating's Lincoln Savings, Scott Mann's Creditbanc Savings, Don Dixon's Vernon Savings, Jarrett Woods's Western Savings, Delta Savings, Lamar Savings and Vincent Kickerillo's UnitedBank.

When Connally filed for bankruptcy in 1987, he showed debts of more than $80 million to 23 savings and loans, most of which had failed. But that didn't stop First Gibralter Savings from lending him $600,000 to buy a luxury high-rise condominium in Houston in 1989.[1]

Connally and Barnes did considerable business with Keating entities. Two months after Keating purchased Lincoln Savings, one of its subsidiaries bought 3,280 acres west of Austin for $56 million at the urging of Barnes and Connally, who were hired to manage the project and got a 50-percent profits participation. Nothing happened; Lincoln lost millions on the deal and ultimately replaced Barnes-Connally as the manager.

In 1985, Lincoln issued a $20 million letter of credit to Chapman

---

[1] *Dallas Times Herald*, December 16, 1990.

Energy, and purchased $3 million in stock in that oil company, which was controlled by Barnes and Connally. In addition, Keating's holding company, American Continental Corp., bought $7 million in stock of American Physicians Service Group, where Barnes and Connally sat on the board of directors.

One of the first projects the two former Texas politicians did together was a condo deal in Ruidoso, New Mexico, where West Texans go to watch quarter-horse racing. Their partner in the project was Houston developer Joe McDermott, the former Mischer employee and close business associate. The group borrowed $12.4 million from Albuquerque Federal Savings and Loan, and then the project flopped, with allegations by the New Mexico Attorney General of questionable sales tactics in trying to unload the condos.[2]

After Connally declared bankruptcy, he was hired at huge retainers by his old friends, Charles Keating, Oscar Wyatt and Charles Hurwitz. In August 1987, he was paid $100,000 as a legal retainer by Keating's American Continental Corp. From 1988 to 1990, he received $160,800 for consulting for Wyatt's Coastal Corp. In 1988 and 1989 he got $250,000 a year for consulting with Hurwitz's Maxxam Group.[3]

There are also some intelligence connections floating around Connally, other than just relationships to Mischer and Beebe. Former Israeli military intelligence officer Ari Ben-Menashe claimed that Connally and other people with strong international political connections were working together in the mid-1980s to procure arms for Iraq, the same country that Connally and Oscar Wyatt visited during the Gulf War.

Ben-Menashe has also stated that money used to procure arms for Iraq came from American savings and loans, including Lincoln.

(It has been confirmed that Ben-Menashe had certain insider knowledge about several notorious savings and loans. In the summer of 1991, Ben-Menashe stated that in 1988 former Republican Texas Senator John Tower approached the Federal Home Loan Bank Board about the possible purchase of Bluebonnet Savings and Loan by Robert Maxwell, the infamous London businessman who died mysteriously off the coast of one of the Canary Islands. The fact that a former Israeli intelligence officer would know, in the summer of 1991, any details relating to a

---

[2] *Texas Monthly*, October 1986.
[3] *Dallas Times Herald*, December 17, 1990.

savings and loan bail-out transaction that was part of the Southwest Plan, along with intimate details about fraud and corruption behind the doors of Maxwell's media empire, seemed questionable. But a lot has happened since that time. It is now widely recognized that Maxwell's organizations were milked to their last dime, prior to his death. And, in June 1992, Danny Wall, former chairman of the Federal Home Loan Bank Board, confirmed to Alan Friedman of the *Financial Times* that Tower had indeed approached him in August 1988, to argue on behalf of Maxwell for a group of 15 failed S&Ls that were sold as a package under the name Bluebonnet.)

According to Ben-Menashe's video-recorded interview with the House of Representatives Committee on Foreign Affairs, taped in May 1991, Ben-Menashe had obtained $56 million in January 1981 from an aide to Saudi Arabian intelligence head Kamal Adham. (Adham was also a BCCI insider, but in May 1991 BCCI was still alive and no one was interested in Adham.) Ben-Menashe stated that the $56 million consisted of $14 million in cash and 40 $1 million bank drafts drawn on Banque Worms in Geneva, Switzerland.

Ben-Menashe further said that he took $4 million of the funds and placed them in an account at Valley National Bank in Phoenix, Arizona, in an account in the name of Dr. Earl Brian, who, as earlier discussed, was involved in the Inslaw PROMIS case.

Prior to Charles Keating's first issuance of A.C.C. junk bonds through Drexel Burnham, Keating obtained a syndicated loan from Valley National Bank in Phoenix. One of the banks participating in the syndication was Saudi European Bank S.A., the small bank in Paris that was involved with Ed Baker, the Houston con man allegedly torched in his Jaguar. In 1985, after the issuance of the A.C.C. junk bonds, Keating, through an offshore entity controlled by A.C.C., purchased a 15-percent interest in Saudi Bank's parent company, Saudi European Investment Corp. (S.E.I.C.).

Sitting on the international board of advisors of S.E.I.C. were John Connally, who was representing A.C.C.'s interest; Robert A. Anderson, the former Secretary of the Navy, who has admitted working with the CIA[4]; Fentress Bracewell, a name partner in Robert Clarke's law firm, Bracewell & Patterson; Philippe Giscard d'Estaing, the brother of former French President Valéry Giscard d'Estaing; and S. P. Hinduja,

---

[4] *New York Times*, June 16, 1987.

whose family has recently been under fire relating to kickbacks from the Swedish arms giant, Bofors.

In July 1992, a Tucson jury awarded the A.C.C. bondholders $400 million in damages from S.E.I.C., regarding its wrongdoing in concert with Keating to avoid regulatory scrutiny of Lincoln.

There had also been earlier questions raised about the big loans— more than $33 million—that Lincoln made to Covenant House, the New York City home for runaways that had been run by Father Bruce Ritter. Covenant House had expanded its programs into Central America, working closely and sharing board members with Americares, a non-profit organization that supplied "humanitarian" aid to Central American countries engaged in internal conflicts.[5]

One of Ritter's and Americares's associates in Central America was Roberto Alejos Arzú, a former partner with Nicaraguan dictator Somoza, and an alleged CIA asset. A board member of both Covenant House and Americares is Robert C. Macauley, one of President Bush's closest friends. The two grew up together, attending school with each other all the way from kindergarten to Andover and to Yale.[6]

It is not known whether any of Lincoln's money went to Americares's or to Covenant House's programs in Central America. Even if it didn't go directly, it would have helped free up other money to be used for such purposes, so that the money could be sent to Central America.

When Connally ran for the Republican presidential nomination in 1980, with help from Keating, one of his campaign workers was a woman named Joyce Downey. After the campaign failed, Downey went to work for Connally and Barnes. She stated that at one time she was actually living with Ben and Nancy Barnes. After Barnes and Connally went down the tube, Downey moved to Phoenix and became executive director of the U.S. Council for World Freedom, working for the organization's head, retired Major General John Singlaub, one of the biggest fundraisers and arms procurers for the Contras.

(Such relationships don't prove that any S&L money went to the Contras, of course, but they do show the closeness of many of the players in both circles.)

Finally, as proof that we Texans have no memory, or no shame, or neither, in 1991 the Texas High Speed Rail Authority approved a high-

[5] *Village Voice*, February 20, 1990.
[6] Ibid.

speed rail link between Houston and Dallas, to be constructed by a French-American team. This group included Ben Barnes, who functioned as spokesman and lobbyist for the group. One of the members of the rail authority board, which unanimously approved the Barnes group, was John Connally.

A good number of the people involved in dirty S&Ls in Texas and Colorado moved on to greener pastures in Southern California. Not only was this the destination of choice for Corson and his cousin, Roy Dailey, it also beckoned Richard Rossmiller, Bill Walters and E. Trine Starnes, who had all filed for bankruptcy yet were still living the good life in luxury. They were able to do this by transferring their assets to their wives or children, thus shielding them from seizure by a rare federal agent who might have the temerity to try to get some of the taxpayers' money back.

One familiar name who allegedly transferred his assets to trusts for his children, according to at least two investigators looking into the matter, was Raymond Hill. Hill, alas, said he was forced to sell his father's mansion in River Oaks and move to a more modest abode. He was also reduced to scrapping for court appointments in the county's juvenile courts, like some C-average law student fresh out of a second-rate law school.

"I'm broke," Raymond Hill tells everyone he meets. What he *doesn't* tell is how much money he transferred to trusts for other members of his family. Furthermore, it doesn't appear that the taxpayers' servants responsible for recovering S&L money have any curiosity about it either.

Carroll Kelly, the old Kappa Sig who ran Continental Savings into the ground for Beebe, got a job with the Houston Shoe Hospital, specializing in shoe repair, and later moved to Fort Worth to practice his entrepreneurial skills there. His younger Kappa Sigma siblings, George Aubin and John Riddle, continued to hang around Houston, probably waiting for the next S&L-like opportunity to be handed to them on a platter by our federal government.

As for their old fraternity, Kappa Sigma, well, in a big story on University of Texas fraternities in the March 1991 issue of *Texas Monthly* it was not even named one of the top six fraternities there, and was only mentioned a few times in passing in the 15-page spread.

Kappa Sigma. *Sic transit gloria.*

23

A Reporter's Toast:
"To the First Amendment!"

In February 1989, the last story by Gregory Seay and myself on Mafia connections to the S&L scandal was published in the *Houston Post*, about one year after the first one ran. It would not be until a year later, in February 1990, that the first stories on the CIA connections to the scandal were printed, even though they were ready to go in the fall of 1989.

In the interim, William Dean Singleton and his partners, who owned the *Dallas Times-Herald* and the *Denver Post*, had purchased the *Houston Post*. Singleton, who was the protegé of Houston banker and former *Washington Star* owner Joe Albritton, is a junk-bond and borrowing patron with a milquetoast personality (except when it comes to cutting staff) and unimpressive intellect who appeared to be fronting for someone else. Speculation centered around his New Jersey partners and Albritton.

Singleton brought in former *Dallas Times-Herald* editor Dave Burgin to be the editor of the *Houston Post*. Burgin, who knew Albritton from his *Washington Star* days, had previously been the editor of newspapers in San Francisco and Orlando, Florida. Burgin is a very smart man, with intense personal loyalties, but also possessed of a volcanic, unpredictable temper. No one ever knew when he would act like a great newsman or when he would erupt and trash everything and everybody in sight.

Burgin usually stood behind me in my investigative work, in particular when I was writing about the huge, powerful Methodist Hospital in

Houston. However, one time he threatened to fire one of the *Houston Post*'s best reporters if she did not change a story to remove something negative about a big advertiser. He also said he would fire her if she told anyone about his threat.

Burgin initially liked the CIA stories. It is doubtful that any of the stories would have seen the light of day without his presence and support. However, Burgin wanted to run the stories one at a time, once every week or so. He claimed he wanted to see what the reaction would be. In particular, he was looking for congressional response. He figured the stories would just fizzle and die without a congressional investigation to piggyback on.

Burgin's decision to simply dribble the stories out was a major tactical error because the material would have had more impact if it had run as a series. In addition—although we couldn't have known it at the time—there was no one in Congress who wanted to pick up the fight.

Not only did Congress not want to investigate any part of the S&L crisis—for obvious reasons—but they weren't about to take on the CIA either. They had seen that what happened to congressional critics of the CIA in the mid-1970s, for example, Senator Frank Church: They had later been defeated for reelection by powerful, well-financed right-wing organizations and opposition.

The first two stories that appeared in the *Houston Post* were too weak to stand by themselves; they were designed to be an introduction to a longer series. As a result of our just running these two by themselves, with no immediate follow-up, many journalists across the country made up their minds after reading the two articles that there wasn't much to the story.

The only fights I had with David Burgin were over comments I made to other journalists—which ended up in print—criticizing the way our stories were dribbled out over a long period of time. Burgin wanted to run the stories intermittently, for another reason: what had happened to him during the Watergate scandal.

Burgin had been City Editor of the *Washington Star* during Watergate and, of course, had gotten his butt beaten badly by the *Washington Post*. (At one time, he told me, he had even been *Washington Post* Watergate reporter Carl Bernstein's roommate.) As a result, he had always considered the *Washington Post*'s coverage of Watergate to be the paradigm of investigative reporting. Since its blockbuster stories appeared sporadically, then by God that's the way ours would, even though their stories were "breaking" ones, whereas the reporting was basically finished on ours.

Nevertheless, I believe the real reason the stories were delayed and published sporadically was that the *Houston Post* editors were afraid to run *everything* we had at once. They wanted to stick their little toe into the water first and see whether anyone tried to bite it off.

More important than that, though, the most significant and interesting information we had unearthed—the story of Walter Mischer and his connections to many of the major players and institutions in the S&L scandal—never appeared in the *Post*. The reason they didn't, and the reason the stories were originally delayed for months, had to do with our newspaper's law firm.

The Houston law firm that read the *Post*'s stories for libel is a firm that keeps popping up in connection with many of the big S&L players: Fulbright & Jaworski, a large, prestigious firm whose name partner for years was Leon Jaworski, the famed Watergate prosecutor. Two of Fulbright & Jaworski's attorneys "lawyered" all the stories I wrote for the *Post*.

Although the stories about the CIA and S&Ls were dribbled out in the *Post* over a period of about nine months in 1990, most of the information had been pulled together by the fall of 1989, and was sent over to Fulbright & Jaworski for their comments. The *Post*'s main attorney there is Rufus Wallingford, a partner and trial lawyer who handles insurance defense work. When Wallingford called back after reading the stories, his first and main objection to writing anything about Walter Mischer was his claim that Mischer is not a "public figure."

(His rationale: Whether or not someone is a public figure is important to a newspaper that is contemplating running an investigative story about them because it is much more difficult for a public figure to prove libel. Whether someone is a public figure depends on that person's prominence in the resolution of public issues. Also, the Supreme Court has held that a person who might not normally be considered a public figure can be considered one if he/she voluntarily injects himself/herself or is drawn into a particular public controversy.)

What Wallingford said about Mischer's not being a public figure was patently absurd, and everyone on the city desk hooted when they heard it. Mischer is probably the most powerful man in Houston and Texas; he has been appointed to various state government agencies by many governors; he was chairman and largest stockholder of the third largest bank in Houston; he was named to all of *Texas Monthly*'s "most powerful Texans" lists; he has been named "The Kingmaker" for his political influence in a book, *Texas Big Rich*, by Sandy Sheehy; he was written about critically in Harvey Katz's book *Shadow on the Alamo*; he had been mentioned in many recent news stories, including one in which he was lobbying members of the City Council not to change a Yellow Cab contract at Houston Intercontinental Airport (Mischer had an ownership interest in Yellow Cab); and his picture graced the front of the *Houston Post*'s Sunday magazine in November 1987, along with the words "Texas Power Broker." In addition, Mischer and his bank were involved in two of the dirtiest S&Ls in the country, Mainland and Continental, whose failures cost taxpayers more than $1 billion. Also, Mischer had many other connections, direct and indirect, to the savings-and-loan scandal, as detailed in this book.

There was obviously something else going on with Wallingford other than merely his interpretation of what a constituted a public figure. Several days later, Assistant City Editor Tim Graham, who was editing the CIA stories, and I went to Fulbright & Jaworski's downtown offices to meet with Tom Godbold, an associate attorney who worked under Wallingford.

Godbold is a quiet, soft-spoken, thoughtful person. However, he instantly started to criticize, vehemently and stridently, our stories on Mischer, and he did so in language obviously intended to give us the impression that his law firm believed we were libeling Mischer and that the paper would get sued and probably lose if we printed the stories. It was very uncharacteristic language for the mild-mannered Godbold, and set off alarm bells with me. I immediately asked him if Fulbright & Jaworski had any conflicts of interest with our stories.

Godbold got very serious and said that he knew of none. He added that Fulbright & Jaworski had represented MBank at one time, but that the bank had been purchased and was no longer in existence. That was all he said; but his reaction to the Mischer material, along with Wallingford's behavior, was enough to scare the *Post* editors away from running the substantive stories on Mischer in the beginning of our exposé, when they *should* have run.

By the end of the summer of 1990, we had printed all of the stories I had initially written, about the CIA and S&Ls, except for the ones on Mischer. I then turned our editor's attention back to those important stories and once again tried to get them into the paper. This time, for some reason, Wallingford, the senior attorney, stayed out of it. But the associate, Godbold, despite additional information and corroboration, continued to object.

Finally, in the winter of 1990, we had a big meeting with Godbold and the top editors of the paper, in which the editors led me to believe that I had answered all of Godbold's objections. We had a new Editor-in-Chief, Charles Cooper, who had taken over for Burgin (who moved to San Francisco to edit a small chain of newspapers). Cooper told Tim Graham and me, after the meeting with Godbold, that he was committed to printing the stories. Graham had been promoted to City Editor and he was completely in favor of printing them too.

It was now Christmastime, and I was on vacation and out of town. The stories were scheduled to run December 31. Graham called me from the city desk saying that Godbold would not sign off on them, but he was approving them anyway, and would so recommend to Cooper. In the end, Cooper, a new editor, decided not to run the stories—based on Godbold's refusal to sign off on them.

I was furious, and told Graham that Godbold's job was probably on the line and if Godbold couldn't stop the Mischer stories he probably wouldn't be made a partner at Fulbright & Jaworski. I then began a leave of absence to work on this book. About six weeks later, I was having lunch with Graham and Executive Editor Ernie Williamson. "Guess what," Graham said, "Godbold just got made a partner."

That's when I began looking in earnest for conflicts of interest at Fulbright & Jaworski with our savings and loan stories. Here is what I found:

(1) As previously mentioned, Fulbright & Jaworski allegedly laundered money for the CIA through the M. D. Anderson Foundation.

(2) The Washington office of Fulbright & Jaworski had represented the Herman K. Beebe-financed, CIA-connected Palmer National Bank in a securities offering. Graham said that Wallingford objected strongly to running our story on Palmer National Bank and wanted to have a sit-down meeting about it.

(3) The Washington office of Fulbright & Jaworski was a client of William Casey when he was in private practice before heading the CIA.

(4) Fulbright & Jaworski helped handle a real estate deal in the mid-1970s involving Herman K. Beebe, Sr., Richard Rossmiller and Surety Savings.

(5) Fulbright & Jaworski represented the campaign of County Judge Jon Lindsay in an effort to retrieve some interest earned on deposits that the FDIC was unwilling to pay the campaign.

(6) Fulbright & Jaworski had represented one of Howard Pulver's companies in a lawsuit. Wallingford had strenuously objected to the *Houston Post*'s running the story about Pulver and Martin Schwimmer being neighbors (discussed in the Chapter 4), which contained a great deal of background about Pulver. Wallingford succeeded in keeping a lot of this detail out of the article.

(7) And, finally, there were the conflicts involving Mischer. First, Wallingford is good friends and a golf partner with Mischer's personal attorney and close friend, Tom Alexander. Every time I would press Wallingford about running the Mischer stories, he would say something like, "Wait until I retire," or "You know we can't run that," or something similar. He would try to make a joke about it or blow it off; but he always seemed worried about how running these stories would affect him personally.

Furthermore, at the same time that Fulbright & Jaworski was telling us we couldn't run the Mischer stories, it was representing the Mischer Corp. in court in a wrongful-death lawsuit against Mischer's company. After I told Graham that I had discovered this, he questioned Godbold about it. The new Fulbright & Jaworski partner told Graham that he hadn't known about the suit, and that Fulbright & Jaworski was brought in by Mischer's insurance company, Aetna.

Two points about those excuses: First, ignorance is not an excuse. Godbold, who had a duty to conduct a conflict-of-interest check, apparently was ethically lax and did not investigate whether his law firm had any conflicts of interest with Mischer, even after I specifically asked him if there were any. And that's giving him the benefit of the doubt—that he actually didn't know of the numerous conflicts. Second, the fact that Aetna was Fulbright & Jaworski's client and had hired the law firm to represent Mischer's corporation makes no difference. Mischer's company is Fulbright & Jaworski's client in the wrongful-death suit and the law firm therefore owes it full loyalty. (At the same time, Fulbright & Jaworski was representing the *Houston Post* in advising us about the Mischer stories and thus, also, owed us full loyalty.)

Also, this was not the first lawsuit in which Fulbright & Jaworski had represented Mischer's company. In 1979, the Mischer Corp. was involved in a suit regarding the garnishment of a worker's wages. Fulbright & Jaworski was hired to represent Mischer's interests.

And a call to Fulbright & Jaworski with the request to speak to the attorney handling Walter Mischer's interests is referred to an attorney in the firm's San Antonio office. A secretary in that office said the attorney there coordinates litigation through other law firms for Mischer Enterprises, an affiliate of Mischer's umbrella company. (One of Mischer's trademark tricks is the hiring of as many law firms as he can, so the firms cannot later be hired by someone fighting him due to conflicts of interest.)

There is little question that Fulbright & Jaworski had a conflict of interest in "lawyering" our stories about Walter Mischer. In addition, they had a duty to determine whether there was a conflict, and a further duty to report this back to us. The Texas Disciplinary Rules of Professional Conduct for lawyers state that in the event of such a conflict the law firm is required to disclose "the existence, nature, implications, and possible adverse consequences of the common representation . . ."

There is something else just as troubling as the Mischer lawsuits. The Texas disciplinary rules also state that a law firm should not represent a person (in this case, the *Houston Post*) if such representation "reasonably appears to be . . . adversely limited by the . . . law firm's own interests." Fulbright & Jaworski intersects with Mischer's circle and nexus of companies, friends and business associates in Houston. A good many of Fulbright & Jaworski's clients have some sort of connection to Mischer, either business-wise or personal. And the law firm probably wouldn't mind representing Mischer in the future. So if it allowed anything adverse to Mischer to be printed, it could be adverse to its own interests and those of some of its other clients.

But such a situation should not have been surprising to the editors at the *Post*. They should never have used the giant Fulbright & Jaworski to lawyer the S&L stories in the first place. After I told *Post* editors about the conflicts I had discovered during my leave of absence, they still continued to use Fulbright & Jaworski. That continued representation was one of the reasons I didn't go back to work for the *Post* after I finished this book. And it was one of the reasons I decided to go to law school. I was determined that no lawyer or law firm would ever again be able to do to me and my work what Fulbright & Jaworski had done.

I did manage to get Mischer's name in one of the stories during the summer of 1990, which by some omission was not sent over to Fulbright & Jaworski. Mischer reacted immediately. He hired famous Houston plaintiff's attorney Joe Jamail, the self-proclaimed "King of Torts," and threatened to sue us. Mischer also simultaneously tried a different tack and began to get closer to the *Houston Post* publisher, Dean Singleton. They apparently became friends, I was told by people inside the *Post*.

When Dave Burgin left to go to San Francisco in the winter of 1990, Singleton threw a party for him in his executive offices. As Singleton walked past me, he told me that I was getting him in trouble with his friends. I asked him which friends he was talking about, and he replied, "Larry Mizel." He further stated that Mizel, the Denver home builder who was in hot water with his dealings with Silverado Savings and some other dirty S&Ls, was a very good friend of his. Singleton's company also owned the *Denver Post*, so I figured that was how he had met Mizel. But I asked him, anyway, how he had first made Mizel's acquaintance. He replied, "Michael Milken introduced us."

It was a miracle that any investigative reporting on the S&L scandal got published in the *Houston Post*.

During the summer of 1990, in the middle of my stories on the CIA-S&L connection in the *Post*, I was contacted by an editor at the giant New York publishing house of Simon & Schuster. He told me his father had seen a write-up of my stories in an alternative California publication and had told him about them. He asked me to send him copies of the stories, which he wanted to show to other editors at the publishing house.

After I sent him the stories, he called me to say that Simon & Schuster wanted to fly me to New York to meet with its top editors to discuss my writing a book for them.

I met with Charles Hayward, the president of Simon & Schuster's massive trade division (who has since moved to Little, Brown), a couple of other editors, and with Alice Mayhew, the company's most renowned editor. I remember the meeting as being very pleasant. I particularly liked Alice, who had edited *All The President's Men* and all of Bob Woodward's other books, as well as those of many leading journalists and writers, such as William Greider. Alice came across as a sharp, tough-talking, no-nonsense professional.

I flew back to Houston and the next day Alice called with an offer. She said Simon & Schuster would pay me a $100,000 advance and that she would get me a contract as good as those she gets for her best writers. I accepted, primarily to have the opportunity of working with such a great editor.

Several days later, I received a contract from Simon & Schuster in the mail. Reading it was like being slapped in the face with a bucket of ice water. It was a "sucker's contract." The most disappointing aspect of it was that the payout of the $100,000 advance was not anything like what Alice had promised over the phone. The terms were significantly more favorable to the publisher. When I pointed out that the advance payout was much different from what Alice had originally promised, they immediately changed it back. But the episode left a bad taste in my mouth that never vanished.

During the contract negotiations I also brought up the fact that it was imperative that the book be published before the 1992 presidential election. At that point in time, it appeared likely that George Bush would again be the Republican nominee and there was a chance that Lloyd Bentsen would be the Democratic candidate. Both men play key roles in the book.

Because of my request, Simon & Schuster modified the contract and agreed to try to publish the book within 12 months of acceptance, rather than their normal lead time of 18.

The book took longer to write than I expected, as Alice accurately predicted, but I submitted it on the deadline date of July 15, 1991. Two months later, in September, I received a four-page editing letter from Alice and one of her associate editors, to whom she had delegated the manuscript. The letter began: "You've got fascinating and important material. The sheer volume of your evidence is impressive, monumental even, and to be honest, overwhelming."

The letter then stated that the structure of the book was "difficult to discern," and suggested an alternate organization, in terms of the "layers that distance both the CIA and the Mafia from the S&L scandals."

"Perhaps," the letter continued, "the final section would take aim at all the government officials and bureaucratic red tape that shut the biggest doors: Keating and his group, Bentsen, Gates, Connally, the Justice Department, the CIA and of course George Bush. Clearly this layer is the most protected, the most circumstantial, and the most damning."

I wrote Alice and her associate a letter back criticizing some of their comments and suggesting a different kind of organization, around the layers of protection and insulation for those involved in the scandal.

They in return responded, saying "We are both a little perplexed but largely encouraged by your memo to us. We think all of us are in basic agreement about what needs doing.

"We did not want or suggest that you invent a 'rip-snorting yarn with a traditional plot.' You have very compelling material, damning in its own right. But you do need urgently to give the reader more guidance, enough to get his bearings and keep him on the central tract and registering the probable implications. Nor are we asking you to pull any punches—we're not at all afraid of toppling giants. We relish that.

"In fact, we do think you accomplished much of what you set out to do—tracing the lineage back to the Mafia and the CIA—but you do it uneconomically."

After several months of trying to restructure the book along the lines suggested, I gave up because it wasn't working. I then began a new presentation along the lines of how I uncovered the stories. This worked better. It took me another three months to finish the restructuring. By then it was February 1992.

During that period I kept in contact with Alice's associate editor. Several times, I expressed my concern and the extreme necessity of publishing before the presidential election. I was assured that Simon & Schuster could turn the book out in two months after receiving the revised manuscript—well before the election.

After I submitted the newly restructured manuscript in February 1992, I waited to hear from my publisher. Nothing. Finally, several weeks later, I called the associate editor to check on the book's schedule. He brushed me off and said he hadn't read the revised version and would read it when he got around to it.

I realized that Simon & Schuster's attitude toward the book had changed—for the worse, and for no apparent reason. Also, around this time I learned that publishers put out in the spring what they call their fall list, a list of the books they plan to publish during the last half of the year. I knew that my book needed to be on Simon & Schuster's fall list if it were to be published before the November presidential election.

I started calling Alice directly, rather than working through her assistants. I sent her letters and faxes, to remind her of the need to publish the book in the fall. I received nothing in response from her or from anyone else at Simon & Schuster: no phone calls, no letters, no faxes. At last, I called her secretary and made an appointment to go to New York, at my expense, to see her. Two days before our meeting, Alice faxed me a message saying she had to postpone it. It was only then that she returned my phone call. She informed me that the fall list was already closed and it was impossible to publish the book before the election.

It certainly seemed that Simon & Schuster had deliberately delayed replying to my communications until after their fall list was closed, so they could present me with a fait accompli: My book would be kept out of bookstores until after the election. Other writers I knew who were familiar with Simon & Schuster and Alice Mayhew said that it could be that Alice just didn't like the book and didn't want to devote any energy to it.

That may be, but during our discussions, she said two things to me that indicated there was more to it. In trying to justify not publishing before the election, she said, "Nobody reads anything in September and October." That struck me as nonsense, and I wondered if she ever told that to her writers whose books she published in the fall.

Then, when I pointed out to Alice that the American public needs and deserves to know—before the election—the facts I had discovered about George Bush and his circle of friends, relatives, associates and backers, she replied, "George Bush is going to win anyway."

Granted, this was before the Democratic nominee had been decided. But what right does any editor have to prejudge who is going to win a presidential election? The American voters make that decision, not Simon & Schuster.

Perhaps Alice truly believed that Bush would really win. But there are several relationships that are worth noting that may explain Simon & Schuster's behavior.

One of George Bush's closest friends, with whom he started Zapata Petroleum back in the 1950s, is Hugh Liedtke, the chairman of Pennzoil. Liedtke is mentioned in this book, in connection with a Houston bank. Liedtke is also a member of the board of directors of Paramount Communications, the parent company of Simon & Schuster.

Paramount Communications is the successor company to the giant conglomerate Gulf + Western. One of Gulf + Western's original founders was Houston businessman John Duncan. Duncan and his brother, Charles, the former Secretary of Energy and before that Deputy Secretary of Defense in the Carter Administration, were involved in the family's business, Duncan Coffee Company, which was merged with Coca-Cola. Charles subsequently became president of Coca-Cola, the company which later would buy 700,000 acres in Belize with none other than Walter Mischer.

When Charles was nominated to be Secretary of Energy, he was introduced to the Senate Committee on Energy and Natural Resources by Mischer's good friend Senator Lloyd Bentsen. And John and Charles are involved in a number of investments and business ventures with Mischer's close associate Jack Trotter and Trotter's wife. Trotter is also a name partner in the Washington, D.C., lobbyist and law firm of McClure & Trotter, one of whose clients is Coca-Cola.

Such relationships do not prove conspiracy. But they show the pervasiveness of the influence of this small circle of Texas businessmen.

As my book was going to print with its new publisher, Simon & Schuster published a book about the Bush Presidency, *Marching in Place: The Status Quo Presidency of George Bush,* written by *Time* magazine's White House correspondents, Michael Duffy and Dan Goodgame, and edited by Alice Mayhew. The book has been billed as the "first hard-hitting critical assessment of the Bush presidency."

There is no doubt that the book contains many incisive and devastating criticisms of Bush's presidential actions and motives. In that respect it is a good book. However, the things that stuck in my mind the most were the little funny, humanizing anecdotes about Bush. And there was not one single mention of Neil Bush, the President's son and the symbol of the $500 billion savings-and-loan scandal, which, itself, was only mentioned a few times in passing.

The book ultimately concludes that, despite his faults and foibles, in Alice Mayhew's words "George Bush is going to win anyway." The final paragraph in the book reads:

"A second Bush term would look a lot like the first: more of the same, only less. Bush would rely on his instincts, reacting to events as necessary. His goals wouldn't be bold, but then his actions wouldn't be imprudent. Like the experienced captain of a cruise ship, Bush would take care to coddle the first-class passengers, and though he would be indifferent to the vessel's course and destination, he could at least be trusted not to sink it."

EPILOGUE

What, then, happened to all that money: the $200 billion-plus that taxpayers are going to have to pay, in addition to more than double that for interest and carrying costs. Any answer is necessarily speculative, because no one has systematicallly tracked it.

In the few cases detailed in this book in which loan-closing documents have been discovered, such as for the Meyerland Shopping Center deal, the Khashoggi Galleria transaction and the St. Joe Paper Co. land sale, it was found that huge sums of money were being sent offshore. In several instances, Mafia associates and CIA assets were transmitting funds to companies on the Isle of Jersey, companies with ties to wealthy Arabs and drug smugglers.

One interesting fact yielded by the few loan-closing documents that have been made public is that a good chunk of the money has been used to pay off prior liens and mortgages held by big banks and big insurance companies. In other words, the taxpayers are now bailing out the savings and loans that were bailing out big banks and insurance companies.

Another interesting fact is that the original landowners—generally rich families and companies—were well taken care of. The Meyers in Houston and the Du Pont companies in Florida got paid more for their land and property than it was worth. Only the integrity and honesty of Leota Meyer Hess in Houston allowed many of the facts to be exposed in the Meyerland Shopping Center deal. In fact, it appears that most of the big land deals financed by S&Ls that generated the huge losses indeed benefitted the rich landowners. They got more money than their land was worth at the time, and considerably more than it is worth today—since the real estate bubble burst. That difference in value was an enormous transfer of wealth from the American taxpayers to prosperous property owners.

Perhaps, in some cases, the property owners were innocent dupes used by the Mafia and CIA front men and middle men to skim off money for their own purposes. But these wealthy and politically influential landowners are certainly not going to complain and raise a ruckus if they made money on the deals. And the big banks and insurance companies are certainly not going to complain if they get their first mortgages paid off and their S&L competition gets eliminated in the storms that follow.

We do not have enough information yet to determine whether the S&L scandal was, in fact, *instigated* by Mafia and CIA operatives, who then made sure that their circle of rich friends got enough of the money to keep them quiet, fat and happy, or whether the scandal was instigated by the privileged cabal, who then cut their friends with the Mafia and the CIA in for a piece of the action—thus buying their formidable protection. It could be that the glue that holds these groups together— money and greed for money, power and lust for power, and the veil of secrecy—makes any distinction between them meaningless.

Despite everything that has been written about the S&L scandal, the American public still knows very little about what really happened. Why?

First of all, it was not the press's finest hour. In truth, the press provided the scandal participants with an additional layer of human protection. This was not the kind of scandal in which the press excels. It wasn't quick and dirty, it was long and drawn-out. The documents either weren't available or were in county courthouses in the hinterlands of Florida, Texas and California, not in New York City or Washington, D.C. No sources were present inside the government and the Washington, D.C., beltway who knew what happened; or if there were sources, they weren't talking, because both political parties were culpable.

Another reason journalists are still unable to follow the money is that some of the crucial documents that would allow them to do so are not public. Federal and state Freedom of Information acts and open records laws exempt the relevant financial documents from disclosure. In our case the necessary records are the loan documents, particularly the title company disbursement sheets. (Title companies collect the loan money from the S&Ls and then cut checks to all the parties getting money.) These documents, along with the federal and state examination reports—which are also not available to the public—are the "Rosetta stones" of the savings-and-loan debacle. Any journalist, federal agent or self-styled expert who claims to know what happened to the money without actually having studied the title company disbursement documents and examination reports is shooting in the dark.

(Congress, of course, has the authority to make these documents public, but during all its discussions of the great S&L crisis no such action was ever mentioned. . . . Well, after all, it's only our tax dollars that we're talking about. Why should the public be able to see what its money was used for? It is interesting to note that about the only other tax dollars the public is not allowed to see are those in the CIA's budget. And, as we have seen, these two categories are intertwined.)

Also, many of the journalists who ended up covering the crisis were business and banking reporters who wouldn't recognize fraud and embezzlement, much less the Mafia and the CIA, if they jumped up and bit them in the butt. And then, too, often the sources for business writers on their S&L stories were business and banking experts and consultants who had a vested interest in not putting the blame on fraud and organized crime. These self-styled experts have no expertise in crime and fraud, and if crime and fraud were significant factors, then they would be out of a job as "experts"—no more getting quoted in newspapers, no more radio talk shows and no more television appearances.

One of the most quoted experts, Bert Ely, actually got paid to testify in court on behalf of some of the S&L looters, repeating his claim that fraud was not a significant factor. The judges and juries who heard the evidence weren't buying this, however, as almost all of Ely's clients lost their court battles.[1]

When savings and loans started dropping like flies beginning in 1985, and it became apparent that these were not random occurrences but something systematic, those who owned the failed S&Ls trotted out an economic explanation: A falling real estate market triggered by economic factors, such as dropping oil prices, did them in. This explanation seemed to satisfy many people as long as most of the failures were

---

[1] *Houston Post*, September 16, 1990.

concentrated in Texas, but it soon lost all credibility as S&Ls in Florida, California, Kansas, Illinois, Pennsylvania and New York also began to topple.

After that, the big lie the S&L owners put forward was that the losses were the result of bad business deals, that they were simply exercising their legitimate business judgments and just guessed wrong. Although any detailed investigations of these "bad business deals" usually revealed business relationships and interconnections between the lenders and the borrowers, as well as criminality in the form of fraudulent, falsified or nonexistent loan documents, those who were charged with S&L crimes continued to use the above excuse at their criminal trials. This kind of business rationalization leads us to the single most important document in the looting of America's savings and loans, and a major protective layer for those who were responsible: the little old innocuous appraisal report.

Every time a savings and loan lends money with a piece of property as security (collateral), it must obtain an appraisal of the property. This appraisal, by the way, is not a public document. The appraisal is an estimate, based on certain time-honored techniques, by a professional appraiser of the fair market value of the property. "Fair market value" is an elastic hole big enough to drive an armored truck through. And that's exactly what happened. It worked like this:

A savings and loan would obtain an inflated appraisal of the property, in cahoots with the borrower and sometimes the property owner. The S&L would pay the appraiser a fee of $5,000 for a job whose standard fee might be $1,000. The borrower might then pay off any prior liens on the property, pocket the remaining money and walk off, leaving the S&L to foreclose on the property. If any questions were raised, the appraiser would simply swear that the inflated value was his best professional estimate at the time.

This is a very simplified version of the basic S&L scam: lending more money than the property is worth. The complications arise when the S&L and the borrower engage in various gyrations to jack up, muddle or hide the value of the property.

One of the most popular ways was through acquisition, development and construction loans (called ADC loans), in which the borrower would buy a piece of vacant land with grandiose plans for development. The S&L would lend the money to buy the land and also the money for the development and construction. The borrower would make a few "cosmetic" plans and maybe do a little construction and then walk off with the rest of the money. The S&L was left with vacant land worth far less than the amount borrowed against it, but the S&L owner was happy because he had collected big up-front fees from the loan (via loan-origination fees, etc.), and, if need be, he could later sell the property to another crooked S&L for a profit. The original land owner was happy because he had gotten more than his land was worth, and the borrower was happy because he had gotten the development money. And if, by unlikely chance, the government came after the borrower, he could put the money in an offshore trust for his children and declare bankruptcy. Such a "bad" business deal was "good" for everybody except the American taxpayers, who guaranteed the S&L's deposits.

Many journalists, including some very good ones, focused on the sizzle of this story, rather than on the meat. Their story line goes something like this: Those who looted the S&Ls were just a bunch of good-old-boy, Texas wheeler-dealer developers who blew all that money on wine, women, song, gambling, fast horses, faster cars, yachts, airplanes, Colorado chalets, California beach houses, etc. . . . . Now, it may be true that these people spent most of the money they got out of the S&Ls on such things, but as mere front men and middle men they only received 1 or 2 percent of what was looted, and rarely more.

For example, consider Don Dixon, the infamous head of Vernon Savings, whose failure costs American citizens more than $1 billion. The federal regulators sued Dixon for more than $350 million for Vernon's failure. But this is ridiculous. Dixon was just a front man and got, at most, 2 or 3 percent of the take out of Vernon: $20 million to $30 million. Granted, that's still a healthy chunk of change, and should be recovered from Dixon, who probably took $5 million or so offshore to save as a post-incarceration nest egg. But most of the American taxpayers' money went elsewhere.

The people who do have the subpoena power to track the money—the FBI and federal prosecutors—have shown little interest in doing so. In one case handled by the Dallas S&L task force, it was found that more than $10 million was wired by a crooked S&L owner to a bank account on the Isle of Jersey. The assistant U.S. attorney handling the case announced that they had tracked down the bank account, and, lo and behold, when they finally got to it, there was no money there. Having come up empty-handed, the Justice Department then apparently gave up.

In fact, the Justice Department itself has become a major layer of protection for the main beneficiaries of the savings-and-loan crisis. FBI agents rarely have the desire or ability to track down piles of complicated, tedious bank records and decipher them. Few have had the accounting, financial and real estate training necessary, and many are young, fresh out of the FBI training academy at Quantico, facing the likelihood of a transfer within a few years.

And even if there is that rare FBI agent who goes after the white-collar S&L crimes, he or she usually runs into a brick wall at the U.S. Attorney's Office.[2] Most federal prosecutors are after the quick conviction, the guilty plea to a lessor felony—chalk it up, and then on to the next case. Not only does this miss the overall picture and those behind it, the crooks who do cop a guilty plea to a short jail term or probation have little incentive to turn state's evidence against those they are fronting for.

Former Attorney General Richard Thornburgh, who presided over the Justice Department's S&L investigations, made the incredible statement on a number of occasions that the fraudulently obtained S&L money cannot be traced. Yet the success of his own department in "Operation Polar Cap" belies his claim. That operation was an attempt to trace some of the Medellín Cartel's drug money—from cash in this country to offshore banks and then back to this country. (Some of the money was deposited in Silverado Savings in Denver, where President Bush's son Neil was a director.) The operation met with fair success under more difficult circumstances than would exist in tracking S&L money, because most S&L theft involves a trail of paper and wire transfers that can be traced.

Thornburgh did have one weapon, the organized crime strike forces, which had conducted successful S&L prosecutions in Florida, Kansas City and New York City. These strike forces had the background, knowledge and experience to delve into the kinds of large-scale conspiracies, with Mafia involvement, that were occurring in S&Ls across the country. And what did the Reagan and Bush Administrations do with these strike force units? They abolished them right in the middle of the S&L crisis.

Furthermore, the S&L scandal, which was crawling with mobsters, was centered in Texas, yet the organized crime strike forces *there* were

---

[2] A notable exception in this area is the team of U.S. Attorney Joe Cage, of the Western District of Louisiana, and FBI agent Ellis Blount of Monroe, Louisiana.

pitifully small. Philip Hilder, the only strike force attorney in Houston, was a lone voice asking for more resources, manpower and assistance to investigate Mafia involvement in S&L fraud. His urgent requests went unheeded.

This point leads to another layer of protection for those behind the scandal. In Texas, there are no experts or repositories of knowledge regarding the Mafia. There exists a widespread myth, which I too believed for many years, that very little Mafia presence and activity exists in the Lone Star State. The readers of this book will have realized that the myth is nonsense. Yet this fiction, along with a lack of law enforcement experts, media experts and public or private organized crime strike forces, has allowed La Cosa Nostra to operate with impunity in Texas.

Congress provided yet another layer of protection by failing to exercise its power to track the flow of money out of S&Ls. Not one Congressman that I am aware of ever asked these simple questions: What happened to all that money, and why don't we try to get it back? Perhaps many of them feared that some of the money would be traced back to their own campaign coffers. And Congress did go easy on its colleagues who happened to get caught with their fingers in the S&L cookie jar. "There, but for the grace of God, go I," they must have thought.

For many of the big S&L failures, the federal regulators hired private law firms to try to track the money and get it back via lawsuits against the officers and directors. As with the suit against Dixon, these lawsuits were usually aimed at the wrong people and have been less than success-ful—except for the purpose of paying the law firms. In some of these cases, putting these firms in charge was akin to putting the fox in charge of the hen house. Many of the firms were intimate with the Republican Administration and had conflicts of interest in going after the real money, as we have seen. So the law firms were just one more effective layer of protection for the good old boys.

Finally, consider the layers of protection offered by the CIA. First, the CIA can simply go to the FBI and say that a person under investiga-tion is working for, or has worked for, the Agency and therefore should not be investigated or prosecuted. The FBI refers to this as a "get-out-of-jail-free" card. Two examples of such occurrences have been detailed in this book.

The CIA also generally receives kid-glove treatment from the press.

Here we have one of the most secretive, expensive, dangerous, infamous and least successful bureaucracies in the American government, and the press does almost no investigative reporting about it. For one thing, it is extremely difficult; it's much easier to investigate improper spending or activities in the Pentagon or HUD. Second, the CIA has control over and access to a tremendous amount of important confidential information and thus is in the position to reward its friends in the press with good stories and punish its enemies by withholding information. This also means that the CIA can keep reporters busy with stories of its own choosing while burying anything that might make itself look bad.

Last, the CIA can withhold most of its documents from the public on the basis—legitimate or not—of national security. Any attempt to get CIA confirmation or documentation on a CIA asset or contract agent is rebuffed.

But what about Congress's investigations into CIA involvement in the S&L scandal? There was a so-called "preliminary inquiry" by a congressional committee into allegations of CIA involvement. In February 1990, the *Houston Post* published the first story detailing some of the allegations. One day later, U.S. Representative Frank Annunzio (Democrat-Illinois) called for CIA Director William Webster to appear before his financial institutions subcommittee and answer questions about the story. Annunzio couldn't have cared less about the facts, all he knew was that it gave him an excuse to deflect some of the adverse publicity he himself was getting on the S&L issue.

Webster refused to appear before Annunzio's committee, saying it was a matter for the intelligence committees, which have oversight of the CIA. But the CIA did more than just refuse to appear before the banking subcommittee. It wrote a letter to Annunzio in which it simply lied about the *Houston Post*'s investigation. The CIA letter stated that CIA officials "have been in contact with Assistant United States Attorney John Smith in Houston, who is quoted in the *Post*. Smith states emphatically that he has never said that there is any connection between his office's ongoing banking investigation and the CIA, and that he is not aware of any such connection. Smith states that he told the *Post* reporter[3] that there is no connection between the CIA and the ongoing banking investigation. The reporter appears to have neglected to include this part of Smith's statement in the article."

But Smith, a man of greater integrity than the CIA officials who

---

[3] The author.

wrote the letter, said the letter did not accurately represent what he told the CIA. "When that guy called me, I told him I wanted that deleted [the part about his allegedly telling the *Post* there was no connection to the CIA], and I wanted them to say something else because I didn't think that part was quite accurate." Smith said he would not make such a statement about an ongoing investigation, which was attributed to him by the CIA. "That is kind of their statement," he said.

After Webster refused to appear before his committee, Annunzio had his staff check out one allegation in the second *Houston Post* story, namely that the CIA had stopped a federal investigation of Farhad Azima in Kansas City. Annunzio's staffers confirmed the *Post*'s article. They talked to the former organized crime strike force prosecutor who made the allegation, Lloyd Monroe. Monroe had quit the Justice Department and was studying at Brown University. The staffers also talked to an FBI agent who had confirmed the CIA's stopping of the Azima investigation for the *Post*. This FBI agent confirmed Monroe's account again to Annunzio's people.

Based on those confirmations, Annunzio wrote a letter to U.S. Representative Anthony Beilenson (Democrat-California), then the chairman of the House Permanent Select Committee on Intelligence, stating:

"As I am sure you are aware, there have been recent press reports, including an extended series by the *Houston Post*, concerning alleged Central Intelligence Agency (CIA) involvement in the failure of savings and loans and banks across the country . . .

"Quite frankly, Mr. Chairman, when I first heard of the media allegations I was not convinced of their total validity. It was for that reason that I asked the CIA to come before the Subcommittee to set the record straight. The refusal of the Agency to respond to the Subcommittee's request and the initial investigative work done by the Subcommittee staff, have led me to believe that at least some of the allegations have validity. . . .

"In that regard, I am writing to ask that your Committee undertake a complete investigation of the allegations that the CIA was involved in the collapse of some financial institutions around the country. I am asking that the Committee conduct a thorough investigation so that there can be no unsettled questions in this extremely troubling area."

In fact, the House Intelligence Committee did not conduct a thorough investigation; it whitewashed the matter. The committee staff concluded that its preliminary inquiry did not justify a full-blown investigation with the calling of witnesses. The staff stated that "the available evidence did not support a conclusion" that funds taken from failed S&Ls by CIA-associated individuals went to CIA-sponsored covert activities not approved by Congress.

However, the committee did not release one iota of the evidence that it used to support this conclusion. Apparently most of the evidence came from the CIA itself.

The biggest problem with the staff's inquiry was that it left undone the one thing that it ought to have done: track some of the money. Without actually tracking the money to its ultimate destination, there was no way they could possibly have known, as they stated, that none of the S&L money borrowed or controlled by CIA assets was used for CIA activities.

The staff also chose to ignore the statements by former Justice Department organized crime prosecutor Lloyd Monroe, and confirmed by me and Annunzio's staff, that the CIA interfered in the investigation of Farhad Azima. A letter from Beilenson to Annunzio said that "all of those interviewed, except the one former prosecutor, recall that the decision not to open a full investigation of this individual [Azima] was based on a lack of sufficient evidence, and the judgment that the individual was only peripherally involved in the underlying case."

This judgment was contradicted by the person probably most familiar with the Indian Springs State Bank case, Kansas City attorney Michael Manning, whose firm was hired by the Federal Deposit Insurance Corporation to investigate the bank's failure. Azima and Global "certainly did contribute to the failure of Indian Springs State Bank," Manning told the *Post*.[4]

The committee staff counsel, Michael Sheehy, said that the FBI agent whom Annunzio's staff and I talked to did not confirm Monroe's story. But what the FBI agent said to Sheehy would depend upon the questions asked of him. If asked a general question on whether the CIA *stopped* the Azima investigation, he might have said, "No." What he would say, if he had been properly asked, is that the FBI was told that Azima was a CIA asset and therefore they knew any investigation and prosecution of him would be a waste of time because he had a "get-out-of-jail-free card."

The intelligence committee staff also completely ignored the state-

---

[4] *Houston Post*, February 8, 1990.

ments by an unrelated federal prosecutor in Texas, who said that a CIA official tried to get him to drop his prosecution of Guillermo Hernandez-Cartaya, a well-known CIA asset, in a fraud case involving Jefferson Savings and Loan. Cartaya was convicted of fraud, as was CIA contract pilot Heinrich Rupp in an unrelated case in Denver in which Rupp said he was working for the CIA. Yet Beilenson's letter baldly states that there is no evidence of "a connection between allegations of fraud and any relationship with the CIA." That, as they say, is a complete lie.

The committee staff also did not interview or question Cartaya, Rupp or Rupp's buddy, Richard Brenneke, the intelligence operative who testified under oath that the CIA surreptitiously used banks and S&Ls to fund the Contras. Brenneke was later acquitted of charges of lying about other statements he made during the same court hearing. Committee staffers indicated that Brenneke refused to talk to them. If they were really interested in getting to the bottom of his statement, they could have subpoenaed him. They didn't.

The committee also made no attempt to investigate the connections between Mafia associates and CIA assets uncovered by the *Post*. In most cases, the same person had connections to both institutions, such as Azima, Lawrence Freeman, Hernandez-Cartaya, Herman Beebe, Mario Renda, etc.

Finally, there was the matter of the intelligence committee staff director himself, Dan Childs. Childs joined the committee in January 1990, one month before the *Post*'s series began, but several months after the CIA became aware of the fact that the newspaper was working on such a series. Childs was a twenty-six-year CIA veteran and former chief financial officer of the spy agency.

Childs said he joined the CIA in 1957 and worked in the administrative branch until 1976, when he went to work for the Senate Intelligence Committee. This was at the time of the devastating revelations about illegal CIA activities by the Church Committee of the Senate. Childs stayed at the Senate committee until 1982, when he left to rejoin the CIA to become comptroller, under Bill Casey.

In 1983, Childs appeared before the Senate Intelligence Committee to answer questions about Casey's moving several million dollars from a secret contingency fund to a fund to aid the Contras.[5] Bob Wood-

---

[5] *Veil: The Secret Wars of the CIA, 1981-1987,* by Bob Woodward (Simon and Schuster, 1987).

ward's book *Veil* portrayed Childs as being nonchalant about the movement of the funds—which irritated the committee head. Childs also testified before the joint congressional Iran-Contra committee in 1987. He has refused to say what he testified about, saying his testimony was taken behind closed doors.

In January 1991, one month after the House Intelligence Committee released its CIA/S&L findings, Childs resigned and returned to work for the CIA as Special Assistant to the Director. He had only served with the committee one year. Apparently the only major investigation the committee staff did during this time was the S&L probe. Regarding that investigation, one of the staff attorneys said, "We've never done anything like this before. We work primarily on legislation."

Unfortunately, this ineffectiveness has come to be expected from the House Intelligence Committee, the same group that sat there like bumps on a log when Oliver North lied with impunity to them about his Contra activities. If it had been up to the House Intelligence Committee, the American public would have never found out about Iran-Contra.

The CIA's placing one of its own on a congressional investigation is not unprecedented. One of the chief investigators on the Iran-Contra committee was Tom Polgar, who had worked for the CIA for twenty-six years, including being chief of six major CIA field installations in Asia, South America and Europe. Polgar is also on the staff of Parvus, the consulting firm loaded with ex-intelligence officers that has as an advisory director, Theodore Dimitry, of the Houston law firm of Vinson & Elkins.

Childs denied that his former CIA position was a conflict of interest in his staff's investigation. "I didn't conduct the investigation," he said. But when asked whether he had any influence on the investigation or discussed it with the staff, he replied, "Of course. They all work for me."

It certainly appears that Childs was brought in specifically to run damage control on the S&L investigation.

Despite all this, there were several interesting revelations in the committee's inquiry. In an extraordinary admission, the CIA acknowledged that five of the individuals, and four of the financial institutions, named by the *Houston Post*, had associations with the CIA. (Such an admission is known in CIA parlance as a "limited hang-out," and is designed to make the American public believe that since the CIA admitted these relationships, then that must be all there is to it.) The committee stopped its investigation with those admissions, taking the CIA's word that there was nothing dirty going on. Committee counsel Michael Sheehy refused to provide the names of the individuals and institutions, saying that they were "classified."

At that point in time, the *Post* had named six CIA assets with ties to financial institutions, including Azima, Corson, Freeman, Khashoggi, Hernandez-Cartaya and Frank Castro.

And the use of at least four fraud-riddled, mob-infested financial institutions for "normal" CIA business raises other questions. These institutions were certainly not pulled out of a hat by the CIA. The Church Committee noted that private commercial financial institutions selected by the CIA would likely earn interest or an investment bonus on the CIA's money. And, the committee found, "selection of these institutions is noncompetitive, rooted in historic circumstances, albeit in institutions that have shown themselves flexible and responsive in providing the Agency services."

The American people have been ridden hard and put away wet, thanks to the savings-and-loan debacle. The final insult is that the Congress and the Justice Department are not tracking down the money stolen from us. Not only do we need to know what it was used for—we need to get it back. The fact that the people who run this country have no desire to do either speaks louder than all the excuses and pious platitudes coming out of Washington, D.C., today.

The Mafia, much like the poor, will probably always be with us. After researching this book, I think that it is as strong as ever, despite all the ballyhooed prosecutions of mob bosses in New York City, Philadelphia and Los Angeles. Many of the second, third and fourth generations have integrated themselves into the legitimate business world, and they love banks and savings and loans. Such places are, after all, as bank robber Willie Sutton remarked long ago, "where the money is."

What about the CIA?

America is better than the CIA; the common people who make this country great are better than the aristocrats who control it and the CIA. We should be teaching the world by our example of what free people can do, rather than by trying to control it through stealth, secrecy, subterfuge and the use of organized criminals to do dirty work—which all too often blows back on us, as it has with the S&L debacle.

The CIA either knew what its contract agents and assets were doing at S&Ls or it didn't know. If it knew, why didn't it stop them or at least sound the alarm? If it didn't know, what kind of intelligence agency is it?

Perhaps one solution is to get rid of contract agents and assets, who all too often are in it for the "get-out-of-jail-free card" and their private gain. Perhaps only full-time employees of the United States government should be able to work for the CIA. Another solution may lie in stopping the CIA from undertaking covert actions, and making it into the intelligence-gathering organization it was intended to be. If the CIA can't do these things, then we should do what President John F. Kennedy said he wanted to do: shatter the CIA into a thousand pieces and scatter it to the winds.

What about George Bush—former spook chief, transplanted Texas gladhander, standard-bearer for the hands-off, blind-eye government policies that made the S&L crisis possible? Reagan-Bush deregulation opened a Pandora's box, and George couldn't close it, and didn't want to, considering all his friends, offspring and political backers who were happily getting richer. As America sank in a sea of S&L debt, the President exhorted us to "stay the course." The Bush course of complicity, non-reaction and denial has left the taxpayers over $500 billion poorer.

Bush is the perfect representative of the real problem in the savings-and-loan crisis: the wealthy businessmen with symbiotic relationships to the Mafia and the CIA. They all used each other to get what they wanted, and most of all they used the government—via semi-monopolistic government charters, government regulation and government deposit insurance—to cheat the taxpayers.

This is nothing new in our history. Consider the words of Andrew Jackson in 1832, when he vetoed the rechartering of a national bank, whose stockholders and borrowers included wealthy, privileged individuals:

"It is to be regretted that the rich and powerful too often bend the acts of government to their selfish purposes. . . . When the laws undertake to add to these natural and just advantages artificial distinctions, to grant titles, gratuities and exclusive privileges, to make the rich richer and the potent more powerful, the humble members of society—the farmers, mechanics and laborers—who have neither the time nor the means of securing like favors to themselves, have a right to complain of the injustice of their Government. There are no necessary evils in government. Its evils exist only in its abuses. If it would confine itself to equal protection, and, as Heaven does its rains, shower its favors alike on the high and the low, the rich and the poor, it would be an unqualified blessing."

ACKNOWLEDGMENTS

I t is not possible to thank adequately all those who helped with this book. However, their assistance does not necessarily imply their endorsement. And any mistakes, errors and omissions are my responsibility.

Because the subject matter is so fraught with difficulty and danger, I am most grateful to the few people who provided me with information and allowed me to quote them by name—without any desire or request for compensation or anything else in return.

At the top of this list is Art Leiser. Art is the former Chief Examiner of the Texas Savings and Loan Department and a veritable treasure-trove of information, sagacity and humor. A feisty bantam rooster now stewing in retirement in Austin, Art went above and beyond the call of duty in helping me.

The law enforcement official who helped me the most was Lloyd Monroe, who quit the Justice Department's organized crime strike force in frustration and disgust and is now at Brown University. A thoughtful, philosophical man, Lloyd was probably more alone in his prosecution work for the Justice Department in Kansas City than I was in my reporting in Houston. Lloyd not only helped me to understand particular events, but kept pushing me to see the bigger picture, not only in terms of criminal activity but also in terms of American society.

The law enforcement officials involved in the S&L scandal most like "The Untouchables" are U.S. Attorney Joe Cage of the Western District of Louisiana and FBI agent Ellis Blount. These two, despite great odds and pressure against them, put Herman K. Beebe, Sr., behind bars and pursued Beebe's powerful associate Edmund Reggie. Cage also introduced me to Dale Anderson, Beebe's former right-hand man. Anderson didn't particularly like me, and disagreed with many of my ideas, but he always returned my phone calls and answered my questions honestly and candidly.

Another law enforcement official who tolerated my questions, and even answered some of them, was Bruce Maffeo, a shrewd, tough, funny, sardonic prosecutor at the Justice Department's organized crime strike force in Brooklyn, New York. Maffeo, who prosecuted Mario Renda and Martin Schwimmer, was one of many talented attorneys who quit the Justice Department after the Reagan and Bush Administrations abolished the organized crime strike forces.

The person most responsible for the CIA portion of this book is Rebecca Sims, who was Robert Corson's accountant. Rebecca quit Corson's employment after she was asked to commit tax and bankruptcy fraud. She then turned her bulldog tenacity and investigative powers on Corson and the CIA, staying the course that destiny put her on at great personal, emotional and financial cost. Rebecca's abilities and knowledge in the fields of accounting, business transactions, financial institutions and the intelligence community are unique and incalculable. In one of the best pieces of investigative reporting I have ever seen, she tracked a Boeing 707 from a company connected to Ian Paget-Brown, a Cayman Islands attorney whose affiliate borrowed money from Mainland Savings, to St. Lucia Airways, a CIA proprietary airline.

Providing great assistance, encouragement and energy from the Miami area was Margie Sloan, a freelance journalist, investigator and tireless worker. Margie also guided me along the inside track to the Denver and Silverado crowds. Among the invaluable information Margie produced were documents linking Denver businessman John Dick to the Compendium Trust, the Isle of Jersey trust fund used by Miami drug-money launderer Lawrence Freeman and S&L looters Robert Corson and Mike Adkinson. In addition to her cheerleading and enthusiasm, Margie tracked down a number of critical records in the Miami area. Margie was also able to find and talk to many insiders who had not previously spoken to any journalist.

Probably the single most important documents to this book, the Florida Department of Law Enforcement reports on Lawrence Freeman and Jack DeVoe, were delivered by Sue Robinson, a free-lance journalist, investigator and general gadfly for truth and justice in the Florida panhandle. Sue also provided me with hundreds of pages of Florida corporation records that yielded much useful information.

If I have been able to see a little further than others, it is because I was standing on the shoulders of some great investigative reporters, primarily Jonathan Kwitny and Stephen Pizzo. Pizzo and his co-authors Mary Fricker and Paul Muolo (*Inside Job*) generously gave me all the information they had, and provided other leads and sources, as well as sympathy and encouragement (mostly from Mary). Pizzo's long-distance wit, good humor and general all-around brilliance lit up many a dull and dreary Houston day.

Other reporters who helped me and kept the journalistic faith with the American public are: Bryan Abas, Dave Armstrong, Dennis Bernstein, Joel Bleifuss, Jack Colhoun, John Cummings, Christopher Hitchens, Anthony Kimery, Robert Parry (who has a new book out, *Fooling America*) and Glenn Simpson. Special thanks also go to Canadian journalist Marci McDonald, who is writing a book about Adnan Khashoggi and who unselfishly provided me with important documents, and to one of Great Britain's best investigative reporters, Michael Gillard, whom I owe $50 because the *Houston Post* would not cough it up to pay for some work Michael did for us in London.

There are two journalists who are unsung heroes, deserving special praise and thanks, for they receive precious little. The first is Jerry Bohnen, a radio reporter from Oklahoma City who is the world's expert on Federal Aviation Administration documents. Jerry tracked down many FAA documents for me, as he has done for countless other reporters, and refused to take any money for it. The other is Don Devereux, an investigative reporter in the middle of unfriendly territory: Phoenix, Arizona. Don's ground-breaking work rarely gets the attention it merits.

A Dallas television reporter, Byron Harris, broke several important savings-and-loans stories for his TV station and in *Texas Monthly*. Thereafter, almost every S&L reporter cribbed scenes from Byron's stories about Don Dixon and Ed McBirney, yet few gave him credit. And a Dallas newspaper, the *Morning News*, stood above other daily newspapers in its coverage of the S&L scandal. This was primarily due to the work and research of two diligent reporters, Allen Pusey and Bill Lodge.

At the *Houston Post* my appreciation goes to esteemed colleagues Gregory Seay (who started it all but who later left for the *Hartford*

Courant), Mary Flood (who later left for Harvard Law School), John Mecklin (who just left for the John F. Kennedy School at Harvard), Bill Coulter (who has gone to the *Houston Chronicle*), Allan Kimball (who moved to central Texas), Kate Thomas, Marge Crumbaker (who moved to the Texas Hill Country), Betsy Parish, Rick Barrs (now with the *Los Angeles Times*), Eileen O'Grady, Mike Cinelli (who is now working for Rice University), Gerald Egger, Leslie Loddeke, Leanne Reidy, Sandra Kinkead (who went back to school), Rebecca Hamilton, Paul Harasim, Jay Dorman, Ken Herman, Doug Freelander, Fred King, Pat Robertson, Lynn Ashby, Juan Palomo, Donald Morris (who has started his own newsletter) and Tom Kennedy, and to the *Post*'s former editorial cartoonist, Jimmy Margulies (who is now with the *Bergen* [New Jersey] *Record*). Also thanks are due the *Post*'s hard-working, competent and long-suffering library staff: Terri Diehl, Margaret Jamison, Carolyn Allen, Linda Bory, Michael Casella, Joyce Lee, Elise McCutchen, Lisa Nickels, Margaret Walker and Harris Worchel.

I have mixed emotions about the editors at the *Post*. They allowed me so much and went so far, yet when the crunch time came on Walter Mischer, they let their fears, fanned by Fulbright & Jaworski, control them. Without Dave Burgin, the Editor-in-Chief, none of the stories would have seen the light of day. City Editor Tim Graham did yeoman work in pushing stories past Fulbright & Jaworski into the paper. And Tim's editing even improved a few of the stories. Thanks also go to Executive Editor Ernie Williamson, to former Assistant Managing Editor Tom Nelson, the best boss I've ever had (and now enjoying the good life in Colorado), and to Managing Editor Margaret Downing, who as city editor patiently allowed me the time the develop the CIA stories. I especially appreciate Margaret's confidence in me.

And also a salute goes to the smart, tough, witty, highly competent Canadians Peter O'Sullivan, Don Hunt and Doug Creighton.

My thanks and gratitude go the following additional people for their help and attention: Medill Barnes, Herb Beebe, Ari Ben-Menashe, Lynn Bernabei, Bill Bertain, Richard Brenneke, Elizabeth Burkhardt, Marjorie Burkhardt, Rico Carisch, Jack Cataneo, P. M. Clinton, Phyllis Cox, John Craig, Deborah Davis, Richard Dechert, Phil Donahue and his superb staff, Hugh Downs, Bill Duncan, Tony Equale, Dr. James Fairleigh, Linda Farrar, Mary Faza, Niki Fox, Phyllis Gapen, Sherrie Glass, Lieutenant Dave Gonzales and Officer Fermin Torres of the Arizona Department of Public Safety, Marcy Gordon, Lynn Gray, Bill Hamilton, Bruce Hemmings, Philip Hilder, John Hinterberger, Ellen Hume, Carl

Jensen, Virgil Knox, Martin Lee, Ann Lehrmann, Betsy McCarthy, Sally McCarty, David MacMichael, Mike Manning, John Mattes, Bill Moyers, Jesse Mullins, Will Northrop, John O'Connor, George Parnham, Tosh Plumlee, Bryan Quig, Terry Reed, Charley Reese, Barbara Reynolds, Cody Shearer, Dan Sheehan, Sheldon Sisson, John Smith, Robert Todd, Andie Tucher, Phil Vogt, Ted Walker, Robert Walters, Steve Weinberg, Eileen Welsome, Gene Wheaton, Bill White, Clyde Wilson and, last but not least, the old Harris County hide inspector himself, Jack Woods. I am also very much indebted to John Craig, who came through when the chips were down and asked for nothing in return—only that the truth be told.

Also thanks go to the National Security Archive and its staff, particularly Malcolm Byrne and Peter Kornbluh. And thank you, Stefanie Scott and Fred Bonavita, of the *San Antonio Express-News*.

There are a number of people who provided crucial help and information that I am unable to thank by name. Their livelihoods and possibly their lives would be in danger if they were identified. They know who they are and they have my gratitude. In particular, there is D.K., a Texas lawman right out of central casting: big, tough, honest, incorruptible, skilled, laconic, dry-witted; D.K. served with my great uncle Eb Riggs, a Texas Ranger and Deputy U.S. Marshal, along the Texas-Mexico border. There is also Leon, who is, with the possible exception of my father, the wisest and most humorous man I have ever known. Finally, there are the Houston police officers from the Criminal Intelligence Division, who opened my eyes to the underbelly of Houston society.

A particular debt is owed to Ken Cureton, the Federal Home Loan Bank Board official who tenaciously pursued his investigation of Robert Corson's Vision Banc Savings. Although Cureton would not talk to me or give me any information, he is responsible for making public many important documents and helping to bring a number of wrongdoers to the bar of justice.

Special thanks are sent to Doug Ireland, media critic of the *Village Voice*, who was the first journalist outside Texas to pick up on the importance of my CIA stories and give them backing and publicity. Doug is also, without doubt, the smartest person I have ever encountered in the world of journalism. (Faint praise, huh Doug?)

I would also like to thank my friends for their support and encouragement, especially Dr. Don Winston, Dave Notzon, Brad Moore,

David Reitz, Mary Flood and Francis Loewenheim, distinguished professor of history at Rice University, as well as fellow law student and troublemaker Katie Moss and Martha Cook, who got me started in this business. And . . . my best friend: the Idiot. Thanks also go to my sons, Mark and Luke, for their patience, indulgence, enthusiasm and candor.

Eleanor Karpf edited this book in three weeks under extreme deadline pressure—an amazing feat. During that short period of time Eleanor displayed a better grasp and understanding of the book than all the editors at Simon & Schuster had managed in eight months. Also, my thanks and appreciation to Sherrel Farnsworth, managing editor and Julian Serer, production manager at S.P.I. Books.

I owe a special debt of gratitude to Jonathan Kwitny, and not just for his previous work in the fields of organized crime and the CIA. When Simon & Schuster refused to publish this book before the 1992 presidential election, I sent a copy to Kwitny to see what he thought. If Kwitny couldn't understand it and its significance, no one could. Jon agreed with me that the book should be published before the election, put me in touch with publisher Ian Shapolsky and gave me great encouragement and assistance.

Ian Shapolsky is everything any writer could hope for, and more: enthusiastic, attentive, open-minded, quick-acting, clear-thinking and courageous. Without his industry and integrity, this book would not exist.

INDEX